PRESERVATION OF CLIENT RIGHTS

PRESERVATION OF CLIENT RIGHTS

A Handbook for Practitioners Providing Therapeutic, Educational, and Rehabilitative Services

Edited by

GERALD T. HANNAH
WALTER P. CHRISTIAN
HEWITT B. CLARK

Fp

THE FREE PRESS
A Division of Macmillan Publishing Co., Inc.
NEW YORK
Collier Macmillan Publishers
LONDON

The Free Press
A Division of Macmillan Publishing Co., Inc.
866 Third Avenue, New York, N.Y. 10022

Collier Macmillan Canada, Ltd.

Library of Congress Catalog Card Number: 80–1644

Printed in the United States of America

printing number

1 2 3 4 5 6 7 8 9 10

Library of Congress Cataloging in Publication Data
Main entry under title:

Preservation of client rights.

    Includes index.
    1. Psychotherapy patients—Legal status, laws, etc.
—United States. 2. Sick—Legal status, laws, etc.—
United States. 3. Hospital patients—Legal status,
laws, etc.—United States. I. Hannah, Gerald T.
II. Clark, Hewitt B. III. Christian, Walter P.
[DNLM: 1. Patient advocacy. 2. Human rights. W 85 P933]
KF3828.P23   344.73′032   80-1644
ISBN 0-02-913820-5

Contents

v

PART III: SAFEGUARDING INSTITUTIONALIZED CLIENTELE

PART IV: SAFEGUARDING RESEARCH PARTICIPANTS

Foreword

As psychosocial and biological methods of changing behavior have become more potent and effective, professionals and paraprofessionals providing human services have been criticized as being manipulative, coercive, and controlling. The specter has been raised of "Big Brother" therapists abusing and exploiting their clients and patients by arbitrarily "drugging" or "conditioning" them to adhere to behavior patterns and values not of their own making. Because behavior therapists overtly specify their goals, interventions, and effectiveness, more concerns have been raised about the ethics of behavior therapy than for other techniques, techniques that may similarly influence behavior and attitudes but do so in more subtle and less effective ways. Behavioral control is with us all of the time, in our daily lives as well as in all therapeutic approaches. It is no more possible to escape behavioral control than it is to obliterate the environmental, historical, and biological matrix within which we live. Since behavior is inevitably determined by its biosocial network, the ethical questions are *how, by whom, for what purposes,* and *with what safeguards* behavior will be influenced.

The editors of this volume have provided the human service fields with a timely and comprehensive handbook on the rights of clients from a wide variety of populations and institutions. The chapters in this book go beyond simple cataloguing of the nature and importance of client rights to presentations of practical, constructive, and clinically tested methods for protecting those rights. It is a basic assumption of the contributors, documented in many places, that actions taken to safeguard client rights will actually lead to more effective as well as more humane treatment.

One of the ways to safeguard client rights is to share with clients —and with their relatives, advocates, and guardians—decisions about behavioral change and treatment methods. This should begin from the point of initial contact, where agreements can begin to be developed on the desired goals of treatment or training. Informed consent for intervention should include the responsibilities of both clients and treatment agents as well as the potential benefits for them. An ideal example of giving clients the power to change their own behavior—which may be approximated with all handicapped populations—occurs when clients choose their own goals, monitor their own behavior, arrange the conditions of their environment to facilitate progress toward the goals, and instruct, evaluate, and reward themselves.

Contemporary human services present a valuable, but incomplete, approach to health and adjustment. The individual client, with encouragement from therapists, agencies, and institutions, can become a primary health care resource. The client's behavior and lifestyle can help bring about beneficial outcomes in social functioning, personal satisfaction, and symptomatic state. Many of the recommendations in this book will facilitate a positive partnership between the client and human-service practitioner, leading to a greater fulfillment of the client's potentials for change. Encouraged by this book's editors and contributors, trends toward self-care will transform the traditionally passive and bemused client into an active, informed, protected, and effective participant in his/her own treatment.

ROBERT PAUL LIBERMAN, M.D.
Professor of Psychiatry, UCLA School of Medicine
Director, Camarillo/UCLA Mental Health Clinical
    Research Center for the Study of Schizophrenia
Chief, Rehabilitation Medicine Service,
    Brentwood Veterans Administration Medical
    Center

Preface and Acknowledgments

In recent years, human-service delivery systems have been confronted with various issues—and with legislation—pertaining to the protection and adequate treatment of persons in their care. Treatment facilities such as psychiatric hospitals, community mental health centers, group homes, retardation institutions, and nursing homes are seeking systems to ensure protection of the client. However, the client-rights literature has not been adequately geared to the needs of the practicing professional and administrator. The literature to date has simply presented a philosophy and assisted in delineating the rights of clients. The present volume has been compiled to provide professional human-services practitioners and administrators with "systems" to ensure the rights of persons receiving psychological, rehabilitative, medical, correctional, and educational services. Each chapter thoroughly examines the client-rights issues and quality-of-treatment concerns for a particular educational, medical, or therapeutic situation. The "systems" discussed are not representative of a particular theoretical approach, but rather are procedures, practices, and technologies that have been shown to be important in the protection and treatment of clients. As will be evident from a perusal of these chapters, many of the systems discussed have undergone extensive experimental analyses, while others are recommended based on their apparent contribution to the protection of client rights in particular situations or settings.

This book has been organized into four major sections, the first of which encompasses a keynote chapter by Mr. Reed Martin, an attorney who has specialized in the legal rights of the handicapped. His article illustrates some of the abuses and neglect that persons have undergone in the name of therapy and rehabilitation. After a review of current trends in legal rights, Mr. Martin proceeds to describe some established standards in providing humane and effective treatment and educational services. He also reminds us of the important role that applied research plays in the continued effort to develop systems that ensure effective treatment and educational services while preserving the rights of the individual.

The second part of this book focuses on the protection and treatment of non-institutionalized client populations—for example, child abuse victims, autistic youths, alcoholics, and sexual abuse victims. Each of the ten chapters of this part provides a comprehensive approach to the protection of the particular client population being addressed. Although there are some commonalities among the systems for protecting and treating these various client populations, each clientele is particularly vulnerable in a different area. Thus unique systems, idiosyncratic to each population, are necessary.

The goal of the third part is similar to that of the second, but the focus is on systems tailored to protect persons who are in various "institutions" of our society. These institutional settings range from sheltered workshops and nursing homes to psychiatric institutions and prisons. As we are all aware, our institutions continue to present a major threat through their abuse of the rights and neglect of those of us in need of treatment and educational services. The eight chapters in this section provide systems uniquely tailored for the protection, education, and treatment of persons in these specialized settings.

The final part of this book addresses the critical role played by applied research and evaluation in ensuring that clients are protected. This section also provides guidelines for the protection of human beings as subjects. The methodology in applied research and evaluation is constantly evolving to encompass (1) more reliable and objective measurement systems applicable to assessment of a larger array of behaviors, (2) more practical experimental designs permitting more "real world" analyses, (3) more sensitive indicators for determining consumer satisfaction, and (4) more sophisticated methods for acquiring societal validation of treatment and educational goals and practices. As these applied research methodologies have become more sophisticated, the sensitivity to subjects' and clients' rights has also improved.

The contributing authors have worked closely with the editors to ensure that their chapters are in concert with this theme of the preservation of the individual's right to humane and effective treatment and education. Although each client population and institutional setting requires certain idiosyncratic systems for the protection of the particular clients, you will find that many of the implemented and tested systems described in each chapter will be applicable—possibly with some modification—for use with a variety of settings and populations.

We would like to express our appreciation to Dr. Robert P. Liberman for his encouragement and support of our professional activities, both through personal contact and through his thoughtfully written foreword to this book. Our editorial consultants at The Free Press, Mr. Robert Harrington and Ms. Kitty Moore, provided us with invaluable guidance throughout the entire course of this book's development. Of course, the tremendous effort by each of the contributing authors is evident throughout. To them we are deeply grateful.

A final appreciation to all practitioners and researchers who ensure the preservation of client rights.

GERALD T. HANNAH
WALTER P. CHRISTIAN
HEWITT P. CLARK

About the Editors

GERALD T. HANNAH, Ph.D., is the Kansas State Commissioner of Mental Health and Retardation, Topeka. Previously he was the Director of the Community Mental Health Division, Vermont State Department of Mental Health, and the Executive Director of the Frank Luton Community Mental Health Center in Nashville. He has also served as an Adjunct Assistant Professor in the Department of Psychology at the University of Vermont, in the Graduate School of Social Work at the University of Tennessee, and in the Department of Sociology/Social Work at Middle Tennessee State University. Currently he is a special consultant to a number of human service and state agencies and to the National Institute of Mental Health.

WALTER P. CHRISTIAN, Ph.D., is Director of the May Institute for Autistic Children, Inc., Chatham, Massachusetts. He holds appointments as Adjunct Assistant Professor with the Department of Human Development at the University of Kansas, Lawrence, and with the Department of Neurology at Tufts University School of Medicine, Boston, and serves as Special Counsel to the State of Kansas Department of Mental Health and Retardation Services. He is the author of *Chronically Ill and Handicapped Children: Their Management and Rehabilitation* (with T. L. Creer) and has written many articles for professional journals.

HEWITT B. "RUSTY" CLARK, Ph.D., is the Director of Children's Behavioral Services, Las Vegas, a comprehensive mental health center for families. He is also the Co-Director of the Desert Region Teaching-Family Staff Training Site and an Adjunct Professor at the University of Nevada. Dr. Clark currently serves on the editorial boards of three psychological journals, recently returned from a Guest Professorship in West Germany (where he was a consultant in adapting new clinical therapies to the culture there), and has published extensively.

About the Contributors

GENE G. ABEL, M.D., is Professor of Psychiatry at Columbia University College of Physicians and Surgeons, New York City, and a Research Scientist at the New York State Psychiatric Institute. He is currently Principal Investigator on HEW grants related to behavioral treatments for sexual aggressives and evaluation and treatment of sexual problems associated with diabetes. He is Co-Principal Investigator on a HEW grant related to the evaluation and treatment of rape and incest victims. His areas of specialization include behavioral medicine, sexual dysfunction, and sexual deviation.

MANUEL BARRERA, JR., Ph.D., is Assistant Professor of Psychology at Arizona State University. His major area of interest is in psychotherapy outcome research, utilization of mental health services, and social support systems. He has published extensively in professional journals.

JUDITH V. BECKER, Ph.D., is Assistant Professor of Psychiatry at Columbia University College of Physicians and Surgeons, New York City, and a Research Scientist at the New York State Psychiatric Institute. She is currently Principal Investigator on an HEW grant related to the evaluation and treatment of rape and incest victims. She is Co-Principal Investigator on HEW grants related to behavior treatment for sexual aggressives and evaluation and treatment of sexual problems associated with diabetes. Her areas of specialization include sexual dysfunction, sexual deviation, and behavioral medicine.

EDWARD J. CALLAHAN, Ph.D., is Assistant Professor of Psychology and Behavioral Medicine at West Virginia University. Professional interests include research on substance abuse and the development and evaluation of psychological services for obstetrics and gynecology patients. He has served on the Board of Editors, *Journal of Applied Behavior Analysis,* and Board of Directors of the Association for Advancement of Behavior Therapy and has published research in human sexuality, behavioral assessment, and addictive behaviors.

MICHAEL F. CATALDO, Ph.D., is Director of the Department of Behavioral Psychology at the John F. Kennedy Institute and is a member of the faculty in the Department of Pediatrics and the Department of Psychiatry and Behavioral Sciences at Johns Hopkins University, School of Medicine where he is director of the Behavioral Medicine Program. He is the author of a number of articles in behavioral medicine and behavioral methodology.

EDWARD R. CHRISTOPHERSEN, Ph.D., is an Associate Professor of Pediatrics at the University of Kansas Medical Center and a Senior Scientist in the Bureau of Child Research at the University of Kansas in Lawrence. In his major area of interest, behavioral pediatrics, he has contributed extensively to continuing education workshops, conventions, seminars, and professional writing. He is also author of the book, *Little People: Guidelines for Common Sense Child Rearing*, H and H Enterprises, Lawrence, Kansas, 1977.

TOMAS L. CREER, Ph.D., is Professor of Psychology and Director of Clinical Training at Ohio University. His interests are in the development of a behavioral health care system for management of asthma and other respiratory disorders. He has published extensively in professional journals.

RICHARD T. CROW, D.S.W., is an Associate Professor in the School of Social Work at the University of Alabama. He has been a probation officer and assistant superintendent of the Detention Center in Indianapolis. In the criminal justice area, Dr. Crow has served as a consultant to the State of South Dakota and the Birmingham Police Department. His key publications include *The Perception of Training Needs of Adult Probation and Parole Officers in Colorado* and *Is the Court Remaking the American Prison System?*

JERRY L. DAVIS is Director of Training for The Bringing It All Back Home Study Center and is an Assistant Professor at Appalachian State University. His current interests center around the development of quality community-based treatment services for youth, development of quality training services for residential treatment providers, and modifications of Teaching-Family technology for a variety of client populations. He has published research and made professional presentations in these areas as well as in the areas of parent training, teacher training, and verbal learning.

JOHN P. DINEEN is a training coordinator in the Child Development and Mental Retardation Center at the University of Washington, Seattle.

Previously, he was located at the Department of Rehabilitation Medicine at the University of Washington where he assisted in the development of a program to aid physically and emotionally handicapped individuals to obtain employment. He is currently involved in assisting sheltered workshops in the replication and evaluation of the training and placement procedures used by the FSVTP.

K. ANTHONY EDWARDS, Ph.D., is presently Assistant Professor of Human Services, Department of Nursing and Allied Health, Northern Kentucky University. He has been a Research Associate and Courtesy Assistant Professor, Department of Human Development, University of Kansas. He is Consultant Editor of *Nursing Homes;* a member of the Board of Directors, Senior Citizens of Northern Kentucky, Inc.; guest editor of *Journal of Applied Behavior Analysis;* and Co-chairperson of the special interest group, Behavioral Gerontology and Geriatrics, associated with the Association of Advancement of Behavior Therapy (AABT).

JAMES E. FAVELL, Ph.D., is the Director of Research at Western Carolina Center. He has conducted applied research on a variety of topics in the area of mental health and retardation, including the development of methods for treating physical aggression, cost effectiveness analysis of teaching methods, and the organization and management of comprehensive development living environments for profoundly handicapped people.

JUDITH E. FAVELL, Ph.D., is the Director of Evaluation at Western Carolina Center. She has published research on a variety of topics in the area of mental health and retardation, and has made important contributions in the non-aversive treatment of self-injurious behavior. Other areas of interest include systems for enhancing service delivery, staff training and management methods, and a wide range of behavioral treatment procedures for highly dependent clients.

RUSSELL E. GLASGOW, Ph.D., is an Assistant Professor of Psychology at North Dakota State University. Dr. Glasgow's primary research interests are in the fields of behavioral medicine and self-control. His publications include studies in the areas of the modification of smoking behavior and evaluations of self-help behavior therapy manuals.

JOSEPH E. HASAZI, Ph.D., is Associate Professor and Coordinator of the Developmental Disabilities Program in the Department of Psychology of the University of Vermont. His teaching and research interests have been primarily in the areas of developmental psychopathology, mental retardation, and applied behavior analysis. His current research is concerned with the relationship of institutional and community residential environments to behavioral development.

ROBERT J. JONES, Ph.D., is Director of Research and Evaluation for The Bringing It All Back Home Study Center and is an Associate Professor at Appalachian State University. His current interests center around the application of behavior technology to delinquency intervention, the development of quality residential treatment for delinquent youth, and the problem of sexual assault against children. He has published research for these areas as well as in the areas of stuttering, family counseling, and the problems of unemployment.

MIRIAM F. KELTY, Ph.D., is Executive Secretary of the Human Development Study Section at the National Institutes of Health. She was formerly on the staff of the National Commission for the Protection of Human Subjects of Biomedical and Behavioral Research, and served as Director of the Office of Scientific Affairs of the American Psychological Association. Her main interest areas are ethics of research, health behavior, and science policy.

PATRICIA J. KRANTZ received her Ph.D. from the University of Kansas in 1974 and is presently Co-Director of the Princeton Child Development Institute, Princeton, New Jersey. Her current work focuses on the evaluation of instruction and treatment strategies for autistic and severe-behavior-problem children and on design of accountability and advocacy systems.

BARBARA S. KUEHN is the Director of Family Training Program affiliated with Jewish Family and Children's Service of Kansas and Missouri. Her current work focuses on teaching child management to parents and on developing programs related to the prevention of child abuse. She received a Master's Degree from the Department of Human Development and Family Living at the University of Kansas.

NECHAMA LISS-LEVINSON received her doctorate in psychology from Southern Illinois University. From 1976 through 1978 she was an NIMH Post-Doctoral Fellow at the Sex Therapy Center of the Department of Psychiatry and Behavioral Science, School of Medicine, State University of New York at Stony Brook. She is presently Assistant Professor of Psychology at Brooklyn College of the City University of New York. Her areas of specialization are human sexuality, the psychology of women, and client rights.

DAVID LUKE, Ph.D., is Director of Sierra Development Center, Sparks, Nevada. His interests are in the application of behavior principles and the management of human service systems. He has published and presented in the areas of program management, staff training, and program evaluation.

REED MARTIN is an attorney active in the field of mental health law. As Director of the Public Law Division of Research Press, he has conducted seminars on mental health law in over two dozen states and consulted with over 100 facilities. He has served on an Institutional Review Board and on the boards of advocacy organizations representing the handicapped and has represented handicapped clients in administrative and judicial proceedings. He is the author of *Educating Handicapped Children: The Legal Mandate* (1979) and *Legal Challenges to Behavior Modification* (1975).

LYNN E. MCCLANNAHAN, Co-Director of the Princeton Child Development Institute, Princeton, New Jersey, has been designing and evaluating prosthetic and therapeutic environments for the past seven years. Dr. McClannahan's previous publications concern the design of living environments for elderly nursing home residents. Currently, she is engaged in research supporting the development of community-based group home treatment programs for autistic children and youth.

JOSEPH NOWINSKI, Ph.D., received his graduate training, in clinical psychology, at Syracuse University and the University of Connecticut. He is currently an NIMH Post-Doctoral Fellow at the Sex Therapy Center of the Department of Psychiatry and Behavioral Science, School of Medicine, State University of New York at Stony Brook. His clinical, teaching, and research interests focus mainly on the areas of marriage and human sexuality. His first book, on male sexuality, was published in 1980.

MARTIN J. POLLACK, Ph.D., is currently a psychologist at Mansfield Training School, where he has done extensive staff training and consultation on severe behavior disorders. Dr. Pollack has considerable experience with special populations including work with delinquent, mentally retarded, and emotionally disturbed children and their families. Current work includes self-control applications with handicapped children, legal and ethical issues, guidelines for behavioral techniques, parenting skills, and home-based treatment approaches.

RICHARD A. RAWSON, Ph.D., is the Director of Substance Abuse Services at the Community Health Projects, Inc., in West Covina, California. He received his Ph.D. in psychology from the University of Vermont in 1974. He has published numerous articles and has done most of his research in the area of substance abuse.

CHARLES M. RENNE, Ph.D., a 1965 graduate of St. Louis University, is Chief of the Clinical Psychology Department within the Behavioral Science Division of the National Asthma Center in Denver, Colorado. His publications and research activity have centered on the application of the principles of learning to health related issues, the behavior management and rehabilitation of chronically-ill children in residential settings, and the measurement of behavior in naturalistic environments.

TODD RISLEY, Ph.D., is Professor of Human Development at the University of Kansas, where he directs the Living Environments Group. His many research articles have recently focused on the development of *complete* environments which serve to continuously maintain and improve the functioning of children and other dependent people in day care and recreation centers, hospitals and institutions, and nursing homes. His most recent books are *The Toddler Center: A Practical Guide to Day Care for One- and Two-Year Olds* (O'Brien, Porterfield, & Herbert-Jackson) and *The Infant Center: A Complete Guide to Organizing and Managing Infant Day Care* (Herbert-Jackson, O'Brien, & Porterfield).

GERALD N. ROSEN, Ph.D., is Clinical Psychologist in private practice, in Seattle, Washington. He is involved in the treatment of phobia disorders and self-help therapies. He has published three books and over 20 articles in professional journals, mainly in the areas of self-help therapies, therapy expectancy sets, and desensitization.

LINDA C. SOBELL, Ph.D., is head of Behavioral Intervention Research Clinical Institute, Addiction Research Foundation, Toronto, Canada. She is the author of three books: *Emerging Concepts of Alcohol Dependence* (with E. M. Pattison and M. B. Sobell), *Behavioral Treatment of Alcohol Problems* (with M. B. Sobell), and *Evaluating Alcohol and Drug Abuse Treatment Effectiveness* (with M. B. Sobell and E. Ward), and of numerous articles and book chapters. She serves on the editorial boards of *Addictive Behaviors, Behavioral Assessment,* and *Behavior Modification* and is a consultant to the National Institute on Alcohol Abuse and Alcoholism.

MARK B. SOBELL, Ph.D., is head of Sociobehavioral Treatment Research Clinical Institute, Addiction Research Foundation, Toronto, Canada. He is the author of three books: *Emerging Concepts of Alcohol Dependence* (with E. M. Pattison and L. C. Sobell), *Behavioral Treatment of Alcohol Problems* (with L. C. Sobell) and *Evaluating Alcohol and Drug Abuse Treatment Effectiveness* (with L. C. Sobell and E Ward), and of numerous articles and book chapters. He serves on the editorial boards of the *Journal of Consulting and Clinical Psychology* and *Addictive Behaviors* and has been consultant to numerous agencies, including the National Institute on Alcohol Abuse and Alcoholism.

Jo-Ann Sowers is the Associate Director of Training and Research for the Vocational Training Program at the Child Development and Mental Retardation Center, University of Washington. Ms. Sowers has numerous presentations and publications related to the area of vocational training, placement, and follow-up of mentally retarded adults.

Jan Sheldon-Wildgen, Ph.D., J.D., is Associate Professor of Human Development at The University of Kansas. Dr. Sheldon-Wildgen has been working with the developmentally disabled for the last eight years and is presently involved in developing and evaluating training programs for the developmentally disabled as well as doing research concerning their legal rights. She has published several articles and two books about legal issues as they relate to dependent populations.

Beth Sulzer-Azaroff, Ph.D., is currently Professor of Psychology at the University of Massachusetts. Besides papers on behavioral approaches to classroom learning and motivation, instructional technology in higher education, professional issues, safety, and others, she is the author of several books: *Behavior Modification Procedures for School Personnel* and *Applying Behavior Analysis Procedures with Children and Youth* (both with G. Roy Mayer), *Making Educational Psychology Work* (with J. Brewer and L. Ford), and *Applying Behavior Analysis* (with E. P. Reese), now in press.

Richard Surles, Ph.D., is Commissioner of Mental Health, for the State of Vermont. His major area of interest is an organizational development, policy analysis, planning, and evaluation. He has served as a consultant in pre-school programs for handicapped, developmental disabilities, and mental health and has published and lectured extensively.

Gary D. Timbers, Ph.D., is Director of The Bringing It All Back Home Study Center and Associate Professor at Appalachian State University. His current interests center around the development of community-based residential treatment programs for delinquent and emotionally handicapped youth; programs for the establishment and training of personnel in group homes, natural homes, and foster homes; and applications of juvenile law as it affects client rights. He has published research and made professional presentations in these areas.

MICHAEL G. VENTURA, J.D., is an attorney at The Johns Hopkins Hospital and a member of the Maryland and Illinois Bar. He actively directed the risk management program and has direct responsibility for the management of all medical–professional liability claims filed against the hospital and its staff.

PART **I**

Keynote

CHAPTER 1

Legal Issues in Preserving Client Rights

Reed Martin

A History of Abuses

THE HISTORY OF CLIENT RIGHTS in public programs in America is unfortunately a history of abuses. Some are obvious, such as the pinching of an autistic youth until he/she is bruised, bleeds, and must be hospitalized. But, amazingly, many practitioners of such "therapy" have not seen it as abusive. It is not unusual to find instances in which individuals have been deprived of food and water in order to force changes in their behavior or to punish them. Again, the practitioners have seen virtue in such deprivation because they considered it effective in bringing about a desired change.

Some abuses are less obvious. In one suburban school district, all entering first graders were given tests that included questions about relations with their parents. Children who, at the age of six, indicated they were not kissed before being put to bed at night were routed into a pre-delinquency prevention project. The school thought this was wonderful and would head off the need for more severe interventions later. In another instance, teenage girls in a state retardation center were in vocational training where they were rewarded with points for their achievements, and then graduated to the next part of the program. But if they failed to stand when program staff entered the room or failed to say "Sir" or "Ma'am" when spoken to, they would not be allowed to advance, despite appropriate vocational skill development.

Some abuses are really hidden from view. A surprisingly large number of children are excluded from receiving educational services on the grounds that the school will not serve them. The rationale is usually that having them there is not fair to the other children, that they are dangerous, or that their parents would really be better satisfied with them being served in some special private facility. However this is presented, it is constructive exclusion; it is illegal; and it is a hidden but

3

widespread abuse all across the country. Another problem of this type occurs in mental health facilities where many clients are in so-called milieu therapy, which provides no individual goals, no treatment, and no growth. There is no possibility that these individuals will ever graduate to a less restrictive community facility. They are condemned, through program ineffectiveness, to a life sentence. Yet the very absence of program makes it hard to find this abuse and uproot it.

What Is Wrong

Some practitioners who read the above will undoubtedly ask themselves how multimillion-dollar facilities and programs with highly educated professionals can commit such abuses in the name of serving our citizens. The answer is threefold: discrimination on the basis of "handicapism"; lack of training about client rights; and lack of continuing legal and therapeutic information.

"Handicapism" refers to discrimination on the basis of handicap.[1] Most of the clients of public programs about whom we are concerned are handicapped. If we think of them as less than human, we then treat them as we would animals in research labs. We determine what is best for them, whether it is working, when to change it, and so forth. And we would never dream of asking permission of the client, let alone informing him/her of our plans. Handicapism is rampant in our society. When our public programs hire persons of dubious background, experience, and training, and then put them in contact with individuals whom they consider less than human, it is almost impossible to run a program without abuse.

As for lack of training about client rights, most staff probably feel that whatever rights a client had were forfeited when he/she entered the program. As I am often told—the biggest client right is the right to effective treatment, so the staff should be unfettered in their attempt to carry out their plans. But clients do have rights, and those rights often conflict with the flexibility with which most practitioners would prefer to carry out their programs. Staff need training in the rights of clients.

With regard to lack of continuing legal and therapeutic information, staff in mental health and education programs are rarely, if ever, given an opportunity to learn about legal developments in client rights and are typically not encouraged or supported in improving their treatment practices. For example, one workshop in which staff hear the current laws can be misleading for months into the future as new regulations

---

[1] I am indebted for this notion to Dr. Doug Biklen of the Center for Human Policy, Syracuse University.

develop. Worse, misunderstandings about legal regulation can create overreactions that cripple programs. The highly useful and supposedly slightly aversive technique of "time out" is barred in many programs because of an overreaction to a few regulatory efforts. Thus, a little information can mislead staff and cripple programs. There must be continuing education systems for updating staff knowledge of client rights and new therapeutic developments.

How Did Clients Get All These Rights So Suddenly?

When staff studied their profession (psychology, teaching, social work, and so forth) in school, they read of programs in which clients were deprived of many rights. Classic studies may have involved deprivation of food or placement in seclusion. As these staff took their positions in the real world of mental health care, they found that these same techniques were no longer allowed.

The clients we are concerned about represent the bottom scale of our society in terms of power—the mentally ill, the emotionally disturbed, the retarded, juveniles, and students. For many years courts did not inquire into their treatment; it was left up to the discretion of administrators.

Suddenly it was recognized that these individuals are citizens and that actions of the staff in public programs involve the state. The U.S. Constitution prohibits the state taking away the life, liberty, or property of anyone without due process of law. Due process of law, basically, requires notice of the intended action and some opportunity for a hearing if the client opposes the action. This recognizes that the client has rights and might in fact have the right to stop the proposed action by the state. With that basic notion of due process in place, courts began to inquire into treatment, and the court decisions come to outline a clear picture of client rights. Congress, reacting to the court decisions, enacted many of these rights into statutes. Acts such as Public Law 93-112, the Rehabilitation Act of 1973; P. L. 94-63, the Community Mental Health Amendments of 1975; P. L. 94-142, the Education for All Handicapped Children Act of 1975; P. L. 94-103, the Developmentally Disabled Assistance and Bill of Rights Act; and P. L. 95-602, the Rehabilitation, Comprehensive Services, and Developmental Disability Amendments of 1978, all establish client rights.

Trends in Rights

Court cases and statutory enactments can give us an idea of the trends that will continue to develop. To illustrate this I have traced several areas of rights—privacy, psychological autonomy, due process, protection against harm, involuntary servitude, least restrictive alternative, individualized treatment, and minimum standards.

Privacy. The concern of our society with privacy was most eloquently stated by Mr. Justice Brandeis, dissenting in *Olmstead* v. *United States:*

> The makers of our Constitution undertook to secure conditions favorable to the pursuit of happiness. . . . They sought to protect Americans in their beliefs, their thoughts, their emotions, and their sensations. They conferred, as against the Government, the right to be left alone—the most comprehensive of rights and the right most valued by civilized men. [*Olmstead,* 277 U.S. 438 (1928) at 478]

What balances against this private right to be left alone? What must an individual do that would allow society to have a legitimate interest in making him/her a client of some mental health service? The only answer can be an overt behavior that qualifies him/her for inclusion in a program. If the behavior does not actually exist, or is predicted only in the eyes of some diagnostician, then the case is very weak for invading that individual's privacy.

Psychological Autonomy. As with the notion of privacy, the First Amendment to the U.S. Constitution has been interpreted as protecting the right to generate ideas. If speech is to be free, then the thought process that produces speech must not be tinkered with. In *Kaimowitz* v. *Michigan Department of Mental Health* a court ruled that an involuntarily committed mental patient could not voluntarily undergo psychosurgery.

> Involuntarily confined mental patients live in an inherently coercive institutional environment. Indirect and subtle psychological coercion has a profound effect upon the patient population. [*Kaimovitz,* 42 U.S.L. Week 2063 (Mich. Cir. Ct., Wayne Cty., July 10, 1973)]

The court found that psychosurgery was too intrusive and would invade the protected privacy area; that the First Amendment "protects the generation and free flow of ideas from unwarranted interference with one's mental processes." After having one's brain cut upon, what would there be left of psychological autonomy?

In *Mackey* v. *Procunier* a prisoner had been involuntarily administered a suffocating drug as part of an aversive treatment program. The court stated that if the events were true as alleged, this would raise

> serious constitutional questions respecting cruel and unusual punishment or impermissible tinkering with the mental processes. [*Mackey,* 477 F.2d 877 (9th Cir. 1973)]

The developing trend is to respect the client's psychological autonomy. As the U.S. Supreme Court summarized in *Stanley* v. *Georgia,*

> Our whole constitutional heritage rebels at the thought of giving government the power to control men's minds. [*Stanley,* 397 U.S. 557 (1969)]

Due Process. When there is a threat to life, liberty, or property there must be due process of law before any deprivation occurs. Courts are beginning to recognize that with the conditions in many institutional facilities, the placement of a client there can shorten life (*Halderman* v. *Pennhurst,* 446 F. Supp. 1295 [E.D. Pa. 1977]). Certainly liberty too is involved: There may be a physical restriction on liberty, as in the placement of a person in an institution; but there is an even greater chance that liberty will be deprived through interruption of freedom of association with others. If, for example, a child in a public school is placed in a class for the emotionally disturbed, even though he is not "locked away" and comes and goes each day his liberty interest has been affected because the freedom to associate with others has been curbed (*Goss* v. *Lopez,* 95 S. Ct. 729 [1975]). And property interests can be affected: A client might when placed in a program have property taken away or have access to it restricted, as could occur in some token economy programs. There is a property interest in educational opportunity also, and if a client's rights are abused in a way that affects his access to education, there has been a property deprivation of constitutional proportions.

Thus due process is required for almost any intervention by the state in the life of an individual. And this means that before changing the status of a client in a program there must be notice and the opportunity for a hearing.

Protection Against Harm. Courts have recognized that the involvement of the state can harm individual clients even when the intention is to help (*New York State Association for Retarded Children v. Rockefeller,* 357 F. Supp. 752 [E.D. N.Y. 1973]). Often an individual loses functional behavior or acquires dysfunctional behavior in a large public program. Such regression has been found to be violative of the Eighth Amendment's prohibition against cruel and unusual punishment. So even though a practitioner might think what he/she intends to do is therapeutic, that does not insulate it from the charge that the overall program is causing harm.

Involuntary Servitude. In the past, when courts did not inquire into the workings of public programs, they allowed a great deal of institution-maintaining labor to be performed by clients. Even in public schools one still finds programs where the retarded are in a "vocational" program that means that they clean up the lunchroom after the other children, or in a "sheltered workshop" where they tend the grounds. Where labor is performed that would be compensated if the laborer were nonhandicapped, courts and regulatory bodies are finding noncompensation for the handicapped to be "involuntary servitude"—a violation of the Thirteenth Amendment to the Constitution. This also raises questions about token economies in which clients must perform tasks but get only tokens, not pay. And it means that any work assignment or work therapy program must fit into an overall therapeutic program or else be viewed very suspiciously.

Least Restrictive Alternative. In *Shelton v. Tucker,* the Supreme Court stated,

> In a series of decisions this Court has held that even though the government purpose be legitimate and substantial, that purpose cannot be pursued by means that broadly stifle fundamental personal liberties where the end can be more narrowly achieved. The breadth of legislative abridgement must be viewed in light of less drastic means for achieving the same basic purpose. [*Shelton,* 364 U.S. 479 (1960)]

This notion of the less drastic means has been popularized as the "least restrictive alternative." It means that choices must exist, and that the least restrictive choice must always be chosen. Once a program is underway, there continues to exist the right to challenge the restrictiveness and ask why the person cannot now be served in a less restrictive intervention. In *Halderman* v. *Pennhurst (supra)* the court found that the very nature of the institution was too restrictive. That court ordered the clients in that institution to be discharged ino community facilities. This raises a real question about the future of institutions.

Individualized Treatment. Many court decisions and several statutes have lead to the formation of the right to individual treatment. No longer can clients be grouped together for the convenience of program managers. There must be individual service plans in writing that specify goals, short-term objectives, and the individual responsible for implementation. One court recently examined programs in juvenile facilities in Texas and found that more was needed to meet this requirement of individual treatment.

> It is not sufficient for defendants to contend that merely removing a child from his environment and placing him in a structured situation constitutes constitutionally adequate treatment. . . . Nor do the Texas Youth Centers' sporadic attempts at . . . behavior modification through the use of point systems rise to the dignity of professional treatment programs geared to individual juveniles. [*Morales* v. *Turman,* 383 F. Supp. 53 (E.D. Tex. 1974)]

Please note that this is not an indictment of token economy systems— these can provide individualized treatment programs within an overall group setting; it is an indictment of group management programs where little or no attention is given to individual needs and goals.

Minimum Standards. More and more courts have examined treatment conditions and found necessary ingredients missing. Beginning with *Wyatt* v. *Stickney* (344 F. Supp. 373 [M.D. Ala. 1972]), courts have listed items that must be in the environment, such as nutritionally adequate diets, personal clothing, reading material, opportunities for privacy, opportunities to interact with others and receive visitors, opportunities for hygiene, and so forth. In meeting these minimum standards, many items that once were restricted in order to cause individuals to change their behavior must now be available without regard to the client's behavior.

Has the Pendulum Swung Too Far?

An expression common in civil liberties debates involves "dying with your rights on." The dilemma is often posed of the potentially suicidal individual who wins release from a restrictive confinement and then accomplishes the suicide. Was the civil liberties attorney right in winning the release? After all, the person was being held in too restrictive a confinement. Or was the practitioner right in wanting to confine the individual indefinitely because of a predicted threat of danger to self?

In being provided these basic rights (e.g., minimum standards, due process) are not clients losing the biggest right of all—the right to treatment so that they can leave the restrictiveness of the program and go back into the community? And, further, does not all this hamper professional choice so that less effective therapies might be used? The only possible rationalization here is that the most effective therapy is the one that will also most adequately protect the clients' rights. Rather than assuming that there is a contest between rights and therapy, professionals must realize that appropriate therapeutic interventions *include* client rights.

What Relationship Exists Between Applied Research and Client Rights?

The documented applied research of the past fifteen years (e.g., in the *Journal of Applied Behavior Analysis* and *Behavior Therapy*) has significantly altered the standards of acceptable practice in the treatment and education of the retarded, delinquent, abused, obese, autistic, learning delayed, and alcoholic, as well as those who simply seek to improve various aspects of interpersonal relationships. In the case of mental retardation and autism this applied research effort is the benchmark upon which backward custodial cesspools are being converted to humane treatment and educational facilities for these handicapped children. Quite obviously, the court and legislative authorities have played an important role in mandating these changes, but it is applied research results that have illustrated the feasibility of humane treatment interventions in assisting these handicapped children in achieving something closer to their individual potential.

It is interesting to note—as is documented in Part IV of this book— that most abuse to clients has occurred in the name of treatment, not science. This is not to suggest that science has never been marred by examples of severe abuse; but it is true that applied research has in recent times come to be extremely sensitive to the rights of clients. The focus now seems to be on the development of the most *humane and effective* practices.

The continued active role of applied research in our treatment and educational settings is critical to solving human problems. On the other hand, clients' rights must be protected. Fortunately, these two goals are not incompatible, as is illustrated in Part IV.

PROTECTING CLIENTS RIGHTS IN TREATMENT AND EDUCATIONAL PROGRAMMING

There is no guarantee that a program will always meet its obligations regarding client rights, or that with new changes in the law it would not need modification. Protection and treatment of clients depends on program personnel being knowledgeable and sensitive to both therapeutic and rights issues. This sensitivity means that program personnel continually review their program, seeking ways to improve its client responsiveness. Many program personnel have found the following questions of value in determining if practices exist that could give rise to legitimate concern.[2]

1. *Should the client in question be in your program?* Check the federal, state, and local eligibility criteria and determine if the client is properly placed. If he/she is not, arguments that he/she is being subjected to an inappropriate therapy would be even stronger. If you discover an inappropriately placed client, attempt to have the placement changed.

2. *Is the goal selected a legitimate target?* All too often behavior is

---

[2] A series of questions similar to these were originally presented in a periodical entitled *Law and Behavior: Quarterly Analysis of Legal Developments Affecting Professionals in Human Services,* written by this author, R. Martin, and published by Research Press, Champaign, Illinois 61820.

shaped for institutional convenience. Is this behavior serious enough to justify intervention? Is it legitimately related to the purpose of your agency? Will changing this behavior aid the client by enabling him/her to move to a less restrictive program?

3. *Have you given adequate notice of the program or the approach that you will use?* Do you tell of possible risks and discomforts? Do you communicate this to the greatest degree possible with the client himself as well as the parent or guardian?

4. *Do you obtain written consent from the proper person?* Do you avoid coercion—such as the suggestion that the recommended procedure is the only alternative? Does the signed consent indicate that the person understands the procedure and that he can revoke consent at any time?

5. *Is there an opportunity for a hearing to air any dispute about the procedures?* Do such hearings in fact work to redress grievances or do they stifle complaints?

6. *If the client is of school age, is he in a full program of education and not just treatment?* Sometimes a child is taken out of a program and put in one that concentrates on only one of his problems. If that program does not have a full educational component then it may violate federal education laws.

7. *Has there been a full assessment of any medical, neurological, or physiological causes for the problem that might suggest an alternative approach?* Courts and administrative bodies seem increasingly sensitive to ensuring that medically correctable deficiencies be addressed as early as possible.

8. *Does placement of the client in your program subject the individual to unequal or unfair circumstances?* Such circumstances might be placement in poorer facilities or with less adequately trained staff.

9. *Does the client receive your therapy as part of an individualized program?* Is the client merely lumped together with others in a general program, or is the technique prescribed specifically for that client's needs?

10. *Is there a periodic review of progress?* Reviews should focus on determining if the results justify continuation, or a change, in the program. Such reviews should be conducted with the client (and his/her representative) and other professionals.

11. *Is the program being offered in the least restrictive alternative that is feasible?*

12. *Do your staff really know what they are doing?* Are the procedures you are using regulated in writing? Are the staff who may use them specified? Are those staff persons trained to a demonstrable level of competency? Are staff supervised as they carry out the intervention?

13. *Is there any reason to consider the approach experimental?* If so, are you in compliance with regulations on human experimentation?

14. *Have you presented your approach for review to any required body?* You may have a research review committee, a treatment review committee, or a human rights committee. If you have no such public body, you might create one to review any approach that you might predict could be publicly, legally, or professionally controversial.

15. *Is your approach corporal punishment?* Courts have defined corporal punishment as the intentional infliction of pain to bring a desired result. Can you distinguish your approach from corporal punishment? If not, you should seek the help of a professional association in refining your approach.

16. *Do you maintain accurate written records?* This includes such things as treatment plans and goals, data on progress, on consent, staff discussions leading to the decision to use a particular approach, progress reviews with the client, approval of any required body, and complaints and follow-up.

17. *Do you investigate any allegations of abuse?* You should have procedures for following-up all complaints, and if necessary for calling upon an investigative panel or professional association to review the situation and recommend immediate action as well as steps to be taken to prevent any future abuses.

18. *Are you sensitive to client rights issues, attempting to improve treatment/education while minimizing possibilities for abuse?* This book has been designed to assist practitioners (e.g., client-care staff, therapists, teachers, administrators, health care personnel, mental health specialists) in improving their treatment/education services by being more responsive to the rights of their clientele. It is hoped that from a reading of this book you will identify and implement numerous ideas that will immediately and directly improve your client services and help prevent any future abuses.[3]

Conclusion

Is it hopeless in these days of client rights to embark on a career in a "helping profession"? Certainly not. But the career must be based on a sensitivity and interest in improving client services and enhancing these through client involvement. Client-care staff, therapists, other practitioners, and administrators must ensure that they keep abreast of new developments in therapeutic practices and client rights. Human-service provider organizations must arrange for continuing in-service educa-

---

[3] In addition to this source book on client rights, you may wish to write the Association for the Advancement of Behavior Therapy (420 Lexington Avenue, New York, N.Y. 10017) for their information on (1) "Professional Consultation and Peer Review Services," (2) "Guidelines for Choosing a Behavioral Therapist," and (3) "Ethical Issues for Human Services."

tional opportunities for personnel in every facet of the care delivery system. Practitioners and administrators alike must come to understand that there is not a dichotomy between client rights and good treatment. Rather, therapeutic practices of good quality encompass a sensitivity to the rights of clients as individuals in a free society.

PART II

Safeguarding
Non-Institutional
Clientele

It might be argued that providers of mental health, education, and health care services find themselves in a position of double jeopardy with regard to client-rights issues. On the one hand, the practitioner must recognize and safeguard rights specific to the *individual* receiving services. For example, providers of services to children must be aware of the special vulnerability of the child as a member of society as well as his/her rights as a client. On the other hand, there are rights issues concerning the *type of service* provided and the *setting* in which clients receive services. For example, more restrictive treatment settings may pose a greater threat to client rights than do less restrictive ones.

In Part II of this book systems for preserving client rights are discussed from the standpoint of the individual receiving services. As noted by Reed Martin in his keynote chapter, the practitioner of mental health, education, and health care services must accept the fact that "clients are people, too" and approach them accordingly. Going a step further, the practitioner must recognize that not all people are equally capable of exercising their rights as clients and individuals.

As Martin has noted, the individuals most in danger of having their rights violated are those at the "bottom scale of our society in terms of power—the mentally ill, emotionally disturbed, retarded, juveniles, and students." It is significant, therefore, that the authors in the following section provide detailed descriptions of how helping professionals can effectively protect the rights of these individuals.

The first four chapters of this section concern the rights of the child client. Christian, Clark, and Luke examine the rights of children as individuals in society, as family members, as students, and as clients receiving community mental health services. They point out that preserving the rights of children in psychotherapy is often complicated by the question, *Who is the client?* In many cases children may find themselves "involuntary" participants in counseling, with the role of client "assigned" to them by their parents. Christian *et al.* discuss several effective strategies for preserving the rights of children as the recipients of counseling services, including client "tracking" systems and case-record review procedures.

Kuehn and Christophersen address the rights of clients in cases of child abuse and neglect by considering the rights of the abused as well as those of the suspected abuser. The authors focus first on the client within the family before considering him/her within the legal and social service systems. They argue convincingly that the most effective strategy in preventing abuse is working to ensure the effectiveness of intervention efforts, and that ineffective intervention in the area of child abuse may result in violations of the very rights that our legal system is mandated to preserve.

The rights of the handicapped child is the subject of both the chapter by Pollack and Sulzer-Azaroff and the one by McClannahan and Krantz. Pollack and Sulzer-Azaroff begin their discussion, "Protecting the Educational Rights of the Handicapped Child," by explaining the historical developments that contributed to the passage of the Education of All Handicapped Children Act (P.L. 94-142) by Congress in 1975. After identifying the educational rights of the handicapped, they present a detailed accout of procedures effective in providing necessary safeguards. Included are strategies for protecting rights during intake, placement, programming, and for obtaining consent for special procedures.

McClannahan and Krantz describe systems for protecting the rights of autistic children and adolescents receiving day treatment and community-based group living services. The special vulnerability of autistic and severely disturbed youths is graphically illustrated in the introductory segment of the chapter, which presents actual responses by autistic youths to questions related to client-rights issues. The authors approach the preservation of client rights through the establishment of program-evaluation and accountability systems, discussing specific ways to measure program processes and products.

The remaining chapters in this part are primarily concerned

with client-rights issues specific to providing mental health and health care services to adults (Becker and Abel, however, do discuss the rights of child victims of sex abuse as well as adults). Hannah and Surles consider the rights of adults receiving clinical services in mental health centers, stressing the importance of adequately informing clients and encouraging client participation in determining goals for treatment and methods to be employed. They also advocate the establishment of an ongoing client-rights policy committee and quality assurance programs in mental health centers to ensure that clients receive effective services within the limits of their rights as clients and individuals.

Liss-Levinson and Nowinski discuss issues and strategies concerning the protection of the rights of clients receiving sex therapy services. They make a strong argument for client advocacy, stressing the importance of adequate training and ethical guidelines for sex therapists. The chapter includes an informative "Bill of Rights for the Consumer of Psychotherapy."

Becker and Abel provide a thorough examination of the rights of clients receiving services related to sex abuse. The discussion highlights issues related to adult sexual assault victims, child sexual assault victims, and sex offenders. The authors provide a number of well-designed consent forms for use with each of these types of client as well as one for use by staff—i.e., a form describing the physical and legal risks involved in providing services to sex offenders.

Protecting the rights of clients seeking services related to substance abuse is the topic of the next two chapters. Sobell and Sobell describe rights issues specific to clients seeking services for alcohol-related problems. The authors present a model for preserving the rights of the problem drinker, which stresses ongoing staff training in client-rights issues and efforts to ensure client understanding of all aspects of the treatment process. The authors also lend their support to the recommendation by other authors in this section concerning the importance of developing quality assurance and clinical-case reviews as systems to safeguard client rights.

Callahan and Rawson's chapter concerns the rights of the addict-client. After reviewing the history of drug use and abuse from the legal and cultural perspectives, they examine the roles of the "client-addict" and the "clinician-jailer." The authors present a detailed explanation of client rights in the treatment of addiction and recommend strategies to ensure their protection. The chapter concludes with the description of the Heroin Antagonist and Learning

Therapy Project (HALT)—a model treatment program involving narcotics-antagonist chemotherapy and behavior therapy.

The final chapter in this section is concerned with the client-rights issues associated with the development and use of self-help psychotherapies. Barrera, Rosen, and Glasgow define self-help as "procedures that assist consumers in making self-directed changes in the relative absence of therapist supervision." The authors document the impressive benefits of self-help therapy, but caution the reader concerning the risks involved and the resultant potential for violation of client rights. The chapter concludes with a critical discussion of the professional responsibilities assumed in prescribing self-help therapies and the ethical standards that should govern the professional's behavior.

The reader will note that the chapters in this section provide encouraging evidence of the present state of our technology with regard to the recognition and protection of the rights of non-institutionalized individuals seeking educational, mental health, and health care services. In addition, the reader will note that the contributors in this section are consistent in stressing three central issues: (1) understanding by the therapist of the rights of clients and their special vulnerabilities as a function of age or handicap, (2) educating the client about his/her rights, about the treatment process, and about the practitioner's recognition of client rights and efforts to protect these rights, and (3) safeguarding client rights as an integral part of service delivery via program-evaluation, accountability systems, and ongoing staff training.

CHAPTER 2

Client Rights in Clinical Counseling Services for Children

Walter P. Christian
Hewitt B. Clark
David E. Luke

The Rights of Children

> The special vulnerabilities of children are well documented in child development research. The impact of experiences in early childhood on later development and behavior is unquestionable. Intellectually and emotionally as well as physically, children are not born to survive independently. In fact, the human infant is probably the most dependent newborn in the animal kingdom. The primacy effect of early experiences, developmental stages, and the critical periods of cognitive and emotional growth create potential behavioral influences that exist for life. As mental health professionals, there is a need for us to apply our knowledge in these areas sensitively and deliberately in our work with children. (*Koocher,* 1976, p. 2)

There is perhaps no other subgroup in our society in a more ambivalent role with more poorly defined rights than our children. Hetznecker and Forman (1974) delineate a number of major conflicts associated with the status of children in our culture—specifically, that while our culture places tremendous value on freedom and independence children are often viewed as "possessions" and may be recognized only as members of groups such as the family or the classroom.

It has been argued that children comprise the largest underrepresented minority group in the United States—having no vote, little affirmative lobbying on their behalf, and virtually no political influence. As Hobbs (1975) observes, "The most obvious and most important limitation is the inadequacy of mechanisms for bringing violations of children's legal rights before the courts." Hobbs further notes, "As long as basic standards remain unwritten matters of judgment which fluctuate with changing resources, priorities, and personnel, the protection of children's legal rights . . . will remain inadequate." Farson (1974) and

Gottlieb (1973), in addressing the issue of children's liberation, emphasize our denial of rights to children. Apter (1976) observes, "politically, economically, legally, and sexually, we have double standards for adults and children." Holt (1972) maintains, "Children have too little freedom of choice and the choices they have are trivial." He defines adult authority as "some kind of general and permanent right and duty to tell children what to do."

Keith-Spiegel (1976) concludes that children are "powerless vis-à-vis society" and that they constitute the most discriminated [against] . . . in terms of legal rights and access to decision making powers over their own destinies." Koocher (1976a) refers to this situation as one of "benign oppression":

> As adults, it is easy for us to think of children as miniature versions of ourselves; indeed, outwardly they appear to be like us, and they do grow up to be like us. The subtle fallacy inherent in this reasoning is that children are not simply small grown-ups. Children are unique in at least two important ways. First, a child's basic equipment for adapting and functioning in the world is quite different from that of an adult. Second, at the very least, children are constantly subjected to benign oppression and to all other violations that any under-represented minority group experiences. (p. 2)

Despite their treatment by society, children indeed have rights and, as we have seen in recent years, there is every sign that the government and the courts are becoming more disposed to identify and protect them. Feshbach and Feshbach (1976) provide a summary of our past and present interest in children's rights: They observe that, in the past, interest in children's rights was limited to the industrial exploitation of child labor (Berger, 1971), gross neglect and sexual abuse (Helfer & Kempe, 1972), and physical harm (Gil, 1970; Light, 1974). To date, only limited attention has been directed to children's rights in therapy (Robinson, 1974), classification and diagnostic labeling (Mercer, 1974), incarceration (Ohlin, Coates, & Miller, 1974), foster care and adoption practices (Berger, 1971; Mnookin, 1974), education practices (Falk, 1941), and privacy and other legal privileges (Rodham, 1974).

Current intensified interest in the rights of children is reflected in the following "challenge" from the Joint Commission on Mental Health of Children (1970):

> If we are to optimize the mental health of our young and if we are to develop our human resources, every infant must be granted: the right to be wanted, the right to be born healthy, the right to live in a healthy environment, the right to satisfaction of basic needs, the right to continuous loving care, the right to acquire the intellectual and emotional skills necessary to achieve individual aspirations and to cope effectively in our

society, and the right to receive care and treatment through facilities which are appropriate to their needs and which keep them as closely as possible within their normal social setting. (pp. 3–4)

In addition to these general considerations, there are a number of more specific children's rights issues of particular interest to the mental health practitioner. The therapist should be particularly familiar with children's rights as family members, as students in education programs, and as clients in psychotherapy.

CHILDREN'S RIGHTS WITHIN THE FAMILY

Feshbach and Feshbach (1976) comment on the lack of attention given children's rights within the family. Much of what attention has been directed toward this area has concerned parental punishment practices. Steinmetz and Straus (1973, 1974) found that corporal punishment is an almost universal practice in England and the United States, with an estimated 84 to 97 percent of parents reporting use of physical punishment at some time in their children's lives.

Feshbach and Feshbach point out that, in the case of severe punishment practices, the child's rights are being violated. They believe that a child too has a right not to be subjected to cruel and unusual punishment—i.e., all forms of punishment that pose negative consequences for the child's growth and well-being. However, in attempting to articulate the child's rights in the home, we are again faced with the subordinate role of the child relative to that of the parent. Such articulation becomes further complicated by the absence of a universally accepted definition and enumeration of the rights and responsibilities of parents and children.

In Feshbach and Feshbach's view, the best resolution to the problem of parent punishment practices lies in teaching parents to choose disciplinary practices that "socialize" without infringing upon the child's rights. They suggest procedures—familiar to every behavior therapist—geared to reinforcing behaviors incompatible with the child's undesirable behavior, rather than physical punishment of the undersirable behavior. Feshbach and Feshbach describe how a community might function as a resource for parents—e.g., providing information, guidance, child care—as well as a protector and advocate for children.

CHILDREN'S RIGHTS IN EDUCATION

Children in many parts of this country have both the legal right and the obligation to attend school. Courts have recognized that the right to an education is fundamental, and that the denial of schooling to a student is a serious act that school officials have the right to perform only in extreme situations and only with strict safeguards against its arbitrariness. The courts have also addressed the issue of the child's right to a quality education. In fact, it may be argued that compulsory education without quality controls is a violation of the child's rights. Recently, several lawsuits in their attack upon the inadequate education provided by certain school districts have tended to support this position (Levine, Cary, & Divoky, 1973).

Other rights issues concerning education that have been highlighted by recent court decisions include the right to due process, the right to be free from arbitrary corporal punishment, the right to equal opportunity as regards the availability and quality of education programs, and the right of students or their parents to have access to school records.

A particularly important development is the recent federal legislation regarding educational programs for the handicapped, since this legislation is concerned with programs for the "emotionally disturbed" and otherwise handicapped child. The Education for All Handicapped Children Act (P.L. 94-142) was signed into law in 1975 and is designed to ensure that all handicapped children have available to them a free, appropriate education emphasizing special education and related services designed to meet their unique needs. In addition, it assures that the rights of children and parents are safeguarded. These safeguards include (1) due process, (2) nondiscriminatory testing, (3) least restrictive environment—e.g., the requirement that handicapped children be educated with nonhandicapped children to the maximum extent possible, (4) education using the child's native language, (5) confidentiality—e.g., the assurance that any information contained in school records will not be released without the permission of the parent, and (6) the right to representation—e.g., the assurance that the child is to be represented by his or her parents, guardian, or surrogate parent. The law further requires that Individual Education Plans (IEPs) be prepared for each handicapped child, with parents participating on the team that draws up the plan. IEPs are to be developed or revised at least once every six months.

CHILDREN'S RIGHTS AND PSYCHOTHERAPY

In providing counseling and psychotherapy for children, the following rights must be identified and preserved in each instance: (1) the right of informed consent, (2) the right to refusal of treatment, (3) the right to an individualized treatment program based on his or her needs (goals of treatment must be objectively stated, regular reviews of progress must be made to determine if the treatment goal is being attained, and the treatment program must be revised as necessary to meet the goal), (4) the right to the least restrictive treatment program, (5) the right to be fully informed of the treatment procedures to be utilized and what each entails (clients must be informed of the history and effectiveness of the treatment procedures with similar individuals and similar presenting problems, the reasonable risks and benefits associated with each treatment procedure, and possible alternative treatments), and (6) the right to confidentiality concerning release of data or other information.

An obvious problem concerns the question *who the client is* in counseling with children. The child is often at best an "involuntary" participant in counseling—his or her participation being "arranged" by parents and therapist. In these cases, there exists a potential conflict of interest between child and parent involving both the status and rights of the client. Koocher (1976b) notes, "In most cases, the child-client is accepted for treatment at the request of the parents, is not asked to decide what he or she wants, and has little control over the goals of the therapy that the grownups establish in consultation with one another." The therapist often finds that he or she must determine what is in the child's best interests—e.g., in cases where the child attempts to exercise the right to refuse treatment.

Koocher (1976b) points out that problems concerning children's rights in psychotherapy are most frequently concerned with omission.

> The problem is not so much that therapists are rushing to trample the rights of their child patients, or even that children are daily being hurt by considerations that are being overlooked. Rather, the key issue is that so much more could be done with greater effectiveness if child therapists recognize their clients' basic rights as a matter of routine. . . . It is not inane to note that children are people and to recognize that they bring to the context of psychotherapy all the uniqueness of individual human beings as well as a special measure of vulnerability. (p. 31)

For example, therapists often neglect preliminary discussions with the child client. Holmes and Urie (1975) observe that such discussions are not only necessary in respecting the client's rights, but also result in more effective treatment outcomes when the child is informed concerning the *how* and the *why* of the therapeutic process.

In addition, confidentiality and privacy are rights often overlooked in work with children. For example, some communications between child client and therapist are not to be routinely shared with family members. Treating the child client as an individual (or as an adult) would require that he or she be informed during preliminary discussions if information is to be shared with parents or family members in order to be able to respond accordingly. It is also important to distinguish children who come to therapy knowing they have problems, suffering as a result of them, and seeking relief, from children brought to therapy only because their behavior is distressing to someone else—e.g., parents or teachers (LoCicero, 1976).

Ross (1974) suggests a set of principles to guide those providing therapy for children. His four basic tenets—as summarized by Koocher (1976b)—are that children have the right (1) to be told the truth, (2) to be treated with personal respect, (3) to be taken seriously, and (4) to have meaningful participation in the decision making that applies to his or her life. In addition, LoCicero (1976) provides an excellent set of guidelines for informing children of the results of clinical evaluations: She stresses the importance of (1) communicating the purpose of the evaluation to the child, (2) "demystifying" the evaluation process for the child, (3) engaging the child in dialogue to the degree possible, (4) discussing family problems within the limits of parental confidentiality, and (5) "translating" technical and interpretive language for the child. This approach not only assists in protecting the child's rights, but also serves as a preliminary step in therapy, providing the therapist with some additional information regarding the nature of the problem. It also helps in establishing rapport between child and therapist.

While most therapists feel comfortable working with children within the limits of their professional ethics, these ethical standards for psychotherapy with children must be expanded and clarified. Koocher (1976b) observes that often ethical standards for professional associations "do not specifically address children as a unique subset of the population," and that "children are unique and [there are] special demands on those who work with children and their families." Indeed, a special set of ethical standards would seem of particular significance for those of us engaged in "socializing" children. In the absence of such standards, we must temper our expectations of the child client with an understanding of his or her ambivalent social status and rights as an individual.

In summary, given their ambivalent social role, limited rights, and "benign oppression" at the hands of society, children are a unique subset of the population. Since children are unlikely to possess the knowledge and assertiveness to adequately recognize their rights as clients and ensure that they are protected, mental-health service providers are in need of reliable systems for quality control and professional accountability in this area. In the remaining sections of this chapter, the essential elements of such an accountability system will be delineated. Basic to the effectiveness of this or any such system is our professional recognition of the child as an individual with rights and privileges that must be preserved.

Preserving Client Rights During Intake Interviews

Any client's first contact with an agency or individual practitioner represents on the one hand, the first opportunity for violation of his or her rights, and on the other, the first opportunity to identify and protect them. This first contact should be an opportunity to educate clients and assist them in maintaining and enhancing their rights and the effectiveness of the therapy to be undertaken.

This section will examine the role of initial contacts—in particular, intake procedures—as they set the tone for the preservation of client rights. If this protection of rights is viewed as a set of skills that clients can learn, then the preservation of client rights requires that clients (1) have a sufficiently accurate knowledge of their rights, (2) have the ability to determine when their rights are being infringed upon, and (3) be able to exercise options to protect their rights.

Thus, one major function of the intake process should be to protect the client's rights by providing information upon which he or she can act. For example, if clear treatment choices are given, then a client will be in a better position to provide truly informed consent. The spirit of informed consent legislation requires that such information be provided in a manner usable to the client.

INFORMING THE CLIENT

The procedures for presenting information to a client can be viewed as an educational process that, as such, is subject to development and examination through the use of instructional technologies. A number of alternative educational approaches can be taken. These include sending descriptive material to clients prior to the intake interview, presenting written material and audio-visual presentations in person, and giving personal explanations to clients.

One approach to assuring that clients can in fact understand their rights involves the use of the Flesch formula (Flesch, 1963), which provides a method for evaluating written material based on factors of ease of reading and interest level. The ease of reading can be measured by extracting samples of written material and subjecting them to analysis that includes tabulating the length of words, sentences, and paragraphs. The level of interest reflects such factors as the use of personal pronouns. This formula yields a grade-equivalent measure of material being given clients.

The primary focus of this evaluative technology has been on adult populations, although alternative approaches are also being developed for children. Treatment materials are being produced in comic book and children's book formats. Recently, Palmer (1977) has published children's books geared at teaching concepts of assertion to children. These books, written for children ages 5–9 and 8–12, teach concepts of liking oneself, using feeling words, asking for what one wants, saying no, and being oneself. The development of these skills would enable a child to participate more fully in decision making in counseling. Similar formats might be used to introduce children to their rights and choices in treatment.

Standardized presentations such as slide projection and videotape can also be used to introduce clients, parents, and guardians to rights issues and describe the services available to them so that they become capable of making an informed choice (Levy & Brackbill, 1979). The advantage of standardized presentations is that information can be efficiently and effectively communicated to clients in a nonthreatening way. These standardized audio-visual presentations free therapists from presenting this information and thus reduce the possibility of unclear or biased presentations. The standardized audio-visual presentation of material can also compensate for a client's inability to read or comprehend material presented through a single modality. Different presentations and materials can be developed that are suitable for specific client populations, including non-English speakers or people from a particular subculture. As has been noted above, it is even possible to develop the materials so they are suitable for direct presentation to children.

One disadvantage of standardized presentation of materials is the lack of certainty that the material is actually being attended to and, in fact, understood. It is therefore important that the therapist be available to ask and answer questions or further clarify topics, in order to ensure that the client can effectively exercise his or her rights.

As previously discussed, an area of special concern in preserving the rights of the child client involves the problem of the parent being the one seeking services for the child. It is therefore important that parents as well as therapists be educated concerning children's rights. More important, parents must be informed of their responsibility to protect the rights of their children. For example, they must see that the child has information and understanding appropriate for him or her to comprehend the need for treatment, the available choices of treatment procedures, the length of the proposed treatment, and the meaning of client responsibility. This is important not only to ensure informed consent on the part of the child, but also to increase the probability of effective treatment. As previously noted, investigators have found that therapy is more effective when children are informed concerning the *how* and *why* of the treatment they are to receive (Holmes & Urie, 1975).

ASSESSMENT BY CLINICIAN

A second major element of intake is the actual assessment provided by the clinician. In practice, this typically occurs during an intake interview in which child, guardian, and therapist discuss presenting problems. At this time the therapist attempts to complete a functional analysis of the problem. There may be a temptation for the clinician to go far afield into historical or peripheral factors that the client may raise. However, from the point of view of client rights, the information solicited should relate as specifically as possible to the problem in question. Morganstern (1976) has suggested that the therapist needs to learn from the client *"everything* relevant to the development of effective, efficient, and durable treatment interventions and, from an ethical standpoint, nothing else." Through limiting the scope of the investigation to problem-relevant areas, the therapist protects the client's right to privacy.

It is encouraging that considerable recent interest has been shown in the area of behavioral interviewing (Evans & Nelson, 1977; Morganstern, 1976; Linehan, 1977). Though it is beyond the scope of this chapter to discuss the intake interview process in detail, it clearly has important implications for safeguarding clients' rights. For example, the intake interview must involve therapist and client in selecting an effective treatment in the least restrictive environment; this requires focusing attention on the specific problem and providing an initial analysis of potential controlling variables. Through this involvement of the client, the clinician's job of systematically collecting relevant data and making recommendations for treatment is more likely to be successful.

The goal of assessment becomes a functional analysis of behaviors and their maintaining contingencies, as well as an investigation of the resources available to change them (Morganstern, 1976). Formats for the intake interview have been developed identifying the major areas to be covered, in order to assure that the major relevant topics are explored. These topics include such things as the client's definition of the problem, antecedent events, consequences, and duration and frequency of behavior.

The value of information obtained during interviewing must be carefully weighed, as suggested in various findings of unreliability in reports by clients. For example, Evans and Nelson (1977), in a review of factors affecting reliability and validity of parental reports, found that retrospective reports are strikingly inaccurate. Further, they suggest that in child rearing practice factual events are much more likely to be accurately reported than attitudes.

With a focus on factual events, the interview can lead to a clear delineation of the behavioral problems and then move on to estimating subjective baselines to provide a picture of the frequency of the be-

haviors. These baselines estimates can be of some use in initially determining the severity of the problem, but lack the advantage of observable
measures. Through interviewing other agents (e.g., grandparents, teachers)
a picture can be obtained of the kinds of procedure that have been
attempted in the past, along with their degree of success.

A concern noted earlier is that the child's status as a client is unclear. The child as a source of information and the child as an individual
may have very different goals. The goals sought by the child must
therefore be clearly recognized and considered in formulating the treatment plan. Though there are no firm guidelines from the courts or the
profession regarding, for example, a child's ability to give consent for
services, ideally the greater the child's involvement (within the limits of
his or her capabilities) the more fully his or her rights as an individual
can be protected.

THE CLIENT-THERAPIST AGREEMENT

A recent innovation, the client-therapist agreement, has provided a
method for ensuring client participation and protection. Though the
therapist may attempt to analyze the presenting problem objectively and
develop a treatment plan that will meet the client's needs, he or she
must recognize that the proposed plan or change in behaviors may not be
satisfactory to the client. Morganstern (1976) concludes that therapists
cannot separate themselves entirely from the important ethical and
societal implications involved in any assessment and treatment. Through
a formalized treatment agreement, the client is offered the protection of
his or her rights along with specification in writing that services to be
received are designed to help the individual achieve the specified objectives.

A variety of practitioners, agencies, and even state governments have
begun to require contract-like agreements for clients receiving services.
Such agreements commonly include commitments by client, guardian,
and therapist to specifically identified goals, procedures to be used, and
methods to assess progress. Also included are mechanisms for periodic
reviews and modifying the agreement. In some cases, fee arrangements
and other elements of the overall treatment context are included. Such
a contract can function as an important educational tool by involving
the client in therapy, as well as helping to limit use of aversive procedures without the client's clear understanding of the range of positive
procedures that have been tried (only after these have been shown to be
ineffective should an aversive procedure be considered).

The use of contractual treatment plans to provide quality services within the limits of the client's rights is discussed in greater detail below, in the section "Record Review."

Client Tracking Systems

In order to preserve the rights of clients in treatment, it is critical not only that assessment occur at the initial intake but that periodic evaluations be made of the client's progress. Unless these reviews occur at intervals specified by state law, agency standards, or good clinical practice, the rights of clients may be violated. Such reviews should involve therapist, client, and legal guardians, and each review should be documented or summarized with the client or legal guardian initialing it to signify that the casenote adequately represents the review. Any additions or comments that the client or legal guardian might want to contribute should be permitted, and in fact encouraged.

It would also seem important for the therapist to review the client's progress periodically with his or her colleagues. Professional peer review is recommended to improve the caliber of treatment as well as provide a type of "public forum" that should help ensure that the least restrictive procedures are being employed. Colleagues can also assist in exploring alternative treatment approaches. Obviously, if a client is not making progress under a given treatment program, it is imperative that this program be changed and a new treatment plan developed in conjunction with the client (Martin, 1975).

To ensure that activities such as these reviews occur and do so in a timely manner, we have found an in-house aid to be of value—an aid we refer to as a "client tracking system." The purpose of this client tracking system is to coordinate services for each client, ensuring that the client receives all the appropriate considerations, periodic reviews, and protections that are his or hers by law and good professional practice. Of course, it is easy for a therapist with a large caseload to overlook a review, the administering of an assessment instrument, or the writing of a summary to document progress. But a tracking system can serve as a therapist's prompter to attend to these activities in a timely manner, which will hopefully affect positively the quality of services provided.

Our experience in the development and implementation of client tracking systems suggests the use of two different types of aid, depending on the information being tracked and its proposed utilization. One system involves the therapist using a worksheet. This prompts the therapist to complete various activities with a given client or group of clients at particular times through the course of treatment. For example, in an individual clinical counseling situation, the form may prompt the therapist to complete the initial assessment during the first session and request that certain baseline data be kept by the client's legal guardians and presented at the second session. During the second session, the worksheet may prompt the therapist to develop at least a preliminary treatment plan with the client (or legal guardian) and begin its implementation. After six sessions the therapist would review the case in a professional staff meeting to determine with colleagues what level of progress is being made and seek other treatment recommendations. If adequate progress is not being made, then another review would be needed with the client, to formulate an alternative treatment plan or seek alternative services for the client. After twelve weeks a complete review of the client's progress and the goals of the treatment plan would be conducted with the client or legal guardian, focusing on the client's awareness of treatment progress. Similar promptings continue throughout the course of the treatment program, with reminders ensuring that all components of the transition from "active" through "follow-up" to "termination" be completed in a timely sequence for the case.

Another type of client tracking system provides an overview of all of the cases for each therapist. The kind of information summarized in this system varies, of course, with the type of treatment service (e.g., residential or clinical). In the case of a residential treatment program, information such as the following would be shown for each client: who holds custody, the date of initial services, dates of periodic case review with staff as well as the client or legal guardian, and proposed dates for discharge. This type of information will be of importance to each therapist and supervisor in tracking the clients, ensuring that they are not lost in the sequence of therapeutic steps.

One additional feature of such a client tracking system is that it can easily be expanded to encompass some relevant fiscal and administrative functions. This is not to imply that these items should necessarily become part of the therapist's responsibility, but they may be shared responsibilities among administrators, therapists, and the business office, with clear delineations as to who is responsible for each component and who has what authority regarding them.

These two systems can be easily combined if an agency has computer capabilities. In our agency (Children's Behavioral Services, Las Vegas, Nevada), the first system simply involves a form for each of the various types of service—with each form tailored to prompt the unique sequence of events for that service. A "memory" typewriter is used to hold all of the information for the second tracking system, which is updated once a month and then redistributed to each of the therapists and administrators for whom this information is relevant. Only through these tracking systems have we been able to ensure that clients receive the greatest protection of their rights.

Record Review: An In-service Training and Quality Control System for Case Records

One of the most potentially valuable safeguards of the rights of the child client is the case-record review system, since in most counseling settings it is the case record that provides documentation concerning frequency of client contact and indicates the quality and effectiveness of services provided. In addition, the case record generally reflects the extent of therapist/agency recognition of a client's rights, a client's or guardian's understanding of his or her rights regarding treatment, and the extent to which these rights are protected in prescribing and administering treatment procedures.

An effective record review procedure can best be established within an environment where systems for treatment planning and record-keeping include aspects of a quality-assurance program: goal-oriented case records, a goal-oriented plan of service, client participation and understanding, ongoing and follow-up outcome measurement, strategic progress review by a co-therapist, and client advocacy.

The case-record review system that we have developed serves three functions: (1) a continuing in-service training program for the staff in client rights and related professional practices, (2) a forum for the discussion of new legislation, client-rights issues, and staff input regarding improvements in professional standards for the agency, and (3) a quality-assurance system to ensure that case records reflect the protection of client rights and delivery of effective services. This case-record review system is capable of addressing all three functions by having all the therapists and clinical supervisory staff participate as case reviewers. Thus the process becomes a peer review system as well as a continuing education activity for quality services.

This program of client-rights review and education is particularly important in children's services, since the child-client is much less likely than the adult to identify potential rights violations or to bring these to the attention of an appropriate party. In addition, the general quality of the case record is of importance when considering its potential use due perhaps to a future need for counseling or more restrictive services as the child matures.

ESTABLISHING CASE RECORD STANDARDS

Review of case records must be based upon standards of record management that should specify in writing information complying with client-rights requirements (e.g., standards for treatment plan, quantity and quality of progress notes, documentation of client informed consent), as well as information required by agency administration or the law (e.g., standards for completion of Title XX forms for client billing). After giving counseling staff an opportunity to become familiar with written-case-record standards, a brief test should be administered to each therapist to ensure his or her understanding of the standards and essentials of acceptable case record management. As new requirements are added to the case management standards, in-service training sessions on them should be held involving all staff. Mastery of the case record standards thus becomes a critical part of the orientation and training of new staff.

DEVELOPING THE RECORD REVIEW FORM

The record review form should be comprehensive but easy to use. Since record review is not typically viewed as enjoyable by staff, a carefully designed review form that can be completed for a case record in no more than thirty minutes is desirable. The form should include several different categories of items. *Quantitative* items should be checked as to whether a required item is present and signed by the appropriate individual—e.g., Is the treatment plan signed by the client (guardian) and therapist?

Qualitative items involve subjective ratings, and may be less reliable —but certainly not less important. Qualitative ratings should be done by a reviewer on two aspects of a case. First, a record should be rated on its "internal consistency." Internal consistency refers to which issues presented in one section of a record are followed up in another (e.g., Do the casenotes reflect that the presenting problems described in the treatment plan are being addressed?) Second, a case record should be qualitatively rated on the extent to which the program of therapy is judged to be appropriate to the client's needs (e.g., Is the client receiving appropriate types of services for the nature and severity of his/her problems? Is the client making adequate progress under this prescription of therapy?).

The record review form should also be designed to elicit input from the reviewer. For example, he or she may be asked to respond to such questions as, How would you improve this case record? or, What did you see as the strongest aspect of this record? Such input is valuable in making the review a constructive feedback process. In addition, eliciting such feedback from the reviewer is advantageous as a subtle, ongoing training experience for the reviewer—e.g., being prompted to think of ways in which even a good record can be improved.

Finally, a good record review form should provide a check of a therapist's compliance with agency policy and procedures as well as with client rights guidelines. One must be prepared to change the record review form as agency procedures change and as new developments occur in the area of client rights.

ESTABLISHING THE RECORD REVIEW COMMITTEE

The record review committee should provide ongoing in-service training for staff in case record management, children's rights, and client-rights issues, in addition to monitoring staff compliance with standards for treatment and documentation. The membership of the committee should include all staff members providing counseling services to clients: the "client advocate," social workers, heads of various service departments (e.g., counseling, educational, residential), interns or practicum students involved with clinical services, medical personnel, and perhaps one or more representatives from the local community (perhaps members of an agency's advisory board or board of trustees).

In settings with no more than ten staff members, one committee meeting on a monthly or bimonthly basis is usually sufficient. However, in settings with larger staffs, several committees should be formed so that everyone is involved in the review process. For example, with a staff of forty therapists, each of the four ten-member committees could meet at different times each month, and possibly—after the quality of records is improved—move to a bimonthly basis, with two committees meeting one month, the other two the next, and so forth.[1]

Detailed information concerning the function of the committee, use of the record review form, case record standards, and client-rights issues should be distributed to each prospective member of the committee so that he or she can become thoroughly familiar with these issues prior to actual involvement in record review.

RECORD REVIEW PROCEDURES

Record review begins with a random selection of cases for review from both active and terminated files. This procedure will be greatly facilitated by a well-organized, up-to-date, centralized filing system. If satellite centers are involved, then arrangements should be made for random selection from their cases as well. Next, cases should be assigned to committee members (two to three cases each) one week prior

---

[1] If more than one record review committee exists in a given agency, with a different person serving as the chairperson of each, then it would be valuable to arrange for all chairpersons to attend each committee meeting. This will help ensure consistency in standards and interpretation across the various case review committees.

to the committee meeting. The assignments are private in that a given reviewer is only informed of the particular cases he or she is to review. Committee members should complete the record review form for each case assigned to them, having no communication about the case with the staff member whose case it is. Completed review forms should then be submitted to the committee chairperson (possibly appointed by the agency director on a rotating basis) at least one day prior to the committee meeting.

At the committee meeting, the chairperson should go over the review form item by item with the committee. As each item is reviewed, the chairperson should actively promote and allow ample time for full discussion by all committee members. Such discussion of an item should include positive feedback as well as identification of difficulties. In other words, comments about the strengths of an innovative treatment program or the thoroughness of a therapist's casenotes should be given equal emphasis with comments about denial of client rights or violation of agency standards. Discretion should be given to use of therapists' and certainly clients' names associated with particular case records being discussed.

VERIFICATION OF RIGHTS VIOLATIONS AND FEEDBACK TO THERAPIST

During the week following a committee meeting, the chairperson should meet with the therapists responsible for the cases reviewed and provide whatever positive feedback is appropriate regarding the quality of the records, and obtain additional information concerning whatever rights violations may have occurred, such as any extenuating circumstances. For example, there may be an instance of a client's (or guardian's) terminating service after two months of attending counseling services; however, the client then again requests service and the case is reactivated the next month. The record review committee may indicate that a three-month review of progress is due after the one month of service following reactivation, at which point it may be argued that the client's termination during the three-month period is an extenuating circumstance in case of omission of the regular progress review, and that no violation of client rights has occurred.

In the case of a client-rights violation, the therapist responsible for the case might also receive feedback from the responsible department supervisor concerning the nature and seriousness of the error. If deemed necessary, the therapist should also be given specific in-service training to ensure that such errors do not recur. In addition, the therapist might be required to submit completed record review forms for each of his or her active clients on a monthly basis until the supervisor is satisfied that the therapist has become sufficiently knowledgeable concerning standards of case management. These additional steps are rarely needed, in that most therapists are sufficiently responsive to the positive and constructive feedback provided through the committee and its chairperson.

In the case of a good report from the review committee, the therapist should receive positive feedback from his or her supervisor and be encouraged to assist with future in-service training sessions for other staff.

In each case, a summary of the staff member's record management skills should be included in the work performance evaluations that determine salary increases. Given the emphasis on positive, constructive feedback and training in such a system, continued violation of client rights by an individual staff member should be considered a serious problem —with the possibility of serious consequences.

NOTIFYING A CLIENT OF THE RIGHTS VIOLATION

The client and guardian must be notified of an instance in which his or her rights have been violated, no matter how trivial the violation may seem to staff. The committee chairperson should meet with the therapist and discuss the violation and the necessity of informing the client of procedures for filing a grievance. A meeting should then be scheduled with the client and guardian, the therapist involved, and the client advocate. In the meeting, the therapist should first carefully identify and define the right in question and in specific terms describe how it was violated. After allowing time for the client and guardian to comment, the therapist should describe the steps required for filing a grievance. A detailed account of this session with the client should then be entered as a note in the case record. A report describing the violation, the circumstances, the action taken to correct it and prevent its recurrence, and the client's and guardian's responses should then be sent to governing authorities where appropriate—e.g., a state human rights commission or the agency's local advisory board.

In summary, an effective record review system involves ongoing education opportunities for therapists in client rights and standards of case record management. Record review can best be accomplished using a carefully designed, comprehensive record review form, a peer review committee that meets on a regular basis, and standard procedures for staff feedback and training based upon the results of review process. Such procedures, thoughtfully implemented, will ensure that case record documentation becomes a method of safeguarding client rights rather than simply another area in which client rights are violated.

Summary: A Coordinated Program for Protecting the Rights of the Child Client

The odds would seem to be against the child in our society; they are most certainly against the child who is handicapped in some way or in need of counseling services. In this chapter we have attempted to identify the importance of recognizing client rights in providing psychological counseling services to children, and to delineate systems for ensuring that these rights are protected. It is not surprising that children's rights are likely to be misunderstood and often violated by adults and, more specifically, by the mental health practitioner. As we have seen, children have an ambivalent social role and suffer from many of the oppressive practices that plague unrepresented minority groups. In addition, client rights are continually subject to change in the ongoing litigation prompted by our country's increasing interest in issues of human rights and individual freedom.

Working with the child client therefore requires special vigilance on the part of the therapist as well as the mental health administrator. With the systems we have described, vigilance in protecting rights and ensuring effectiveness of services delivered is best accomplished when these systems are conducted in a setting with active in-service training programs and policies ensuring that client rights are everyone's concern.

IN-SERVICE TRAINING ON CLIENT RIGHTS ISSUES

Regular in-service training for counseling staff on children's rights, client rights in general, and agency policy is an essential part of an effective safeguarding program. It is important in teaching staff how to effectively implement such safeguard procedures as client procedures, systematic record review, and assessment procedures described above. Several recent publications can be used in conjunction with in-service training programs to keep staff current on rights issues. For example, Reed Martin in his periodical *Law and Behavior: Quarterly Analysis of Legal Developments Affecting Professionals in Human Services* has provided an excellent learning aid, and the "handbook" series published under the auspices of the American Civil Liberties Union (e.g., Levine *et al.*, 1973) provides information concerning the rights of mental health patients as well as students, prisoners, and minority groups.[2]

---

[2] A few additional materials that might be appropriate for in-service training are:

BARTON, W. E., & SANBORN, C. J. (Eds.). *Law and the mental health professions: Friction at the interface.* New York: International Universities Press, 1978.

DESIGNING FORMS FOR AGENCY USE

In addition to educating staff about these issues, agency policy and procedures should be formulated with the goal of protecting client rights. For example, forms such as treatment plans and authorizations for service can be carefully designed so that client rights are identified and protected. There are a number of sample forms available that are designed to protect client rights, such as Stuart's *Client-Therapist Treatment Contract* (1975).

We ourselves have developed a comprehensive "Clinical Service Agreement" which not only carefully delineates the "obligations" of client and therapist with regard to the treatment program, but seeks to inform the client to the extent possible concerning the nature of and justification for the treatment procedures employed. Specifically, here each client receives (1) a summary of the rationale for each treatment procedure to be utilized, (2) a detailed account of previous use of the procedures to resolve similar problems (including reference material available on the premises for client inspection), (3) an account of the possible "reasonable risks" and "potential benefits" of each treatment procedure, and (4) criteria and procedures for evaluating client's progress toward treatment goals.

While our Clinical Service Agreement covers much of the same material as Stuart's treatment contract (1975), more attention has been given to specifying criteria for success to be used in assessment of progress toward treatment goals. The agreement can be easily revised to that new procedures and service programs can be implemented when indicated in regular review of the treatment plan with the client.

In addition, service authorization forms must be designed to ensure that, independent of a treatment plan for a specific problem, the client give the agency and therapist permission to conduct "counseling sessions" and evaluation and assessment as necessary to determine his or her treatment needs. More important, however, such authorization forms provide the client and guardian with a mechanism for specifying in writing what information the therapist or agency may share with specified parties—e.g., physicians, schools, welfare agencies—thus ensuring confidentiality.

GROSS, B. & GROSS, R. (Eds.). *The children's rights movement: Overcoming the oppression of young people.* Garden City, N.Y.: Anchor Books, 1977.

KRAPFL, J. E. & VARGAS, E. A. (Eds.). *Behaviorism and ethics.* Kalamazoo, Mich. Behaviordelia, 1977.

MARTIN, R. *Legal challenges to behavior modification.* Champaign, Ill.: Research Press, 1975.

STOLZ, S. B. & ASSOCIATES. *Ethical issues in behavior modification.* San Francisco: Jossey-Bass, 1978.

STUART, R. B. *Trick or treatment: How and when psychotherapy fails.* Champaign, Ill.: Research Press, 1970.

After designing forms with the specificity and clarity necessary to keep the client informed and protect rights in treatment, staff training in the use of these forms should be conducted. Training is especially important whenever changes in treatment forms are made and whenever a new therapist joins the staff. Staff understanding of the forms and their use is then monitored by the regular case-record review committee process previously described.

RIGHTS COMMITTEES

In this chapter we have described a variety of procedures that require coordination to ensure their effectiveness. This coordination can best be accomplished through the establishment of committees to oversee activities such as in-service training, monitoring developments in the areas of client rights and human rights in general, conducting grievance procedures when rights are violated, and monitoring and supervising the various safeguard systems that may be in operation.

As previously described, the record review committee would be designed to meet several of these needs. Specifically, it would provide ongoing in-service training for staff in case record management and client-rights issues relative to case-record documentation, treatment, and assessment. The record review committee would also monitor the operation of safeguard systems. For example, a review of the case record would reveal the extent to which client-oriented procedures are being followed by the therapist and the nature of assessment and follow-up procedures employed.

A human rights committee could then be charged with monitoring developments in the area of children's and clients' rights, conducting grievance procedures when they are violated, and working to correct policy and procedures that might result in violations. A client advocate would work closely with this committee, receiving, investigating, and attempting to resolve complaints from clients. The advocate, with the assistance of the committee, would attempt to resolve a complaint to the client's satisfaction. Given the likelihood of a child's being a "passive" participant in terms of knowledge and understanding of his or her rights and helping to safeguard them, the role of the client advocate becomes critical.

With input from the client advocate and the record review committee, the human rights committee would collect information relative to potential violations of client rights and formulate changes in policy and procedure necessary to avoid them. In this way, the committees would work together to coordinate systems for identifying and protecting client rights.

An obvious theme of our discussion has been that safeguarding client rights is very much a technology of quality control and accountability. The future of children's rights would seem to be encouraging, given our commitment to improving technology in mental health and society's increased sensitivity to human-rights issues. With improved technology and increased concern for individual rights, there remains the ultimate challenge for us as mental health practitioners—giving the child client the benefit of our respect as well as our expertise.

References

APTER, S. J. The rights of children in teaching institutions. In G. P. Koocher (Ed.), *Children's rights and the mental health professions.* New York: John Wiley & Sons, 1976.

BERGER, N. The child, the law, and the state. In P. Adams (Ed.), *Children's rights.* New York: Praeger, 1971.

EVANS, I. M., & NELSON, R. M. Assessment of child behavior problems. In A. R. Ciminero, K. S. Calhoun, & H. E. Adams (Eds.), *Handbook of behavioral assessment.* New York: John Wiley & Sons, 1977.

FALK, H. *Corporal punishment: A social interpretation of its theory and practice in the schools of the United States.* New York: Teacher's College Press, 1941.

FARSON, R. E. *Birthrights.* New York: MacMillan, 1974.

FESHBACH, N. D., & FESHBACH, S. Punishment: Parent rites versus children's rights. In G. P. Koocher (Ed.), *Children's rights and the mental health professions.* New York: John Wiley & Sons, 1976.

FLESCH, R. *How to write, speak and think more effectively.* New York: Harper & Row, 1963.

GIL, D. G. *Violence against children: Physical child abuse in the United States.* Cambridge: Harvard University Press, 1970.

GOTTLIEB, D. (Ed.). *Children's liberation.* Englewood Cliffs, N.J.: Prentice-Hall, 1973.

HELFER, R. E., & KEMPE, C. H. (Eds.). *The battered child and his family.* Philadelphia: Lippincott, 1972.

HETZNECKER, N. & FORMAN, M. A. *On behalf of children.* New York: Grune and Stratton, 1974.

HOBBS, N. *The futures of children: Report of the project on classification of exceptional children.* San Francisco: Jossey-Bass, 1975.

HOLMES, D. S. & URIE, R. G. Effects of preparing children for psychotherapy. *Journal of Consulting and Clinical Psychology,* 1975, *43* 311–318.

HOLT, J. *Freedom and beyond.* New York: E. P. Dutton, 1972.

Joint Commission on Mental Health of Children. *Crisis in child mental health: Challenge for the 1970s.* New York: Harper and Row, 1970.

KEITH-SPIEGEL, P. Children's rights as participants in research. In G. P. Koocher (Ed.), *Children's rights and the mental health professions*. New York: John Wiley & Sons, 1976, pp. 53–81.

KOOCHER, G. P. (Ed.). *Children's rights and the mental health professions*. New York: John Wiley & Sons, 1976a.

KOOCHER, G. P. A bill of rights for children in psychotherapy. In G. P. Koocher (Ed.), *Children's rights and the mental health professions*. New York: John Wiley & Sons, 1976b.

LEVINE, A., CARY, E., & DIVOKY, D. *The rights of students: An American Civil Liberties Union handbook*. New York: Avon Books, 1973.

LEVY, M. & BRACKBILL, Y. Informed consent: Getting the message across to kids. *APA Monitor*, March 1979, p. 3.

LIGHT, R. Abused and neglected children in America: A study of alternative policies. In *The rights of children*. *Harvard Educational Review*, 1974, Series 9, 198–240.

LINEHAN, M. M. Issues in behavioral interviewing. In J. D. Cone & R. P. Hawkins (Eds.), *Behavioral assessment: New directions in clinical psychology*. New York: Brunner/Mazel, 1977.

LOCICERO, A. The right to know: Telling children the results of clinical evaluations. In G. P. Koocher (Ed.), *Children's rights in the mental health professions*. New York: John Wiley & Sons, 1976.

MARTIN, R. *Law and Behavior: Quarterly Analysis of Legal Developments Affecting Professionals in Human Services*. Champaign, Ill.: Research Press.

MARTIN, R. *Legal challenges to behavior modification*. Champaign, Ill.: Research Press, 1975.

MERCER, J. R. A policy statement on assessment procedures and the rights of children. In *The rights of children*. *Harvard Educational Review*, 1974, Series 9, 328–344.

MNOOKIN, R. H. Foster care: In whose best interest? In *The rights of children*. *Harvard Educational Review*, 1974, Series 9, 158–196.

MORGANSTERN, K. P. Behavioral interviewing: The initial stages of assessment. In M. Hersen & A. S. Bellack (Eds.), *Behavioral assessment: A practical handbook*. New York: Pergamon Press, 1976.

OHLIN, L. E., COATES, R. B., & MILLER, A. D. Radical correctional reform: A case study of the Massachusetts Youth Correctional System. In *The rights of children*. *Harvard Educational Review*, 1974, Series 9, 120–157.

PALMER, P. *The mouse, the monster, and me: Assertiveness for young people*. San Luis Obispo, Calif.: Impact Publishers, 1977.

ROBINSON, D. Harm, offense, and nuisance: Some first steps in the establishment of an ethics of treatment. *American Psychologist*, 1974, 29 (4), 233–238.

RODHAM, H. Children under the law. In *The rights of children*. *Harvard Educational Review*, 1974, Series 9, 1–28.

ROSS, A. O. The rights of children as psychotherapy patients. Paper presented at the American Psychological Association Meeting, New Orleans, La., 1974.

STEINMETZ, S. K. & STRAUS, M. A. The family as a cradle of violence. *Sociology,* 1973, *10,* 50–56.

STEINMETZ, S. K., & STRAUS, M. A. (Eds.). *Violence in the family.* New York: Dodd, Mead, 1974.

STUART, R. B. *Client-therapist treatment contract.* Champaign, Ill.: Research Press, 1975.

CHAPTER 3

Preserving the Rights of Clients in Child Abuse and Neglect

Barbara S. Kuehn
Edward R. Christophersen

INTEREST IN THE AREA OF CHILD ABUSE and neglect has increased dramatically during the past twenty years. During this time professionals have found that reconciliation in these situations is continually complicated by the fact that abuse and neglect are circumstances involving the entire family environment. This means that the rights of parents, the abused child, and his siblings are all affected and must all be considered in assessing consequences, needs, and treatment goals. The ideal goal is for each family member to receive treatment in accord with his/her individual needs. However, frequently for one person's needs to be met another's must be compromised. At this point the process of case management involves decisions concerning whose needs and rights deserve priority.

This chapter will discuss both issues and procedural systems that are relevant to professionals working with clients experiencing abuse and neglect circumstances. The underlying philosophies that have influenced the development and refining of legislation concerning abuse and neglect will provide an historical matrix from which current practices affecting client rights can be more clearly viewed. The discussion of this main issue of rights, however, will focus on the client first within the family and then within the legal and social service systems. Finally, the technological and systematic procedures which have been developed to protect the rights of clients will be presented.

For the ensuing discussion, three basic definitions of rights will help clarify what is meant in the various rights issues. These include nurturing—the right to affirmative acts of personal care to promote a child's normal physical and emotional development; custody—the right to be cared for by adults chosen for their capacity to meet a child's needs and protect his interest; and freedom from abuse—the right to family interaction that is not damaging, harmful, or threatening to a child's physical integrity (Beck, Glavis, Glover, Jenkins, & Nardi, 1978).

Two Models for Protecting Children

The two models presented here are reflections of the theoretical and procedural frameworks that have evolved historically in the legislative and judicial process concerning abused and neglected children. Traditionally, the responsibilities of parenting within the family unit have been viewed by the legal profession as analogous to a trust. Thus, the court has been directed to protect the "best interest of the child" as being of paramount importance. Legislation concerning child abuse and neglect has therefore been construed to define an affirmative duty on the part of parents similar to that of a trustee "who must act with the care and skill [of a person] of prudence, discretion, and intelligence . . . in the light of circumstances existing at the time of the act" (Beck et al., 1978, p. 724).

The apparent emphasis of this model concerns the behavior of parents as it pertains to responsible child-rearing practices. However, the effects of these actions on the child have been of secondary consideration. Therefore as recently as 1970 Gil, a major authority in the field of child abuse and neglect, advocated permanent removal of children from the home of the natural parents "when there is clear evidence or even persuasive evidence of abuse with a child under three" (p. 44). Further, he recommended that "whenever a child is removed from a family because of evidence of battering or sexual abuse the nonguilty parent should be placed on probation and forbidden to remove any other children they have from the possibility of continuous and intensive surveillance by the court or jurisdiction" (p. 45). These recommendations have also been endorsed by Beck et al. (1978). Implicit in this model is the concept that the best interest of a child can best be served by first considering consequences and remedies affecting the parents.

Mnookin (1973) points out that the "best interests" approach does not allow the court to take into account the complex variables involved in removal of the child from the natural home or prescription of consequences solely affecting the parents. This approach requires predictive information concerning removal of the child or interruption in regard to his family relationship, since the court must predict the child's future relationship with a surrogate family, the effects of periodic contacts with the natural family, and find surrogate families that must be experienced in this process. In contrast, more predictive information may be available concerning the past behavior of the natural family, the child's natural psychological attachment to the family, and the motivational advantages of leaving him at home. However, the court can neither predict nor discount the individual child's unique reaction to each environment (Skolnick, 1973).

This quandary has led to the development of another model for writing and interpreting abuse and neglect laws, known as the "least detrimental alternative." This approach involves—and may facilitate—weighing the advantages and disadvantages of specific alternatives. The task at hand is always to salvage as much as possible from an unsatisfactory situation. Goldstein, Freud, and Solnit (1973) state that the least detrimental placement alternative "maximizes in accord with the child's sense of time and on the basis of short-term predictions given the limitations of knowledge, his or her opportunity for being wanted and for maintaining on a continuous basis a relationship with at least one adult who is or will become his psychological parent" (p. 53). The intent of this approach is that the service delivery system be guided to look at the whole picture: the parents' actions, the child's welfare, the home environment, the child's response to all of these, and the available alternatives and their probable consequences for the child. Ideally, this full-spectrum perspective would encourage decisions made in the child's true best interest within a complex developmental environment rather than in an effort to provide consequences for parents' acts of commission or omission.

The "least detrimental alternative" model has opened up new horizons for the social service fields by bringing the focus of intervention with the abused or neglected child back to meeting his needs in the complex family environment. This shift in emphasis has led current authorities to suggest its use in such cases. This approach, while focused more directly on the child's needs, allows courts and professionals to encompass the rights and needs of the entire family unit when developing and evaulating systems and technologies for working with these families. The remainder of this chapter will focus on this process and present alternatives and procedures that have evolved in the attempt to maximize the protection of client rights in abuse and neglect situations.

The Child's Rights Within the Family

Although it is impossible to entirely segregate the child's interests from those of his family (Wald, 1975), *Wyman* v. *James* (1971, 400 U.S. 309) was a landmark case that set the precedent for distinguishing between the child's interests and those of the parents (Burt, 1971). Utilizing this separate-but-equal guideline, it is of foremost importance that dispositions in abuse and neglect be made on a case-by-case basis, taking into account the home environment and the child's response to it, what programs and resources the court has to offer, and the dynamics of each specific family situation (Wald, 1975). There is a substantial theoretical and data base that supports the position that a child's intellectual, physical, emotional, and social development is significantly affected by and adaptable to his home environment, a fact not to be skimmed over lightly pending a decision to remove him (Freud, 1965; Jencks, Acland, Bane, Cohen, Gintis, Heyns, & Michelson, 1972).

However adaptable each child may be he still has a right to a certain standard of treatment and care until old enough to assume those responsibilities for himself (Katz, 1975). The view that the child is legally entitled to care and support that represents the minimum accepted community standard (Paulsen, 1962) seems to be the most commonly held guideline. Intervention in the interest of upholding this standard requires two things: identification and documentation that the child's care is substandard, and a willingness by the court to intervene (Fraser, 1976).

The idea of the minimum accepted community standard encompasses more than just food, clothing, and shelter. Goldstein points out that children are "dependent and in need of direct, intimate, and continuous care by the adults who are personally committed to assume such responsibility" (1973, p. 11). Denying a child of his nurturing deprives him of reasonable opportunities for development. The effects of this can go so far as to cause growth retardation, delay in intellectual achievement, and autistic social responses (Patton & Gardner, 1963). This response pattern is referred to as failure to thrive. Similarly, when a parent exceeds the bounds of reasonable discipline and abuses his child, the child's right to physical security is infringed (Beck et al., 1978). This right is further jeopardized if, as a result, the state removes him from his familiar surroundings rather than removing the offending adult. Since removal of the adult is unlikely, due to society's current priorities, the most positive alternative here might be to introduce services so that the child would be protected while remaining in a safe, familiar setting with his psychological parent (Goldstein et al., 1973).

The right to nurturing also requires that parents ensure every reasonable opportunity for normal physical development. Parents who ignore medical treatment for their children are not adhering to a reasonable minimum level of care for them (Beck et al., 1978). This right to a reasonable opportunity for normal physical development places crucial responsibility on the parents that begins when the child is first conceived. In humans, the number of brain cells is thought to increase in a linear fashion from conception until birth and then more slowly until the age of six months (Vore, 1973). Research indicates that deficits resulting from prenatal malnutrition are apparently permanent. This means that a mother who does not acquire adequate prenatal care or nutrition may be limiting or even damaging the child's potential for development. Miller and Merritt (1979) have shown that this potential can also be compromised by smoking or consuming alcohol during pregnancy. Scrutiny must be given as well to those cases where the mother uses drugs during pregnancy, particularly those resulting in the infant's addiction to these substances at birth.

The concept of the parents' responsibility to nurture demands some fine discrimination by the parents. There is a very fine line between a close mother-child bond where the mother meets the child's needs and a situation where the child becomes responsible for meeting the mother's needs—e.g., the need for someone to love her, for someone to share her worries, and so on (Alexander, McQuiston, & Rodehoffer, 1976). This situation deprives the child of abilities and opportunities for his own physical and emotional development. The result is that, later on, as a parent himself the deprived child will be unable to give his own children the care and affection necessary for their normal development (Beck et al., 1978).

These rights to a minimum accepted community standard of care in the home—including emotional care and nurturing, medical treatment, and adequate prenatal care—are the basic areas where the courts support the child's interests as distinct from those of the parents. These rights are still paramount in the discussion of children's rights as children enter the social service system because of a violation of these rights in their own homes.

The Child's Rights Within the Social Service System

As the child enters the social service system, the observance of his rights is still of primary importance. As he comes into contact with more people through the system, there are necessarily more opportunities for rights to be compromised. In the interface with social services the primary area of risk for such compromises is the child's involvement with the foster care experience, including the rate at which decisions concerning the family's fate are made and implemented.

Concerning the foster care experience, there are several guidelines and considerations of importance. To begin with, temporary removal should be the exception and not the rule (Sameroff & Chandler, 1975). Unlike most adults, children's behavior is not guided by a consistent rational understanding of events. As they mature, their understanding of events, tolerance for frustration, and need for caring, support, stimulation, guidance, independence, and restraint evolve asymmetrically but concurrently with regard to their cognitive and rational abilities. Since the dissonance created by these alternately dominant aspects of development is not readily reconciled, it is extremely important that at least the environment have some consistency for these children (Katz, 1969).

Once the decision has been made that foster care is appropriate, difficulties with the child's identity problems and anxieties about his future may be ameliorated by placement in one home rather than by allowing many placement changes (Weinstein, 1969). Katz (1969) points out that the court supports the concept of the need for continuity in foster children's lives. In a related decision, *In Re Jewish Child Care Association* (1959), the Supreme Court of New York affirmed children also have a right to a home where a bond or psychological relationship can develop with foster parents. It is extremely important to children's emotional development for them to have a psychological parent with whom to identify and rely on for consistency and concern (Weinstein et al., 1960; Goldstein et al., 1973).

Ironically, the development of such a nurturing relationship, affirmed by the legal system, is hindered by the social service system. Initially, when couples enter a foster care program, they are required to agree to two conditions: that the relationship can never be anything beyond foster parent and foster child, and that the agency may terminate the placement at its own discretion without providing justification to the foster parents (Goldstein & Katz, 1965). These requirements probably have a retarding effect on the bonding process because of the walls foster parents are likely to put up to protect themselves from being hurt if the child leaves.

The speed—or lack of it—with which the social service system in some cases works is also a threat to client rights. The slowness of the decision-making process in cases of outside placement may impede the settlement of each foster situation and delay the beginning of the bonding process (Goldstein et al., 1973). Speedy decisions, in addition to facilitating bonding, would show deference to the fact that a child's sense of time is much different than that of adults. That which may seem only a short period for adults may be an extreme hardship to a youngster separated through no particular fault of his own from all the things and people familiar to him. Faster decisions would also reduce the time children spend waiting in foster placement for the system to return them to a safe, stable home. This is especially important since data indicate that once a child has been in foster care for twelve to eighteen months, he has a greatly reduced likelihood of returning home (Maas & Engler, 1959). Eisenberg (1962) found that of 140 foster children seen in a psychiatric clinic, only 10 percent were functioning at age-appropriate levels in school. Additionally, 70 percent of the cases were referred to the clinic for aggressive behavior. Although this finding does not indicate whether these problems developed prior to or during foster placement, they do signify that these children probably have more complex problems than they would have had otherwise. This increases the probability of failure in any foster home—as does the length of time a child remains in foster care, regardless of whether this is a result of his own home conditions or the speed of the system.

Family Rights Within the Social Service System

In 1935, the Social Security Act (42 U.S.C., par. 601) mandated the provision of protective services. It set the guidelines that the state "must encourage the care of dependent children in their own homes by enabling the state to furnish financial assistance and rehabilitation and other services to needy dependent children and the parents with whom they are living to help maintain and strengthen family life."

Bronfenbrenner has suggested that meeting the environmental prerequisites for healthy and effective family functioning (e.g., providing the family with adequate health care, nutrition, housing, and employment) is probably the most powerful technique for significantly improving both the parents' use of reasonable child-rearing skills and the child's development. His suggestions are derived from extensive longitudinal research into the effectiveness of early-intervention programs. He concludes that for many poor families

> the conditions of life are such that the family cannot perform its childrearing functions even though it may wish to do so. Under these circumstances no direct form of intervention aimed at enhancing the child's development or his parents' childrearing skills is likely to have much impact. Conversely, once the environmental prerequisites are met, the direct forms of intervention may no longer seem as necessary (1974, p. 59).

If a plan to meet environmental needs is possible of implementation, it might help parents to interrupt the cycle of venting the frustrations of dealing with "the system" on their children (Steele, 1970; Wasserman, 1967). As it is, Bronfenbrenner's ideal is far removed from the reality of its implementation.

In light of the present-day reality in dealing with child abuse and neglect, there are three areas of heightened concern as regards the abridgment of these families' rights as they interact with the social service system. These include the training and attitudes of those who are making decisions in child custody situations, the information about the social service system itself utilized in making those decisions, and the efforts made to maintain the family unit. Although the state of current legislation is not sophisticated enough to include these concerns, it reflects rights that need to be acknowledged and advocated as our social-service delivery system evolves.

First and foremost is the problem of the common notion that the social service system is omniscient and omnipotent, with a merciful and benevolent intention. In reality the system is made up of individuals with private agendas, who have come into their positions as judges, guardians *ad litem,* prosecutors, social workers, and psychologists from a myriad of different cultural and educational backgrounds.

These people comprise the decision-making body in abuse and neglect situations. Many judges, especially in rural areas, are farmers, merchants, or businessmen with no legal, psychological, or child-development training at all. Clients have a right that these decision makers, when stepping into the family unit to alter it in any way, be educated as to the needs and dynamics of the family unit and the special dynamics in abuse and neglect situations (Wald, 1975). Since laws do not specify what harms to intervene for, it is essential that those deciding how others should and should not behave in their own homes be relevantly educated and trained for these decisions (Smith, 1974).

Every effort must be made to educate decision makers about current concepts of family and child development, including those regarding emotional and developmental needs (Campbell, 1970). Such education and training should help to reduce the tendency of decision makers to project personal values about child-rearing, values that have little or no support from scientific evidence (Handler, 1973; Cheney & Beaton, 1966; Phillips et al., 1971; Bowlby, 1965).

To avoid infringing on client rights, these decision makers also need information on the relative effectiveness of the soft and hard services offered by the social service system (Kadushin, 1967). The decision makers must realize the limitations of their ability to help or else risk nonproductive or nonbeneficial interventions. It is a reality that for some families intervention by an inefficient system may cause more upheaval and turmoil than is merited by the seriousness of the initial concern or the effectiveness of any given intervention experience.

Additionally, Wasserman (1967) has pointed out the very relevant concern for the stability of the service delivery system itself. Typically, turnover rates for both social workers and judges are extremely high. This means a lack of continuity in case management because of, for example, the differing value orientations of the new decision makers. This high rate also detracts from the amount of training each person has for his own role. Unfortunately, the effect of this instability and low level of education or training support sets the scene for a low level of motivation among workers in providing the services and endeavoring to make up for the inadequacies of the system (Mnookin, 1973). Although these aspects of the service delivery system do not approach an optimal level, this is not an indictment of the system. The decision makers must be aware of the shortcomings of their situations and utilize that knowledge in their daily decisions concerning the lives of their clients.

The final focus for our attention regarding the preservation of the family's rights within the system is the importance of making every effort to maintain the family unit. The strongest rationale for this stand is that at this time social service systems have no guarantees that separation will be any less harmful than the child remaining with his parents. Partially because of the way in which the foster care situation is managed, there is no way to predict how any given foster placement will progress; the important psychological bond may or may not develop. But if it does not there is an increased likelihood the placement will fail for a lack of commitment between foster parent and child.

Placement in foster care should be viewed as a last resort for another reason: Many children tend to perceive the whole placement process as punishment for things that are vague or undefined (Goldstein et al., 1973). The child is removed from all that is familiar and secure and from those with whom there is a commitment, to an unfamiliar, frequently changing living situation. Unfortunately, a parent, when as a child his life was frequently disrupted, will tend to treat his own children in a similar fashion (Steele, 1970; Wasserman, 1967). And so the chain tends to be self-perpetuating, unless efforts to change it are diligent and constant.

Furthermore, when parents are having a difficult time handling their children, taking the children away hardly seems like an educational experience. Child-rearing is not a skill that is typically learned in the absence of children. Unfortunately, once children are placed out of their homes, the tendency has been for programs not to offer parents any further services (Mnookin, 1973). This arrangement not only strains the attachment between the parents and their child but possibly even decreases the prognosis for improved functioning once the family is reunited.

Since the early 1970s, efforts have been progressing to develop some alternative support systems to alleviate the need for placement in some instances. Studies have shown that emergency homemakers and emergency caregivers can be utilized to help families get through a crisis period without requiring placement for the children. This approach costs no more money and still maintains the family unit (Burt & Balyeat, 1974).

The next step is the maintenance of the clients' rights concerning actual service alternatives. As custody and placement decisions are made, it is essential that all available services and factors be considered. These guidelines are essential for the sake of the family for several reasons. The most important of them is that no judge can predict what the foster care experience will be like (Mnookin, 1973). As Goldstein et al. (1973) have so eloquently pointed out, the child's emotional growth (and in extreme cases physical growth as well) is dependent on the psychological bond that he develops with his parents or guardian. The negative effects of deliberately weakening or breaking this bond (Klaus & Kennel, 1970) must certainly be justified by the alternatives chosen for the child.

As decisions are made altering these clients' lives, the clients will be benefited most if the service providers involved work diligently to improve the family's ability to utilize services and to work with the system for the child's (and thereby the family's) best interest (Morse, Hyde, Newberger, & Reed, 1977). Possibly, if the parents gain any skills in this area, as a result of the intervention they will be able to utilize them in the future when dealing with any of the systems in our society to help increase their effectiveness in obtaining what they want from each experience.

This endeavor would be a first step toward Bronfenbrenner's ideal of helping to raise families' general functioning level, thereby decreasing external pressures and the probability of further abuse or neglect.

Granted, there is a long way to go in any move to help alleviate problems of child abuse and neglect. There are some who advocate turning our backs on abused children today and focusing our energies on the next generation (Helfer, 1977). Helfer's thought is that the changes needed are of such great magnitude that we can never help in time for those children growing up today, but if we work hard on education and system reforms we can look for a better outlook for their children. Although this long-range view may have some validity, parents and children today still deserve our very best effort to respect their rights and mitigate the harsh circumstances in which they find themselves, by a supportive, well-educated, and coordinated intervention effort.

In order to point out the complex interaction of the child, his parents, and society (represented by the child protection agency), and the rights involved in such interactions, the authors will now review some typical processes that are involved when an abuse report is filed.

In cases of suspected child abuse and neglect a rather rigid set of procedures for processing each reported concern has been legislatively mandated. Although the specific methods of service delivery vary from state to state, there is a general agenda that each state utilizes as a guideline for offering child protective services.

Once concern is expressed for a child's situation, the severity of the concern and immediacy of the need are evaluated by the local protective service agency. When the abuse is severe—where, for example, a child has unusual burns or broken bones—an investigation is begun immediately. In all cases of serious concern, a concerted effort is made to make contact with the family within twenty-four hours. Investigations of the majority of other cases are initiated within seventy-two hours after the referral is received. In some states, the police have the authority to take a child into protective custody for forty-eight hours. In severe cases, the police can accompany the social worker in case the child has to be removed from the home immediately. In these cases, a "deprived" petition is filed by the district attorney's office, the child is removed to a temporary group or foster placement, and there then begins the due process of detention hearings, collateral investigations, dispositional hearings, and the ensuing treatment toward the child's return home.

In less clear-cut cases the investigation, including collateral contacts, is made prior to the decision to temporarily place the child out of the home. If this investigation reveals that placement is uncalled for, then supportive services are offered to the family to help ensure that the situation precipitating the referral does not recur.

In the cases where there is no reason for concern for the child's safety or where the parents themselves request help, existing supportive services are discussed and made available to parents as needed. Throughout the process, as stated previously, it is necessary to distinguish between the parents' and the children's rights. The decisions for placement or involvement with therapy are made in an effort to ensure that the child will be maintained in a safe home environment consistent with minimum accepted community standards.

While the court is gathering the data necessary for deciding whether an out-of-home placement is indicated, parents have many rights that need to be observed. Parents have a right to legal representation from the time the social worker first approaches them to discuss the concern. Although this is their right, families only rarely request legal counsel at this point. This failure to exercise a constitutional right can certainly be reduced by an insistence that child protection workers inform alleged child abusers of their right to a court-appointed attorney.

During the investigative interview the family has a right to several kinds of information. First, they have a right to know just what the concern is that is being investigated. Although this does not entitle them to know who expressed the concern, it does help define the specific problem being investigated.

In addition, each parent has a right to know what can happen as a result of the investigation. This includes the alternatives available to the worker and to the family—e.g., legal representation, placement, therapy, and so on. The parents also have a right to be informed of the due process that will ensue if the court becomes involved. If the parents decide at any point that they want legal representation, the court is obliged to provide counsel if they cannot afford their own. As discussed previously, the parents also have a right to have adequately trained and educated professionals make the decisions concerning their families.

After the initial visit, when the level of concern has been assessed the case may be handled at one of three levels. The court may either assume temporary custody of the child and place him in foster care, assume temporary custody and return the child to his parents' home with protective service supervision, or the family may be encouraged to seek treatment without court intervention while protective services continues its monitoring. In either of the first two options it is the family's right to have periodic reviews by the court to ensure that all reasonable efforts are being made to prepare it for the child's return home or the withdrawal of court intervention.

These periodic reviews serve the best interest of both parents and children. They help to ensure that the social service agency is encouraging therapy for the parents such that they will become eligible for their child's return. An all-too-common tendency has been to place a child and then neglect to provide any services for parents during that placement (Mnookin, 1973; Morse et al., 1977). The periodic reviews also protect parents against the negative effects of the high staff turnover rates that prevail in most social service agencies. The reviews help to formally state in a permanent record what will be expected of the parents prior to their child's return. This record is then a consistent factor, even if the workers who manage the case change.

On the child's behalf, these hearings help set the structure through which proceedings for severance-of-parental-rights petitions are initiated. If therapy contracts and visitation arrangements are continually ignored by parents, and the court is able to follow this pattern from one review to the next, then support has been provided for recommending termination of their rights. This in turn allows permanent placement plans—ideally adoption—to be made for the child. Such placement is essential to the child's development of new psychological ties (Goldstein et al., 1973). Additionally, this will help to get him reestablished in a consistent environment where he will have the basics for normal cognitive (Katz, 1969), emotional (Weinstein, 1960; Goldstein et al., 1973), and physical development.

Children have a right to treatment during their foster placement, when appropriate. Because of children's perception that they are being punished when placed in foster care (Goldstein et al., 1973), treatment may be necessary to help them overcome guilt for their removal from home. Therapy may also be necessary to help them process what is taking place with their parents and the effects of that on their behavior. There is sufficient evidence to suggest that a child's development is affected by his home environment and may be adaptable to it (Skolnick, 1973). However, the changes from the abuse environment and the skills required to cope with it may be tremendous. Therapy may be necessary to smooth this transition so that foster placement has a chance of success. If the child's behavior patterns are the same when he is returned to his parents as prior to his removal, he may reinitiate the abuse cycle.

After parents have consented to seek treatment they have the right to be informed of the types of treatment available to them. Social workers who deal with services throughout the county can be good resources for educating parents about these services. If the parents have this knowledge they can make an informed choice about the treatment they receive, and this may enhance their participation and the likelihood of success in therapy.

Client Rights During Treatment

When this choice is made by parents and a therapist has agreed to work with the family, the issue of parents' right to an informed consent to therapy becomes pertinent. In order for them to reasonably sign an informed consent-to-therapy agreement, eight major issues must first be delineated.

1. Parents have a right to know what approach will be used in treatment—e.g., transactional analysis, behavior modification, psychotherapy, and so on.

2. The client has a right to know approximately how long the treatment will last.

3. The client has a right to know in advance approximately how much the therapy will cost and if there are any alternatives available to aid in paying for the service. This point is especially important since typically these are multi-crisis families where money is frequently one source of hardship on family functioning.

4. The client must be informed that he does have the right to refuse treatment. With this right, however, he must also be informed of the possible consequences of refusal—e.g., if he is re-referred to protective services, the fact that counseling had been previously refused might not support a claim that the parent should still have the child at home. Even though protective services endeavors to maintain children in the natural home, such a lack of willingness to change the circumstances at home could be negatively interpreted in a second or third referral investigation.

5. Similarly, the client has a right to know what, if any, consequences there may be for terminating the therapy prior to its completion. Typically this would require that a written summary of the therapy progress and the reason for termination be submitted by the therapist to the protective-service agency. (This is always the case when the state has helped provide payment for the therapy sessions.)

6. The client has a right to know what the scope of confidentiality will be regarding therapy. It is not infrequent that information is shared during treatment concerning ongoing instances of abuse in the home. The law mandates that professionals report knowledge of any such incidents to protective services. The therapist must therefore inform the client of his criteria for reporting. This agreement is as important for the therapist as the client, for he must be concerned with ensuring that the children are in a safe environment while allowing the latitude essential in any therapy for clients to progress. These mechanisms need to be defined in advance for handling situations when clients are not meeting the minimum accepted community standards of care.

7. The client has a right to input in deciding the treatment goals. Since changes can only be brought about by a conscious and continual effort by the parents to learn new skills, it is essential that the priorities of treatment be in agreement with the needs of the parents. In deciding these goals the parents should be allowed a great deal of latitude.

8. The client has a right to know what the criteria for completion of his therapy will be. This may be most explicitly delineated in behavioral terms such that the parents are made aware of what things they are expected to be saying and doing to be ready to terminate therapy. Frequently, once the client has met criteria for termination, a monitoring period ensues to ensure that they are able to continue using their new skills without frequent contact with the therapist. The client's understanding the. criteria for termination is important not only so he can minimize expenses in therapy but also so he may have clear-cut goals for which to strive in his efforts to improve family functioning.

These eight issues need to be discussed and defined with a client before he can sign a truly informed consent to treatment. They help to provide a sound basis for treatment no matter what treatment modality is being utilized.

Once parents have signed an informed consent for treatment, the concern of preserving their rights broadens. The authors have identified nine variables that are important for consideration in any discussion of client rights. But they are especially important in abuse and neglect cases for two reasons. First, in these cases the families are not asking for help in the traditional way; although their consent to treatment is voluntary, it is not as though they had the idea unprompted and pursued it themselves. Second, these rights are important because in abuse and neglect situations we are concerned with the basic unit of our society— the family. The magnitude of this undertaking demands careful control of how it is approached philosophically and implemented clinically. Following are the nine variables that need to be monitored in the endeavor to preserve client rights.

1. Parents and children in abuse and neglect situations have a right to appropriately educated and trained therapists. This means that therapists' education should have included sufficient courses in child development that they may recognize whether a child's physical, emotional, or developmental needs are being met (Smith, 1974; Campbell, 1970). In addition, therapists in abuse and neglect should be trained to understand the dynamics that initiate, maintain, and perpetuate the abuse syndrome (Wald, 1975).

2. Clients have the right to approve the treatment techniques that are being utilized with them. In order that a client will maximize his

participation and cooperation with the treatment program, he must be comfortable with the techniques he is being asked to utilize.

3. Clients have a right to undergo treatment techniques that have a reasonable data base. It is especially important in abuse and neglect that clients receive services that have an established likelihood of effectively improving the family's functioning. Although throwing darts at doll figures may feel good for venting frustration, it is unlikely that this would help parents to not abuse their children in the future. At any rate, there is no evidence that demonstrates the effectiveness of this procedure. The seriousness of the situation in these families demands that they receive services that have been demonstrably effective for making the home environment safer for children.

4. Clients have a right to a periodic review of their treatment progress. This review can help them to be more aware of how they are benefiting from their involvement in therapy. This may also help to motivate parents, as they see on a regular basis how they progress toward their stated goals compared with the amount of energy they have invested. Periodic review will also allow them to reevaluate how helpful the therapist has been and make an informed decision concerning their involvement with any given treatment approach or therapist. The client has a right to request a change in therapists if no progress is being made. Without such a periodic review the clients tend to become embroiled in the demands of the moment and lose perspective on their goal of making their home environment safe for their children.

5. Clients have a right to be given specific procedures rather than general principles. For example, rather than simply telling a mother to place her child's inappropriate baby talk "on extinction" (a principle of behavior modification that requires the removal of all reinforcing consequences for a stated behavior), the therapist should give her the following explicit guidelines:

- When your child uses baby talk, do not answer him.
- Do not provide him with what he is requesting until he makes an effort to use age-appropriate speech.
- Do not give him eye-contact when he uses baby talk.

Clients need explicit instructions for using the tools of any therapeutic technology being utilized for structuring the therapist's interactions with the family and interactions between family members. Anything less is tantamount to giving a non–mechanically inclined person a disassembled engine and expecting him to make it work.

6. Clients have the right to have treatment procedures modeled for them. If a therapist is expecting a parent to utilize a procedure with a child—e.g., redirecting his attention to an appropriate activity following an inappropriate behavior—then it is essential that the therapist show the parents how to implement that procedure. In treatment the therapist must assume that if the client knows how to utilize the skill he would do so, and the fact that he is not using it is a demonstration of his inability. If the therapist asks the parent to praise his child for playing quietly, and then fails to praise the child at similar appropriate times himself, he is failing to provide the parent with a consistent model for that behavior.

7. Clients have a right to be given procedures for handling specific situations where problems typically occur. Parents in abuse and neglect circumstances frequently encounter situations and settings where they perceive social pressures as controlling their children's behavior. These may include grocery stores, restaurants, the doctor's office, and so on. Since these are situations that can increase stress and, in turn, increase the likelihood for abuse to occur, clients have a right to procedures to help them in these situations as well as in the therapist's office and at home.

8. If modeling these procedures in the office or clinic is not effective, then home visits may be necessary to demonstrate how to effectively utilize them. It is nearly impossible during an office visit to demonstrate the patience and consistency that is essential for resolving bedtime problems. The therapist, who has the training and expertise in the use of the treatment procedures, has the responsibility for detailing procedures to fit each family. One cannot reasonably expect the family to generalize all the skills they learn in the office to the greatly complicated and unpredictable home environment (Stokes & Baer, 1977).

9. Each client has a right to learn skills that he may utilize in handling future situations. Treatment providing less than this for any client cannot claim to help prevent future abuse or neglect or to make the home environment safer for the children.

Fortunately, the issue of protecting client rights is compatible with the provision of treatment alternatives, informed consent, and so on. In fact, the protection of client rights will, almost by definition, result in improved service delivery systems.

Summary

Professionals working in the area of child abuse face an enormous challenge. For the first time, mental health professionals and various governmental agencies are being forced to work together in an effort to provide comprehensive and effective services to families demonstrating that they cannot function adequately on their own. The judicial system is being forced to make monumental decisions that affect the very lives of the children they serve. Social service agencies must provide the courts with accurate and comprehensive information while either providing or overseeing the various services to the families, and mental health professionals must provide services that are effective.

These services, offered through the courts, social welfare, and private and public mental health practitioners, must also be provided without compromising the rights of the child or parents. The various rights discussed in this chapter present a unique dilemma to service providers. For years, discussions about the effectiveness of social intervention systems received only minor attention, most of it from those professionals holding academic positions. Some of the vital issues (e.g., comparisons of several intervention strategies, cost effectiveness, and recidivism rates) were never adequately addressed. Rather, professionals squared off in senseless pedantic debates, never arriving at any practical decisions. Now society is called upon to produce an effective, cost-efficient system of intervening with families involved in abuse. Judges borrowed from family, civil, or criminal court are hearing cases of abuse and neglect in juvenile court. Social service personnel are providing services to families—hoping, without knowing, that their efforts will reduce the likelihood of further abuse while protecting the child from psychological harm. Mental health care providers, long accustomed to operating in settings where little if any emphasis has been placed on accountability, are now attempting to adapt or restructure their services as they help combat this problem, one of the most heinous of all social psychological maladies—the abuse of one's own offspring.

Perhaps these new pressures will be good for the professions involved. Perhaps now the courts, social service agencies, and mental health professionals will be forced to critically evaluate their services, dropping or culling out ineffective and wasteful procedures and concentrating their efforts on the delivery of effective treatment procedures.

In the area of child abuse, outcome is the variable that is of paramount importance, both immediately and in the long run. Why? Because we have come to realize—apparently for the first time—that troubled individuals, be they the abusing parents or the abused child, have a *right* to a positive outcome of effective services. No longer are we dealing with academic debates. Now that we recognize that we are actually dealing with children's lives and their futures, we cannot settle for a popular or a faddish intervention. To do so would violate the very rights the system is mandated to protect.

References

ALEXANDER, H., McQUISTON, M., & RODEHOFFER, M. Residential family therapy
     In H. P. Martin (Ed.). *The abused child: A multidisciplinary approach to
     developmental issues and treatment.* Cambridge, Mass.: Ballinger, 1976.

BECK, C., GLAVIS, G., GLOVER, S., JENKINS, M., & NARDI, R. The rights of children: A trust model. *Fordham Law Review,* 1978, *46,* 715–780.

BOWLBY, J. *Child care and growth of love* (2nd ed., abridged and edited by Margaret Fry). London: Penguin Books, 1953.

BRONFENBRENNER, U. Is early intervention effective: A report on longitudinal evaluations of preschool programs. *I. 2. Health Education and Welfare Monograph,* No. (OHD) 74–25, 1974.

BURT, R. Forcing protection on children and their parents: The impact of *Wyman* v. *James. Michigan Law Review,* 1971, 1259–1285.

BURT, R., & BALYEAT, T. New systems for improving care of abused and neglected children. *Child Welfare,* 1974, *53,* 167–179.

CAMPBELL, S. The neglected child: His and his family's rights under Massachusetts law and practice and their rights under the due process clause. *Suffolk Law Review,* 1970, *14,* 641–645.

CHENEY, M., & BEATON, G. Safeguarding legal rights in providing protective services. *Children,* 1966, *75,* 86–92.

EISENBERG, L. The sins of the fathers. *American Journal of Orthopsychiatry,* 1962, *32,* 5–17.

FRASER, B. The child and his parents: A delicate balance of rights. In R. E. Helfer and C. H. Kempe (Eds.), *Child abuse and neglect: The family and the community.* Cambridge, Mass.: Ballinger, 1976.

FREUD, A. *Normality and pathology in childhood: Assessment of development.* New York: International Universities Press, 1965.

GIL, D. *Violence against children: Physical child abuse in the United States.* Cambridge: Harvard University Press, 1975.

GOLDSTEIN, J., FREUD, A., & SOLNIT, A. *Beyond the best interests of the child.* New York: Free Press, 1973.

GOLDSTEIN, J., & KATZ, J. *The family and the law: Problems in decisions in the family law process.* New York: Free Press, 1965.

HANDLER, J. *The coercive social worker: British lessons for American social services.* Chicago: Rand McNally College Publishing, 1973.

HELFER, R. Invited address, Second Annual Governor's Conference on Child Abuse and Neglect, Wichita, Kansas, 1977.

JENCKS, C., ACLAND, H., BANE, M., COHEN, D., GINTIS, H., HEYNS, B., & MICHELSON, S. *Inequality: A reassessment of the effect of family and schooling in America.* New York: Basic Books, 1972.

KADUSHIN, A. *Child welfare services.* New York: Macmillan Co., 1967.

KATZ, S. Foster parents vs. the agencies: A case study of the judicial application of "the best interests of the child" doctrine. *Michigan Law Review,* 1969, *65,* 145.

KATZ, S., HOWE, K., and MCGRATH, T. Child neglect laws in America. *Family Law Quarterly,* 1975, *1,* 63.

KLAUS, M., & KENNELL, J. Mothers separated from their newborn infants. *Pediatric Clinics of North America,* 1970, *17,* 1016.

MAAS, H., & ENGLER, R. *Children in need of parents.* New York: Columbia University Press, 1959.

MILLER, H. C., & MERRITT, T. A. *Fetal growth in humans.* Chicago: Yearbook Medical Publishers, 1979.

MNOOKIN, R. Foster care: In whose best interests. *Harvard Educational Review,* 1973, *43,* 599–631.

MORSE, A. E., HYDE, J. N., NEWBERGER, E. H., & REED, R. Environmental correlates of pediatric social illnesses. *American Journal of Public Health,* 1977, *67,* 612–615.

PAULSEN, M. The delinquency, neglect and dependence jurisdiction of the Juvenile Court. In M. Rosenheim (Ed.), *Justice for the Child.* New York: Free Press of Glencoe, 1962.

PATTON, R., & GARDNER, L. *Growth failure in maternal deprivation.* Springfield, Illinois: Charles C. Thomas, 1963.

PHILLIPS, M. H., SHYNE, A. W., SHERMAN, E. A., & HARING, B. L. *Factors associated with placement decisions in child welfare.* New York: Child Welfare League of America, 1971.

SAMEROFF, A., & CHANDLER, M. Reproductive risk and the continuum of caretaking causality. In F. Horowitz (Ed.), *Review of child development research* (Vol. 4). Chicago: University of Chicago Press, 1975.

SKOLNICK, A. *The intimate environment: Exploring marriage and the family.* Boston: Little, Brown & Co., 1973.

SMITH, S. Profile of juvenile court judges in the U.S. *Juvenile Justice,* 1974, *25,* 27.

STEELE, B. Parental abuse of infants and small children. In J. Anthony & T. Benedek (Eds.), *Parenthood: Its psychology and psychopathology.* Boston: Little, Brown & Co., 1970.

STOKES, T. F., & BAER, D. M. An implicit technology of generalization. *Journal of Applied Behavior Analysis,* 1977, *10,* 349–367.

VORE, D. Prenatal nutrition and postnatal intellectual development. *Merrill-Palmer Quarterly,* 1973, *19,* 253–260.

WALD, M. State intervention on behalf of "neglected" children: A search for realistic standards. *Stanford Law Review,* 1975, *27,* 985–1040.

WASSERMAN, S. The abused parent of the abused child. *Children,* 1967, *14,* 5.

WEINSTEIN, E. *The self image of the foster child.* New York: Russel Sage Foundation, 1960.

CHAPTER 4

Protecting the Educational Rights of the Handicapped Child

Martin J. Pollack
Beth Sulzer-Azaroff

So MUCH ATTENTION is currently being given to issues of the rights of handicapped children, and so heavily have those issues begun to dominate the popular media, that few but those directly affected may recall that the topic was virtually ignored in the not-too-distant past. Previously, children unable to profit from the typical public school education were treated in one of two ways: Either they were benignly tolerated and permitted to learn as best they could, moving along via "social promotions" with their chronological peers or being retained at a grade level as their physical maturation and that of their classmates gradually separated; or else, if they became too obtrusive or disruptive or began to tax the human and material resources of the system, they were excluded. Some compensation may have been provided in the form of home tutoring or other limited efforts. But this was often inadequate, since allocated sessions were often brief and intermittent and personnel frequently lacked the training that would permit them to meet the child's educational needs. This system reflected a philosophy that handicapped children could benefit little, if at all, from a formal education.

During the sixties and early seventies, this all began to change. One could begin to see a great groundswell of social concern for the rights of the individual. Paralleling the emerging concept that individual citizens could question participation in the Vietnam War was a developing concern for the rights and dignity of those persons whose vulnerable position had permitted them historically to fall victim to the social power structure. Writers and philosophers began to advocate social change in behalf of minorities, women, and the mentally, physically, and emotionally handicapped. The influence of such people as Martin Luther King,

Betty Friedan, Szasz (1961), Wolfensberger (1972) and other social reformers caused citizens to begin to raise issues hitherto ignored. The concern for handicapped children was reflected in a fundamental question: "Does providing severely handicapped children the most rudimentary basic necessities adequately fulfill society's responsibility to them?" The question led to discussion, and the discussion led to action: action in the courts; action in the congress and state legislatures; changes in administrative policy.

Therein lay the impetus for the modification of social policy toward the rights of the handicapped child. Issues were clarified and redress sought through the courts and legislation. It was noted that no system was in place for providing services to these children. The handicapped child was recognized to have been denied adequate services in that educational programs tended to focus on the common denominator rather than the individual. Educational decisions about identifying handicapped children and about how to deliver services, where they should be provided, and for what age range, needed to be addressed. The public began to realize that programs for handicapped children lacked appropriate facilities, curricula, and fiscal support, as well as adequately trained personnel. Roles and functions of professionals serving handicapped children were in need of refinement and redefinition. The sources and functions of social influences had to be identified and utilized, and the school and consumers in the community had to be involved and their concerns considered.

As these and related issues began to be addressed, the rights of the handicapped child started to be clarified. The courts handed down judicial decisions, many of which were to serve as the nuclei for legislative action. In this chapter some of these major issues will be considered and their influence on public policy traced. By analyzing this material it will be possible to identify numerous rights and safeguards that now exist for the handicapped child. But laws and policy do not ensure their own execution; the preservation of rights requires the concerted effort of concerned individuals. It is toward that end that the latter section of this chapter is directed, via the presentation of a series of promising strategies for the preservation of the rights of the handicapped child.

The handicapped child, for purposes of this exposition, is a child with a disadvantage that makes achievement unusually difficult. The disadvantage may be physical, emotional, or intellectual. Such children usually require special services if they are to profitably interact with their educational environment. Some of the major events affecting the handicapped child, and how they relate to some of the critical issues, will be briefly examined here.

In 1954 the U.S. Supreme Court arrived at the decision that was to play one of the most significant roles in the United States educational arena—its ruling on *Brown* v. *Board of Education of Topeka*. That decision established the concept that educational opportunities for children are tied to success in life. Thus, with the statement "Such an opportunity, where the state has undertaken to provide it, is a right which must be made available to all on equal terms," schools were no longer permitted to racially segregate educational programs.

It was nearly two decades later that concern over the denial of educational opportunity for handicapped children reached a magnitude sufficient to inspire significant action. Basing their case in part on the *Brown* school desegregation ruling, the Pennsylvania Association for Retarded Children (PARC) contested in 1971 a school's right to exclude children on the basis that they are considered unable to benefit from an education. Having heard expert testimony that mentally retarded children can indeed profit from educational programs, the court found that the state laws denied the excluded mentally retarded children equal protection and due process, two critical constitutionally guaranteed rights. The following year this finding received further support when in *Mills* v. *District of Columbia* the court found that all handicapped children, regardless of handicapping condition, had the rights to a *free appropriate public education*.

So the *PARC* and *Mills* decisions left little doubt that courts would treat seriously the arbitrary exclusion of handicapped children from school. But these decisions had an even broader impact, for they began to specify procedural safeguards that would serve to lay the groundwork for the elaboration of appropriate service delivery systems. For instance, *Mills* specified methods for student identification, notification, assessment, placement, review, curricula, educational objectives, and personnel qualifications.

Just as the *Brown* decision caused far-reaching modifications in civil rights laws and policies (e.g., the Civil Rights Act of 1964), it also had an important impact on legal protection of the rights of the handicapped. Public Law 93-112, the Rehabilitation Act of 1973, referring to programs assisted by the Department of Health, Education and Welfare, provides in Section 504 that "no otherwise qualified handicapped individual . . . shall solely by reason of his handicap, be excluded from participation, be denied the benefits of, or be subjected to discrimination under any program or activity receiving federal financial assistance."

Since these regulations provided a definition of handicapped individuals from the perspective of employment, the law's discrimination prohibitions were widely interpreted as limited to employment situations. This interpretation was clarified in 1974 with the enactment of P.L. 93-516, in which Section 504 was amended to broaden the definition of handicapped individuals to "any person who (A) has a physical or mental impairment which substantially limits one or more such person's major life activities, (B) has a record of such impairment, or (C) is regarded as having such an impairment." This language now became essentially the same as that incorporated in the antidiscrimination provisions of the Civil Rights Act of 1964, but with direct application to educational services. Since Section 504 is endowed with funding jurisdiction over any program or activity receiving federal financial support, it is, in effect, the enforcer for compliance with all other educational legislation.

Also in 1974, Congress enacted an amendment to the Elementary and Secondary Education Act of 1965 through the passage of P.L. 93-380. This law established the national policy of equal education for all Americans (Section 801), and addressed several of the critical issues related to the rights of handicapped children. A system of service delivery began to emerge, with provision for identification, assessment, placement, and due process rights.

It was in P.L. 94-142 that the most complete redress of grievances for handicapped children and their parents was provided. This act, the Education of All Handicapped Children Act—passed by Congress in 1975—contains specific and detailed provisions for implementation into law. (See *Federal Register*, August 23, 1977.) Here issues of individualization, appropriateness of location, funding policies, priorities, and dates for implementation were addressed. A free, appropriate public education was mandated, with special education and support services defined. Due process provisions were elaborated: Parents could now have major input into the system of education that would affect their handicapped children. Their involvement was guaranteed via mandated contacts and options existing throughout the process, including access to records, which would have to be written in a form comprehensible to them; the right to independent evaluations whenever questions of objectivity or accuracy arise; receipt of comprehensible written notice at several key points in the process; and giving consent as required in certain early steps. The importance of parental participation is emphasized by provisions for parent surrogates to advocate for the child in the absence of natural parents.

Handicapped children are now protected—by P.L. 94-142—from being arbitrarily segregated from their nonhandicapped peers. In fact, the law stipulates that handicapped children should be educated in the *least restrictive environment* appropriate to their situation. The regular classroom is to be the starting point in placement consideration, and handicapped children are to be educated with nonhandicapped children to the maximum extent appropriate. Rather than placing the burden of proof on the child's parents or advocate to demonstrate that placement in a regular class setting would be reasonable, the burden is shifted to the school to justify separation from that setting. If the educational objectives set for the child can be judged as potentially achievable in the regular class, that is where the child belongs. Decisions to separate the child are subject to review, and due process provisions permit a mechanism for the resolution of conflict over such judgments. P.L. 92-142 specifies—in Section 121a.550— "special classes, separate schooling, or other removal of handicapped children from the educational environment [constitutes separation, and separation] occurs only when the nature and severity of the handicap is such that education in regular classes with the use of supplementary aids and services cannot be achieved satisfactorily." (See *Federal Register,* August 23, 1977.[1])

Other stipulations of this law also support the concept of least restrictiveness. Alternative services and placements are conceptualized as a continuum from the regular classroom to the hospital or institution. For example, a child judged unable to profit from education in a regular class would not be immediately institutionalized. Rather, he might be served by a specialized program within the school, neighborhood, or region. Every attempt would be made to keep him as close to home as possible in selecting a placement appropriate to his educational needs, and the decision would be subject to review. Justifiable nonacademic and extracurricular services and activities are to be made available as well. So if a youngster is clearly unable to function in a regular classroom due to severe developmental delay in language and social skills, he might be placed in a program provided by the collaborative efforts of several school systems in his region. There, in addition to any academic skills, he might be provided language and specific social skills training.

Compliance with the provisions of P.L. 94-142 is required of private as well as public educational agencies; personnel need to be given technical and training assistance to permit that compliance. The state education agency is charged with the responsibility of monitoring educational facilities and making those corrections that will assure compliance with the law.

The evidence that each handicapped child is recognized in P.L. 94-142 as having unique educational requirements is embodied in the Individualized Educational Program (IEP). P.L. 94-142 requires that each handicapped child, whether in public or private facilities, be provided with a program plan that addresses his or her individual, complex educational and related needs. Conceivably, however, IEP program planning meetings could meet the letter but not the spirit of the law by formalizing previously existing practices within the IEP plan. To protect against such nonresponsive planning, all closely involved parties are included in the meeting. The burden for assuring parent participation at this meeting belongs, once again, to the educational agency

---

[1] Henceforth referred to as "*FR,* August 1977."

rather than the child, the parents, or the advocate. The law does not simply require passive acceptance of parental attendance at the meeting but insists that the agency strenuously encourage parents to attend and asks for documentation of such efforts. So, for instance, if parents are employed efforts must be made to schedule a meeting at a time and place that enables them to attend without jeopardizing their position at work.

While no specific measures or procedures are mandated for evaluation of IEPs, the law does require that appropriate objective criteria be applied to evaluation procedures. A schedule for review of achievements is also to be included. Since no specific rate of progress is specified for the IEP, the educational agency cannot be held liable for failure to achieve all objectives. However, the law does require that the agency make "good-faith efforts" to achieve the objectives as written. Parents are not restricted in their right to request revisions or in their utilization of all due process procedures to guarantee those "good-faith efforts."

Through its blending of rigour and flexibility the IEP permits the conception, implementation, and evaluation of programs that should meet the educational needs of each handicapped child. When utilized as intended by the spirit of the law, the IEP should permit the objective gathering of valid evidence of student performance in light of the instructional methods and curriculum that have been provided.

Given this historical and philosophical perspective, providers of educational services to handicapped children will appreciate the care with which they must proceed. In the following section we recommend a series of strategies for protecting the educational rights of these children during intake and other placement and programming phases, as well as under circumstances that may require restrictive procedures or in which research activities are planned.

The suggested strategies below should be considered as a set of guidelines that may be adjusted within the bounds of legally mandated procedures and as administrative policy and individual student circumstances warrant.

Strategies for Protection of Handicapped Children's Rights

DURING INTAKE

1. *Identification.* Contrary state laws or court orders are the only conditions that preclude the right to a free and appropriate public

education according to the 1978 and 1980 guidelines of **P.L.** 94-142.

Strategies:

a. Educate yourself and your staff about each handicapping condition that requires formal identification. These are named and defined in Section 121a.1-11 (*FR,* August 23, 1977). Follow the rule that any child experiencing difficulty in learning due to physical, sensory, or learning deficits should be served.

b. Make your search effort a "child-find" program that is demonstrably vigorous and active, by including a variety of tactics. For example, utilize television, radio, and newspapers to educate the public and stimulate inquiries by parents of handicapped children; provide toll-free telephone lines for initial contacts; use brochures, postings, public speaking programs, and other outreach efforts in each community.

c. Anticipate problems in receipt of information by residents of your community unable to benefit from standard communications.

d. Utilize professionals in direct contact with students as a resource for identification. Teachers, consultants, and supervisory staff should submit written recommendations for consideration as handicapped regarding any child indicating such needs. Supervisors and administrators should solicit new information in this area through an annual survey of all staff reasonably able to offer identifying information.

2. *Evaluation.* Once a child becomes a candidate for evaluation to determine special education and related needs, parent notification must occur.

Strategies:

a. Design pre-evaluation notices to include the following:

   i. Use easily understood, native language unless not feasible. Be prepared to meet any communication needs.

   ii. Prepare a brochure or other written notice to inform parents of all due process safeguards afforded them and their children. (See Sub-Part E [*FR,* August 23, 1977].)

   iii. Inform parents of all decisions made to date, with a rationale for each.

   iv. Describe in detail the evaluation planned, including procedures and instruments to be used. Where precise advance knowledge is not feasible, provide a strategy and the most probable methods that would follow each type of finding. Be prepared to demonstrate informed consent for evaluation methods selected.

      v. Figure 1 indicates a time-frame appropriate for evaluation and placement. Notices should conform to the time-frame requirements listed in Figure 1. Pre-placement evaluation notices should reach parents within seven days of referral.

b. Obtain informed consent prior to initial pre-placement evaluations.

c. If natural parents are unavailable, negotiate with surrogate parents. If "parents or guardians are not known, unavailable, or the child is a ward of the state" surrogate parents should be appointed (Sub-Part E [FR, August 23, 1977]).

    Figure 2 presents a series of steps to follow in requesting a surrogate parent. Surrogate parents participate as the legal authority for all educational decisions. Professionals should be prepared to recommend changes when observing either conflicts of interest between surrogate parent and child or inadequate representation.

d. Focus evaluation efforts on outcomes that relate to specific educational needs. Identify performance levels in all relevant areas of functioning. Establish a sufficient foundation to permit prescriptive recommendations for placement and program needs addressed in the IEP.

e. Organize a multidisciplinary team. Include at least one teacher or other specialist with knowledge in the area of the suspected disability or handicap. Encourage contributions by all relevant persons, especially parents and others having significant contact with or knowledge of the child. Where appropriate in the evaluation process, include the child as an active participant as well as the subject of formal evaluation. Establish a cooperative relationship among all participants to maximize ongoing benefits to the child.

f. In conducting an evaluation, procedures and instruments should be
    i. valid for the purposes used, and should assess the specific and related areas of need;
    ii. selected with consideration for the child's particular impairments;
    iii. administered by a qualified person, and—unless not feasible—in the child's native language; and should
    iv. include multiple measures rather than any single measure of functional level. Favor prescriptive information and avoid labels such as IQ scores used alone. For example, use adaptive behavior summaries, aptitude and achievement test data, social and cultural background information, teacher recommendations.

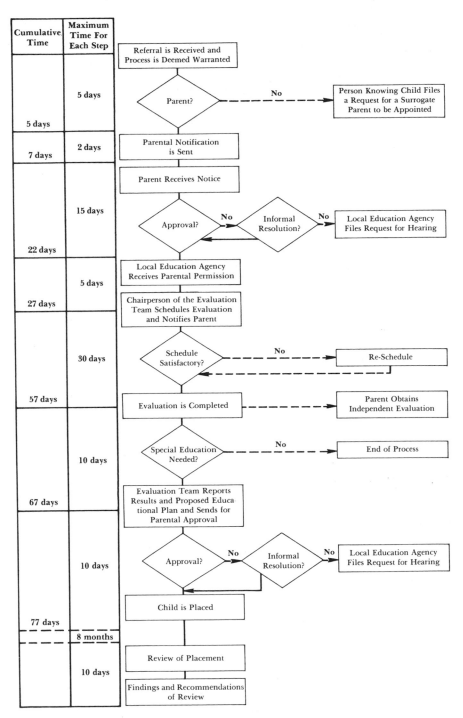

FIGURE 1. Time requirements for each step in the evaluation and placement process.

From Abeson, Bolick, and Hass (1976). The authors wish to thank the Council on Exceptional Children for use of materials in this figure.

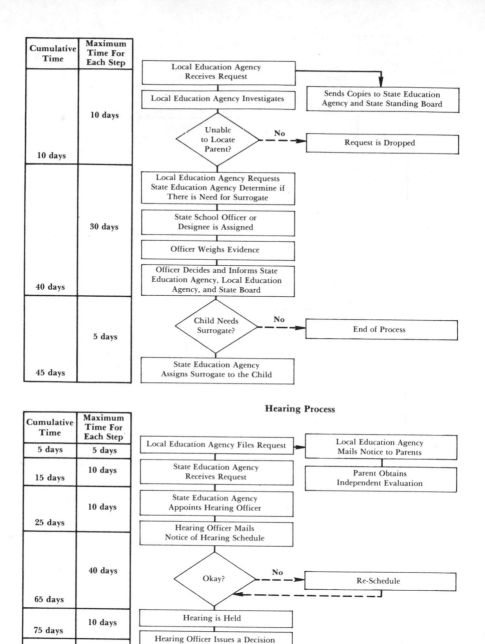

Cumulative Time	Maximum Time For Each Step
	10 days
10 days	
	30 days
40 days	
	5 days
45 days	

Local Education Agency Receives Request

Sends Copies to State Education Agency and State Standing Board

Local Education Agency Investigates

Unable to Locate Parent? — No → Request is Dropped

Local Education Agency Requests State Education Agency Determine if There is Need for Surrogate

State School Officer or Designee is Assigned

Officer Weighs Evidence

Officer Decides and Informs State Education Agency, Local Education Agency, and State Board

Child Needs Surrogate? — No → End of Process

State Education Agency Assigns Surrogate to the Child

Hearing Process

Cumulative Time	Maximum Time For Each Step
5 days	5 days
15 days	10 days
	10 days
25 days	
	40 days
65 days	
75 days	10 days

Local Education Agency Files Request

Local Education Agency Mails Notice to Parents

State Education Agency Receives Request

Parent Obtains Independent Evaluation

State Education Agency Appoints Hearing Officer

Hearing Officer Mails Notice of Hearing Schedule

Okay? — No → Re-Schedule

Hearing is Held

Hearing Officer Issues a Decision

Parent Approval? — No → Appeal is Initiated for Judicial Review

Issue is Resolved

FIGURE 2. Time requirements for each step toward appointment of a surrogate parent.

From Abeson, Bolick, and Hass (1976). The authors wish to thank the Council on Exceptional Children for use of materials in this figure.

     v. Instruments and administration should be racially and culturally fair, and in all respects nondiscriminatory.

g. Permit independent evaluations. When parents wish to have an independent evaluation, its source and cost and use of the results need to be considered.

     i. Prepare a list of resources that parents may request and use at their discretion. Include resources for all handicapping conditions. To guarantee independence, avoid resources that lead to a conflict of interest.

     ii. Prepare to bear the cost of an independent evaluation unless the parents agree to pay or the local educational agency ("LEA") chooses to contest the payment responsibility via a formal hearing. (See Sec. 121a.506 [*FR,* August 23, 1977].) LEAs should seek to resolve differences over cost informally, if at all possible.

     iii. Include findings from independent evaluations in developing IEPs regardless of who assumed the cost.

h. Schedule periodic reevaluations.

     i. Schedule a reevaluation *at least* once each three years, but more often if warranted. Anticipate questions regarding the usefulness of current evaluative information. Be prepared to receive requests for updates. Initiate reevaluations in the absence of specific requests from parents, if warranted by program feedback.

     ii. Anticipate questions about the usefulness of current evaluative information, and be prepared to justify any omission in current diagnositic information for each IEP.

     iii. Initiate reevaluations when appropriate without parental prompting, to demonstrate responsiveness to each child's needs. Maintain a detailed written chronology of all actions taken in behalf of the child since the last IEP planning/review meeting. Establish a cooperative, trusting relationship with parents by sharing information and responding to inquiries patiently. Thoughtfully anticipating and quickly responding to parents' concerns will avoid the need for time-consuming and trying defensive operations.

i. Prepare evaluation reports and access to records. When it is determined by the evaluation team that special education or related services are needed, the following should take place:

     i. Schedule a meeting to develop the IEP.

     ii. Prepare a report on the findings of the evaluations. The report should be made available for parent review prior to the IEP.

    iii. Update all school records for the child in anticipation of review by parents or their representatives. Meet requests prior to the IEP or within a maximum of forty-five days.

    iv. Prepare to comply with reasonable requests for explanation or interpretation of records.

    v. Routinely provide information during months in which IEP meetings are less heavily scheduled. Maintain regular contact with teachers and parents to prevent demands on professional time from concentrating at one particular time (e.g., teachers and principals are particularly busy at the start of a school year).

    vi. Communicate reports in easily understood language (and try to use the parents' native language, unless that is not feasible). Use specialized communications where required.

    vii. Maintain a detailed record of all communications with parents (correspondence, telephone calls, visits), including dates, discussion topics, outcomes, materials or records provided, and other significant details. Use this record as a guide to maximize the effectiveness of contacts and schedule appropriate events throughout the year.

DURING PLACEMENT AND PROGRAMMING

1. *Placement.*

    a. Be prepared to defend a student's removal from the regular educational setting and document the inability of that setting to achieve service needs. (See Section 121a.500, [*FR*, August 23, 1977].)

    b. Place each handicapped child in a program that conforms to the principle of "least restrictive environment." All handicapped children should be educated with nonhandicapped children to the "maximum extent possible."

    c. Establish a continuum of service settings, beginning with the regular classroom and utilizing support or supplementary services before placement in any of the successively more restrictive settings.

    d. Implement a system that encourages movement in the less restrictive direction and requires adequate justification for movement in a more restrictive direction.

    e. When alternative placements are required, locate children as close to home as possible.

    f. Consider potential harmful effects and limits on the range of services, as well as the potential benefits, resulting from placement in any setting alternative to the regularly assigned school.

2. *Program and Service Options.*
   a. Provide opportunities for handicapped children to benefit from the variety of educational programs and services equal but not restricted to those offered nonhandicapped children—including art, music, vocational education, and industrial arts.
   b. Provide those nonacademic and extracurricular activities offered to all students that are potentially beneficial to handicapped students. Examples of nonacademic services are counseling and health services, recreation, athletics, special interest groups and clubs, employment opportunities arranged through the school, and transportation services.
   c. Provide a physical education program appropriate for each child's needs. Place the highest priority on inclusion in regular programs, but design special programs if necessary. Approach physical education as an integral part of the program for each handicapped child, not as a luxury or optional component.

3. *Priorities.*
   a. First, provide a free, appropriate public education ("FAPE") for all handicapped children currently receiving no services.
   b. Second, improve services to those children currently receiving inadequate services for their needs, beginning with those with the most severe needs within each handicap area.

4. *Individualized Educational Programs (IEPs).* As mentioned earlier, an IEP plan must be written and implemented for each handicapped child, regardless of placement.
   a. Initiate and conduct the meeting for the development, review, and revision of the IEP. Conduct at least one such meeting per year for each child. These IEP-meeting responsibilities may be delegated to outside agencies providing services, but, regardless of who has undertaken this activity, develop an accountability system to assure due process in these functions. Ultimate responsibility remains with the home LEA.
   b. Schedule IEP meetings sufficiently far in advance of the beginning of the school year to permit implementation without unreasonable delay. Hold IEP meetings for newly identified children within thirty days of identification.
   c. Where appropriate—as when a large number of children are involved—begin preparations early in the year. Maintain a list of children for whom IEPs are needed and project the number of additional IEPs that will probably be needed for children not yet identified. Prepare a tentative schedule to permit ade-

quate attention to each child's needs and to parental rights. Complete IEPs for all identified children by the end of the school year, to permit adequate planning for in-service programs, hiring of new staff, and other preparations.

d. Activate each IEP by the beginning of the school year or as soon as possible following the meeting in which it is developed. Immediate implementation is the rule, with minimal delay permitted only under special circumstances to work out details of implementation.

e. Provide copies of IEPs and minutes of IEP meetings to parents on request.

f. To achieve its objectives, assure full participation in each IEP meeting. The IEP meeting should be attended by the child's teacher, a special educator or supervisor, one or both parents, a representative from any outside agency being considered as a placement site, the child (if appropriate), and others at the discretion of the LEA and the parents. Should these be initial evaluations for the child, a member of the evaluation team should be present to explain procedures and interpret findings. If too many people are attending to permit productive planning, we recommend that the varied professional input be coordinated by a single qualified representative.

g. Vigorously encourage participation by parents. Make special arrangements for this participation if necessary, such as conference calls, alternate representation, and so on. Document all efforts to accommodate and persuade the parents to participate; keep detailed records of telephone calls attempted and the conversations and outcomes, correspondence, and visits to parents' home or office and their outcomes. However, conduct the IEP meeting without parents if they cannot be persuaded to participate.

h. Consider the following factors when determining the appropriateness of the child's attendance and participation: the child's age, his or her ability to cope with the demands of the meeting, the severity of the handicap, and the potential for contributing to the IEP. If attendance is not advisable, consider alternative ways to involve the child—such as through a prior meeting with a more select group.

i. Include in the IEP
   i. a description of the child's present level of functioning in all areas, including those not traditionally part of the educational program, such as self-help skills;
   ii. annual goals, including short-term instructional objectives;
   iii. specific special education and related services to be provided;

      iv. the extent of the child's participation in regular educational programs (e.g., number of hours per day, uses of regular versus special programming, and so on);

      v. projected dates for initiation and anticipated duration of services; and

      vi. appropriate objective criteria and evaluative procedures. Plan a program-review schedule corresponding with individual objectives, to assess achievement and maximize benefits from refinements and revisions of methods or objectives.

j. Demonstrate accountability by making "good-faith efforts" to assist in achieving the objectives included in each child's IEP. Include administrative and direct service activities. While no guarantee can be made that progress will occur at the projected rate and neither agencies nor individuals are liable for objectives not achieved, "good-faith efforts" are required by law. To demonstrate credible "good-faith efforts" professionals should adhere to quality educational standards, including the following practices:

      i. Respond to each problem addressed in the IEP. Consider especially fundamental needs—those which if not substantially met would prevent the accomplishment of other important objectives for the individual.

      ii. Use objective criteria and evaluation methods to assess the accomplishment of annual goals. Employ methods that are current and of demonstrated merit. This may require utilizing previously untapped resources (e.g., consultants) to design or review accountability systems for individualized programs. Examples include instructional technology or behavior analysis specialists.

      iii. Incorporate a data collection and monitoring system in the plan to implement the IEP. The system should gather valid and reliable data from which teachers and other professionals may obtain regular feedback. Data should accurately reflect overall progress and the effectiveness of specific methods.

      iv. Select methods to achieve objectives that would pass the scrutiny of peer review. Consider both ethical factors and the technical integrity of the practices.

      v. Document professional responsiveness to monitored data, including continuation of effective methods and refinement or revision of less effective methods.

      vi. Document the use of methods to maintain and extend demonstrated positive changes. Introduce new objectives in order of priority, as criteria are reached.

STRATEGIES FOR USE WITH AVERSIVE OR RESTRICTIVE PROCEDURES

Certain procedures may require considerably more detail specific to their use, beyond the generally applicable guidelines below.[2] Ethical and safe use of specific procedures should be determined by individual research, including consultation with professionals experienced in their use and knowledgeable about sophisticated issues surrounding them.

1. Confirm and document the operation of an overall positive learning environment, including functional incentives or rewards as a precondition for any nonpositive approaches.

2. Document the ineffectiveness of positive approaches used by themselves for this problem.

3. Justify the use of any aversive or restrictive procedures by their therapeutic/educational merit for the individual (e.g., specific benefits to be gained).

4. Rule out all possible medical (i.e., physiological) causes of the problem or medical contraindications of procedures.

5. Conform to all local, state, and federal policies, regulations, and statutes.

6. Document the use of "least restrictive alternatives" through evidence of the inadequacy of less restrictive efforts.

7. Select procedures on the basis of demonstration of effectiveness (preferably professionally published) with this or a similar problem.

8. Select procedures that provide an acceptable balance of degree and speed of effectiveness, durability, and positive side effects against degree of restrictiveness or aversiveness and negative side effects.

9. Prepare contingency plans for any potential negative side effects.

10. Obtain informed consent for each procedure from the legally responsible authority (e.g., parents, guardians, surrogate parents, courts) and if possible from the child for each procedure.

11. Obtain approval from a human rights committee or other adequately skilled, impartial review board.

12. Establish an adequate monitoring system to document proper implementation, refinements or revisions, and phase-out when the criterion is reached.

13. Train staff to a standard of demonstrated proficiency and ethical use—not merely knowledge—of each procedure employed.

14. Aim towards establishing the child's self-control over the previously maladaptive behavior.

---

[2] These and subsequent strategies are based on federal regulations and administrative policies, such as those developed at the Mansfield Day Treatment Center and other agencies, combined with recommendations derived from the authors' own experiences.

15. Maintain updated information to be shared with consenters upon request.

16. Include the procedure in the IEP if possible.

Aversive Procedures.   The requirements of P.L. 94-142 and related legislation were designed to protect children's educational rights by emphasizing nonpunitive and nonrestrictive conditions. There are times, however, when children under these conditions will fail to acquire the skills that would enable them to reach their potentially optimal quality of life, given the limitations of their handicapping conditions. Sometimes they fail to make the effort necessary to surmount hurdles; sometimes they may engage in behaviors that may either seriously impede their own or their classmates' ability to progress or be dangerous to themselves or others. In either event alternative approaches must be considered. But under these circumstances it is absolutely critical that measures be taken to protect the child from arbitrary or vengeful procedures. Below we present some guidelines designed to offer such protection. Since consent requires informing clients or their advocates as to any potential risks or discomfort, consent strategies for aversive procedures need detailed attention.

Strategies for Obtaining Consent to Aversive Procedures

1. Follow accepted standards for eligibility of consenters—that they be competent, legally authorized, voluntary, informed, and free from conflicts of interest.
2. Include a precise description of target behaviors.
3. Include a complete description of aversive stimuli and procedures.
4. Include a description of previously attempted approaches and unsuccessful outcomes observed.
5. Provide a rationale for this procedure, including the prediction of best possible outcomes from withholding this treatment and continuing reliance on other procedures.
6. Include a description of the monitoring procedures to be followed; provide baseline data (consisting of a series of measures prior to the intervention).
7. Include a description of potential side effects or risks of this procedure and precautionary actions to be taken.
8. Provide a statement of anticipated benefits and the estimated time required to realize them.
9. Include a description of the qualifications of the staff using the procedures.
10. Include an assurance that the emphasis will remain on positive

areas—such as increasing adaptive skills—even when the restrictive procedure must be in effect.

11. Where a special apparatus or setting is involved, indicate that as part of the informing process consenters (e.g., the student, parents) were provided a demonstration, simulation, or actual opportunity to experience the procedure (as in role playing being placed in a time-out room).

12. Include a statement that indicates voluntariness on the part of the consenter (i.e., a noncoercive disclaimer).

13. Include acknowledgment by the consenter that he or she has been informed of the right to refuse to consent and the right to withdraw consent at any time without penalty or retribution.

14. Include an acknowledgment that all questions regarding the procedures to be used have been answered to the consenter's satisfaction.

RESEARCH ACTIVITIES

The mandate to educate all handicapped children will challenge instructional planners. For while much has been accomplished in the recent past in developing curriculum materials and procedures for special-needs students, much more remains to be accomplished. Responsible procedural development requires the collection of objective information under conditions of experimental control. Technically such endeavors fall under the heading "research," and clients should be protected and consent obtained.

Strategies for Protection in Research Activities

1. Establish a review board to screen research proposals involving children as subjects.

2. Establish criteria for determining the scientific merit of proposed research including

    a. potential for increasing factual information about one or more handicapping conditions, and

    b. potential benefits to these and other handicapped children.

3. Obtain informed consent from the subjects or a legally authorized person. Include an acknowledgment of having informed consenters of right to refuse consent and withdraw consent at any time without penalty or retribution.

4. Any risk to subjects participating should be matched by the importance of achieving the objectives of research and by benefits to the

subjects. For example, applied research involving treatment of children exhibiting severely self-injurious behavior may justify greater risk than less dangerous problems.

5. Permit only qualified individuals to assume responsibility for each research project.

6. Assign a competent, objective individual to monitor the research and safeguard the rights of research subjects.

7. Establish procedures to guarantee confidentiality.

8. Establish a vehicle to make outcomes of research available to subjects or their legally authorized representative at the earliest time possible without introducing bias into the research.

9. Include in the consent process full disclosure of potential short- and long-range consequences to participants.

10. Use the safest procedures to minimize harm or discomfort.

Strategies for Obtaining Research Consent from Research Review Board and Participants

1. Include a brief rationale for research support.
2. Include a description of the procedures involved for the subjects, or, if such a description would compromise the research, be prepared to provide this information later.
3. Provide an indication of what is expected to be gained from the research.
4. Provide assurances of confidentiality, ethical practices, and qualified professional supervision.
5. Include a description of what is required by the subject, and any discomfort or risks that would not otherwise be present.
6. Obtain permission to use results for publication.
7. Consent should be voluntary and informed, with a statement assuring the right to refuse participation and the right to withdraw consent at any time without penalty or retribution.
8. Offer to provide complete information on research procedures and outcomes when the risk of bias to the experiment is over.
9. Include a statement that a review board must approve all research on the basis of its merit, and that the research will be monitored for compliance with that approval and for safety of subjects.

Trends

Legislation and litigation should lead to refinements of the law over the next few years. Failure to sufficiently meet the letter of the law will certainly result in some court actions; much litigation is also to be expected as the limits of the law are interpreted. Areas in which litigation is highly probable have been suggested by Turnbull (1978) and Melcher (1976). Such litigation should impact on virtually all major tenets of the law. It is likely that test cases will emerge in areas such as scope of services available, including early intervention and extended school programs; access to barrier-free environments; quality of services, including tests of "good-faith efforts" and standards for implementing the IEP; use of nondiscriminatory evaluation, with validation for the purposes intended posing major problems; and the appropriateness of specific mainstreaming efforts and the absence of appropriate placement opportunities.

The role of children as advocates for their own best interest is likely to be strengthened. One indication of this trend is already found in the more extensive regulations governing informed-consent procedures (e.g., Protection of Human Subjects, [FR, November 1978]). Children's right to oppose decisions made for them by their parents requires clarification.

Any test of quality in educational programs will reflect on the training of professionals. More technically skilled professionals sophisticated in ethics and the law are needed. Universities and service centers will need to train staff cooperatively, since training staff to function in actual service settings enables them to learn to cope with demands of those settings. Cooperative training offers the additional advantages of exposing trainees to newly emerging roles and providing resources for in-service training.

The former adversary relation between community and school is becoming more cooperative. The advocacy movement, represented by the action of parents and community groups, appears to have strengthened the relationship. According to Fanner (1977) this has resulted in greater community access to the school, reduced combativeness between the school and the community, and improved services to children. As teachers recognize the inevitability of regular contact with parents, they should begin to make increasingly greater efforts to become skilled in forming a trusting and cooperative relationship with them.

Summary

The foregoing discussion has narrated how historical events and changing philosophies of education for the handicapped have coalesced within the past few years, culminating in the Education of All Handicapped Children Act (P.L. 94-142). This act mandates the education of all handicapped children over a minimum age, but goes much further in specifying procedures for insuring due process and other modes of rights protection for those individuals.

In this chapter we have attempted to provide a set of guidelines for implementing strategies that provide maximum protection of the rights of the handicapped child. But a word of caution: Lest one become so enmeshed in the web of protective devices that inaction is the result, one must continually consider handicapped children's right to receive the best possible education. Such a goal requires that optimal methods are selected.

Educators will need to constantly strive to maintain an open mind about possible procedures. They may, for instance, not like the idea of providing small treats, tokens, or special activities as rewards for educational accomplishments. And yet for some students this very thing may be the key to progress. Educators thus must be willing to innovate and put promising procedures to a fair test, remembering that it is the environment (e.g., teacher-student interactions, curricula) that shapes the child's progress. The ultimate educational right of handicapped children is to progress toward those goals that are in their own best interest, while the ultimate responsibility of the schools is to provide the talent and resources that will enable them to do so.

References

ABESON, A., BOLICK, N., & HASS, J. *A primer on due process: Education decisions for handicapped children.* Reston, Va.: The Council for Exceptional Children, 1976.

Brown v. *Board of Education,* 347 U.S. 483 (1954).

FANNER, P. The new relationship between parents and schools. *Focus on Exceptional Children,* 1977, *9,* 5, Denver: Love Publishing Co.

Federal Register (Part II), August 1977, *42,* 1963. Washington, D.C.: Department of Health, Education and Welfare.

Federal Register (Part III), November 30, 1978, *43,* 231. Washington, D.C.: Department of Health, Education and Welfare.

Federal Register (Part IV), May 1977, *42,* 86. Washington, D.C.: Department of Health, Education and Welfare.

MELCHER, J. W. Litigation and handicapped children. *Exceptional Children,* November 1976, *43,* 126–130.

Mills v. *District of Columbia Board of Education,* 348 F. Supp. 866 (D.D.C. 1972).

Pennsylvania Association for Retarded Children (PARC) v. *Pennsylvania,* 334 F. Supp. 1257 (E.D. Pa. 1971) and 343 F. Supp. 279 (E.D. Pa. 1972).

Public Law 93-380. *Education Amendments of 1974.* Sec. 611–621, 20 U.S.C. 1221-1.

SZASZ, T. S. *The myth of mental illness* (Rev.) New York: Harper and Row, 1974.

TURNBULL, H. R. The past and future impact of court decisions in special education. *Phi Delta Kappan,* April 1978, pp. 523–527.

WOLFENSBERGER, W. *Normalization: The principle of normalization in human services.* Toronto, Canada: National Institute on Mental Retardation, 1972.

CHAPTER 5

Accountability Systems for Protection of the Rights of Autistic Children and Youth

Lynn E. McClannahan
Patricia J. Krantz

NOT LONG AGO, we invited fifteen children to participate in brief interviews about their rights. The respondents ranged in age from three to fifteen years, and all attended school at the Princeton Child Development Institute, an education and treatment program for autistic children and youth.[1]

The children were first asked, "Do you like to come to school?" In response to this question, fourteen children answered yes, and one child did not make a verbal response. When asked, "What else do you like?" one child did not answer; the responses of the other fourteen children were: "I like to do work," "Lunch," "I will like to play toys," "School," "To go to Room Number 14," "Do exercise," "I like my chicken, chicken is my favorite kind. I eat chicken off the bone. They were just delicious," "I like to play with the Letter Train," "For God so loved the world," "Jumping," "PCDI," "Ed," "Bathroom," and "Like school."

The third question was "Are your teachers fair to you?" Twelve children said yes, one child said, "Fair to you," one said, "Fair to," and one did not answer. This item was followed by the inquiry, "What does it mean to be fair?" When this question was posed, two children repeated the word "fair" and two gave no answers. The other children's responses were: "It means to be fair—I don't know," "Nothing," "What's this?" "It means going to Room Number 7," "Because Beth is fair—so did

[1] Research and development activities related to this work were partially supported by a grant to the Princeton Child Development Institute from the Community-Based Programs Division of Father Flanagan's Boys' Home, Boys Town, Nebraska.

The authors wish to also express their appreciation to the teachers and therapists of the Princeton Child Development Institute, whose commitment to the education and treatment of autistic children has greatly facilitated the development of accountability systems.

83

Sharon," "Because she tries to tell you," "My pair—my socks are white," "I don't know," "PCDI," "Stan," or "Teacher."

These mini-interviews were concluded by making a direct inquiry about the children's rights. When asked, "Do you have your rights?," ten children said yes, three repeated the word "rights", one said "hand," and one did not offer an answer. The final question, "What are rights?" evoked no verbal response from two children; three children repeated the word "rights," and two said "right hand." The others' replies were: "I don't know," "Nothing," "What's this?" "You can write on math or spelling or SRA Reading," "R—rights—rabbits," "I love school, and I take the chocolate milk and the regular milk and the skim milk," "Louie," and "All right."

These brief interviews serve to illustrate how the language characteristics of autistic children and youth pose special problems that must not be neglected in designing systems to protect their rights. While many— adult mental patients, persons in correctional facilities, individuals in alcohol or drug treatment programs, and educable mentally retarded children and youth—may benefit from direct instruction about their rights and be taught to make use of review and appeal processes, many autistic children and youth display a lesser ability to profit from such direct instruction, particularly at the outset of intervention. Thus, one child who participated in our interviews was unable to make any verbal response, although consistently responding with vocalizations. For him the newly acquired ability to vocalize in response to a question from another person represented substantial progress, but it will be some time before he achieves readiness for instruction about his rights.

It may also be noted that, when confronted with closed-ended questions requiring yes or no answers, most of the children made agreeing responses. These agreeing answers were offered even though children's responses to the open-ended items (e.g., "What does it mean to be fair?" and "What are rights?") revealed that they did not understand the questions. While learning to say yes, to agree, and to cooperate with others has been an important component of these children's treatment programs and has greatly improved their relationships with peers, siblings, parents, and teachers, this pattern of agreeableness does not place them in a favorable position vis-à-vis questions whether their rights have been violated.

Examination of children's answers to open-ended questions indicates a broad array of language delays, deficits, and excesses. Several children interviewed were echolalic, repeating portions of the questions that were asked. Some of the children displayed perseverative speech—as in going "to Room Number 14" or "to Room Number 7." Many of the children offered one-word answers or brief phrases, having not yet developed the skills requisite for complex, descriptive, or "paragraphic" speech.

While an important program goal must be to assist children in acquiring the linguistic and conceptual skills that will enable them to receive direct instruction about their rights, participate in the selection of educational and treatment goals, and give informed consent, their current language development problems must be taken into account in developing more immediate procedures for the protection of their rights.

In addition to the language characteristics discussed above, a variety of other behavioral characteristics of autistic children and youth tend to limit their access to traditional protective mechanisms. Many children entering treatment display severe behavior problems such as physical aggression, self-injurious behaviors or destruction of home furnishings, and highly repetitive self-stimulatory responses such as twirling, rocking, or spinning objects; these behaviors tend to evoke disengagement, disapproval, or even active hostility from others.

This difficult situation is often compounded by many youngsters' affective deficits—that is, they do not enjoy the company of others and have not learned to value adult attention. They must be taught, first to tolerate, and later to enjoy physical contact; to express affection or liking for others; to give compliments; and to value social attention and praise.

The absence of appropriate affective behavior from children's repertoires is especially salient because it portends that they are unable to employ those social interaction skills that could serve to attenuate others' disapprobation and hostility. Unfortunately, these "others"—parents, guardians, teachers, and treatment personnel—who display disappointment and disengagement are often precisely those individuals who have the greatest responsibility for safeguarding the children's rights and for giving consent and making decisions regarding treatment goals and strategies.

The serious implications of this interaction between children's behavior problems and adults' responses to them must not be underestimated; even the most competent parents, teachers, and therapists occasionally report feeling that children's extreme inappropriate behaviors are maliciously directed *at* them. Although almost all parents and human-services providers probably experience such feelings occasionally, it does not seem unreasonable to hypothesize that this experience may be encountered somewhat more frequently by persons working with autistic children and youth, due to the severe and extraordinary problems characteristic of this population. An adequate system for the preservation of children's rights must undertake to protect them from decisions that may be made during adults' periods of disappointment or disengagement.

Finally, autistic children's dependency tends to limit their access to traditional protective systems. In this respect, their problems resemble those of chronic institutionalized mental patients, nursing home residents, or severely or profoundly retarded persons. Deficits in self-care, home maintenance, or community-living skills contribute to placement in institutions, special education programs, or treatment agencies where, unless special precautions are taken, individuals may have low visibility to other members of society and low access to reviewers and advocates. Some very special systems are needed to protect the rights of persons who cannot yet count the number of meals served per day, have not yet learned to discriminate between clean and dirty bed linen, and do not yet understand the uses of banks, post offices, and stores.

From Ethical Concerns to Functional Protective Systems

Although the literature pertaining specifically to the rights of autistic persons is still quite small (Lovaas, 1978, p. 377; National Society for Autistic Children, 1975; Ritvo, 1976; Sullivan, 1976), there is growing consensus in the human services field as a whole about those ethical issues that require attention. Questions that must be continuously raised and answered include these: Is intervention justified? Has informed and non-coerced consent been obtained? (Martin, 1975.) Are treatment goals and methods appropriately selected and sufficiently specified? Are client rights of confidentiality and anonymity protected? Is the adequacy of treatment evaluated? (Association for the Advancement of Behavior Therapy, 1977.) Are there individualized habilitation plans for each client? Are there adequate provisions for ongoing program monitoring, program review, and program evaluation? (National Association for Retarded Citizens, 1976.)

It is not always easy to translate ethical concerns and program guidelines into effective systems for the protection of client rights. How can the consumers or potential consumers of program services know whether a treatment agency really offers individualized instruction and treatment programs? How can consumers and other members of the community make informed judgments about whether treatment goals have been appropriately selected? Assuming that individualized programming is available, how can large numbers of individualized programs be effectively reviewed and their results summarized? (The problem of how to evaluate the data obtained from many single-subject interventions has been a troublesome issue for some time.) How can someone external to the treatment agency know whether there is a need for the services being provided, and whether the program is responsive to consumers' input and feedback?

Just as there has been growing consensus about ethical issues pertaining to the rights of autistic persons, so has there been increasing agreement on the importance of developing accountability systems that can protect those rights. Programs that currently offer individualized habilitation plans may already be producing data on treatment effects and client progress. Indeed, the day-to-day operation of a good human-services agency usually produces a broad array of data about program processes and products. To the extent that such data can be efficiently collected, accurately summarized, and effectively disseminated, they can serve as an assurance of program accountability and protection of client rights, by facilitating ongoing public review by consumers and various other community representatives.

The Annual Report: Framework for a Protective System

The use of an annual report to convey information about a program's personnel, accomplishments, new or expanded services, and funding problems or prospects is not a new idea. Many agencies already have annual reports that serve as newsletters, financial reports, funding requests, or informational brochures. However, insofar as the annual report is also used as a vehicle for presenting specific, objective data to outside parties— parents, representatives of referral or funding agencies, members of advisory or review boards, peer reviewers, potential consumers, and other members of the community—it may also serve as a system for preserving client rights [2] (Martin, 1975, p. 100).

The types of data to be included in an annual report that can function as a protection system should be determined primarily by (1) the professional literature on program development and operation, treatment strategies, and the ethics of intervention; (2) current legal standards; (3) federal and state program guidelines and guidelines developed by such consumer groups as the National Society for Autistic Children and the National Association for Retarded Citizens; and (4) local community norms and expectations about behavior problems and appropriate treatment services.

Some types of program data, such as staff turnover rates, staff-client ratios, absenteeism, lost-time accidents and work-related injuries, are probably already being collected on a regular basis and are easily summarized and presented. Other data (e.g., data on internship programs) may be regularly collected, but are perhaps less readily summarized. Still other measures, such as measures of follow-up services or information dissemination activities, may require the development of new data collection procedures. And finally, certain aspects of the proposed protection system—such as measures of the acquisition of new skills that would help autistic children and youth participate in the protection of their

---

[2] A model for an annual report and training sequences relevant to the implementation of the protective system can be obtained from the authors.

rights—may require the development of new services, new data collection activities, and new procedures for summarizing and reporting data.

Perhaps most difficult, the program administrator, advocate, or human-services professional will be faced with the need to balance the desired comprehensiveness of the protective system against current parameters of cost and personnel resources. Although these tasks are not always easy, the outcome, effective preservation of the rights of autistic children and youth, is laden with social significance.

Components of the Protective System: Measures of Program Processes and Products

While some students of program evaluation contend that variables pertaining to program processes are unimportant, and that only client behavior change should be studied in assessing program accountability, we do not share that assumption. Services to autistic children and youth have a relatively recent, brief history, and the absence of comparative data from different treatment agencies means that there are few guidelines for determining what levels of behavior change constitute "good" or "poor" outcomes for this difficult-to-treat population. Under these circumstances, it appears important to include data on the independent variables (e.g., amount and types of service, utilization of personnel and financial resources) as well as the dependent variables (e.g., skills acquired, inappropriate behaviors controlled, and post-treatment outcomes) in an overall evaluation of program effectiveness and monitoring of client rights.

The sections that follow outline several broad areas of program operation and outcome that provide raw material for the construction of data-based accountability systems critical to the protection of client rights. Within each of these areas, specific measures are enumerated and described, and rationales for selecting such measures are discussed.

MEASURES RELATED TO THE PROVISION OF EDUCATION AND TREATMENT SERVICES

Numbers and Types of Individualized Instruction and Treatment Programs. An individualized instruction or treatment program may be said to exist if the client's file contains (1) a written response definition that provides an objective description of the skill deficit or behavior problem, (2) a specified data collection procedure, (3) a specified teaching or treatment procedure, and (4) data sheets and a graph or other form of data summary. It often proves useful to maintain each of these sets of documents as a separate section in the client's folder, so that data on numbers and types of individualized programs can be readily retrieved. Data summarization is straightforward and merely involves listing each individualized program of each client. It will be useful for program reviewers and community representatives to know the total number of individualized programs implemented during the reporting period, as well as the mean number of individualized programs per client. These measures offer documentation that the agency does in fact provide individualized habilitation plans.

In addition, a complete list of individualized programs could be reported. This can be done in tabular form showing the number of clients for whom each type of program has been implemented. In the case of autistic children, it is especially important that lists of instructional and treatment programs should include both new skills acquired and behavior problems overcome. Ideally, these two types of program will receive at least equal attention. An agency that places a great deal of emphasis on treatment of inappropriate behavior but little emphasis on skill acquisition programs may run the risk of creating an unpleasant environment for clients, and may be perceived by community members as unnecessarily punitive.

The availability of this list of individualized programs enables consumers and program evaluators to make their own decisions about whether children's instruction and treatment goals have been appropriately selected, thus helping assure that this area of client rights is monitored. Experience suggests that community representatives can be excellent judges of the social validity of behavior change goals.

External Evaluators' Ratings of Individualized Programs. The reader will have noted that we have not thus far discussed the success or failure of individualized programs, but merely how many and what types of program are provided. Unfortunately, current technology in the field does not offer solutions to all of the problems presented by autistic children, and even the best of human-service professionals occasionally discover that they do not know how to teach a particular child to use functional speech, or how to teach another child to read, or how to help a particular youth control facial grimacing or noncontextual giggling. Since most practitioners working with autistic populations will from time to time experience failure with respect to certain treatment goals for particular children, and since little is known of what constitutes a "high," "average," or "low" failure rate, it seems appropriate to employ some measures that are related not to treatment outcome but only to the availability of services that autistic children have a right to receive. On the other hand, neither can issues concerning the effectiveness of treatment be ignored; there is no rationale for the existence of a treatment agency that does not change behavior, and it is therefore necessary to examine the effects of individualized programs.

The problems of how to evaluate large numbers of individualized educational and treatment programs were mentioned previously. Single-subject designs do not at first glance appear to lend themselves to the development of generalizations about the effects of treatment, but since they usually constitute the real substance of autistic children's treatment it is important to develop methods that permit summary of these data. One solution to this problem is to select an evaluator external to the treatment agency and request that this individual examine the individualized programs for each client and rate each of these programs along certain dimensions. Dimensions to be evaluated and rated might include (1) Does the client's record contain a written-response definition that provides a specific and objective description of the skill to be acquired or the behavior to be changed? (2) Is there a written description of the data collection procedure? (3) Has the data collection procedure been appropriately selected for this client and this behavior? (4) Is there a written description of the instruction or treatment procedure? (5) Has the intervention procedure been appropriately selected for this client and this behavior? (6) Does the client's record contain a graph or other form of data summary that displays previous and current levels of the target behavior? (7) Has the client's behavior changed since the intervention procedure was implemented? If so, was this behavior change in a desired or an undesired direction? and (8) Are changes needed in data analysis or summarizing procedures? The results of such an evaluation are readily summarized, and are easily understood by most lay and professional audiences.

Several words of caution may be in order as regards undertaking this evaluation procedure. First, the selection of an evaluator external to the treatment agency is a rather sensitive task. The evaluator should have widely recognized professional credentials, should be known and accepted in the field, and should be personally acquainted with the literature on autism and with the characteristics of autistic populations. It is also important that there be mutual respect between the evaluator and members of the governing and review boards, program administrators and staff members, and consumers and their parents or other representatives. Unless there is broad agreement on the selection of the evaluator, the results of the evaluation may receive little credence.

Second, definitions of the evaluator role and the functions of evaluation may be significant determinants of how well the evaluation will be received by staff members. Evaluation of large numbers of individualized programs almost inevitably brings the evaluator into contact with teachers, therapists, and other direct-service personnel who have primary responsibility for designing and implementing client programs and gathering and analyzing performance data. With adequate preparation, the evaluation can become an important part of the agency's staff-development program, since it sets the occasion for practitioners to receive acknowledgment of their work as well as specific feedback about instructional strategies and treatment technology. Thus, it is important to select an evaluator who can achieve warm and reassuring interactions with program personnel and deliver corrective feedback without becoming excessively demanding or punitive. Finally, to further guarantee that the evaluation can serve a staff-development function, program administrators should provide strong assurances that omissions or errors in programming that come to light during the evaluation will not set the occasion for informal punishment or fomal disciplinary action but will be used to design additional learning opportunities for program personnel.

Third, the administrator must attempt to reconcile the completeness of the evaluation with the costs incurred. Experience suggests that an appropriately qualified evaluator may be able to examine and rate as many as twenty-five or thirty different individualized programs for autistic children in one work day. In a small group home, school, or treatment program, it may be necessary to purchase only from one to three days of a consultant's time in order to obtain a complete review of *all* individualized programs. This level of completeness is highly desirable because it verifies that each individual receiving program services has a set of individualized programs, and that the appropriateness of each of these programs has been examined. In a larger treatment agency, however, funds may be insufficient to purchase the amount of consulting time needed to review every individualized habilitation program, and it may therefore be necessary to enlist the consultant's aid in devising a method of randomly selecting a subset of client programs for evaluation. In the latter case, the evaluation can retain its in-service training function as well as its protective function if the records are sampled not only by the evaluator but also by the staff member responsible for providing programs and collecting and recording data.

Finally, those who instigate and participate in this type of evaluation should acknowledge at the outset that not all findings will be positive. There are no perfect human services programs. However, it is only by disseminating complete evaluation data that the evaluation process serves a genuine protective function. And, if presented in their entirety, the data can contribute to the achievement of a broader goal—the development of a body of normative data on program operation and outcome that will eventually enable consumers, reviewers, and community representatives to make more informed and enlightened decisions about what constitutes a "good" or "'poor" behavior change program for autistic children and youth.

Test-Retest Scores on Standardized Instruments.   Traditional uses of standardized tests with autistic children and youth present a discouraging picture; a large majority of children are designated "untestable" on standardized intelligence tests such as the Stanford-Binet and Leiter, and they typically score between the second and third year on instruments such as the Vineland Social Maturity Scale (Rincover, Koegel, & Russo, 1978). In the present context, however, these traditional uses of standardized tests are perhaps less interesting than the possibility of employing them as repeated measures of the children's acquisition of new skills as they progress through a treatment program.

For example, the Peabody Picture Vocabulary Test, Vineland Social Maturity Scale, or Preschool Attainment Record may be administered to an autistic child upon his or her entry into treatment, and then periodically readministered in order to document the child's acquisition of language or social skills that were not displayed at the outset. Similarly, children may be initially tested and periodically retested on standardized measures of academic achievement (e.g., Key Math Test or Peabody Individual Achievement Test), so that their educational progress may be regularly reviewed. These test scores, like other measures discussed earlier, could contribute to the development of a body of normative data on treatment outcomes for autistic children, while simultaneously serving as a benchmark in the evaluation of individual service agencies.

Anecdotal Accounts of Children's Progress.   The earlier emphasis on measurement of program processes and products notwithstanding, it often happens that not all consumers, board members, or community representatives have acquired a taste for data. These individuals may, however, be quite responsive to case studies. Thus it may be possible to substantially broaden the audience for the annual report (and concomitantly for the protective system) by including descriptive materials relevant to autistic children's progress.

Such case study information should be generated by describing the earliest and most recent data points on children's behavior change. This approach permits empirically inclined reviewers and evaluators to validate the written descriptions by tying them to the original data from which they were derived. Most programs for autistic children and youth seem to have favorite "success stories," and the telling of these is often important to parents, staff members, and members of the governing board, who should be encouraged to take active roles in the protection of children's rights.

Measures of Parent-Training Services.   Many established and well-known programs for autistic children place heavy emphasis on parent-training activities (Freeman & Ritvo, 1976; Hemsley, Howlin, Berger,

Hersov, Holbrook, Rutter, & Yule, 1978; Lovaas, 1978; Lovaas, Koegel, Simmons, & Long, 1973; Nordquist & Wahler, 1973; Rincover & Koegel, 1977; Rincover et al., 1978). Given the severity of these children's problems and their difficulties in generalizing new skills, the ongoing involvement of parents can be critical to their survival in community environments. Trained parents, serving as at-home tutors and therapists for their own children, can significantly increase the total amount of intervention available, and can ensure continuity of program implementation. Thus, the provision of effective parent-training services contributes importantly to the protection of autistic children's rights, by maintaining children in "least restrictive" education and treatment environments (i.e., families and day schools, as opposed to institutional placements).

Process measures of parent-training services may include (1) number of parent-training meetings held, (2) number or mean number of parents in attendance at group training meetings, (3) number of individualized parent-training sessions, (4) mean number of individualized training sessions per family, (5) number of hours of individualized parent-training services delivered, and (6) mean number of hours of individualized training per family.

Some important outcome measures of parent training include the number or mean number of home instruction and treatment programs implemented by parents (employing the definition of "individualized program" advanced on p. 88). A variety of definitions of "implementation" is possible, but one of the most straightforward is based upon the number or percentage of completed home data sheets submitted by families to the parents' trainers or home programmers. Including also a list of these home instruction and treatment programs implemented by parents in this outcome reporting will make an important contribution to the protective system, by enabling professionals, community representatives, and parents of referred children to examine home treatment goals and assess their appropriateness and social significance. In addition, if parents' data on home programs are regularly graphed or summarized, external evaluators and reviewers can employ the rating procedure described above, in order to determine the effectiveness of home programs in achieving child behavior change.

Measures of Community-Entry Services. Most persons acquainted with the problems of autistic children and youth agree that a "sink or swim" philosophy is not the preferred approach to helping them enter the mainstream. Typically, these children require extensive special programming if community entry is to meet with success. One strategy for helping them become integrated into public school classes was reported by Russo and Koegel (1977); after some pretraining sessions to establish tokens as reinforcers, a therapist attended the child's kindergarten classroom to provide treatment. After ten weeks the classroom teacher was trained in behavioral techniques, and later was able to maintain the child's appropriate classroom behavior. Although some retreatment by the therapist was required at the beginning of first grade, the child's performance was maintained during her second and third grade years with different teachers. A primary advantage of this approach is that it may circumvent the extreme restrictions of stimulus control and generalization deficits that are characteristic of autistic children (cf. Koegel & Rincover, 1974).

An alternative mainstreaming strategy involves the provision of individualized programs of gradual transition from special treatment environments to "normalized" community settings. For example, children enrolled in the programs of the Princeton Child Development Institute who achieve readiness for community entry attend the Institute's special education classes for part of each day, and participate in normal preschools, in public school classrooms, or in after-school recreation programs for the remainder of the day. In these cases, transition programs include special monitoring and reporting procedures (e.g., school notes and direct observation of the children in community programs), as well as special instruction and therapy in the treatment environment or in the mainstream setting. As children's appropriate performances become more stable, the amount of time spent in normal settings is gradually increased, and the extrinsic reinforcers, such as tokens, are faded.

Since special programming appears critical to autistic children's successful community entry, it is essential to provide public reports on the availability and effectiveness of these services that try to help them move to and remain in "least restrictive" environments. Process measures of community-entry services include the number of children to whom transition services have been provided, as well as the number of individualized transition programs implemented. It is also relevant to report the number of training or consulting sessions provided to receiving personnel—such as public school teachers, scoutmasters, recreation directors, and others. And, finally, some measure of the number of hours of direct observation of the children participating in community programs is important. These data are critical to the development of child protective systems, because they document that children are not segregated from normal peers who may serve as role models, nor are they deprived of exposure to regular classroom curricula and materials (Russo & Koegel, 1977). In addition, such data offer evidence that human services agencies are not stable and self-perpetuating but instead encouraging of movement through and out of their programs.

Outcome data on community entry may be based upon out-of-house reviewers' evaluation of data on the children's performance in community settings, as described previously. Of course, the best outcome measure of community-entry services is the number of children who receive positive discharge from special treatment programs, and the number who continue to function effectively in the community. These considerations lead to a final area of measurement of instruction and therapy services.

Follow-up Measures. A now-classic discussion of generalization and follow-up measures (Lovaas et al., 1973) offers convincing evidence that autistic children discharged to nontreatment environments (such as state hospitals) lost what they had gained during treatment, whereas children discharged to their parents (who had been trained in behavior management procedures) maintained their new skills or showed further improvement. These data strongly suggest that parent-training and transition services are necessary conditions for follow-up measures to yield encouraging results.

This pioneer work by Lovaas *et al.* (1973) employed measures of self-stimulation, echolalia, appropriate verbal behavior, social nonverbal behavior, and appropriate play obtained before, during, and after treatment. Although these investigators used an automated button-panel with a direct computer hookup to measure frequency, duration, and interaction of target responses, agencies with lesser access to hardware may find that a procedure of time-sampling within intervals produces similar information with only minor revisions of the original protocols.

Not infrequently, social, economic, and political contingencies influence children's treatment in ways that render the interpretation of follow-up data difficult. In some cases, compliance with conditions of funding may prohibit a human services agency from rejecting a referred child who has been inappropriately diagnosed as autistic. And although it appears obvious that a child whose parents seek training will be in a better position vis-à-vis outcome than one whose parents reject it, and that a child removed from a program during the early months of intervention will fare less well on follow-up than one who completes treatment and pursues a planned program of community entry, many agencies may have little control over parent involvement or child tenure in their programs. Since such issues strongly affect outcome, it is incumbent on treatment agencies to develop reliable definitions of positive and negative discharge. Definitions of positive discharge often rest on performance data indicating that a child has achieved treatment goals and is able to display target skills in community settings as well as the treatment environment. Discharges may be defined as negative if, for example, (1) a youth has attained a chronological age that requires exit from the program, although performance data indicate that treatment goals have not been achieved, (2) a child develops a chronic illness or other severe handicapping condition requiring transfer to a medical facility, although treatment goals have not been met, (3) the child's parents fail to exhibit a specified level of participation in training activities over a specified period of time, (4) parents or guardians request the child's discharge, although performance data indicate continued need for intervention, or (5) after extended enrollment in the program, data on the child's individualized programs show little or no progress in achieving treatment goals. Although differing program philosophies and differing referral and funding sources may require differing definitions of discharge, careful attention to discharge taxonomy should contribute to the understanding of follow-up data and should also facilitate the development of a body of descriptive data on post-treatment outcomes against which individual agencies can assess their follow-up results.

While the importance of direct observation of children's post-treatment performance cannot be underestimated, additional follow-up data may be obtained by asking parents, foster parents, or other responsible adults to periodically rate the child's performance with regard to each of their original treatment goals. For example, parents of children positively discharged from the Princeton Child Development Institute are interviewed three, six, twelve, eighteen, and twenty-four months post-treatment, and annually thereafter. During these interviews, parents are asked to assign satisfaction ratings to each of the target behaviors treated. This rating procedure appears to pick up low-rate or situation-specific behavior problems (e.g., sleep disruptions, feces smearing, attacks on particular persons) that might not occur during follow-up observation sessions but might be critical to children's ability to remain in "least restrictive" environments. A follow-up system providing early detection of such problems permits the delivery of consultation and re-treatment services that contribute to children's survival in community placements. Because of their potential contributions to the protection of children's rights, the presence of these follow-up systems should be noted in the annual report.

MEASURES OF EXTERNAL PROGRAM MONITORING

For the most part, programs for autistic children and youth may employ the same instruction and treatment strategies offered children with other handicapping conditions, although programming must often be more highly structured, systematic, and continuous. Under these circumstances many autistic children will respond well to intervention, but some, unfortunately, will not. These exceptions are encountered sufficiently often to merit considerable attention. Indeed, it appears that a characteristic of autistic populations—in comparison with other populations of disabled children—is their comparatively higher rate of failure to respond to a rather standard set of behavior management procedures, such as positive reinforcement (Foxx, 1977; Foxx & Azrin, 1973) and time-out from positive reinforcement (Plummer, Baer & LeBlanc, 1977). Acknowledging these treatment problems, the National Society for Autistic Children recently reported that autistic children's presenting behavior problems "may be persistent and highly resistant to change, often requiring unique management, treatment, or teaching strategies" (1978).

Aggressive behavior, self-injury, and excessive self-stimulation often head the list of difficult-behavior-management issues. It has been noted that when self-stimulatory behaviors decrease, other more appropriate behaviors may increase (Risley, 1968), and some investigators have reported autistic children who did not exhibit discrimination learning or appropriate play behaviors until self-stimulation was suppressed (cf. Koegel & Covert, 1972; Koegel, Firestone, Kramme, & Dunlap, 1974). Such data have lead some researchers to the hypothesis that "elimination of self-stimulatory behavior may be a necessary prerequisite to the establishment of new appropriate behaviors" (Koegel & Covert, 1972).

It is assumed, of course, that behavior reduction procedures will not be attempted by responsible researchers and professionals unless other avenues of intervention have been fully explored and documented as ineffective in producing a behavior change considered critical to a child's present welfare and continued progress. It is also evident that some punishment procedures are highly preferred over others, based upon the extent to which the variables included in a treatment package lend themselves to precise measurement and replication. Further, it is assumed that aversive procedures should be implemented only if informed and noncoerced consent has been obtained.

Apart from all of these important precautions, however, the continuation of particular interventions and indeed the continued existence of particular treatment agencies may ultimately rest upon how treatment processes are viewed and interpreted by community representatives. Because programs for autistic children must be highly structured, and because behavior reduction strategies must sometimes be employed, misunderstandings sometimes arise. Regular on-site contact with visitors, observers, parents, interns, members of governing and review boards, and others can serve both preventive and ameliorative functions by providing essential information about how treatment activities are perceived by persons outside the program. Positive feedback from persons external to the agency can offer social validation and the assurance that treatment strategies are viewed as meaningful and appropriate. Negative feedback from these community members can offer opportunities for error correction and program revision in order to ensure the maintenance of good community relationships.

In most cases, external monitoring is easy to arrange. Many parents, educators, medical and nursing personnel, and members of the media find autism an intriguing and unfamiliar area, and frequently request opportunities to visit the treatment setting. High school and college students who are developing careers in psychology, special education, speech or occupational therapy, or other disciplines may welcome opportunities to intern in the program. And, finally, local professionals such as attorneys, advocates, social workers, and politicians often find that service on the agency's governing, advisory, or review boards contributes to their experience and credentials. The interest typically displayed by these individuals of diverse backgrounds recommends them as observers of program processes, and permits a variety of measures of external program monitoring.

Parents' Visits. Parents are especially important visitors because their observations of their own children's instruction and treatment programs helps guarantee that informed consent has indeed been obtained. Both the number of children whose parents have visited and the number of visits are easily reported.

Internships. Local high school and college students and community volunteers who wish to participate in on-site internships or field experiences can enhance the agency's programs in many ways—by serving as observers, data collectors, or teacher aides. In addition, since many of these young people will be preparing for human services careers, they are particularly valuable as program monitors; frequently, they approach internship experiences with a great deal of humanitarian concern for autistic children's rights and welfare, and tend to ask many questions and display interest in many different dimensions of program operation. Their presence in the treatment setting often places regular staff members in the roles of trainers and models demonstrating the correct implementation of instruction and therapy procedures for the benefit of the trainees. And since many undergraduate and graduate students earn academic credit for their on-site experiences, their participation in field-work seminars and their reports to faculty members may occasion informal (and cost-free) program review by professionals in the community.

Measures of interns' program-monitoring functions may include (1) number of students or community volunteers who participated in internships, (2) days of the week when interns were on site, and (3) number of hours of on-site observation completed. To the extent that interns' institutional affiliations and educational levels are perceived as related to program-monitoring capabilities, it may be useful to provide consumers with this information as well.

Visitors.   Some programs regard visits as interruptions in the routine delivery of services; in programs for autistic children, however, outsiders' visits to the treatment setting may be turned to advantage by using them as opportunities for children to practice specific social skills, such as greetings, introductions, and descriptions of their usual activities. The presence of new faces offers chances to help children achieve stimulus generalization with regard to many different social interaction tasks. And visitors, like parents and interns, can contribute to program monitoring. Obviously, a program receiving only 2 visitors per year would be regarded quite differently than would a program receiving 200 visitors; consumers and community representatives would rightly perceive the former agency as closed and insular, and the latter as more open and concerned with community education and coordination of services.

Press Coverage.   The mysteries of autism's etiology, the extreme disparities in skill levels displayed by some autistic children, and the extraordinary success of some lend themselves to human-interest stories. Media reporters, whose training encourages them to look beyond press releases and public statements, can serve as excellent program monitors. Thus, in the annual report that serves as a protective mechanism an additional measure that may be included is the number of times that newspaper, magazine, radio, and television coverage has been obtained. With sufficient attention to the process and outcome measures discussed earlier, it would ideally be unnecessary to report the ratio of favorable to unfavorable media presentations.

The measures of external program monitoring enumerated above are by no means comprehensive; it is also important to report, for example, on peer review processes and meetings of the agency's governing and advisory boards. Most of us have heard stories of human services agencies whose intervention programs were regarded as grossly inappropriate; in most cases, these "deviant" agencies tend to be clothed in secrecy and cut off from public review and feedback. Attention to external monitoring of program operation can help to ensure that services to autistic children remain consistent with local community norms and expectations, and are integrated with larger human services systems in the county and state.

CONSUMER EVALUATION

There is a rapidly growing literature on consumer evaluation (e.g., Clark, Greene, Macrae, McNees, Davis, & Risley, 1977; Minkin, Braukmann, Minkin, Timbers, Timbers, Fixsen, Phillips, & Wolf, 1976; Stokes & Fawcett, 1977; Willner, Braukmann, Kirigin, Fixsen, Phillips, & Wolf, 1977). Consumers, their representatives, and members of the larger community are increasingly being invited to participate in evaluating the social significance of treatment goals, the appropriateness of intervention procedures, and the importance of treatment results (Wolf, 1978). In this context, the Teaching Family Model of group home treatment deserves special attention, because it offers tested and readily adaptable strategies for obtaining consumer feedback (Lassiter, 1978; Phillips, Phillips, Fixsen, & Wolf, 1972; Schneider & Lassiter, 1978). Implementation of this evaluation paradigm involves asking the members of various consumer groups to respond to brief questionnaires, indicating their satisfaction or dissatisfaction with program services on Likert-type rating scales. This procedure yields a great deal of evaluation data at relatively low cost.

It is advantageous to use the broadest possible definition of "consumer," since this results in maximum feedback and—if the data are publicly disseminated via the annual report—maximum protection of children's rights. In programs for autistic children, the most immediate consumers of program services—the children themselves—are often unable to respond to evaluation instruments of the type under discussion, and must therefore be represented by parents, foster parents, guardians, or responsible relatives. Parents' sustained and intimate interactions with their children and their regular associations with program personnel give them an excellent vantage point from which to assess program operation and outcome. Representatives of referral and funding agencies (e.g., social workers in public agencies and personnel in the children's local school districts) are also primary consumers, and similar data may be obtained from them. Since neighborhood sentiment can potentially determine the initial development and continued operation of community-based programs, neighbors' feedback is also significant. Neighbors are in an optimal position to evaluate the program's impact on, and acceptance by, members of the local community.

Beyond these obvious consumer groups, there are several other groups frequently and extensively influenced by program quality. The appropriateness and effectiveness of program services directly affect members of the governing and review boards. Similarly, students participating in internships and teachers and therapists employed by the program are regular consumers of training services, as well as consumers of one anothers' work activities. These individuals, who observe the effects of policy decisions as well as the moment-to-moment implementation of instruction and treatment programs, are especially well qualified to evaluate program administration, co-workers' professional skills, and service delivery.

In sum, consumer feedback can be an invaluable program resource, permitting ongoing revision of service delivery systems, correction of errors, and development of new services. Dissemination of consumer-satisfaction data via the annual report can contribute significantly to the protection of autistic children's rights.

CONSUMER DEMAND FOR SERVICES

Helping agencies should not be self-perpetuating but should provide specific services for which there is consumer demand. Reporting the number of referrals received and the number accepted or rejected per year assists in documenting the level of community need for the agency's services, and enables persons outside the program to evaluate the appropriateness of shrinkage, expansion, or maintenance of intervention activities. And because even the most well-meaning service providers have been known to become ensnared in bureaucratic entanglements to the detriment of their clients welfare, it is important to also report the mean number of days in the period from the time a referral is received to the time a decision on acceptance or rejection is made and communicated to the client or representatives. A relatively short mean time between receipt of referral and communication of decision shows that clients who may be badly in need of service are not being wait-listed and denied opportunities for early or rapid intervention.

Professional ethics binds service providers to offer intervention without regard to religious affiliation, race, or national origin. Beyond these obviously important considerations, agency policy may require that decisions on acceptance or rejection be made within specific parameters or age, gender, financial eligibility, place of residence, and so on. Reporting on receipt and disposition of referrals by age, sex, ethnicity, residence, religious preference, and similar variables can document that agency policy is being correctly implemented, and can simultaneously show that no subgroups within the referral pool are targets for discrimination. Nondiscriminatory decision-making on referrals can be further documented by public presentation of the reasons for rejection of referred children.

HELPING CHILDREN PROTECT THEIR OWN RIGHTS

Prior to intervention, most autistic children and youths display a virtual absence of self-protection resources. As children embark upon treatment programs that will help them learn to follow instructions, control undesired behaviors, engage in motor and verbal imitation activities, and begin to use functional speech, their learning experiences should also include skill-building activities expressly designed to help them protect their own rights.

At the most basic level, language development programs should include training in the correct use of "yes" and "no," how to request and transfer information, giving accounts of everyday events, and expressing simple desires (cf. Lovaas, 1977). As children display increasing skill, training may broaden to include more detailed descriptions of activities and events, recall of events that are temporally more remote, and expressions of appropriate disagreement—e.g., "No, this is not a————," "No thank you," "I'd rather not," or "I don't think so."

Because many autistic children do not initially enjoy social contact, they are often excluded from the ongoing personal interactions that help normal children learn to attend to and report on their physical and emotional states. Consequently, autistic children may need special instruction on how to report illness or injury or how to communicate emotional affect, as in statements of happiness, pride, worry, anxiety, anger, fear, or affection. In addition, they may also need training in order to identify certain situations or events as "dangerous," "bad," "threatening," "illegal," or "punishing."

Before treatment, many autistic children have been passive recipients of care, rarely expressing preferences or making choices among objects, events, or activities. Therefore, training in decision making is often needed. Such instruction may begin at the level of asking children to make simple choices between a few visible objects: "What shall we have for snack—these cookies or this can of beets?" or "What do you want to buy with your tokens?" As children gain proficiency they should be encouraged to make more complex choices, such as where to go on an outing, what to buy with allowance money, or what to wear to a party. Decision-making skills should be gradually elaborated to lead toward participation in self-government (see Phillips et al., 1972).

As children acquire the requisite skills, they should also receive explicit instruction on day-to-day human rights. Even children in comparatively early stages of language development can learn to respond to questions about fairness, such as "Is it fair for Johnny to take your toys away?" "Would it be fair if you didn't get to play outside?" or "Is it fair for you to have a nice lunch?" Of course, children at more advanced levels of receptive and expressive language development should receive direct instruction in client rights and in review and appeal mechanisms. And, commensurate with their readiness, children's programs should include expanding contacts with community members and increasing opportunities to gain awareness and understanding of the roles of police officer, social worker, bank teller, physician, attorney, and advocate. Finally, programs for helping children protect their own rights should cultivate those skills that will ultimately enable some clients to participate in consumer evaluation of program services (cf. Phillips, et al., 1972; Quilitch, 1978; Willner et al., 1977).

Conclusion

The above-described measures of program processes and products are by no means inclusive; many additional measures could contribute importantly to the protective system. For example, measures of staff performance—including praise rates, nag rates, teacher-generated opportunities for children's response, and minutes of transition time between scheduled instructional activities—could give program reviewers and community representatives additional information to be used in the evaluation of program services. Similarly, measures of information dissemination—such as listing community organizations in which program staff members regularly participate, number of professional meetings attended, number of presentations made at conventions, and number of manuscripts accepted for publication—may help others outside the program evaluate the extent to which program personnel share information, cooperate with other human services agencies, and keep abreast of current developments in their fields.

All such measures can serve a double protective function: First, they provide program staff with data-based feedback that facilitates program development and modification; and, second, they enable others to evaluate program processes and outcomes. Neither of these opportunities should be overlooked. Obviously, data are useful to program personnel only insofar as they are carefully scrutinized and subsequently utilized in program monitoring, troubleshooting, and making policy and clinical decisions. And it is equally obvious that data are useful to community representatives and external reviewers and evaluators only if they receive broad public distribution. Construction of the proposed system for the protection of children's rights is a worthwhile activity only if agency heads commit themselves to the widest possible dissemination of data, via the annual report or a similar vehicle.

Those who anticipate adoption of this protection system should be forewarned that maintenance must be programmed if the system is to remain viable and operative. Initial attention to the issues of when, where, how, and by whom data are to be gathered and recorded will have long-term positive results. In addition, teachers, therapists, home programmers, secretaries, and administrative assistants who feed data into the system will need initial and ongoing training in order to insure complete and correct data collection. Although the foregoing pages do not include discussions of reliability, most of the measures described above readily lend themselves to reliability estimates; presentation of levels of interobserver agreement on each of these variables will greatly enhance the overall credibility of the protective system. Last but not least, program administrators or their designees must plan to allot sufficient time for the preparation of the annual report that disseminates these data.

Although the proposed system undeniably involves certain costs in terms of materials, time, effort, and commitment, such costs can be regarded as a sound investment in preservation of the basic rights of autistic children and youth.

References

Association for the Advancement of Behavior Therapy. *Ethical issues for human services.* New York: Association for the Advancement of Behavior Therapy, 1977.

CLARK, H. B., GREENE, B. F., MACRAE, J. W., McNEES, M. P., DAVIS, J. L., & RISLEY, T. R. A parent advice package for family shopping trips: Development and evaluation. *Journal of Applied Behavior Analysis,* 1977, *10,* 605–624.

FOXX, R. M. Attention training: The use of overcorrection avoidance to increase the eye contact of autistic and retarded children. *Journal of Applied Behavior Analysis,* 1977, *10,* 489–499.

FOXX, R. M., & AZRIN, N. H. The elimination of autistic self-stimulatory behavior by overcorrection. *Journal of Applied Behavior Analysis,* 1973, *6,* 1–14.

FREEMAN, B. J., & RITVO, E. R. Parents as paraprofessionals. In E. R. Ritvo (Ed.), *Autism: Diagnosis, current research and management.* New York: Spectrum Publications, 1976.

HEMSLEY, R., HOWLIN, P., BERBER, M., HERSOV, L., HOLBROOK, D., RUTTER, M., & YULE, W. Treating autistic children in a family context. In M. Rutter & E. Schopler (Eds.), *Autism: A reappraisal of concepts and treatment.* New York: Plenum Press, 1978.

KOEGEL, R. L., & COVERT, A. The relationship of self-stimulation to learning in autistic children. *Journal of Applied Behavior Analysis,* 1972, *5,* 381–387.

KOEGEL, R. L., FIRESTONE, P. B., KRAMME, K. W., & DUNLAP, G. Increasing spontaneous play by suppressing self-stimulation in autistic children. *Journal of Applied Behavior Analysis,* 1974, *7,* 521–528.

KOEGEL, R. L., & RINCOVER, A. Treatment of psychotic children in a classroom environment: 1. Learning in a large group. *Journal of Applied Behavior Analysis,* 1974, *7,* 45–59.

LASSITER, R. B. Developing and maintaining good consumer relations. In L. Thompson & K. Carlson (Eds.), Community-Based Programs Monograph Series VI. Boys Town, Nebr.: Community-Based Programs Division of Father Flanagan's Boys' Home, 1978.

Lovaas, O. I. *The autistic child: Language development through behavior modification.* New York: Halsted Press, 1977.

Lovaas, O. I. Parents as therapists. In M. Rutter & E. Schopler (Eds.), *Autism: A reappraisal of concepts and treatment.* New York: Plenum Press, 1978.

Lovaas, O. I., Koegel, R., Simmons, J. Q., & Long, J. S. Some generalization and follow-up measures on autistic children in behavior therapy. *Journal of Applied Behavior Analysis,* 1973, *6,* 131–166.

Martin, R. *Legal challenges to behavior modification.* Champaign, Ill.: Research Press, 1975.

May, J. G., Risley, T. R., Twardosz, S., Friedman, P., Bijou, S. W., & Wexler, D. Guidelines for the use of behavioral procedures in state programs for retarded persons. *M. R. Research,* 1976, *1* (1), 1–73.

Minkin, N., Braukmann, C. J., Minkin, B. L., Timbers, G. D., Timbers, B. J., Fixsen, D. L., Phillips, E. L., & Wolf, M. M. The social validation and training of conversational skills. *Journal of Applied Behavior Analysis,* 1976, *9,* 127–139.

National Society for Autistic Children. Definition of the syndrome of autism. Washington, D.C.: National Society for Autistic Children, 1978.

National Society for Autistic Children. White paper on behavior modification with autistic children. Washington, D.C.: National Society for Autistic Children, 1975.

Nordquist, V. M., & Wahler, R. G. Naturalistic treatment of an autistic child. *Journal of Applied Behavior Analysis,* 1973, *6,* 79–87.

Phillips, E. L., Phillips, E. A., Fixsen, D. L., & Wolf, M. M. *The Teaching-Family Handbook.* Lawrence, Kans.: Bureau of Child Research of the University of Kansas, 1972.

Plummer, S., Baer, D. M., & LeBlanc, J. M. Functional considerations in the use of procedural timeout and an effective alternative. *Journal of Applied Behavior Analysis,* 1977, *10,* 689–705.

Quilitch, H. R. Communication: Client participation in the evaluation of a residential treatment program. *Journal of Applied Behavior Analysis,* 1978, *11,* 124.

Rincover, A., & Koegel, R. Research on the education of autistic children: Recent advances and future directions. In B. B. Lahey & A. E. Kazdin (Eds.), *Advances in clinical child psychology.* New York: Plenum Press, 1977.

Rincover, A., Koegel, R. L., & Russo, D. C. Some recent behavioral research on the education of autistic children. *Education and Treatment of Children,* 1978, *1* (4), 31–45.

Risley, T. R. The effects and side effects of punishing the autistic behaviors of a deviant child. *Journal of Applied Behavior Analysis,* 1968, *1,* 21–34.

Ritvo, E. R. Primary responsibility: With whom should it rest? In E. R. Ritvo (Ed.), *Autism: Diagnosis, current research and management.* New York: Spectrum Publications, 1976.

Russo, D. C., & Koegel, R. L. A method for integrating an autistic child into a normal public-school classroom. *Journal of Applied Behavior Analysis*, 1977, *10*, 579–590.

SCHNEIDER, K., & LASSITER, R. Evaluation in the cooperative group home. In D. Weber & L. Thompson (Eds.), Monograph Series. Boys Town, Nebr.: Community-Based Programs Division of Father Flanagan's Boys' Home, 1978.

STOKES, T. F. and FAWCETT, S. B. Evaluating municipal policy: An analysis of a refuse-packaging program. *Journal of Applied Behavior Analysis*, 1977, *10*, 391–398.

SULLIVAN, R. C. Autism: Current trends in services. In E. R. Ritvo (Ed.), *Autism: Diagnosis, current research and management*. New York: Spectrum Publications, 1976.

WILLNER, A. G., BRAUKMANN, C. J., KIRIGIN, K. A., FIXSEN, D. L., PHILLIPS, E. L., & WOLF, M. M. The training and validation of youth-preferred social behaviors of child-care personnel. *Journal of Applied Behavior Analysis*, 1977, *10*, 219–230.

WOLF, M. M. Social validity: The case for subjective measurement, or how applied behavior analysis is finding its heart. *Journal of Applied Behavior Analysis*, 1978, *11*, 203–214.

CHAPTER 6

Client Rights in Clinical Counseling Services for Adults

Gerald T. Hannah
Richard C. Surles

Introduction

A STORY TOLD BY A FORMER DIRECTOR of a mental health center exemplifies current professional concerns about safeguarding the rights of clients. It seems that during a counseling session in this mental health center a male client, a welfare recipient, became angry over the inadequacy of his income and abruptly terminated the session by announcing that he was going across the street to the local public-welfare office and "get them" for not providing more assistance. As he stormed out the door, the mental health therapist called the welfare office to warn them of the imminent arrival of the client. When the welfare worker asked for the client's name, the therapist responded by saying, "I can't tell you that because of confidentiality, but he's walking across the parking lot toward your office right now, he's wearing a red shirt, and he's madder than hell."

This illustrates the real dilemma mental health professionals face in safeguarding clients' rights. During the early 1970s, the advocate of human services integration usually found the mental health professional cautious about such concepts as "co-location" and "single portal of entry." At that time, mental health professionals resisted efforts to unify or centralize computerized management-information systems. Today, federal and state courts have taken positions that control many clinical-practice and administrative policies of mental health centers.

Community mental health centers were developed so that a variety of skilled professionals can be part of an organization capable of responding to client needs in a comprehensive manner. The comprehensiveness of the response requires twenty-four-hour emergency services, outpatient and inpatient services for citizens of all ages, day treatment programs, and therapeutic-community-based residential programs (P.L.

107

94-63). The comprehensive nature of centers requires an organizational structure that permits professionals to deliver clinical and educational services with some control over professionals through supervision, co-ordination, and monitoring of services to clients. In order to preserve the rights of clients, a mental-health center administration must ensure that center staff and clients are aware of the rights and responsibilities of both parties. The mental health center does, in fact, enter into a contractual relationship with each client.

Individuals seeking mental health treatment for the first time are usually just as apprehensive about entry into the mental health center as about the emotional and behavioral problems they are experiencing. The stereotyping of both the mental health professional and client produces fears that frequently act as deterrents to treatment and other related services. One way to minimize a client's apprehension is a written statement signed by both parties stating that both the seeking of assistance and the delivery of service will be done with total confidentiality, along with a clear understanding of the center's and the client's responsibilities.

From a clinical and legal sense, one of the greatest potential problems for a mental health center is the failure to state clearly the intended outcome of the therapeutic relationship with the client beyond the client's expression of the need for support and treatment. The obligation of the center, then, is to develop an organizational structure that will permit the establishment of consistent actions by staff that will provide the client with (1) a clear understanding of the desirable outcome of treatment (that is, desirable to the client), (2) a specific description of the center's expectation for the client regarding services received and cost responsibility; and (3) an understanding of the ethical, professional, and legal obligations under which the center operates.

While a center may expect each therapist to negotiate a relationship of trust with each of his or her clients for the purpose of treatment, the center's staff will best serve clients if conditions for use of the center are understood and accepted by the client prior to treatment. Although such an understanding is inappropriate in emergency situations, most clients will be seeking services under conditions that would permit the center to specify center procedure and practice.

One of the best means of establishing the nature of the client-center relationship is through the use of a contract, such as an "informed consent" form. The contract need not be a written legal document (Stuart, 1975). Instead, a contract can be an overt behavior initiated by the center for ensuring that they have fully apprised the client of their expectations and reviewed the client's expectations for services requested.

For example, an intake worker would describe the range of services provided, the client's rights and financial responsibilities, and would answer questions. However, the intake worker should inform the client that if he or she has any concerns regarding the center, these should be discussed with the therapist. Overall, there is no "best" procedure for establishing the center-client relationship, but latitude should be given to the therapist to negotiate on behalf of his or her client should any center policies jeopardize treatment. While means for developing a contract may vary, the contractual relationship should address at least the following: (1) expected duration of service, (2) services to be performed, including stated goals of service and treatment techniques to be used, (3) assurance of professional standards by the mental health center, (4) special terms, if any, under which services will or can be delivered, (5) the cost and terms of payment for services, (6) a description of the procedures for confidentiality, and (7) an agreement governing the use of client information in reports such as statistical summaries of services and research-evaluation documentation.

Several federal court decisions have attempted to define the rights of mental patients. *Rouse* v. *Cameron* (1966) was the first legal decision to deal with the right-to-treatment issue. The Rouse decision not only suggested constitutional facets to the right of treatment, but also extended the importance of this right by stating that continued failure to provide treatment was not justified by an insufficiency of resources. The decision asked that an individualized treatment program be established and periodic evaluation be conducted. The *Wyatt* v. *Stickney* (1971) decision addressed the issue of adequacy of care and treatment. The *Donaldson* v. *O'Connor* (1974) case suggested that an individual has the right to "effective" treatment for the purpose of being cured or improving his mental condition.

The case of *Tarasoff* v. *Regents of the University of California* (1974) has had significant impact on mental health professionals by addressing the issue of confidentiality versus the rights of others in society. *Tarasoff* was heard by the Supreme Court of California in 1976. The court reported that on October 27, 1969, Prosinget Poddar killed Tatiana Tarasoff. Civil action was brought by Tatiana's parents, alleging that two months before Tatiana's death Poddar, who was a voluntary outpatient of a mental health facility operated by the University of California, had confided to his therapist that he intended to kill Tatiana. The therapist requested that Poddar be held by police. The police briefly complied, but released Poddar when he appeared rational. The therapist's superior, a psychiatrist, directed that no further attempt be made to detain Poddar. No one warned Tatiana of the threats on her life. The court stated that Tatiana's parents had a right to bring civil action against the therapist and his superior, the psychiatrist, asserting that they had

> determined that the daughter's killer presented a serious danger of violence to her, or pursuant to the standards of their profession should have so determined, but nevertheless failed to exercise reasonable care to protect

her from that danger *(Tarasoff* v. *Regents of the University of California,* 1976, p. 1166).

The responsibility of the therapist in a case where there is serious danger of violence to another individual was found by the court to require that the therapist take action to effectively warn the intended victim. The court took note of the argument that there are limitations to the ability of mental health professionals to detect the difference between a situation where a patient is making threats with no intent to act versus and one with threats and an intention to act. The finding of the court was as follows:

> Within the broad range of reasonable practice and treatment in which professional opinion and judgment may differ, the therapist is free to exercise his or her own best judgment without liability; proof, aided by hindsight, that he or she judged wrongly is insufficient to establish negligence. In the instant case, however, the pleadings do not raise any question as to failure of defendant therapists to predict that Poddar presented a serious danger of violence. On the contrary, the present complaints allege that defendant therapists did in fact predict that Poddar would kill, but were negligent in failing to warn *(Tarasoff,* p. 1177).

While the California case is not at the time of this writing the law of the land, it does establish a precedent. Responsibility of the mental health professional is extended by this ruling to include violent acts committed by a client if the professional had knowledge that such acts might occur. It is important that professionals be aware of their responsibility and potential liability. Obviously in this case the court is placing the right to be spared violence at a higher priority than the right to confidentiality in the therapist-client relationship.

However, the court did repeatedly indicate a sensitivity to protecting client rights when seeking mental health services. It discussed the right of confidentiality of clients who do not threaten violent action. The court warned therapists to yield to disclosure only to avert a clear and present danger to others. In other words, the ruling in the case indicated that liability occurs only when the therapist considers the client's threats serious enough to take some steps toward confinement and commitment, but then fails to follow through on those attempts and fails to warn the intended victim.

Safeguarding client rights is important in maintaining the credibility of the mental health professional. However, failure to use good judgment when a client clearly indicates a plan of violence against society or an individual can legally implicate the therapist should the client act in a manner that the therapist had predicted.

Mental health professionals in private practice have the same responsibility for assuring client rights; but in general private therapists are not as subject to pressure for client information as are public agencies or private nonprofit mental health centers that rely on community, county, state, and federal funds. For this reason, this chapter focuses on the mental health center and the procedures that might be used by center staff in safeguarding client rights. Nevertheless, most of these procedures for good clinical treatment and protection of client rights are also directly applicable to private practitioners.

Initial Phone Call

The client's first contact, usually by phone, with a center or individual therapist presents the first opportunity for protecting client rights. This initial phone call from a potential client should provide each client the opportunity to choose the needed professional services and feel that he or she can trust the contacted clinic. Rosen has stated that a trusting relationship between client and service provider has long been viewed as an essential and central feature of the treatment process (1953).

During the initial call the individual is seeking information regarding type of service, cost of service, center hours, and an indication that he or she needs professional services. The information given to a potential client should be consistent and easy to understand.

The center staff member assures the individual of the center's confidentiality policy before seeking any information from the client. Once the client indicates his or her understanding of confidentiality, the staff member begins answering the individual's questions. After the client's questions are answered, the staff member informs the client that the following information must be recorded: (1) the caller's name, address, phone number, (2) a brief statement regarding the nature of the client's problem, and (3) an appointment date for the intake session. The center also requests permission to contact the client, if needed, and explains procedures for contacting, such as calls at home or work between certain hours. The client is also informed that the center is never identified when an attempt is made to contact the client.

Safeguard procedures for assuring client rights during the initial phone call are as follows:

1. Center staff member reads a brief statement describing the center's confidentiality policies, such as: "As a client of this agency, no disclosure of your record to outside agencies or other professionals will be made without your written consent. Basically, we have an organizational system for safeguarding your rights and this will be fully explained during your first interview."
2. Center staff member records some brief information about the client, and

3. Seeks instructions from client for contacting the client.
4. Initial phone contact information is placed in a number-coded folder and forwarded to medical records department for filing under intake interview information.
5. The client's name and code number is recorded in the intake interview appointment book.

Client Records System

Most clients bring both hope and anxiety into the first interview session (Rosenbaum, 1975). This interview should focus on the client's needs for services, his or her expectations from the center, and informa-

EXHIBIT I.   Initial Phone Call: Information

Staff _____

Date _____

    I. *Checklist*
       1. Read statement about the center's services and office hours   _____
       2.. Read confidentiality statement   _____
       3. Received instructions for contacting the client by telephone   _____
       4. Made an appointment for first interview   _____

   II. *Client Information*
       1. Client name_____ Client number_____
       2. Address_____
       3. Home number_____ Office number_____
       4. Type of services client requested
          a. outpatient counseling   _____
          b. inpatient   _____
          c. day treatment   _____
          d. day hospital   _____
          e. community residential   _____
          f. home visit   _____
          g. educational/training classes   _____
          h. diagnostic/evaluation   _____
  III. *Instruction for Telephone Client*
       Call office/home (circle) during these hours: _____.
       Identify the client by_____.

   IV. *Appointment*
       Date_____
       Time_____

tion about the center (Korchin, 1976). Sullivan recommends that it is wise to start the interview by telling the client what you know about him or her, either from his own self-report or from information provided by others (1954). During this session, considerable time is needed to explain client rights—primarily the right of confidentiality and to receive or refuse treatment.

Confidentiality is one of the prerequisites to the establishment of trust in a therapeutic relationship (Noll, 1974). The American Medical Association, the National Association of Social Workers, and the American Psychological Association maintain respect for the confidentiality of client communications and for the individual's right to privacy in clinical interviews (Noll & Hanlow, 1976; Stolz & Associates, 1978). Greenwalt defines confidentiality as the right to be left alone (1974), while Westin describes it as a process that excludes the public to a certain extent (1967). In other words, confidentiality simply means being able to tell someone something in confidence, with the assurance that it not be repeated to anyone. Thus, it is vital for a mental health center to describe in writing its confidentiality policies and procedures for the client.

The issue of confidentiality is complicated by the increasing emphasis now being placed upon the ready accessibility of fiscal and clinical information. During the past several years, various methods of collecting client data have been developed, ranging from checklist forms (Elpers & Chapman, 1973; Fox & Rappaport, 1972; Nelson & Morgan, 1973) to centralized mental-health computer systems (Crawford, Morgan, & Gianturco, 1974). Community mental health centers have become large "storage banks" of client data. There is some uneasiness among consumers and mental health professionals about the possible intrusion on the right to privacy through this collection and storing of client data. There is particular concern about the increasing requirements to report detailed client information to various organizations such as (1) state and federal health agencies, (2) employers curious about the psychological history and present ability of their employees, (3) police departments anxious to learn the identity of individuals being treated for drug addiction, (4) life insurance companies interested in potential suicide risk, and (5) professional standards organizations requiring reviewer access to medical and clinical records (Gobert, 1976). While community mental health centers widely recognize the constraint to not release client information to other agencies without written consent from a client, some centers apparently feel such constraints are not necessary for the various governmental agencies or those within their own organizations.

Client information must be protected from internal and external demands. Moreover, clinical information on a client should be factually and carefully recorded. Noll has discussed the dangers in diagnosing or labeling clients (1974). Client records should be coded for filing, and carefully monitored whenever removed from secure record files. Clinical supervision does require the therapist to discuss certain client information, but the therapist should be discreet in selecting clinical data about the client when discussing the case with the supervisor or clinical group conference. In addition, the client should be informed in advance that certain agency senior clinical staff will review his or her case.

A community mental health center has staff who have access to client information—file clerks, business office staff, statisticians, clinical staff, and so on. Some centers feel confidentiality is protected by ensuring that only their employees or contacts with the community mental health center have access to client records. However, this is not the case. The possibilities for disclosure are increased with the creation of a centralized mental-health computer system because of the increased number of individuals involved in collecting, filing, coding, and recording data. Some staff are not under stringent professional ethical obligations to keep such information confidential. Furthermore, information can be obtained directly from the computer. Hence, there is a danger here that client information—which may include name, psychiatric diagnosis, previous treatment history, and condition at termination—will become available to unauthorized parties and individuals.

Because of external considerations, clients are often asked to relinquish their privacy with regard to their clinical record. Traditionally it has been held that clients retain the power and right to waive the confidentiality existing between them and the therapist (Shah, 1970). Recent Supreme Court decisions have recognized the existence of this right. The court has invoked the right of privacy to protect a pregnant woman's decision to choose an abortion, and the right to obtain contraceptives. In the *Roe* v. *Wade* (1973) decision, in which the issue was whether a woman had the prerogative to terminate her pregnancy, the court held that such a decision is protected by a woman's constitutional right of privacy. In the mental health center the client waives this right by providing the therapist with signed consent that permits or authorizes the therapist to release relevant information to a third party. Over the past several years there has been an increase in the number of requests for information from mental health professionals regarding former clients (Halleck, 1971). These requests originate largely from (1) a third-party payer who might insist on scrutinizing a client's record before remitting payment, (2) a therapist who requests permission to seek additional information about a client from another agency, or (3) a governmental funding agency that might require a review of records to ensure accountability. However, when clients grant such consent by signing a waiver, they have opened the clinical record for the therapist to choose material to be given to the external agency. Hence, the therapist is converted to a "double agent." The kind of information that the therapist formulates will determine how much harm could be caused the client (Noll, 1974). Halleck has described the dilemma which a therapist faces:

> Initially we were honest in our replies and tended to give agencies whatever information they requested. We soon learned that our cooperation was hurting some of our former patients. Then we decided to provide information only when we could say something favorable about the client (1971, p. 127).

Thus, a client has the right to control the dissemination and use of information concerning his or her psychological state (Gobert, 1976). Before any client information can leave a therapist's office, the client should authorize in writing who can see the information and where and how the information can be processed and stored.

Safeguard procedures for protecting client information are as follows:

1. Client receives a written document describing in detail the mental health center's policy and procedures for insuring confidentiality.
2. Clinical records describing a client are written in short, concise, and accurate form.
3. Client is consulted on review of the clinical information for purposes of supervision and for clinical conferences.
4. Client is permitted to review his or her record.
5. Client is permitted to enter written statements into the record in case of disputes.
6. No disclosure of a client's record to external agencies or individuals may be made without written consent. The written consent must specify who receives the information, the purpose of the disclosure, the nature of the information disclosed, and the consequences of refusal to consent. Provision may be made for limited disclosure without consent when to obtain consent is impossible due to client incapacity and necessary in order for client to receive benefits. Limited disclosure of information may also be made for statistical or research purposes if client has been informed in advance that such action might be taken so long as no client-identifying information is released (see p. 116).
7. A center provides a list to the client of all possible staff who might see the client's name and clinical information. The client checks these names for approval.
8. Clients are assigned number codes, and separate files are kept— one, identified by number, containing diagnostic and treatment information; the other, containing name and code number, address, and telephone number, to be used in the business office.
9. If a computer is used, one set of coders and key punchers should work on the name-number files and another on the mental health data files. In this manner, no single computer technician could learn private facts about a particular client (Gobert, 1976).
10. A computerized system outside the community mental health

EXHIBIT II.   Client Written Consent

Client Name _____

Date _____

Witness (staff member) _____

Date _____

I.   I hereby give consent to the _____ Center to release the attached (copy) information to _____ (agency) _____ (staff member) for the purpose_____

     _____ .

II.   I refuse to release any information regarding me. I understand that the following consequences could occur if I refuse to release this information:
   1. Nothing   _____
   2. Possible lack of continuity of care from the requesting agencies   _____
   3. Legal issues from the court   _____
   4. The _____ Center may not receive governmental and/or private funds for not being able to provide demographic client data   _____

_____   _____

Client Signature   Date

_____   _____

Staff Member   Date

     center should not receive the client's name, address, or other information that might clearly identify the client. Such systems should only receive the coded number and certain demographic, treatment, cost, and attendance data (any datum is acceptable if it does not identify client).

11. A community mental health center should have an attorney appointed to represent the center and client in case a client's name and folder is requested from outside.

12. States should pass statutes levying heavy penalties—including fines and mandatory jail terms—for unauthorized disclosure, receipt, or use of mental health data (*Hancock* v. *State,* 1966).

13. Client information that includes the client's name, social security number, address, etc., should eventually be destroyed. The time period before destruction may vary for different types of information.

14. Client should be informed of the times when he or she will not be able to prevent disclosure of records or communications. Such

conditions may include the following: (a) a mental examination ordered by the court, (b) a proceeding brought by the client against the therapist, (c) determination by the therapist that involuntary hospitalization is necessary to prevent physical harm, (d) necessary facilitation of guardianship, (e) communications made in the course of treatment being called on to determine client's fitness to stand trial and only with respect to that issue, and (f) the client introducing his or her mental condition as an issue during court proceedings (Shlensky, 1977).

Treatment Agreement

The American Psychiatric Association's board of trustees in its December 1976 meeting, upon recommendation of its Task Force on the Right to Treatment, stated that adequate care and treatment should be available to all individuals requiring it, both in the hospital and in the community (APA Board, 1977). This issue has implications for both inpatient and outpatient agencies.

Since the previously cited litigations in Alabama (*Wyatt* v. *Stickney,* 1971) and Florida (*O'Connor* v. *Donaldson,* 1974), the "right to treatment" has been a difficult issue for both the legal and mental health professions. The Constitution does not describe a "right to treatment." It does guarantee an individual explicit basic rights as described by the Bill of Rights, such as freedom of speech and free exercise of religion. With the exception of the Sixth Amendment's provisions regarding criminal prosecutions and trial rights, the Constitution is silent concerning such governmental functions and services as mental health, health care, and welfare. Thus, a state may terminate funding for mental health services, since such services are not mandated by the Constitution. As long as a state government implements the Fourteenth Amendment's equal protection and due process clause for all citizens, it is protected from private complaint against reductions of human welfare services (McGough & Carmichael, 1977). However, though a right to treatment does not appear verbatim in the Constitution, it has grown out of basic rights through the process of judicial interpretation and application (McGough & Carmichael, 1977). Thus, an individual does have the right to treatment from a mental health center if such services are provided, and the right to participate to the extent possible in decisions affecting his or her treatment.

The client has a right also to be informed. The right to be informed has generally focused on confidentiality and informed consent, which ensure the client that information supplied by him or her will be guarded. Based upon recent trends in federal legislation, informed consent has been expanded to mean that a client has a right to be aware of and to formally approve his or her treatment plan. A prime component of this federal legislation is an assurance of client involvement in the selection of appropriate treatment strategies and approval of the final treatment plan. For example, P. L. 94-142 requires that all children receive an education appropriate to their needs and provides parents the opportunity to review and approve the treatment plan prepared by education professionals. Rehabilitation legislation proposed in 1978 (U.S. Sen. 2600) would require the development of an individualized treatment plan acceptable to the client and would not allow treatment to begin until the client approved. Even if federal and state laws do not follow this pattern of mandating client involvement in treatment planing, mental health centers would be well advised to institute policies and practices that inform clients as to the purpose and expected outcome of treatment. Moreover, when feasible, treatment plans that contain statements of strategies to be used should be reviewed prior to implementation and signed by the client, signifying his or her acceptance of the plan. Such a practice would not only promote good clinical practice but provide useful documentation at some future date should legal action occur. Also, informed consent allows some data to be used for research purposes.

Recent court decisions have ruled that clients have a right not to be harmed. This issue is far more complex than informed consent, because, unlike the situation with informed consent, administrative procedures to avoid harm are difficult to define and develop. The legal principle related to harm has been developed primarily from legal actions in which states were maintaining twenty-four-hour custody of institutionalized persons. In a New York State case, attorneys for the plaintiff documented to the satisfaction of the court that the individual had been adversely affected by treatment such that plaintiff was worse as a result of treatment (*Nysarc and Parisi* v. *Carey,* 1975). While case law related to actions in this area against mental health centers is limited, one suit filed in Vermont (*Anonymous* v. *Washington County Mental Health Service,* 1978) alleges that outpatient treatment in a community mental health center resulted in mental harm, increased anxiety, and depression for the plaintiff.

Furthermore, it is important that an agency protect the client's right to choose a preferred type of treatment. The client has the right to refuse certain treatment procedures. While the clinical staff may disagree or choose to refer the client to another more appropriate agency, the client does have the right to refuse treatment except for emergency situations (*Wyatt* v. *Stickney*). Although treatment seeks to help the client, it can be repulsive to the client, and the client's preference should be respected

(McGough & Carmichael, 1977). The best results from any treatment are obtained when client and therapist engage in a collaborative effort (Sehdev, 1976).

Safeguard procedures for assuring treatment rights are as follows:

1. Client participates with the therapist in planning treatment goals and type of treatment technique.
2. Clients can refuse treatment except in an emergency situation.

Quality Assurance

The mental health service-delivery system continuously attempts to improve its performance by monitoring and evaluating its results. Performance feedback permits the mental health profession to extend and improve services. Moreover, clients have a right to know the quality of services they receive. Thus, the public relies on professionals to carefully monitor themselves and be monitored by outside health care agencies. This is the essence of quality assurance.

Mental health and other counseling agencies have received increased pressure for accountability. The most visible evidence is provided by the various governmental monitoring requirements which focus on both the cost and quality of service rendered. Recently, consumer groups and third-party payers have requested information describing the quality of services. But the most persistent group behind the pressure for accountability has been the courts, which have concentrated forcefully on the issue of quality (Jacobs, Christoffel, & Dixon, 1976).

A community mental health center needs to establish a quality assurance review in which the main purpose is to assure that the services received by the client are of optimal achievable quality. It should provide reliable feedback to client and therapist indicating the areas of positive and negative results. Such data provide therapist and client the opportunity to measure the welfare of the client against the standard requiring that services rendered to a client be primarily concerned with producing the largest possible improvement in the shortest period of time (Risley, 1969).

Imagine entering a mental health center's lobby and observing a bulletin board that displays clinical information describing various clinical-program or other service-outcome results (for example, the percentage of treatment goals reached across each clinical program) and consumer feedback results. A client has the right to know such information.

The safeguard procedure here is that an agency publish an annual consumer report that is given to each client.

Summary

The mental health field during the seventies has witnessed tremendous emphasis in the areas of service delivery accountability and client rights. As discussed in this chapter, clients have basic rights which include protection of confidentiality to the fullest, control of the dissemination and use of information describing their psychological states, the opportunity to participate in treatment goals and techniques, the option to refuse treatment, and accessibility to consumer information about the organization providing services. Mental health practitioners cannot assume that the issue of safeguarding client rights is just a "fad" or that the courts will become silent. We have just begun the task of designing, implementing, and evaluating the mental health delivery system in a way that protects client rights while providing effective services.

This chapter has attempted to describe some client rights issues and procedures for safeguarding these rights. To ensure that such a system functions, a mental health center should establish an ongoing client-rights policy committee which would have the responsibility of coordinating in-service staff training, conducting grievance procedures when rights are violated, and developing new safeguard procedures. Further research is needed for demonstrating the impact of these safeguard procedures.

The future in the mental health field as regards safeguarding client rights appears to be a tremendous challenge. To meet this challenge, mental health professionals need to know when to develop new administrative and clinical procedures and, in some situations, agree to be retrained in the areas of client rights and legal developments (Martin, 1975).

References

American Psychiatric Association Board of Trustees. The Task Force on the Right to Treatment. *American Journal of Psychiatry*, 1977, *134*, 354–355.

Anonymous v. *Washington County Mental Health Services et al.*, Washington Superior Court, S379-77WnC (Vermont, 1978).

CRAWFORD, J., MORGAN, D., & GIANTURCO, D. (Eds.). *Progress in mental health information systems: Computer applications.* Philadelphia: Bellinger, 1974.

Donaldson v. *O'Connor*, 493 F. 2d 507 (5th Cir. 1974).

ELPERS, J., & CHAPMAN, R. Management information for mental health services. *Administration in Mental Health*, 1973, *2*, 12–25.

FOX, P. & RAPPAPORT, M. Some approaches to evaluation in community mental health services. *Archives of General Psychiatry*, 1972, *26*, 172–178.

GOBERT, J. J. Accommodating patient rights and computerized mental health systems. *North Carolina Law Review*, 1976, *54*, 154–187.

GREENWALT, K. Privacy and its legal protections. *Hasting Center Studies*, 1974, *2:3*, 45–63.

HALLECK, S. L. *The politics of therapy.* New York: Science House, 1971.

Hancock v. *State,* 402 S.W. 2d 906 (Tex. Crim. App. 1966).

JACOBS, C. M., CHRISTOFFEL, T. H., & DIXON, N. *Measuring the quality of patient care: The rationale for outcome audit.* Cambridge, Mass.: Ballinger, 1976.

KORCHIN, S. J. *Modern clinical psychology.* New York: Basic Books, 1976.

MARTIN, R. *Legal challenges to behavior modification.* Champaign, Ill.: Research Press, 1975.

McGOUGH, L. S. & CARMICHAEL II, W. C. The right treatment and the right to refuse treatment. *American Journal of Orthopsychiatry,* 1977, *47,* 307–320.

NELSON, C., & MORGAN, L. The information system of a community mental health center. *Administration in Mental Health,* 1973, *2,* 26–38.

NOLL, J. O. Needed: A bill of rights for clients. *Professional Psychology,* 1974, *5,* (1), 3–12.

NOLL, J. O., & HANLOW, M. J. Patient privacy and confidentiality at mental health centers. *American Journal of Psychiatry,* 1976, *133* (11), 1286–1289.

Nysarc and Parisi v. *Carey,* 393 F. Supp. at 719 (New York 1975).

RISLEY, T. R. Behavior modification: An experimental therapeutic endeavor. In L. A. Hamerlynck, P. O. Davidson, & L. E. Acker (Eds.). *Behavior modification and ideal mental health services.* Alberta, Canada: University of Calgary Press, 1969.

Roe v. *Wade,* 410 U.S. 179 (S.D.N.Y. 1973).

ROSEN, J. *Direct psychoanalysis.* New York: Grune & Stratton, 1953.

ROSENBAUM, C. P. Initial interviewing. In C. P. Rosenbaum & J. E. Beebe III (Eds.), *Psychiatric treatment: Crisis clinic, consultation.* New York: McGraw-Hill, 1975.

Rouse v. *Cameron,* 373 F. 2d 451 (D.C. 1966).

SEHDEV, H. S. Patients' rights or patients' neglect: The impact of the patients' rights movement on delivery systems. *American Journal of Orthopsychiatry,* 1976, *46,* 660–668.

SHAH, S. A. Privileged communications, confidentiality, and privacy: Confidentiality. *Professional Psychology,* 1970, *1,* 159–164.

SHLENSKY, R. Informed consent and confidentiality: Proposed new approaches in Illinois. *American Journal of Psychiatry,* 1977, *134,* 1416–1418.

STOLZ, S. B. & associates. *Ethical issues in behavior modification.* San Francisco: Jossey-Bass, 1978.

STUART, R. B. *Client-therapist treatment contract.* Champaign, Ill.: Research Press, 1975.

SULLIVAN, H. S. *The psychiatric interview.* New York: Norton, 1954.

Tarasoff v. *Regents of the University of California,* 17 Cal 3d 425, 131 Cal. Rptr. 14, 551 p2d 334, 83 ALR 3d 1166 (1976).

WESTIN, A. F. *Privacy and Freedom.* New York: Atheneum, 1967.

Wyatt v. *Stickney,* 344 F. Supp. 373, 374 (M.D. Ala. 1971).

CHAPTER 7

Client Rights in Sex Therapy

Nechama Liss-Levinson
Joseph Nowinski

SHOULD THE RIGHTS OF CLIENTS in sex therapy be considered as apart from the rights of clients in any other therapeutic modality? Is sex therapy somehow different from marital therapy, family therapy, or individual therapy? The answer to both questions is a qualified yes. Perhaps more so than any other form of psychotherapeutic intervention, sex therapy calls for sensitivity and extraordinary care on the part of the therapist if client rights are to be truly preserved. In fact, one might go so far as to suggest that it is the sex therapist's proper place to be a client advocate.

By its very nature sex therapy concerns an area of personal and interpersonal functioning that lies at the heart of a person's sense of self. As a result, persons seeking sexual therapy generally feel—and consequently are—extremely vulnerable. A most important consideration to be kept in mind is that these clients are seeking counsel for problems that lie within a sphere of thought and action still subject to cultural taboo. Because of this taboo most persons lack knowledge, for which they unfortunately often have substituted prejudice and superstition. More likely than not the client will reflect the culture at large and lack accurate information, possess wrong notions, and feel distinctly uncomfortable in openly discussing the intimacies and intricacies of sex. If it is a couple that is seeking therapy together, each partner is likely to have disclosed less than the totality of his or her background and current sexuality to the other. All in all, such conditions make for a good deal of anxiety on the part of the prospective client. This anxiety is not only of clinical import; it also has implications for the ethical conduct of sexual treatment programs. The position of the therapist at the outset of sex therapy is perhaps more markedly different from that of the client than is the case in any other treatment modality. In sex therapy, the therapist is presumed to (and most likely does) possess a great deal more factual knowledge than the client. Moreover, the therapist is presumed to have more practical knowledge as well, since the client is not used to talking with people about sex but the therapist is. Partly as a result of accurate knowledge, the therapist may hold significantly different sexual attitudes from the client's. In sharp contrast to the client's reticence stands the therapist's apparent ease in openly discussing this most tabooed of subjects. Each of these differences contributes to the sex therapist's aura of expertise, maturity, and authority.

All in all, then, the sex therapy situation places the therapist in a decided position of advantage with respect to the client. The client feels bad. Her or his self-esteem suffers from a severe wound as a direct result of the sexual problem. The therapist is perceived as sexually functional and probably more than adequate. The client is naive and knows it; the therapist is sophisticated. It should come as no surprise then that same-sex clients may be intimidated by the sex therapist, while opposite-sex clients may be drawn toward the sex therapist. In either case the result is really the same: The client feels inferior, immature, vulnerable, and perhaps even helpless in relation to the therapist. In short, endemic to sex therapy is the possibility of the therapist assuming an inordinately powerful role within the therapeutic relationship, and this places extra burdens on the therapist with regard to ethics and client welfare.

The cultural taboos surrounding sexuality work also to seal off from communication the client who is seeking therapy or who may be dissatisfied or skeptical in any way about the treatment. People often select sex therapists on the basis of minimal information. Because they may be uncomfortable talking about their problem they do not consult friends or even authoritative sources, and because they feel ignorant they are not likely to ask a lot of questions of a referral source or even of the prospective therapist. Such basic issues as credentials, cost, treatment technique, and prognosis often go unmentioned. By the time they overcome their inhibitions and finally do seek out treatment, prospective clients are usually quite anxious—if not desperate—for relief, and in this position can be easily convinced of the efficacy of just about any "treatment" one can imagine, at nearly any price. At the same time, the cultural taboo inhibits the client from seeking a second opinion or taking complaints to an external authority. Quite to the contrary; the client with a sexual dysfunction almost invariably has great concerns centering around confidentiality and wants as few people as possible to be knowledgeable concerning his or her difficulties. Abuses of the therapeutic relationship, breaches of the therapeutic contract, and other lapses in ethical conduct will not in all probability come to the attention of any external authority. This, too, places an extra burden of responsibility on the sex therapist.

Another factor that sets sex therapy apart from other forms of psychotherapy is that in this particular instance knowledge by third parties can be damaging to the client. As Harry Stack Sullivan once noted, no one in our culture is apt to feel good about needing or seeking out psychotherapeutic services; nor would they be anxious to disclose the fact to others (1954). When the therapeutic focus is on other concerns— be they individual, family, or even marital—the effect of accidental disclosure would not be nearly so severe as would disclosure of the fact that a person is seeking help for a sexual problem. The client whose employer, family, or peers discover that she or he is in sex therapy will almost certainly be subject to unflattering gossip at the very least, and quite possibly humiliation and defamation of character.

All psychotherapists frequently find themselves in a position of having information that a client would not want disclosed to anyone else, including his or her sexual partner. In sex therapy, which often involves work with a couple, the therapist may be—in fact, often will be—privy to the sexual secrets of each partner. Some therapists balk at this prospect and avoid all individual discussion with clients seen as a couple. Others will meet individually with partners but preface such discussions with a statement that all information given is subject to disclosure to the partner by the therapist. Still other therapists grant individual partners complete confidentiality, in the belief that it is therapeutically vital that the therapist have the most accurate and complete information available. It is not within our purview to debate therapeutic technique; our purpose is only to point out that sex therapists frequently end up in possession of "hot" material: information about clients that could be extremely upsetting to all concerned were anyone else, including the client's partner, to have it. Once more this places a special burden on the sex therapist if the rights of clients are to be preserved.

Individuals seeking out sex therapy generally do so having one or more specific and delimited goals in mind; for example, to be able to experience erections again, become orgasmic, or enjoy sex more. They usually assume that sex therapy will focus on these circumscribed goals. More important, they are prone to assuming that the effects of the therapy, if successful, will be limited to this one sphere of their lives. They do not enter sex therapy with the expectation that, for instance, becoming orgasmic may dramatically affect their marriage. Yet it is the experience of sex therapists that, even when the scope of its interventions are limited, sex therapy exerts a secondary but powerful influence on many other aspects of clients' lives, including the sense of self and the nature of their relationships. The sex therapist needs to remain cognizant of the potential impact of sexual changes, and also to make ethical choices concerning the issues of risk and treatment format. For instance, whether to see a couple in which one partner is engaged in an extramarital affair and whether to see a client individually or conjointly with her or his partner are ethical as well as clinical decisions.

In the past, the practitioner offering sex therapy services had few clearcut guidelines to fall back on when confronted with dilemmas such as those described above. Prior to 1970, when sex therapy was provided by individual physicians, psychologists, or ministers, the practitioner regarded himself or herself as bound by the ethical code of a particular profession. Most existing professional codes, however, had no specific provisions regarding the rights of clients in sex therapy. The American Psychological Association, for example, exhorted practitioners "to respect the integrity and protect the welfare of the people and groups with whom they work." The ethical standards provide additional guidelines regarding confidentiality, professional competence and maintenance of standards, and pursuit of research activities. However, it was only in the most recent revision (in 1977) that a clearcut policy was ennunciated prohibiting sexual contact between client and therapist (Principle 6A). While acceptable as general statements of ethical philosophy, most professional ethical codes, such as the APA code cited above, lack specificity.

With the increase in the number and variety of persons offering sex therapy came increased possibilities of abuse of the therapy relationship and outright quackery. At present the title "sex therapist" does not belong to any one profession; nor is it regulated by any state licensing laws, as for example are the titles "psychologist," "physician," or "social worker." Many responsible sexologists do feel the need for specific ethical guidelines in order to avoid wholesale mistreatment of client populations. In the absence of other regulatory agencies, the American Association of Sex Educators, Counselors, and Therapists (AASECT) took upon itself the job of training and certifying sex educators, counselors, and therapists. Some professionals have applauded the work of AASECT, while others see the organization and its goals as primarily self-serving. While it is not our goal here to render judgment on AASECT, we must agree with LoPiccolo's observation that any agency that presumes to both train and certify may be hopelessly entangled in a conflict of interest (1978).

A second response to the vacuum vis-à-vis an ethical code for sex therapists and researchers was the convening in 1976 and 1978 of two conferences, under the auspices of the Reproductive Biology Research Foundation (now the Masters and Johnson Institute). At these conferences, major representatives from such disciplines as medicine, psychiatry, psychology, and nursing gathered to discuss the ethical issues confronting sex therapy and research. This group finalized and published a code, "Ethical Guidelines for Sex Therapists, Counsellors, and Sex Researchers," which was subsequently adopted by AASECT.

Client Rights in Sex Therapy: Issues and Strategies

What follows is a discussion of ethical issues and specific strategies that can be used to insure ethical practice and to protect the rights of

clients in sex therapy. These include strategies for both clinical and research settings. In order to adequately insure client rights, it is essential
for the practitioner to be fully aware of the range and content of those
rights.

Table 1 presents a full "bill of rights" for clients in sex therapy. All
of these rights overlap with client rights in any general outpatient therapy setting. Those issues that have a unique application to sex therapy
are asterisked and discussed more thoroughly in the text that follows.

TABLE 1.   Bill of Rights for the Consumer of Psychotherapy

ISSUE	RIGHTS
Credentials	The right:
	*To be fully informed of the therapist's qualifications to practice, including training and credentials, years of experience, personal therapy, etc.
	*To be fully informed regarding the therapist's therapeutic orientation.
	*To be fully informed regarding the therapist's areas of specialization and limitations.
	*To ask questions about issues relevant to your therapy, such as the therapist's values, background, attitudes, and life experiences; and to be provided with thoughtful, respectful answers.
Confi-dentiality	*To be fully informed of the limits of confidentiality in the therapy setting—With whom will the therapist discuss your case?
	*To be fully informed of the extent of record-keeping regarding the therapy, in both written and taped form, and knowledge concerning accessibility of those records.
Treatment Methods	To be fully informed regarding the therapist's estimation of the approximate length of therapy required to meet your goals.
	*To be fully informed regarding specific treatment strategies employed by the therapist (talking, body exercises, homework assignments, medications, etc.).
	*To be fully informed regarding potential risks and contraindications for therapy.
	To be fully informed regarding format of the therapy (individual, group, etc.).
	*To refuse any intervention or treatment strategy.
Fees	*To be fully informed regarding the fees for therapy, and the method of payment (including acceptability of insurance).
	To be fully informed regarding the therapist's policies on issues such as missed sessions, vacation time, telephone contacts outside of the therapy hour, emergency coverage, and so on.
Complaints	*To know which ethics code the therapist subscribes to.
	To terminate therapy at any time.
	*To solicit help from the ethics committee of the appropriate pro-

TABLE 1 (*Continued*)

ISSUE	RIGHTS
	fessional organization in the event of doubt or grievance regarding the therapist's conduct.
Other	To ask questions at any point.
	To specify or negotiate therapeutic goals and to renegotiate those goals when necessary.
	To be fully informed of your diagnosis (if the therapist uses such categories).
	To refuse to answer questions at any time.
	To request that the therapist evaluate the progress of therapy.
	To discuss any aspect of your therapy with others outside of the therapy situation, including other therapists.
	To require your therapist to send a written report regarding services rendered to any qualified therapist or organization upon your written consent.
	To be provided with copies of written files concerning your therapy, upon your written request.
	To give or refuse to give permission for the therapist to use aspects of your case as part of a presentation or publication.
	To get a written contract specifying the conditions of therapy, including the therapeutic goals.
	To request, if you are seen in a clinic setting, a specific therapist or type of therapist (e.g., male versus female).
	To request, if you are seen in a clinic, to speak with the clinic director or administrator regarding any aspect of concern to you.

Adapted from A Consumer's Guide to Non-Sexist Therapy *by the Psychology Committee, National Organization for Women (New York Chapter), 1978.*

ISSUE #1: CREDENTIALS

As it has become more popular and lucrative, more practitioners are interested in practicing sex therapy. In order to competently practice sex therapy, however, one needs specific knowledge and skills in addition to those required in such areas as sexual anatomy and physiology, developmental sexuality (through the life span), sex roles and sexuality, sociocultural factors in sexual values and behaviors, diverse sexual lifestyles, medical factors interfacing with sexuality (including effects of illness, disability, drugs, pregnancy, contraception, and fertility), and ethical issues in sex therapy. Specific skills that are necessary include techniques of sex therapy, techniques of marital and family counselling and familiarity with methods of outcome evaluation. The therapist needs, finally, to feel relatively comfortable with his or her own sexual adjustment.

According to the Masters and Johnson code, the above foundation in skills requires training and *supervised* experience in *both* human sexuality and a psychological or bioclinical field. Professional training as either a medical doctor, psychologist, or social worker is *not* in itself sufficient. It is clearly stated that training must include supervised experience in sex therapy. Additionally, prospective sex therapists must be able to act with professional dignity and integrity.

Strategies

1. Clearly inform the client at your initial meeting of your training and experience in the practice of sex therapy. Training and experience should be in both a psychological or bioclinical field as well as in sex therapy specifically. Only cite training or experience from an accredited institution, it is inaccurate and unethical to claim that sex therapy training took place through attendance at a lecture, demonstration, conference, panel discussion, workshop, seminar, or other similar teaching presentation. Be clear in stating whether you are presently in training.

2. Be prepared to discuss your own values regarding issues of central importance to the client's interest. For example, if a homosexual man is having difficulties in his sexual relationships, you may be legitimately asked to state your views on homosexuality.

3. APA ethics cautions the psychologist against practicing beyond the limits of one's competence (Principle 2). Make sure that your confidence does not exceed the boundaries of your own competence. Even if you have been trained in sex therapy, certain problems may require consultation (with a gynecologist or urologist, for example) or referral (to a marriage or family counselor perhaps).

4. Develop a referral network and skill in giving referrals. Be aware of other competent professionals in the community and their areas of expertise. Only refer clients to persons who you know are sensitive to professional ethics. Develop contact with community resources such as rape crisis centers, battered-wives shelters, and Planned Parenthood. Know the availability of self-help groups such as Alcoholics Anonymous, Parents Without Partners, and Women's Centers.

5. Keep abreast of current developments in the field by reading appropriate journals and through involvement in continuing education and attendance at professional workshops and conferences.

ISSUE #2: CONFIDENTIALITY

Due to the particular vulnerability many persons feel regarding their sexuality, extreme care must be taken by the therapist with respect to preserving client confidentiality. This confidentiality extends to the very existence of a client-therapist relationship. It includes all aspects of the relationship, from initial inquiry to treatment records kept following termination of therapy.

Strategies

1. Inform the client at the initial meeting of the limitations of confidentiality. This includes all circumstances under which you, as a therapist, would disclose either details or generalities regarding the case. Include a discussion of emergency circumstances, supervision, observation, staff training or consultation, and insurance reimbursement. (See APA ethics [Principle 5] and AASECT code for further discussion of these issues.)

   a. Special provisions must be made regarding confidentiality of one spouse if his or her partner requests a release of information. The therapist is responsible to maintain the confidentiality of the spouse. This extends even to the existence of the therapy relationship.

   b. In a group setting, the therapist needs to emphasize the need for confidentiality. However, since the group members are not legally bound by professional ethics, the therapist also needs to warn the group regarding risks of possible disclosure by other group members.

2. Inform clients at the initial interview of the kind and extent of record-keeping, whether clinical or financial, written or taped. Clients must voluntarily give consent for any audio- or video-taping of sessions to occur. They should know the length of time that records are kept and have knowledge regarding who has access to them. Finally, they should be informed as to how they might have access to their records.

3. All records should be kept in locked files. Only personnel essential to the running of the clinic or practice should have access to these files.

4. Records should use a numerical coding system so that names of clients do not appear anywhere on them. The key to the coding system should be kept in a separate locked file, to which access should be granted on a strict *"need-to-know"* basis.

5. Written consent of the client is necessary to get information from or give it to other professionals, including psychiatrists, psychologists, physicians, or clergy. Written permission should be obtained even to contact the referring agent or insurance company regarding diagnosis and reimbursement.

6. Special training regarding confidentiality is necessary for all students, trainees, and support personnel who may be involved in the therapy setting, including the receptionist, secretaries, typists, file clerks, and office assistants.

7. Permanent records should be kept to a minimum. At the conclusion of therapy, only those records that seem essential for research or future clinical referral should be retained. All other records should be disposed of in a secure manner.

8. Permission must be obtained from clients in order to publish details of their treatment or personal histories in the form of case studies. Clients should be specifically informed of methods used to insure their privacy when such reports are written for publication.

ISSUE #3: TREATMENT PROCEDURES

Although sex therapy has been popularized in the media, knowledge of actual treatment strategies varies greatly. Clients implicitly trust the therapist to provide ethical services. Given their lack of knowledge, they may be unable to differentiate unethical sexual abuse from an appropriate treatment plan. The power differential in the therapist-client relationship must be kept in mind, and it is up to the therapist to provide integrity—that is, to earn and deserve the trust he or she so often receives unconditionally.

Clearly, what is defined as appropriate treatment is partly a function of the prevailing value system of the society. Cultural flux and moral pluralism, however, do not justify thoughtless or irresponsible experimentation. Any deviation or variation from commonly accepted sex therapy practices must be contingent on special circumstances which include the presence of all of the following criteria: (1) important theoretical justification, (2) ongoing research evaluation, (3) peer review by eminent professionals in the field of sex therapy–research, (4) review by a panel of interested community consumer advocates, and (5) informed consent by all participants.

Strategies

1. You should have fully informed clients, by the first or second visit, of actual treatment strategies you plan to use. For example, do you require talking, body exercises, homework assignments, or use of hormones or medications? Also, inform the client of the probable length of therapy. Because of the proven efficacy of short-term sex therapy, you need to justify any estimates longer than six months.

2. Inform clients of their right to refuse any treatment strategy. Listen carefully to their refusal. Do not interpret all refusals clinically—i.e., as resistance. Clients should be encouraged to leave therapy or change therapists if they feel consistently pressured to perform activities that they find morally objectionable.

3. Clients should be fully informed of the risks of sex therapy. It is not uncommon for persons in sex therapy to change their value system, at least with respect to sexuality. Religious values may also be affected. Equally important is the potential for changes in the client's relationship with his or her partner. Extant areas of conflict may be considerably exacerbated by sex therapy, often with accompanying negative affect. Should clients decide to dissolve their relationship during the course of sex therapy, they should be fully informed regarding alternatives to continuing treatment, especially marital counseling with a different therapist.

4. Sexual contact between client and therapist is regarded as unethical by both the APA (Principle 6A) and AASECT codes of ethics.

5. Nudity on the part of client or therapist during therapy, or viewing of sexual activity of the clients by the therapist, is considered unethical except in very unusual circumstances. (See p. 125; nudity of clients is of course permitted during a physical exam by a licensed nurse or physician; however, this should not include purposeful sexual stimulation of the client being examined.)

6. The use of sexual surrogates in sex therapy is extremely controversial. The AASECT code permits their employment in extremely limited circumstances (as outlined on p. 129). In any case, it must be clearly recognized by the client that surrogates are not sex therapists and are not legally bound by professional ethics. It should also be recognized that endemic in the use of surrogates is the potential for exploitation of the client.

ISSUE #4: FEES

Due to the combination of high consumer interest in sex therapy and a relative paucity of adequately trained professionals, fees in sex therapy are often exorbitant, tremendously out of proportion when compared with other forms of outpatient psychotherapy. One could argue that this situation amounts to exploitation of the consumer.

Strategies

1. Fully inform the client of fees and method of payment at the initial visit, without waiting for him or her to inquire regarding the issue.

2. Fees should not differ significantly from local fees for other outpatient marital counseling or couple therapy services. Appropriate additional amounts may be charged to offset the cost of additional training in sex therapy and materials (e.g., films), but such increases should not be disproportionate to the professional's investment.

3. Therapists should take the personal circumstances of the client into account when setting fees, and should provide a portion of their services at reduced or no cost for those in limited financial circumstances (see AASECT code and APA code, Principle 6D).

ISSUE #5: ETHICAL PROCEDURES

Most clients are unaware of their rights in the sex therapy setting. Due to the previously mentioned power differential, most clients never assert themselves to find out their rights. Because of embarrassment regarding sexuality, they may be reluctant to pursue any complaint with outside agencies. It becomes the responsibility of the therapist to apprise clients of their rights in the therapy situation as well as encourage them in pursuing fully any ethical complaints.

Strategies

1. All clients should be provided with a written bill of rights similar to the one shown in this article (Table 1).

2. All clients should be provided with a written contract explaining the terms of therapy, including fees, treatment strategies, policies, and so on.

3. All clients should be informed of the professional organizations to which the therapist belongs as well as the ethical codes to which he or she adheres. Copies of the ethical codes should be available upon request.

4. Procedures on filing grievances should be provided to the client early in therapy, including names and addresses of appropriate persons or agencies.

5. If at all possible individual therapists, private-practice groups, and clinics should employ an ombudsman to be involved in preservation of client rights.

6. In clinic settings a community consumer advocate should be in a responsible administrative position, such as member of the governing board, and should be involved in setting clinic policies.

ISSUE #6: THE RIGHTS OF CLIENTS
IN RESEARCH SETTINGS

Ongoing research that involves the development and evaluation of clinical treatment programs is in the public interest. However, when it happens that clinical service is offered as part of the therapist's (or someone else's) research program, additional ethical considerations arise. Although the clinician is encouraged to design and implement research, ethical obligations as a clinician must take precedence over his or her needs as a researcher. It is only when the clinician-researcher assumes this basic attitude that clients will feel assured that their personal welfare will remain the final criterion in settling any potential conflict between clinical considerations and issues related to research design. The ultimate aim—an ethical one—of research is to improve the efficacy of clinical services, but this end does not justify cavalier treatment of clients' immediate needs. On several points we substantially agree with the guidelines regarding the welfare of research subjects delineated in the previously mentioned AASECT code. When doing clinical outcome research in the area of sexual therapy, the following ethical guidelines should be strictly observed in order to assure preservation of client-subject rights.

Strategies

1. For each research project at least one person—but preferably several—not directly affiliated with the research program or the researchers should be given authority to review and oversee the study with respect to ethical issues. This committee might be composed of both peers and community representatives. The names and addresses of these persons should be provided to the prospective client in writing in advance of his or her participation. It should be made clear to the client-subjects that this person or committee exists for their benefit and is available for consultation at no cost, and that availing themselves of such services will in no way affect their ongoing treatment.

2. Participation in clinical research must be strictly by informed consent. At a minimum, client-subjects must be provided—in writing and in advance—with the following information: the general purpose of the study, the nature and extent of their participation, risks and possible contraindications, and alternative, non-research-based clinical resources available in the geographic vicinity.

3. The client-subject must be clearly informed that participation in research is not a prerequisite for treatment (although it may be a contingency for a fee reduction); nor should a client's subsequent decision to withdraw from research participation affect in any way his or her continuing treatment. With respect to fees, the clinician-researcher must remember the aforementioned obligation to take a client's financial situation into consideration.

4. Permission from clients must be obtained in advance in order for clinician-researcher to publish personal history data and clinical treatment material in the form of individual case studies.

5. Client-subjects must in no way be led to hold expectations for treatment effectiveness that are inconsistent with the researcher's own

expectations. In short, the researcher must share straightforwardly his or her best prognostic estimates, and not proffer or even suggest a false prognosis.

6. Client-subjects who are being offered an experimental variation of an existing standard treatment of proved effectiveness must be so informed. If the client would prefer the standard procedure, he or she should be referred to a competent therapist within the geographic area. If no alternative clinical resources are available in the vicinity, and if the clinician-researcher is competent to provide the standard treatment, it should be offered on a limited basis.

In addition to the above special considerations, all of the previously discussed ethical responsibilities of the clinician apart from research apply to the researcher in clinical research settings. When many persons have access to client records—as is often the case in research settings—or when computer storage and retrieval methods are used, special security precautions to guarantee client-subjects' confidentiality are in order. In such cases numbers only—never names—should be used for purposes of identification.

Implications of a Consumer Model for Practicing Sex Therapists

As has been noted elsewhere (Hare-Mustin, Marechek, Kaplan, & Liss-Levinson, 1979; Van Hoose & Kottler, 1977) the function of professional ethical codes traditionally has been to help a profession preempt external control by adopting a policy of voluntary self-control. Although we are not without sympathy for the professions in their desire for autonomy, one cannot help but note the potential dangers of such a unilateral approach to regulation. Too often it leads to a philosophy of establishing "minimum" requirements for ethical practice, whereas from the consumers' point of view the idea of therapists aiming for a minimum in ethical conduct is hardly a desideratum.

In the area of sex therapy, the very content of the therapeutic work lends itself, at least some of the time, to temptation on the part of both the therapist and the client. To think otherwise—e.g., to argue that the "mature" therapist is beyond the lure of transference or countertransference—is not merely a fantasy, but a potentially dangerous one from the consumer's perspective. When such an attitude is adopted by a profession, it leads to a lack of vigilance at best and bald denial or rationalization at worse.

In this chapter we have encouraged the therapist to adopt a somewhat different posture from the above when approaching the issue of professional ethics and client rights. It has been suggested that a shift in attitude from a defensive stance toward one of consumer advocacy, might in the long run better serve both the clinician and the interests of clients seeking therapy. Nowhere does such a shift in perspective seem more appropriate than in the field of sex therapy. Therapists who are sympathetic to such a philosophy would do well to begin asking themselves, were they clients, what sorts of information they would want to know about a given therapist and a specific form of treatment prior to entering sex therapy themselves. That many clients seeking treatment do not ask for such information does not exempt the ethical therapist from giving it voluntarily.

Some information that is, we feel, particularly pertinent has been summarized in this article. Beyond this the therapist can work to insure client rights by educating clients in a consumer perspective. Providing prospective clients a list of consumer resource materials or even the materials themselves, has proven helpful. Although some professionals fear that consumer advocacy will create problems, this approach often serves to enhance the therapeutic relationship.

The fundamental principle underlying the current consumer movement is that of social responsibility. Sex therapists, like other professionals, have a responsibility to the community in which they live and practice. Their particular responsibility is to bring their own unique knowledge and skills to bear toward achieving the ends of public education and social welfare. Since it is in the common social interest, the sex therapist or researcher has an ethical responsibility to freely share relevant knowledge with the interested lay public, and to actively pursue opportunities to do so. Ideally, this kind of outreach will lead in the long run to a general improvement in couples' sexual functioning and sense of personal fulfillment.

References

American Psychological Association. *Ethical standards of psychologists.* Washington, D.C. 1200 17th Street, N.W.: APA, 1977.

Reproductive Biology Research Foundation. *Ethics guidelines for sex therapists, sex counselors, and sex researchers.* St. Louis: RBR Foundation, 1978.

HARE-MUSTIN, R. T., MARECEK, J., KAPLAN, A., & LISS-LEVINSON, N. Rights of clients, responsibilities of therapists. *American Psychologist,* 1979, *34,* 3–16.

LoPiccolo, J. The professionalization of sex therapy: Issues and problems. In J. LoPiccolo and L. LoPiccolo (Eds.), *Handbook of sex therapy.* New York: Plenum, 1978.

SULLIVAN, H. S. *The psychiatric interview.* New York: Norton, 1954.

VAN HOOSE, W. H., & KOTTLER, J. A. *Ethical and legal issues in counseling and psychotherapy.* San Francisco: Jossey-Bass, 1977.

CHAPTER 8

The Rights and Treatment of the Sexually Abused Client

Judith V. Becker
Gene G. Abel

RAPE AND CHILD MOLESTATION have become increasingly visible social problems and a focus of national concern. The rate of rape is currently 40–70 rapes per 100,000 women at risk. The FBI indicates that approximately 55,000 rapes are reported each year. These figures, however, do not accurately reflect the high incidence of sexual assault in this country, since 2.2 rapes are committed for each one reported (Curtis, 1975). Crimes involving sexual aggression are thus frequent and effect the lives of many women and men.

Over the past ten years tremendous strides have been made in attempting to meet the needs of sexual assault victims and sex offenders. Special sex-crime squads have been instituted within police departments; for rape victims, rape laws have been reformed; rape crisis centers have been organized, and a National Center for the Prevention and Control of Rape has been established as a part of the Department of Health and Human Services. For the sex offender more than two dozen new treatment programs have been established, with new assessment and treatment techniques. Each of these agencies has learned that working with sexual assault victims or offenders is an extremely sensitive endeavor.

Since rape is a felony, the therapist who treats victims or offenders must be aware that information regarding the client might be subpoenaed by the criminal justice system. Therefore, it is imperative that therapists be knowledgeable about the potential risks involved in recording certain types of information from these clients, while at the same time requiring information to facilitate the therapeutic process.

The purpose of this chapter is to highlight issues relating to client rights with (1) adult sexual assault victims, (2) child sexual assault victims, and (3) sex offenders, and to suggest strategies for protecting client rights.

Adult Victims

An understanding of what the victim of a sexual assault undergoes is helpful to the therapist. The client has probably been attacked at random either in her home or outside, without benefit of witnesses to the crime. She has been overpowered, and during the rape has temporarily lost control of her life. After her assault she frequently must defend herself from the interpretations others may give as to how she became a victim. These myths about rape include assumptions that women enjoy being raped, a woman can really stop herself from being raped if she wants to, rape victims dress in a manner to provoke their own rape, and so on.

The guiding principal for therapists treating sexual assault victims is to help them *regain control* of their lives. Various authors have described the typical rape victim's reactions following the assault (Becker & Abel, 1977; Burgess & Holmstrom, 1974; Fox & Scherl, 1970). The typical victim has a pattern of reaction to the rape that can be broken down into three successive categories: In Category 1 the victim is stunned, shocked, and unable to organize how she is going to cope with her assault. This first category or stage usually lasts from one to ten days. In Category 2 the victim begins to deal with the impact of the rape. Vacillations of mood here are common; her emotional responses are attenuated. She copes primarily by avoiding conflictual areas. This stage usually lasts from one to seven weeks and ends with the victim reestablishing a steady state of functioning. However, if the victim fails to resolve her fears and anxieties during Category 2, she may chronically maintain her symptoms and enter Category 3. In this third stage she usually is able to function physically again, but her emotional response to the assault persists in the form of sexual dysfunction, phobias, or high anxiety levels (Becker & Abel, 1977). Knowing which category the victim is in will help the therapist better understand her coping style and how it interfaces with client-rights issues.

A widely accepted form of treatment for sexual assault victims is rape crisis counseling, which aids the victim in *regaining control* of her life by generating a supportive, empathic relationship in which problem-solving behaviors can be learned.

Victims in Categories 1 and 2 typically feel responsible for the assault; counseling focuses on assuring them that they were not responsible, and outlining for them the type of symptoms that can be expected as a result of the rape trauma. Counselors also encourage—but do not force—the victim to express her anger, fear, and depression related to the rape. Counseling the victim experiencing Category 2 symptomatology includes providing support without challenging the defenses the victim has constructed during this self-protective period. Counseling the late stages of Category 2 and Category 3 involves a working through of the victim's feelings about herself and the assailant, and helping her gain self-respect. (For further information regarding crisis counseling, the reader is referred to Burgess & Holmstrom, 1974; Hilberman, 1976; Nass, 1977.)

The therapist's responsibility to his or her client is to (1) be informed of the sympotmatology rape victims typically experience, (2) be aware of state statutes regarding crimes of sexual aggression, and (3) provide the client with the best treatment available.

The adult consent form shown here is a model for those counselors and therapists who use crisis counseling. The relevance of the consent form for the victim is to (1) explain the treatment procedure, (2) outline the potential benefits and risks in the treatment, and (3) inform her of her rights regarding the therapeutic alliance. Thus, before treatment can even begin, the victim is given ultimate control over the proposed therapy by first deciding whether she wishes to participate.

Consent-to-Treatment Form: Adult Sexual Assault Victims

1. I understand that I will be receiving treatment for the emotional problems I have experienced as a result of being the victim of a sexual assault. The treatment involves my talking with someone about the fears, anxiety, depression, possible sexual problems or other problems I have experienced since the assault and specifically how I might deal with these problems. This treatment, in over 50% of victims, causes some emotional upset, anxiety, anger, and nervousness since one may relive many of the same experiences of the assault. This working through of the experience, however, has been found to be very helpful in coping with the experience and is the usual form of treatment for this problem. If this form of therapy, which is called Crisis Counseling, is not effective at alleviating my emotional problems, then I will be offered another more specific form of therapy.

2. In addition to this form of treatment, I will be asked to complete certain paper and pencil tests, pre- and post-therapy. These tests will help my therapist evaluate the effectiveness of the treatment being used. I will also be asked to keep track of my daily thoughts referable to the assault, such as how often I think about the assault, how often I have had dreams about it, how often I feel comfortable with my male friends, etc. This information allows the therapist to keep very close watch on how I am doing. Keeping track of such things, however, may make me more nervous, depressed, and anxious than before. Although these symptoms are usually mild, they do happen (in about 20% of assault victims). If this does occur, I am to call my therapist and help will be provided to me as soon as possible.

In addition, I will also be asked to rate how nervous certain brief phrases make me feel. I will be asked to rate such phrases as "I see a strange man approaching my car" or "My loved one is holding me close in his arms." Such information is to help my therapist understand exactly how I am feeling so he/she can know what treatment is helping me the most and which isn't. Thinking about such scenes, like keeping track of my thoughts, may make me more nervous, upset, angry, or depressed. Although these symptoms are usually mild, this can happen to about 20% of assault victims. If this occurs, I am to contact my therapist immediately. I understand that failure to keep such measures will in no way jeopardize my right to treatment.

3. I understand that if I elect to have family members or significant others participate in my therapy, this may represent a risk to me in the following areas: (1) Family and friends may have incorporated some of the destructive myths regarding rape, and knowledge of this may serve to further upset me. (2) Telling others that I am in therapy may increase the risk of my records being subpoenaed to court if, in fact, I have pressed charges. On the other hand, I realize that the problems I am experiencing may be apparent to my family and friends, and that including them in my therapy may be beneficial to all concerned. The final decision as to whether to include family and friends will be left up to me. Furthermore, I realize that I don't have to disclose to anyone that I am participating in therapy.

4. To insure that my therapy goes as smoothly as possible, every effort will be made to make my treatment go easily for me. If I am dissatisfied with my therapist, for example, or simply would like to see a different therapist, I will convey this to my therapist, whose responsibility it is to refer me to another therapist.

5. My therapist is concerned about the confidentiality of my records. For example, there may be some things about my own assault that I may not want to be known to the legal authorities. The best safeguard about this information is for me to provide it to no one. Information I report during my evaluation/treatment may be sensitive—i.e., I may not want my family or others to know about it. All such information will be locked up in my therapist's files. My therapist has the right of "privileged communication," which means it is extremely unlikely that anything I have said to him/her would be repeatable. A therapist cannot be absolutely certain that this information can't be requested by legal authorities, but every effort will be made (short of breaking the law) to protect my records. I understand that I have access to my records at any time. Furthermore, if any agency should request my records, my therapist will not forward any material until I have read and co-signed any reports or notes dealing with my assessment/therapy.

6. This form of therapy/counseling will last approximately _____ therapy sessions. Each session will be _____ minutes in duration. My therapist's fee per session is _____ per hour. At the end of _____ sessions my therapist and I will evaluate the progress which has been made and a decision will be made regarding whether further therapy is needed. I understand that if I cannot keep a therapy session, I will inform my therapist 24 hours in advance.

7. If I have any questions about this therapy, I have written those questions in the space below and have discussed them to my satisfaction with my therapist.

Therapist/Counselor _____

Patient/Client _____

Auditor/Witness _____

Date:_____

Therapist's Phone #: _____

Reconsenting to the consent form above after 2 therapy sessions:

Therapist/Counselor   _____

Patient/Client   _____

Auditor/Witness   _____

Date:_____

If I have any questions about my therapy, I have written those questions in the space below and have discussed them to my satisfaction with my therapist.

Therapist/Counselor   _____

Patient/Client   _____

Auditor/Witness   _____

Date:_____

Statements on completion of therapy. I sincerely wish to know if I have been accurate in my description of what this therapy would involve, what you were expected to do, the problems encountered. Were these problems handled properly? Should anything be changed about this therapy? Please comment about any or all of these items and any additional issues that you feel would help me understand any problems you have had while participating in this form of therapy.

Therapist/Counselor   _____

Patient/Client   _____

Auditor/Witness   _____

Date:_____

The consent form has been divided into seven sections. Section describes the type of treatment that will be used. A possible risk to the client is that by discussing the assault she may initially experience more emotional discomfort than before. This is especially relevant to victims in Category 2, who are attempting to rebuild defenses and deny to themselves the impact of their sexual assault. The therapist's dilemma here is that the best form of therapy includes discussion of the assault, which may be contrary to the wishes of the victim. Informing her in advance of the treatment, however, allows her to make her own decision about receiving this therapy (which preserves her rights) and thus to maintain her control over the therapy itself (which is therapeutically sound for her). The client is also informed that crisis intervention therapy is not always 100 percent successful and if she does not respond to therapy an alternative therapy will be made available.

The therapist must constantly assess the impact of treatment, treatment which in the case of rape victims may itself increase the client's emotional discomfort. Section 2 of the consent form explains this to the client so that once again she can make an informed judgment as to whether she wishes to do this or not. Her rights are once again preserved, while she maintains control over this decision.

A sexual assault can severely traumatize the victim, but knowledge of the assault also can have a tremendous impact on the victim's family and significant others. Even if others are not aware of her rape, they usually are sensitive to the change in her behavior after the assault—i.e., avoidance, crying, fears, change of residence, and so on. The victim's family and friends are a vital element of her existing support system, and their incorporation into the treatment process can be quite helpful. On the other hand, this same support system may harbor many of the traditional societal myths about rape, and therefore the enlistment of help from family and others may backfire, should, for example, the family choose to blame the victim for her own rape or others believe that she was not raped but participating voluntarily in a consensual sex act.

Section 3 of the form outlines the solution to this dilemma. Informing the client of the risks and benefits of incorporating family members in therapy protects her rights and again helps her maintain control.

Section 4 explains the client's rights regarding terminating therapy with her therapist. Many sexual assault victims verbalize that their therapist was insensitive to them. Since therapists are subject to the same myths about sexual assault as are the rest of our society, it is not surprising that they might verbalize these to their rape-victim clients and thus appear insensitive to them. If a therapist believes that he or she has a specific bias regarding sexual assault victims, he or she should refer the client from the very first. This can be a difficult task for the therapist, because it involves admitting a bias to oneself and the possibility that one cannot be of assistance to all clients. A client's verbalized dislike for her therapist can also prove problematic to the therapist, because basically therapists want to be liked by their client and to feel that they are helping them. It is however, the right of the client to express her feelings regarding the therapist, to terminate if she wishes, and to be referred to another therapist.

The confidential nature of the client-therapist communication is discussed in Section 5 of the form. Victims who press charges against the offender face the risk of having their therapy records subpoenaed. This issue needs to be made explicit to the client, because it may be a factor in her decisions to seek treatment and to press charges.

The length and cost of therapy and the client's responsibilities regarding appointments are discussed in Section 6.

Irrespective of the amount of detail and thoroughness of any consent form, further issues may arise from the client that need further clarification. A blank section at this point in the consent form allows documentation of these issues, so that the therapist and client are protected regarding consent for these as well.

The signing of the consent form (Section 7) should be witnessed.

Normally, this is done after the witness has heard the consent form read to the client. In cases of rape—where such knowledge could be a further source of embarrassment—it is more prudent to have the witness simply indicate observation of the signing.

No matter how detailed the description of therapy is, the only real way to insure that the client knows what treatment will be like is to actually have her experience it. After two treatment sessions, it is therefore advisable for the therapist and client to reread the consent and resign it, since there is minimal doubt at that time regarding what the client is consenting to.

Finally, the therapist continually needs feedback regarding the effectiveness of the rape crisis counseling. The final portion of Section 7 allows the client to provide this.

The consent form and the therapeutic interchange are focused on helping the client regain control over her life. They should also, however, serve as a model to help the client interact with people and institutions. For example, victims usually will come into contact with the medical profession; following a sexual assault, they need to be examined for injury, venereal disease, and pregnancy. It would therefore be helpful for the therapist to discuss the victim's rights and how to maintain them in interacting with the medical profession, since the principle is identical—consent while maintaining as much control as possible.

A number of victims elect to prosecute the perpetrator. The majority of victims describe this interaction with the criminal justice system as traumatic. To help the client prepare for court the therapist should have knowledge of (1) the state laws regarding sexual assault, (2) the availability of rape crisis centers providing advocates to help the client prepare for court, and (3) the impact a court proceeding may have on her attempts to regain control. Once again, the best way of teaching the client about her rights within the judicial system is to model that type of interaction during the client-therapist interactions.

Child Victims

The sexual abuse of children is a distressing social issue. It is neither a new nor rare phenomenon. The exact incidence of child sexual abuse is unknown, but our best estimates range from 100,000 to 1 million children sexually abused yearly (Gager & Schurr, 1976). The emotional, physical, and legal stress on the child and the family can be overwhelming.

The effect of sexual abuse on a child varies as a function of four major factors. The first factor is the nature of the relationship between offender and victim. Some incidents of sexual abuse committed by a stranger are less traumatic to a child that those committed by a relative. Parents typically are supportive of the child when the offender is a stranger. They believe the child's report of abuse, and hold the offender completely responsible for the assault. If they overreact to the assault, it is generally because they believe they have not adequately protected their child. The parents' anger is directed at the perpetrator, not the child.

However, when the child is the victim of intrafamily sexual abuse, repercussions to the child are more devastating. For example, when a daughter reports being sexually abused by her father to her mother or an authority, she is often overcome with guilt if they blame her for the incest. When the courts take action to protect the child, it is often the child who is removed from the home, not the assaultive father. This is very confusing to a child, who views her removal from her own home as punishment rather than protection. Also, the removal of the child or father from the home may have severe emotional implications for the child who may, for future emotional wellbeing, require that this relationship be normalized through therapeutic rather than legal means. Incestuous sexual abuse thus is more traumatic to the child and more disruptive of the family.

The second factor is the degree of violence used against the child. If the child's assault was quite brutal and painful and her physical injuries were severe, the short- and long-term effects would be more serious than otherwise (MacFarlane, 1978).

The third factor is the frequency of the sexual abuse, and the more complex problems that develop when abuse is chronic. In incestuous relationships extending over months and years, the offending father or stepfather is frequently able— due to his powerful, authoritative role in the family—to convince the victim that the secret of the incestuous relationship must be kept from others. Furthermore, these sexual interactions between the child and the aggressor may be the only situations where the victim receives attention from a parent, and the victim herself is thus sometimes reluctant to report the incidents and disrupt this inappropriate yet sole opportunity for parental contact.

Unfortunately, when long-standing incestuous relationships become public knowledge, social agencies, schools, and family members begin treating the victim as if she were an adult with knowledge and understanding of the inappropriateness of incest. The public environment points out how wrong the involvement was especially since "she allowed it to continue so long." The net result is that even greater guilt is placed upon the innocent victim as opposed to the aggressor.

The final factor is a facet of the reaction of the child's parents, siblings, and friends on learning that the child has been sexually assaulted. Parents typically feel quite guilty on learning of their child's assault. They wonder if they could have done something different that would have prevented it. They also become extremely angry, because an assault on their child is almost like an assault on them. When parental reactions are extremely excessive the child absorbs the parental message that the assault was a devastating event for the victim. As a result, the child's reaction, which initially may have been minimal, can become markedly exaggerated as she incorporates her parents' attitudes. In other situations parents' zealous attempts to locate and punish the perpetrator can divert parental attention and concern for the child.

In cases of intrafamily sexual abuse this issue is even more complicated. If the mother is appropriately supportive of the child, holds the father responsible, and demands that he be removed from the home to protect the victim, the mother may at the same time be jeopardizing the financial stability of the family, since typically the father is the sole source of financial support in these families. The nonabusing parent, on learning of the possible abuse of her child by her husband, is faced with a dilemma: Whom should she believe, blame, and support? Some parents choose to blame the child, which increases her guilt and shame and traumatizes her further. If a decision is made to remove the child from the home by a Child Welfare Agency, the separation from her family and friends can be devastating to the child. Irrespective of which final decisions are made, in cases of incest the effects on family members can be devastating.

The behavioral manifestations of sexual abuse on a child are similar to those in an adult, although their expression may be somewhat different. Some children regress to earlier developmental stages—i.e., they may exhibit eneuresis, thumb sucking, fear of the dark, of strangers, or of new places. Eating and sleeping patterns may be disturbed. The child may wish to avoid school and friends and males in general (Burgess, Groth, Holmstrom, & Sgroi, 1978).

Treatment for child abuse victims and their families is crisis counseling similar to that described earlier for adult victims, with the modification that the means of allowing the child to talk about the assault must be adapted to the child's developmental level.

Burgess et al. (1978) further note the following modifications: (1) The child may be a reluctant client. She is frequently brought in for help without having requested it, which may be a breach of her rights. (2) The child may be uninformed or misinformed by her parents as to why she is seeing the therapist. (3) The child may not feel that she has a problem needing treatment. These are three critical issues to consider in working with child victims, from the viewpoint of both the client's rights and therapeutic needs. Other relevant issues concern (1) the age at which a child can give informed consent, (2) how to obtain informed consent, and (3) the language used in consent forms.

The U.S. Department of Health and Human Services has ruled that proxy consent is insufficient when research subjects are seven years of age or older (Levy & Brackbill, 1979). A task force of the American Psychiatric Association has developed a model law regarding confidentiality, a portion of which mandates that twelve years of age be established as the minimum consent age. Therapists should check with their states to determine if these model laws or others have been adopted.

If the child is of the age to give consent, the issue becomes what the most appropriate means is to present consent information to the child. Levy and Brackbill (1979) describe the use of a brief documentary videotape as an aid in describing potential benefits and risks to children. If a written consent form is used, it is imperative that it be written in a style that the child can understand.

The accompanying consent form for child victims is a model which was developed in crisis counseling with children around twelve years of age. The goals of the form are to (1) explain what treatment involves, (2) outline the benefits and risks in the treatment, and (3) discuss the role the parents will play in treatment. The basic issues—involving confidentiality, feelings about the therapist, reconsent, and so on—are similar to those discussed under the section on adult victims, and therefore will not be repeated here.

As with the adult victim, the guiding therapeutic principle with the child victim is to assist her in gaining control over her proposed therapy.

Consent-to-Treatment Form: Child Sexual Assault Victims

1. Some children feel guilty or responsible after they have been sexually abused. My parent or guardian knows that I am not guilty and wants to make sure that I don't feel that way. That is why they have brought me to the counselor. Some children also have other feelings about themselves after an assault which they didn't have before the assault. I know that I will be talking with a counselor about my feelings about what happened. When we talk I might feel a little bit funny inside because I've never talked with a counselor about this before, but the counselor's job is to help me, so if I feel funny I just tell the counselor that what we're talking about is making me feel funny.

2. I know that the counselor may want to talk with my parent(s) or guardian. I know that if I wish to have family members take part in my therapy that it will probably make me feel better; however, having them present may also cause me to be upset. For example, they might talk about feelings that I didn't know they had. The final decision as to whether they will be included will be left up to me. Furthermore, I know that I don't have to tell anyone that I am in counseling.

The counselor may ask me or my parent(s) or guardian to take certain tests or to keep records of how I am feeling. This information helps the counselor keep close watch on how I'm doing. Keeping track of such things, however, may make me or my parent(s) more upset. Although this rarely happens, if it does occur I am to call my counselor, who will provide help to me as soon as possible. I also know that I can decide not to keep such records and will still receive counseling.

Whatever I or my parent(s) tell the counselor will not be told to anyone else unless I or my parent(s) ask the doctor to tell someone else.

If I feel funny or upset in between the times when I see the counselor, I or my parent(s) can call the counselor and he/she will help us.

If this treatment doesn't seem to make me feel better, my counselor, parent(s), and I will decide whether another form of treatment should be used. If I wish to stop treatment at any time, I can.

If I feel that my counselor isn't helping me or if I don't like my counselor, then I will tell my parent(s) and they will ask the counselor to send us to another counselor.

I know that I will come to see my counselor for _____ minutes, _____ days a week for about _____ weeks. Part of the time the counselor will talk to me and part of the time he/she will talk to my parent(s) or all of us together. My parent(s) will pay the doctor _____ per hour for this counseling.

If I have any questions about this treatment, I will ask them now and the doctor will answer them.

Therapist/Counselor   _____
Patient   _____
Parent(s)   _____
Witness   _____
Date:_____ Therapist's Phone #: _____

Reconsenting to the consent form after 2 therapy sessions:

If I have any questions about my treatment, I have asked or written those questions in the space below and they have been answered.

Therapist/Counselor   _____
Patient   _____
Parent(s)   _____
Witness   _____
Date:_____

Statement on completion of treatment. I sincerely wish to know if I have been accurate in my description of what this counseling would involve, what you were expected to do, the problems encountered. Were these problems handled properly? Should anything be changed about this counseling?

Therapist/Counselor   _____
Patient   _____
Patent(s)   _____
Witness   _____
Date:_____

Section 1 of the consent informs the child that she is not responsible for the sexual assault. Furthermore, it defines why her parents have brought her to see a counselor. The type of treatment is described and the child is informed of a possible risk—feeling "funny" (a word that a twelve-year-old can relate to for becoming more upset). The child is given the ultimate decision regarding whether she wants to involve herself in counseling. Her rights are preserved, and she maintains control. She also learns that obtaining her voluntary consent is mandatory before an adult (the counselor) can interact with her. Since sexual assault involves an adult forcing an interaction either verbally or physically, the child frequently loses trust in adults. The counselor must establish himself or herself as an adult who can be trusted to help and protect the child by giving control to her as to whether their interaction will continue.

Section 2 of the consent informs the child of the benefits and risks of incorporating the parent or other family members in therapy. When the child is an incest victim she is especially at risk if her parents are included in therapy, since discussion of her sexual abuse in her parents' presence may upset her further and disrupt intrafamily relationships further. On the other hand this relationship has already been disrupted, and for it to remain intact counseling is necessary. The therapist's dilemma stems from the fact that the best form of therapy includes counseling the victim *and* her family members. It is important to inform the client of this issue and then leave the final decision to her.

Sexual Offenders

Only 13.3 percent of individuals charged with rape are found guilty of the crime and incarcerated. Therefore, the majority of sex offenders are residing in their communities, residing there without benefit of treatment. Emphasis should be focused on their receiving treatment.

The psychological treatment needs of rapists and child molesters have received minimal attention. Even the very idea of treatment for sex offenders is sometimes seen as an alien concept. The high incidence of sexual aggressive behavior, the low incidence of conviction, and high recidivism rates, however, point to the need for treatment programs.

For the past three and one-half years the authors have been conducting a clinical research project involving the assessment and treatment of sexual perpetrators. The project is presently operated as an outpatient clinic at the New York State Psychiatric Institute in New York City. To become a client-subject, the individual must be (1) a voluntary participant and (2) capable of giving informed consent. If there are any questions regarding the client's ability to give informed consent—for example, if the person is on parole and it was recommended that he receive treatment—he is referred to a client advocate who, with the help of a community advisory board, determines if the client is indeed under coercion to receive treatment and is therefore not a voluntary client. If the client is voluntary and able to give informed consent, the consent form, "Assessment of Sexual Interests" is read to the client in the presence of an auditor witness, after which he reads it to himself.

Consent-to-Treatment Form: Assessment of Sexual Interests

1. I understand that I am being asked to participate in a research project specifically to evaluate my sexual interests. I will be extensively questioned regarding my past history with specific details being asked about my sexual behavior. I will also be asked to fill out numerous questionnaires, paper and pencil tests that explore my general emotional state as well as my sexual behavior and interests. I will be asked to keep track of my sexual thoughts, how frequently they occur, and the nature of these thoughts. During the course of such interviews, questioning or recording, I may become anxious, nervous, depressed, or uncomfortable because the investigators are gaining knowledge about my sexual interests, sexual interests that are rather personal.

My sexual interests will also be measured by recording my erection response while I look at explicit sexual films or listen to sexual material. This sexual material will be very explicit and will depict a man and a woman having sexual intercourse, a male having sexual intercourse with a woman against her will, or a male physically assaulting a woman. While I observe these sexual materials, my erection will be measured by a small penile transducer, an apparatus that I place around my penis in the privacy of the laboratory. This device only records my penis size and cannot hurt me physically. This device is thoroughly cleaned with an antiseptic to kill germs, such as those that cause venereal disease and other infections. Although it is remotely possible to get diseases from the device, this has never occurred during the 9 years we have used it.

2. Because I haven't had erection measures recorded before and because the investigators will know my erection responses, I may feel uncomfortable about such recording. I may worry about whether I am going to get an erection or not, or be uncomfortable in the laboratory surroundings. I subsequently may feel anxious, uncomfortable, depressed, nervous, or angry. Although these symptoms are possible, they occur to a significant degree in fewer than 5 subjects out of 100.

My fears about sexual performance in the laboratory may cause me to have fears about my sexual performance outside of the laboratory after such measures are taken. I may develop difficulties getting an erection or may be unable to get an erection at all because of the measurement experience. Although the investigators have not seen this during the measurement of over 250 subjects' erection responses, it is still possible.

Should I develop any emotional reaction to such measurements, I understand that the investigators are highly trained in the treatment of anxiety, depression, fears about whether I will or will not get an erection, or the actual inability to develop an erection following the measures. An investigator will be at hand at all times for treatment of these problems, should they develop during the study or afterwards.

3. The benefits of such an assessment are that it will be able to identify exactly which (if any) treatment is needed because of my sexual interests and arousal. The results of such an assessment will be communicated to me at the end of this study. Alternative means of evaluation include interviews and psychological testing similar to that described above but without the direct measurement of my erection response. I may wish to choose that form of evaluation if I have excessive concerns about measurement of my erection response during this study.

At any time during any stage of my assessment, I may voluntarily withdraw my consent regarding this study and withdraw from the study without penalty of any kind or prejudice to my future medical care.

4. If I have any side effects during or after this study, I am to call any of the therapists whose telephone numbers are listed below.

Therapist's name and phone # _____

Co-Therapists's name and phone #_____

5. The confidentiality of your records is of extreme concern to the investigators. The researchers want to make it very safe for you to participate in this evaluation-treatment. A number of safeguards have been taken, including:

   a. Don't tell anyone connected with your evaluation-treatment *about the specifics* of any illegal act (rape). If you have raped someone or anyone suspects you have, don't tell us any of the particulars about it—for example, don't tell us when it allegedly occurred, what time of day, where, who the victim was, what she looked like. *Not telling us any information about a possible illegal act is your best protection.*

   b. Any information you give us, by telling us or by the numerous tests and penile recordings made, will go into your chart. You will be given a special identification number. All your information can be recognized by that code number, so don't tell anyone what it is unless you want them to get or give you that information. The evaluation-treatment team takes your name and your identification number and sends them to a special place outside of the United States. It is extremely unlikely that this material (your name and identification number) could be retrieved from outside of the United States, but it is remotely possible and therefore a possible risk to you.

   c. If you tell someone what your number is, that is giving them possible access to the information in your chart. All your testing and erection measures in that chart may be damaging to you, so be careful.

   d. Your records with your code number (not your name) will be carefully locked up. If the courts ask us or the hospital for your records, we will tell them we can't give them unless *you* tell us you want us to give them to the courts and *by telling us what your identification number is.* If you tell your identification number to someone, you are also saying it's alright for them to know everything in your chart. Since your erection measures may indicate that you are a rapist, don't tell your number to the law unless you want to give them proof that you may be a rapist.

6. I understand I have some responsibilities as a participant in this and any further study I give my consent to. These include:

   a. If I can't come in for my appointments, I am to call the therapists above and tell them so, at least 12 hours in advance. Failure to do this on three occasions may lead to my being dropped from participation in this study, even though I want to continue.

   b. A specific way in and out of the hospital will be described to me. *Failure to follow that route once* may lead to my being dropped from participation, even though I want to continue.

   7. The psychologists and psychiatrists involved in this and further studies have responsibilities as well, including

   a. to give me treatment that they believe to be just as good as the best treatment available for the problem described in the Consent Form,

   b. to explain anything about the evaluation-treatment or Consent Forms that I have questions about, and

   c. to write in how often and how long any evaluation-treatment is that I consent to in the space at the bottom of each Consent Form for that.

Should I request a formal report of the results of these studies, however, this report will be advanced only to me. In this fashion, I will know the exact results of my assessment, and can make a decision on my own as to whether to advance that information to any third party.

   8. *Questions and Comments Section:* If I have any questions about the assessment, I have written in these questions in the following space and discussed them to my satisfaction with the person in charge of my evaluation listed below. My signature indicates I have read and understood all of the above.

Signature of client _____

   I understand that to insure the confidentiality of the subject's assessment and/or treatment, I as a parent or guardian *will not* be provided with any information regarding the results of the subject's evaluation, treatment, or ongoing contact of any type with the research project. This means that once the subject has entered the research project, I will not be provided any information regarding how he is doing. I will not even be told whether he is still in the research project or not.

Person in Charge
of my Evaluation: _____Client/Subject:_____
Auditor/Witness: _____Date: _____

   The consent form is divided into eight sections. Section 1 gives a detailed description of what the assessment consists of and its potential risks—i.e., the client's becoming nervous, depressed, and so on. Our particular program evaluates a client's progress in part by assessing his arousal by deviant sexual acts, such as rape and child molestation. This psychophysiologic assessment is effected by the client wearing a penile measurement device. Since various anxieties can develop, these risks are outlined for the client.

   Section 2 describes the impact that assessment may have on the client's sexual functioning outside the laboratory. Since client-subjects have not undergone measurement of sexual arousal previously, a risk involves potential negative feelings generated by their preformance or lack there-of in the laboratory. In our experience we have noted this to occur in less than 5 percent of the subjects. It is the client's right to know that this may occur, and that should he experience any sequelae the investigators will treat any such problems.

The benefit of the assessment to the client are outlined in Section 3. The subject would be receiving what is to our knowledge one of the most valid assessment techniques available; but should the client not wish to avail himself of this form of assessment, alternative means of evaluation are explained.

The client has the right to withdraw consent at any point in the assessment. This can present a dilemma to the therapist who knows that the client has deviant sexual arousal and is capable of engaging in sexual aggressive behavior. On the one hand the therapist will want to insist that the client continue the assessment and receive treatment, while on the other hand it is the client's right to discontinue participation without penalty. In addition, it is the therapist-researcher's responsibility to ensure that the client is aware of other referral sources. This issue will be complicated even further if the client informs the therapist that he intends to assault a specific individual. The California Supreme Court ruled (Stone, 1976) that it is the obligation of a psychotherapist, once he or she has determined that the client presents serious danger to another individual, to take reasonable care to protect the intended victim against such danger.

Rada (1978) in discussing the applicability of this ruling to therapists who treat rapists, states, "When treating a rapist whom the therapist believes represents a clear danger to a specific potential victim, the therapist incurs the responsibility of warning the victim or using other methods (e.g., commitment) to protect the patient from acting out in a manner which could be harmful to himself or others" (p. 376).

Roth and Meisel (1977) deal with this issue by advocating that the therapist at the start inform the client that in the event he should represent a danger a warning will be given to the third party. This agreement can be formalized by way of a consent form.

Confidentiality is discussed in Section 5 of the form; the issue of confidentiality with sex offenders is particularly crucial because of the nature of information regarding possible past criminal offenses that they may have committed but not been apprehended for.

The issue of confidentiality of records has posed a perplexing problem to both individual therapists and institutions. Rada (1978) notes that some therapists and institutions keep two sets of records—one for their personal files, the other in public files. Some therapists have even stopped keeping formal written records. Further guidelines need to be established to help therapists and institutions deal with issues relating to confidentiality.

In the authors' clinical research project confidentiality of data is protected by assigning a number to each subject. When a subject enters the project, he is read the consent form. The subject is then asked to read the consent form to himself. If the subject agrees to participate, the therapist-researcher then assigns the subject a number. The subject signs the consent form and writes his number next to his name. The therapist-researcher then cuts off the bottom of the consent form (which contains the subject's name and number) and mails that portion of the consent form to a person outside of the United States who has agreed to guard the confidentiality of subjects' names and numbers. The therapist-researchers do not keep a list of clients' names or try to remember the names that correspond with the numbers. The client's number is written on a file and all clinical interview materials, lab data, and paper and pencil tests are placed in the client's numbered file. When the client is seen for assessment or therapy, he is asked for his number; the therapist or lab technician then pulls the numbered file, and that day's therapy notes or data sheets are placed in the client's file. Should the client forget his number, the therapist then asks the client for his name and contacts the person outside of this country holding the names and numbers and requests the number that goes with the name, assuring the contact that no authorities have requested the records.

Using this method, should a court request information about a particular individual it would be impossible for us to release it unless the client provided his number.

Furthermore, we advance evaluation and treatment reports only to the client. Should he desire to share that report with a third party, it then becomes his responsibility to do so. Finally, federal law prohibits our research personnel from being compelled to testify in any court in the country regarding information given us by any client-subject in this program.

At the authors' present location concern was expressed by hospital staff about the possible risk that having sex offenders on the premises might present to them. The authors have established a system in which offenders are instructed to call the therapist from a pay telephone located near the hospital prior to their appointment. The therapist or technician then meets the client at the entrance and escorts him to and from the research-therapy unit. The client is never left unattended while in the hospital. If the client fails to follow the entry procedure or is found wandering around the hospital he is subject to being terminated from the project.

The therapist's responsibilities are outlined in Section 7 of the consent form. The client's rights are best protected when he is informed about the nature of the assessment procedure, can elect alternative means of assessment, and is given the therapist's best available treatment.

The remainder of the consent form is for questions the client has and for signatures of client, witness, and therapist.

At the completion of the assessment, recommendations are made to the client regarding therapy. Before a specific form of therapy is instituted the client signs a consent form for that form of therapy. For example, if a client needs three components of therapy—(1) therapy to decrease his deviant sexual arousal, (2) therapy to increase his nondeviant sexual arousal, and (3) social skills training—the client signs a separate consent form for each component of therapy, which outlines the benefits and risks associated with that component.

As mentioned previously, our program includes a client advocate and an advisory board comprised of professional and lay members of the community. These individuals protect the rights of the client-subject by insuring that he is a volunteer client and is knowledgeable of alternative forms of treatment. Prior to entering treatment the client meets with the client advocate, who discusses the treatment with him. If the advocate questions the client's ability to give informed consent or the form of treatment he or she takes these issues to the advisory board, which then decides whether the client should be involved in that form of treatment.

Historically, issues of informed consent have focused on the client-therapist relationship. However, in working with sexual perpetrators who are potentially dangerous, staff should be informed of the potential risks to them. Although we have never had a staff member assaulted by a client in our nine years of working with sexual perpetrators, the potential risk still exists. Therefore, all staff members are requested to sign a consent form prior to being hired.

Consent Form: Staff Participation in Research Related to *The Evaluation and Treatment of Sexual Aggressives*

1. As a staff contributor to the above-named project, the following are risks involved in my participation in this project. I may be working with sexual aggressives, near them, or with their data, all of which may pose dangers to me.

The subjects themselves will be sexual aggressives, some of whom have used force against their female or male victims. By working with them, I run a risk of being raped, injured, or verbally threatened by them. Although this has never happened during the last 9 years that Dr. _____ has worked with over 250 sexual deviates, many of whom have identical sexual problems, it is still remotely possible. To prevent the occurrence of such an incident, I am to (a) maintain a professional relationship with the subjects at all times, (b) never identify myself by last name or if I do, to never reveal my home address, (c) never reveal the last names or addresses of others associated with the research unit or at the hospital, (d) never enter with the subject a room that is lockable from the inside, (e) never participate in any portion of the research that I feel uncomfortable with, and (f) notify Drs. _____ immediately of any event involving the above.

2. Equally as dangerous is my working with the subject's data. Possible knowledge of the subject's data or history may lead to my being subpoenaed to court, with an attempt by the prosecuting attorneys to uncover information about the patient's specific unlawful acts. Relaying such information would be dangerous for the subject. To prevent such disclosure, I understand I am to (a) never ask a patient about the specifics of any illegal act such as rape (e.g., what address were you at, what did the victim look like, how did you hold the victim down, what specifically did she say?), (b) never attempt to learn the subject's identification number, (c) report any possible breakdown in the data concealment process to Drs. _____ _____, (d) read subject Consent Form #1, "Assessment of Sexual Interests," and (e) tell no one information about any subject or about any of the conduct of the research project.

3. If subpoenaed into court I will be provided legal counsel only to the extent provided any Psychiatric Institute employee, which is *very limited.* In other words, I will have to provide most of my own legal counsel if subpoenaed. In the nine years that Dr. _____ has worked with sexual deviates, many of whom were charged with sexual crimes, such subpoena into court to reveal such information *has never occurred.* Still it remains a possibility. The best protection is to never ask for such information.

4. During the course of my involvement with this research project, there are further psychological and social complications that could occur. I may become depressed, nervous, upset, or anxious during my interaction with the subjects. Colleagues and associates may view my participation in the project as a reflection of my own preoccupation with sex or perverse sexual topics. I may receive social pressure to stop this type of work due to its content. Although these complications occur in less than 5 cases per 100, they are still possible. If any of these problems develop, the investigators are responsible for arranging psychological counseling if I desire same.

5. Furthermore, if I should desire to withdraw from this project because of any of the above consequences of my participation or any unexpected consequences, I may withdraw at any time without penalty and nothing will appear on my work record reflecting same.

Questions and Comments: If I have any questions about this study, I have written them in the space below and discussed them to my satisfaction with the research staff member listed below. The comments listed below reflect my knowledge of what I am consenting to. My signature indicates I have read all of this form and understood it, and have read the subject's Consent Form #1.

Research Staff Contributor:_____
Date: _____
Research Staff Member
Explaining Consent Procedure: _____
Auditor/Witness: _____

This consent form is divided into six sections. Section 1 outlines the risks to the staff members and provides guidelines for interacting with clients. Section 2 describes the legal risks involved in handling client's data. Here staff members are given instructions on how to interact with clients relevant to their data.

Section 3 defines the legal support that the hospital will provide to the staff member in the event that he or she is subpoenaed. Since the hospital is limited in the legal counsel it can provide, the staff member is advised of this. The staff member is advised in Section 4 of the possible psychological risks to him or her. Frequently family or peer group members are curious about why an individual would want to work with sexual perpetrators. This curiosity can be manifested, for example, as ridicule, hostility, or fear for the safety of the staff member. Should the staff member develop psychological problems that are work-related, psychological counseling will be arranged.

The staff member is free to terminate employment with the project at any time. If the termination is related to psychological stress as a function of the work, efforts will be made to help the employee find other employment.

Section 6 is for recording any questions the staff member has, and for signatures.

In summary, in working with sexual perpetrators focus is placed on (1) informed consent, (2) dangerousness, (3) confidentiality and privileged communication, and (4) informed consent for program staff.

Conclusion

Mental health care professionals have been under increasing pressure to attend to issues involving protecting the rights of their clients. This chapter has reviewed some of the client rights' issues for sexual assault victims and offenders. The intent here has been to share with the reader some of the issues the authors have dealt with in their own practice and solutions to the problems that have arisen in working with both victims and offenders. The consent forms provided are meant to serve as a guideline or model for health care providers who work in research or clinical settings.

Looking to the future, the authors feel that greater emphasis should be placed on client-advocate committees and peer-therapist review committees. Clients are not always aware of their rights regarding treatment, and it is often difficult for them to confront their own therapists about issues involving their rights. A system needs to be developed whereby clients are provided with information concerning their rights prior to entering into a contractual treatment agreement. And greater emphasis needs to be placed on the use of peer review boards and continuing education for mental health professionals.

References

BECKER, J., & ABEL, G. The treatment of victims of sexual assault. *Quarterly Journal of Corrections,* 1977, *1,* 38–42.

BURGESS, A., GROTH, N. HOLMSTROM, L., & SGROI, S. *Sexual assault of children and adolescents.* Lexington, Mass.: Lexington Books, 1978.

BURGESS, A., & HOLMSTROM, L. *Rape: Victims of crisis.* Bowie, Md.: Robert J. Brady, 1974.

BURGESS, A., HOLMSTROM, L., & McCAUSLAND, M. Counseling young victims and their families. In A. Burgess, N. Groth, L. Holmstrom, and S. Sgroi (Eds.). *Sexual assault of children and adolescents.* Lexington, Mass.: Lexington Books, 1978.

CURTIS, L., Victimization: Intolerant people, intolerant statistics. Paper presented at the Sixth Annual Symposium on Justice and Behavioral Science, University of Alabama, Tuscaloosa, Ala., January, 1975.

FOX, S., & SCHERL, D. Patterns of response among victims of rape. *American Journal of Orthopsychiatry,* 1970, *40,* 503–511.

GAGER, N., & SCHURR, C. *Sexual assault: Confronting rape in America.* New York: Grosset & Dunlap, 1976.

HILBERMAN, E. *The rape victim.* Washington, D.C.: American Psychiatric Association, 1976.

LEVY, M., & BRACKBILL, Y. Informed consent: Getting the message across to kids. *APA Monitor,* March 1979, 3.

MACFARLANE, K. Sexual abuse of children. In J. Chapman and M. Gates (Eds.), *The victimization of women.* Beverly Hills, Calif.: Sage Publications, 1978.

NASS, D. *The rape victim.* Iowa: Kendall/Hunt, 1977.

RADA, R. Legal aspects in treating rapists. *Criminal Justice and Behavior,* 1978, 5, 369–378.

ROTH, L., & MEISEL, A. Dangerousness, confidentiality, and the duty to warn. *American Journal of Psychiatry,* 1977, *134,* 508–511.

STONE, A. A. The *Tarasoff* decisions: Suing psychotherapists to safeguard society. *Harvard Law Review,* 1976, *90,* 358–378.

CHAPTER 9

Client Rights in Alcohol Treatment Programs

Linda C. Sobell
Mark B. Sobell

THIS CHAPTER ADDRESSES the protection and welfare of individuals who seek treatment for alcohol-related problems. While some client-rights issues are applicable across several client populations, others are relevant only to clients who seek treatment, rehabilitation, or evaluation services for alcohol-related problems. (Hereafter, these individuals will be referred to as alcohol clients.) Also, since drinking frequently gives rise to legal problems, the preservation of client rights in treatment sometimes generates ethical and legal conflicts. These and other issues will be discussed at length in this chapter.

Historically, the protection of client rights had its origins in the medical profession, where physicians are bound by professionally imposed ethical standards (e.g., privileged communication between doctor and patient). When other professional groups (e.g., psychologists, social workers) began providing mental health services, they followed the model of the medical profession by enacting their own professional and ethical codes. Unfortunately, the enforcement of ethical standards by professionals is a difficult task. For example, the process of deciding whether ethical violations have occurred is often a subjective one, and when sanctions are imposed for professional misconduct they are often less than punitive.

In order to more assuredly protect client rights, states have enacted licensing laws that (1) restrict the practice of certain professions (e.g., medicine, psychology, nursing, etc.) to qualified practitioners and (2) establish review boards that have the power to withdraw or deny licensure for those professionals who violate ethical standards. In the mental health field, however, similar restriction and review of clinical practice have been compounded by the diverse backgrounds of service providers as well as the advent of paraprofessionals, who claim no specific professional affiliation. As a result, in many states paraprofessionals have not been regulated in the provision of services by any peer group or licensing provisions. Efforts to deal with this problem have included enacting state and federal regulations governing *everyone* (including administrative and secretarial staff) who encounters clients in therapeutic settings. In summary, without regulations or professional accountability there can be little enforcement or protection of client rights other than through lawsuits—which are not only expensive but rarely pursued by the kinds of client whose rights are likely to be violated.

A Historical Look at the Alcohol Field

A short discourse on the special nature and treatment of alcohol problems will aid the reader in understanding some of the recent state and federal guidelines and regulations protecting alcohol clients' rights. Historically, our society has had diverse beliefs about alcoholics' drinking behavior. For instance, excessive drinking has at times been considered morally corrupt and illegal (the latter usually resulting in incarceration). Others, however, have viewed alcoholism as a physical disease—an illness and a pervasive health problem. Currently, the specific etiology of alcoholism is unknown; consequently, there remain competing theories and opinions about how to label and treat individuals so afflicted.

EARLY RECOGNITION OF THE NEED FOR CONFIDENTIALITY IN TREATMENT

The mid-1930s witnessed the first successful organized effort to help alcoholics—the establishment of Alcoholics Anonymous (AA). Interestingly, at the time of AA's conception, the founders obviously had concerns about confidentiality, as reflected in the title of the organization as well as in its practices. The use of the word "anonymous," for example, was probably not fortuitous, but rather reflected a concern about societal attitudes regarding people with drinking problems.

Societal ambivalence about the labeling of persons with drinking problems forms the basis for the stigmatizing image of alcoholics as "no-good, weak-willed bums who can't handle liquor yet can't stay away from it and should be locked up." These and similar stereotypic impressions and attitudes have probably led to a marked hesitancy on the part of individuals with alcohol problems to seek treatment. Moreover, when such individuals do seek treatment, they are often fearful that information about their treatment will become known to others and result in negative consequences.

Less than fifty years ago the only treatment for alcoholics was provided by physicians, who usually limited their treatment to the physical complications of the illness—alcohol withdrawal symptoms and organic damage. Psychotherapy, as we know it today, was not provided. In an effort to provide more humane treatment for persons with drinking problems, the American Medical Association in 1956 declared that alcoholism is a disease (AMA, 1956), and recognized hospital treatment of alcoholics as legitimate. Following this initial recognition, there has been extensive development of a network of treatment agencies and resources for individuals with alcohol problems. These have ranged from outpatient alcohol programs in mental health centers to private alcohol-treatment programs to halfway houses operated and supported by recovered alcoholics.

Many of the alcohol treatment programs have not followed the traditional "medical model" in their structure, however, and are not always directed by licensed professionals. In fact, as a result of the early influence of AA, the paraprofessional concept is very pervasive in the alcohol treatment field. This brings us back to a point made earlier: Many service providers in the alcohol treatment field today are not bound by any professional codes or explicit ethical standards. Furthermore, since some alcoholism counselors have had little formal education and training in their specialty, their exposure to and understanding of professional issues and problems such as client rights are limited and sometimes lacking. This problem was in part resolved in 1975, when the Public Health Service of the U.S. Department of Health, Education, and Welfare (HEW) issued general provisions for ensuring confidentiality, "Confidentiality of Alcohol and Drug Abuse Patient Records" (42 CFR Part 2, [*Federal Register*, 1975a]). These regulations apply to the handling of all client treatment activities and client records by all individuals and programs that receive any federal support (direct or indirect) and are involved in education, training, treatment, rehabilitation, or research relating to alcohol or drug abuse.

REGULATORY BODIES FOR SAFEGUARDING CLIENT RIGHTS

The federal confidentiality regulations and rules are quite comprehensive; when one considers the potential and unchecked abuses that might occur without such regulations, the need for them becomes obvious. The federal regulations clearly delineate the conditions and circumstances under which disclosure of information is allowed, and the penalties for those violations that occur. (Violations are punishable by fines of up to five hundred dollars for the first offense and not more than five thousand dollars for each subsequent offense ["Confidentiality," 42 CFR Part 2, § 2.14(a)—FR, 1975a].)

It is important to note that even though the federal government has issued these regulations and established penalties for violation of confidentiality, decisions as to whether client rights have been violated are the province of the courts. Therefore, until these regulations are tested in the courts the actual degree to which they can and will be enforced is uncertain. Moreover, the number of cases of violation of client rights that are taken to court is probably minuscule compared to the number of actual violations that occur. Finally, a paramount need for ensuring observation of client rights is educating clients about the extent of their rights, what constitutes violation of those rights, and, most important, what avenues can be pursued if violation occurs.

Two additional means of safeguarding client rights have recently evolved. The first involves outside accreditation or program standards. Many agencies receive some portion of their revenues from local, state, or federal governmental agencies; these governing bodies can exercise control over the quality of care and preservation of client rights in programs they support. Along these same lines, many treatment agencies are now seeking reimbursement from third-party payers (e.g., Medicaid, Medicare, insurance companies), and many of these third-party payers are mandating that treatment programs be accredited in order to be eligible for reimbursement. The best-known accreditation body is the Joint Commission on Accreditation of Hospitals (JCAH), which has established guidelines for reviewing and accrediting alcohol treatment programs. Also, government-supported programs are usually site visited or audited by their respective funding agencies to assess whether they are in compliance with state and federal regulatory and funding standards. These reviews include examination of whether client rights are being preserved (e.g., reviewing client charts, speaking with clients).

The second avenue for protecting client welfare involves certification of paraprofessional counselors in the alcohol and drug fields. At present, such efforts are just beginning, and certification is neither federally mandated nor mandatory across states. In some states, however, counselors are being required to take written and oral examinations to qualify for certification. While certification is different from licensure, there are legal provisions for certified counselors to be bound by ethical and professional canons similar to those governing physicians and psychologists. Similarly, provisions are set forth for disciplining, individuals who do not follow the code of their profession, and eventually will be established to prevent uncertified persons from engaging in alcohol or drug counseling.

In summary, several regulatory mechanisms have evolved for preserving and assuring client rights: (1) federal regulations (HEW) for the confidentiality of alcohol and drug client records; (2) state licensing and review standards for treatment programs; (3) accreditation agencies and third-party payer standards for reviewing and accrediting treatment programs; (4) professional and paraprofessional associations and boards, which can review, censure, or expel an individual from professional practice for violation of client rights, and (5) legislative and judicial action.

Client-Rights Issues Specific to Alcohol Treatment Programs

In alcohol treatment programs, many clients are referred for services by others (e.g., courts, employers, relatives) who want them to receive treatment. While it is ultimately the client's decision in these cases to voluntarily seek treatment, one wonders whether these individuals would have done so in the absence of coercion. The courts often refer people with alcohol problems for treatment, the premise being that treatment is a favorable alternative to incarceration. While this may be the case, in a day and age when the conditions under which clients are treated *must* be voluntary, except in life-threatening circumstances, court-referred alcohol clients pose an interesting dilemma: How voluntary is participation in treatment by individuals who are coerced?

From both a legal and treatment standpoint clients are voluntarily requesting services, even though the choice a judge may have confronted them with was treatment or jail. The major problem here relates to the situation when clients fail to follow through with or are dismissed from treatment, with information to that effect being communicated to the courts. Technically, since the client usually has given written permission for the treatment program to provide information to the court, the program is free of responsibility; any abridgment of client rights occurs in the context of the original agreement between the client and the criminal justice system that referred him or her to the program. From a treatment program's perspective, the decision to allow information to be transmitted to the court is thus the client's and the court's responsibility. If the courts are unable to obtain information on some referrals, they could assume one of two things: either the client did not request treatment and did not receive it, or the client refused to give written permission for the program to communicate with the courts. In either case, it would be the courts' prerogative to gain the referred client's cooperation, similar to that with someone who fails to pay a court fine.

If treatment agencies do not wish to provide treatment under what they may consider "coercive conditions," then they should make this known to referral agencies. However, before making this decision, an agency should recognize that if other treatment programs similarly refuse to treat court-referred clients then no treatment alternative to incarceration will exist. Thus, the court-compelled abrogation of clients' rights to confidentiality may be a secondary concern, in contrast to the need to provide treatment rather than incarceration.

Another case of "involuntary" treatment for alcoholics concerns commitment to a state hospital. In most states, involuntary commitment of alcoholics is usually only possible if the individual is evaluated by a physician as presenting a danger to himself or others as a result of his drinking. In the case of danger to others, if a client communicates an intended threat to someone's welfare or life, then involuntary commitment can occur. In the case of possible harm to self, excessive drinking in and of itself is usually not considered sufficient grounds for commitment unless the person has communicated an explicit threat of suicide. However, when emergency treatment for serious withdrawal symptoms from alcohol seems indicated, involuntary commitment is sometimes possible.

In reading the above one might surmise that the laws have been designed to allow alcoholics to drink themselves to death. However, it was not always thus. Attitudes toward the issue of involuntary commitment have drastically changed only in the last decade, and this change has been in favor of client rights. Several years ago, almost anyone could commit an alcoholic to a state hospital for treatment simply as a result of the alcoholic's drinking behavior. Frequently, people were committed for as long as six months with no due process, and this commitment often brought more comfort to the client's family than the client. Today this could not happen, as there are specific time-frames within which a committed individual can appeal his or her case before a judge. If, for example, an individual who is drinking heavily is judged to be suicidal or making threats against the lives of others, and is then involuntarily committed, when that individual is no longer intoxicated and manifesting hostility or threats he or she can request discharge from treatment or at least a court hearing to challenge continued commitment. Such a court hearing would undoubtedly rule that the client is no longer a danger to self or others, and as a result the client would be discharged from treatment. While alcoholics are no longer being committed en masse, the recent policy change has caused frustration for friends and relatives of alcoholics who can neither persuade them to stop drinking nor have them involuntarily hospitalized.

Special regulations relating to the confidentiality of minors (persons under eighteen years of age) and legally incompetent and deceased individuals are also outlined in HEW's above-mentioned provisions ("Confidentiality," 42 CFR Part 2, § 2.15–§ 2.16-1 [FR, 1975a]). In the case of a legally incompetent individual, the legal or court-appointed guardian may give consent for services. In the case of minors, the signatures of both the minor and a parent or guardian are usually required. Some states, however, authorize treatment for minors without parental consent. In those states, when a minor applies for treatment, disclosure to a parent or guardian is prohibited without the client's consent. The only exception is when the applicant lacks a capacity for rational choice or his or her health or life is threatened.

CLIENT RIGHTS AND THE CLIENT-THERAPIST RELATIONSHIP

With the growing focus on client-rights issues, there has been an increasing concern about the resultant threat of protective provisions to the "sacrosanct" therapeutic setting. One of the major concerns involves conditions under which therapists might have to violate confidentiality, and, further, how this would affect the therapeutic relationship. One situation where a client's confidentiality might be violated involves life-threatening matters where therapists must take steps to prevent the client from harming others. This issue will not be elaborated here, as it has been the subject of two California Supreme Court decisions and consequently has been discussed at length in the professional literature (Leonard, 1977; Stone, 1976). In this type of clinical situation decisions about the preservation of client rights are complex, especially when there is an overriding question of whether those rights should be preserved at the risk of harm to client or society. In such cases, therapists would be advised to seek professional or legal counsel, rather than make unilateral decisions that might later result in liability. (Consultation can occur without identifying the client.)

DISCLOSURES OF CLIENT INFORMATION

With a few exceptions, federal confidentiality guidelines prohibit any unauthorized disclosure of information about a client's treatment in or association with an alcohol program. The requirements for a valid consent and what information can be released or disclosed are clearly specified (*FR*, 1975a), and the interested reader is referred to these regulations for further detail. For the reader's reference, Appendices 1 and 2 of this chapter are copies of two different release-of-information forms currently being used by the Alcohol Program of the Dede Wallace Center in Nashville, Tennessee. Appendix 1 is an example of a release that the client would sign in order for the program to give information to someone needing information or inquiring about the client. Appendix 2 is an example of the release the program would use to request information about the client from another source. Both releases are in compliance with federal regulations (*FR*, 1975a, § 2.31 and § 2.31-1).

All written disclosures of information to any person or agency must always contain the following statement (see *FR*, 1975a, § 2.32):

> This information has been disclosed to you from records whose confidentiality is protected by Federal Law. Federal regulations (42 CFR Part 2) prohibit you from making any further disclosure of it without the specific written consent of the person to whom it pertains, or as otherwise permitted by such regulations. A general authorization for the release of medical or other information is NOT sufficient for this purpose.

This regulation prevents one agency from releasing another agency's records intact without the consent of the individual in question. Someone needing access to the original records must obtain a written release from the client for that specific information.

Other situations that might involve or require release of client information involve third-party payers, outside funding agencies, court testimony, child abuse, medical emergencies, research, audits and evaluations, and, in an alcohol treatment program, drunk driving—that is, driving away from the program when known to be legally drunk (in most states, 100 mg. ethanol per 100 ml. blood). Each of these situations will now be briefly discussed with respect to whether the client's consent is needed to disclose information.

Third-Party Payers. With third-party payers and other outside funding agencies becoming important sources of financial reimbursement for treatment services, some communication with these agencies about clients' treatment is necessary. In this regard, however, federal regulations only allow disclosure of client information to third-party payers (e.g., Medicaid, Medicare, insurance companies) with the written consent of the client (see *FR*, 1975a, § 2.37 and § 2.37-1), and even then only information that is reasonably necessary for the discharge of the obligations of the third-party payers can be provided (e.g., attendance, diagnosis, types of treatment received, and dates of services).

Despite the current safeguards and confidentiality regulations, problems remain; one contemporary confidentiality issue relates to submitting insurance claims for reimbursement for alcohol treatment. In our experience, several clients have independently raised the concern that if they use their insurance information about their treatment will not be kept confidential, and this information may be transmitted to their employer or supervisor and result in their being terminated or dealt with unfairly (perhaps not for the specific reason feared, but then subtle pressure and hidden agendas for dismissing employees are not un-heard-of).

Many community mental health centers and other treatment pro-grams are mandated to both charge clients on a sliding fee basis (based on ability to pay) and collect from third-party payers. Therefore, the need to collect from third party payers is crucial to the financial stability of many treatment programs. For example, consider a client who pays five dollars a session on a sliding fee scale, but whose insurance will re-imburse the program at forty dollars per session. If the client refuses to sign a release of information to the insurance company, this puts the treatment program in a double-bind. The question here is, Should clients be denied services if they are insurance eligible but refuse to sign a release? Should these clients be charged full fee for services even though some cannot afford these costs, or should the program suffer a consider-able monetary loss because of the clients' refusal to have information about their treatment communicated to their insurance company? While no court case has yet addressed these questions, they certainly raise an interesting issue as to whether a treatment agency can require clients to use insurance, thereby forcing a release of certain information about their treatment to the insurance company.

Audits and Research. Specific provisions are set forth in the HEW code (§ 2.52 and § 2.52-1) that allow for qualified personnel to examine client records with or without client consent "for the purpose of con-ducting scientific research, management audits, financial audits, or pro-gram evaluation" (*FR,* 1975a, p. 27815). Those examining such records must give written assurances to the program that they will not identify, directly or indirectly, any client in any report of research, audit, or eval-uation, or otherwise disclose client identities in any manner.

Court Orders. Courts and other agents of the legal-judicial system sometimes request information about a client's treatment and diagnosis, because they think it might be relevant or beneficial to court proceedings involving the client. The HEW code contains specific regulations and rules regarding requests for information from courts and the procedures necessary for the release of such information (*FR,* 1975a, § 2.61 through § 2.65-1). A thorough reading of the section on court orders is necessary to understand the scope of these regulations. However, court orders in and of themselves are not sufficient to release information about clients. In fact, a special hearing apart from the regular court proceedings must be held in order to show that there is good cause for releasing the clinical record. If such an order is granted, it can only require disclosure of objective data (facts and dates of enrollment, discharge, attendance, and medication, and similar objective data) relevant to the court action in question. Other client-therapist communications, even though part of the clinical records, are not subject to release by court order. An example of a court order conforming to federal regulations appears as Appendix 3 to this chapter.

Medical Emergencies. In the case of a bona fide medical emergency, information can be disclosed to medical personnel without the client's consent. As discussed earlier, information can be released without the client's consent when the client poses an imminent danger to himself or herself, or to others. In Tennessee and some other states there is a third situation which requires disclosure of information regardless of client consent. This would involve knowledge or reports of child abuse or neglect. In Tennessee, anyone who fails to report instances of possible child abuse or neglect can be charged with a felony.

Drunk Driving. Another situation where client confidentiality might have to be violated is unique to outpatient alcohol programs; it involves clients driving to the program with a blood alcohol concentration ("BAC") that would legally be considered under the influence of alcohol. If these clients drive away from the program and are stopped by law enforcement officers, they undoubtedly will be arrested for drunk driving. The relevance of this problem here is not that the client drove to the program legally drunk, but rather that if a staff member has determined (e.g., through breath alcohol testing procedures) that a client has a BAC that would qualify him or her as legally drunk, then allowing the client to drive under these conditions, would be tantamount to, at best, allowing a misdemeanor to be committed and, at worst—if the driver fatally injures someone else—creating conditions conducive to vehicular homicide. This problem, of course, only occurs when a program uses breath alcohol testing devices, and a drunken client, despite being informed of his or her condition, insists on driving away from the facility. In such cases, staff are obligated by law to report the client's intended behavior of committing a crime (albeit probably just a misdemeanor) to the police, since the concept of privileged communication applies only to crimes that have already been committed, not to those that might be or are about to be committed. However, communicating with the police about a client's intended behavior without written permission from the client is obviously in violation of the federal confidentiality regulations. Interestingly, in this double-bind situation one must either break confidentiality or be liable for prosecution for not reporting a crime about to be committed.

In the situations where a client drives to a treatment program when drunk in legal terms, we suggest two alternatives to avoid this double-bind: (a) find an alternative way for the client to be transported, or (b) have the client wait until his or her BAC drops below the level that would be considered legally under the influence of alcohol when driving. Using these alternatives in our program, we have only had to call the police one time in eight years.

Unfortunately, if a client drives away from a program when known to be under the influence of alcohol, there are no judicial precedents to guide us with respect to violation of client confidentiality. A partial solution to this double-bind can be achieved by using written informed consent wherein all clients, as a condition of entering the program, agree that if they drive away from the program while legally under the influence of alcohol, their confidentiality will be broken by the program informing the police of their actions. At present, in order to be admitted to the Alcohol Program of the Dede Wallace Center all clients are asked to read and sign an informed-consent statement which explains the program's policy regarding occasions when someone is found to have driven to the program under the influence of alcohol. A copy of this statement appears as Appendix 4 to this chapter.

Clearly, when clients are informed in advance of the conditions under which their confidentiality will be broken, we have gone a step further in preserving client rights. On the other hand, some would argue that informing clients of the limitations on their confidentiality might create an environment that is not conducive—perhaps even counterproductive—to the original tenets of psychotherapy. It can also be argued that when we inform clients of situations that would require breaking their confidentiality, we run the risk of their refusing to discuss those situations in therapy.

PROTECTION OF CLIENT RIGHTS IN RESEARCH PROJECTS

Research that involves retrospective examinations of client records for scientific purposes (e.g., to determine referral patterns, to identify the types of client who drop out of treatment against medical advice, and so on) is usually not planned in advance, and consequently it is difficult or impossible to obtain clients' informed consent or permission, since most will have already terminated treatment. In such cases, the HEW code (§ 2.56 and § 2.56-1) contains specific provisions allowing the examination of client records for the purpose of conducting scientific research, management audits, financial audits, or program evaluation (*FR,* 1975a). However, although written consent from the patient is not required here, the examiners must provide written assurance that they will make no direct or indirect disclosures of client identities.

Research that involves clients currently in treatment, however, must adhere to more stringent criteria. While the federal regulations only apply to research supported at least partly by HEW (45 CFR Part 46

[*FR,* 1975b]), many institutions now require that all studies involving human subjects follow similar procedures in order to minimize risks to subjects. Investigators are typically required to submit to an institutional review committee a research proposal describing the planned study. While proposals will vary in format, the following topics are usually addressed: (1) summarization of the study's objectives and research protocol; (2) explicit descriptions of all procedures that will be carried out with each type of subject; (3) criteria for selection of subjects for the study, including the number, ages, and sources of subjects to be studied; (4) anticipated risks or inconveniences to subjects that might be associated with the study's procedures; (5) precautions that will be taken to safeguard subjects' welfare with regard to procedures that may place them at risk; (6) steps that will be taken to insure subjects' rights, privacy, and well-being; (7) plans for maintaining the confidentiality of documents and data and restricting access to such; (8) a description of the nature of any type of deception of subjects that might occur and its justification, and procedures to undo (counteract) it (e.g., debriefing after the study); (9) an indication of how the participants' informed consent will be obtained—usually by providing a copy of the actual statement that will be read or heard by subjects prior to giving their written consent; and (10) a signed statement by the investigators that they will adhere to the procedures outlined and implement any changes in format only after committee approval. Lastly, the investigators are required to immediately notify the committee of any adverse effects experienced by subjects who participate in the study.

As with the confidentiality of patient records, HEW has issued specific guidelines and regulations for the protection of human subjects in research studies (45 FR Part 46, 1975b; HEW, 1971). The regulations require that all institutions that receive funding (direct or indirect) from HEW and conduct research with human subjects are obligated to obtain and document informed consent from subjects prior to the conduct of research. The Institutional Review Board, which must be approved by HEW, must establish that the procedures used to gain informed consent from subjects are adequate and appropriate. By definition, "informed consent" means that when subjects or their legal guardians consent to participate in any research study, they do so by exercising free power of choice without undue inducement or use of any element of force, constraint, or coercion. The required components of an informed-consent statement are as follows (HEW, 1971):

1. a fair explanation of the procedures to be followed and their purposes, including identification of any procedures that are experimental
2. a description of any attendent discomforts or risks that subjects might expect

3. a description of any benefits to science and mankind that can reasonably be expected
4. a disclosure of any appropriate alternative procedures that might be advantageous for subjects
5. an offer to answer any inquiries concerning the procedures
6. an instruction that subjects are free to withdraw their consent and discontinue participation in the project at any time, without prejudice

Appendix 5 to this chapter is an example of an informed consent statement that we have used with subjects in a recent alcohol-treatment evaluation study.

OUTCOME EVALUATION OF CLINICAL TREATMENT PROGRAMS

Until recently, mental health programs have enjoyed a fair degree of autonomy in their provision of clinical services. However, as a result of recent state and federal mandates requiring health-services account-ability, increased attention has been given to evaluating the effectiveness of clinical treatment in mental health programs, including alcohol and drug programs. The ultimate accountability would mean making treat-ment outcome evaluation a routine part of alcohol treatment programs. The implementation of such procedures will require careful planning, as clinical and research settings differ substantially.

However, the procedures used for obtaining informed consent from clients in outcome evaluation studies of clinical programs will likely be very similar to those used in research projects. When following up with clients, trying to gather information from significant others, or checking record sources, care must be taken to ensure that proper and valid re-leases of information have been obtained from all clients and that im-proper disclosure of information does not occur. While the required safeguards for conducting follow-up studies are few, the risks of dis-closure (violating confidentiality) are great. Thus, the same caution and concern that operate in the clinical setting must also apply when con-ducting follow-up and treatment outcome evaluations.

Special Client Rights Issues

PRIVATE TREATMENT PROGRAMS

Since the federal confidentiality rules and regulations discussed throughout this chapter only apply to programs that receive direct **or** indirect federal support, the preservation of client rights in other alcohol treatment facilities and agencies (e.g., private hospitals, self-help groups such as Alcoholics Anonymous, halfway houses and missions) is a problem that needs to be addressed. In the case of private hospitals that operate alcohol detoxification and rehabilitation programs, JCAH (Joint Commission on Accreditation of Hospitals) accreditation is usually necessary for reimbursement by insurance companies and other third-party payers to occur. This, however, still leaves many other alcohol treatment programs with few, if any, regulations regarding client rights. It is to be hoped that, with increasing state and federal requirements for program and counselor accreditation, it will soon be necessary for all alcohol treatment programs to abide by provisions and regulations ensuring the preservation of client rights.

RIGHTS OF MINORS

Another area where clearer guidelines are needed concerns treatment services for children. The major argument against treatment for minors without parental consent is that such treatment may cause injury to the family unit—that is, treatment might be provided to minors without full knowledge of the familial situation or input from family members. This argument, however, could be similarly applied to adult clients whose spouses are not—at the clients' request—involved in the ongoing treatment. Although views on children's rights have been changing, until recently parents have had ultimate legal control over their children. Currently, two trends can be identified that are intended to further protect children's rights. The first relates to obtaining the child's—as well as the parents' or guardian's—consent in research studies. The second involves providing children with separate legal counsel. Perhaps these trends point to a special need to ensure and safeguard children's rights and confidentiality (e.g., a children's "bill of rights").

DISCRIMINATION FOR ALCOHOL ABUSE

Three other issues deserve some mention. These relate to alcohol client rights and possible discrimination as a result of their disability. The first issue (which was discussed earlier) involves reimbursement from insurance companies for a client's treatment in an alcohol program: Some clients have refused to allow treatment programs to process their insurance forms because they fear their jobs will be threatened if their employers or supervisors find out that they have an alcohol problem or are in an alcohol treatment program. One way to address this problem is for companies and businesses to let employees file their own medical claims with the insurance companies, thereby avoiding any insurance-related information coming to the employees' place of work. Another method would be for companies to adopt a formal policy of nondiscrimination regarding employees who receive services for alcohol problems.

The second issue also involves insurance companies. Some insurance companies will not pay for outpatient therapy for clients with certain diagnoses, such as alcohol addiction. The reasons for this discrimination are unclear; treatment for some disabilities is just not reimbursable. At present, several alcohol constituency groups are attempting to deal with this problem on the federal level. However, until changes occur, insurance companies will continue to be essentially defining what types of psychiatric and medical problems qualify for reimbursement. This is the type of situation where client advocacy groups could be influential.

The third issue relates to the requirement of some state vocational rehabilitation programs that two diagnosed problems are needed in order for them to accept clients into their program. If alcohol treatment programs are to send clients with a primary alcohol addiction diagnosis to some state vocational rehabilitation programs, then these clients must also be given secondary diagnoses to be eligible for vocational rehabilitation services. The reasons for requiring two diagnoses are unclear, other than the assumption that alcohol addiction in and of itself is not sufficient to warrant vocational rehabilitation services. This situation is in many ways similar to that of insurance companies denying reimbursement for certain psychiatric diagnoses. Here therapists are faced with a choice of contriving another diagnosis or being unable to get their clients vocational counseling and rehabilitation services. Since these are state government programs, the only recourse clients seem to have is to take their case to court to argue against this requirement of two diagnoses—or, practically speaking, the implicit requirement of a contrived secondary diagnosis.

Since such diagnostic discrimination currently exists, the question also arises as to how alcoholics are treated under other diagnostic labels. When this happens, a client's record would contain a diagnosis that were it not for insurance reimbursement or a need for vocational services, would not be there. This being the case, the following questions must be addressed: (1) While clients might want their vocational rehabilitation or treatment paid for, do they want it at the expense of another, contrived diagnosis? (2) Are clients aware of the diagnoses that are submitted to outside agencies or contained in their clinical records? (3) Most important, are these kinds of "second" diagnosis ethical or clinically warranted?

INVOLVING CLIENTS IN THEIR
OWN TREATMENT PLANNING

One last special issue relates to involving clients in their own diagnostic formulation, treatment, and goal setting. While involving clients
in their own treatment planning is not a new concept, relevant documentation of such activity is lacking. One way to document a client's
involvement in treatment planning and goal setting is to ask him or her
to delineate written goals and objectives; then the client and therapist
could jointly write and sign the treatment plan. However, not all therapists feel that all clients should have access to their records or can effectively participate in their own treatment planning. Even though clients
now have the right to read and review their clinical records, some therapists argue that certain information (e.g., diagnoses, psychological test
results) might be "injurious" to the client. It is argued that if clients
become aware of some diagnostic information in their clinical records,
that information might interfere negatively with the therapeutic relationship and have social labeling consequences. While the reasons for
these attitudes have not always been well formulated, they could be
perceived as a response to the invasion of what some therapists call "the
sacrosanct therapeutic milieu."

A Model for Preserving Alcohol Clients' Rights

For all programs that receive federal support (either directly or indirectly) the preservation of client rights is not an option but a mandate.
With the exception of private programs and practitioners, it is the case
that almost all alcohol treatment programs are subject to federal purview; thus, for them federal requirements apply. Since the federal regulations are complex, presented in legal terms, and subject to legal challenges and judicial interpretation, one of the best ways that clinical
staff can be assured of preserving client rights is to understand what is
required of them. To this end, we suggest that all staff, especially new
staff joining treatment programs, be *required* to complete in-service
training on client rights and confidentiality. Further, copies of all laws
and regulations that govern or apply to client rights should be readily
available to all staff (administrative and support staff, as well as
clinicians).

Another way of preserving client rights is to assure that clients understand the conditions under which they are seeking treatment. For example, when individuals first decide to enter treatment, they should be
aware of the conditions under which they will engage in treatment,
those under which their confidentiality could be broken, and the possible

risks and benefits of various treatments (e.g., medication, group therapy, individual therapy). Clients should also be made aware of federal and state confidentiality regulations and the need for obtaining releases for requesting, as well as providing, information.

Further safeguards for the preservation of client rights can be accomplished through quality assurance and clinical case reviews. These are both peer review mechanisms that have been created to better ensure that therapists provide quality clinical services to clients.

Since regulations regarding client rights are of recent origin and have rarely been tested in court, the best method that programs and practitioners have for preserving client rights is to be familiar with all existing regulations and changes that occur, and, further, to seek legal counsel when questions arise.

Future Trends and Issues

The preservation of client rights and development of model procedures to ensure these rights have been very recent developments. Certainly, as with no other era, this is an age of civil liberties. Many groups of people whose civil rights might well be subject to violation because of their special problems or classification have received significant attention and advocacy since the early 1970s.

While there has been considerable recent federal and state legislation and regulation governing client rights in alcohol treatment programs, the major concern of civil libertarians should now be the enforcement of these rights. Putting the onus totally upon service providers—who may not be aware of certain violations that they commit—or accreditation committees—which usually give advance notice of their reviews—does not seem sufficient. What seems most lacking are client advocacy groups—groups which insure that client rights are being safeguarded from the client's perspective. For example, while programs may use proper and valid informed consents and releases of information, the language in these documents may not be understandable so that clients can competently make decisions to engage in treatment or allow disclosure of information.

Another issue concerns the mental state of the client. Can we assume that all clients are of sufficient intellectual ability and knowledge to understand their rights? Further, since many alcohol clients seek treatment when intoxicated, can documents signed when someone is intoxicated and presumably impaired by alcohol be taken as sufficient and binding? These two questions point to the need for procedures to insure and safeguard the rights of clients who at certain times may be unable to fully understand their rights and give fully informed consent. Client advocacy groups could develop policies to deal with cases such as these, especially if some members of these groups are individuals who were once clients themselves.

Conclusion

In summary, the last ten years has witnessed a morass of legal changes and controls for preserving client rights. As a result of various rulings, the alcohol field, as well as other fields dealing with client-rights issues, has been tremendously affected. Most alcohol-treatment service providers who were working in the field a decade ago would probably agree that the new requirements and regulations are necessary. And, no doubt, changes in this area will continue. Thus, clinical service providers will need to keep abreast of all new rulings and regulations.

References

American Medical Association (AMA), Committee on Alcoholism. Hospitalization of patients with alcoholism (Reports of Officers). *Journal of AMA,* 1956, *162,* 750.

Department of Health, Education and Welfare (HEW). *The institutional guide to DHEW policy on human subjects.* HEW Publication No. (NIH) 72-102. Washington, D.C.: U.S. Government Printing Office, 1971.

Federal Register (40 *FR* 27802). Title 42, Code of Federal Regulations, Part 2 (42 CFR Part 2). Confidentiality of alcohol and drug abuse patient records. *FR,* July 1, 1975a. Washington, D.C.: HEW.

Federal Register (40 *FR* 11854). Title 45, Code of Federal Regulations, Part 46 (45 CFR Part 46). Protection of human subjects. *FR,* March 13, 1975b. Washington, D.C.: HEW.

LEONARD, J. B. A therapist's duty to potential victims: A nonthreatening view of *Tarasoff. Law and Human Behavior,* 1977, *1,* 309–317.

STONE, A. A. The *Tarasoff* decisions: Suing psychotherapists to safeguard society. *Harvard Law Review,* 1976, *90,* 358–378.

APPENDIX 1: Consent for Release of Information

WRITTEN CONSENT FOR RELEASE OF INFORMATION SIGNED BY THE CLIENT. (If other than client indicate below the relationship to the client and the reason for other than the client's signature).

Re: _____

Date of Birth: _____

I give my permission to the _____
(name and address of the treatment program)

to release to: _____
(Name of person, organization or agency to which disclosure is to be made)
Address: _____
Phone: _____

This information is needed to aid in the clinical treatment and evaluation of this person as a client in the program. The specific type of information to be disclosed is as follows:

NOTE: *In order for this release to be valid, one column must be checked for each of the following areas:*

Area of Disclosure	Yes	No
1. Summary of Initial Intake Evaluation of alcohol-related dysfunction and treatment recommendations .... ____		____
2. Participation and progress in treatment .... ____		____
3. Results of Antabuse Screening/Evaluation .... ____		____
4. Results of Psychological Testing .... ____		____
5. Information required to process insurance claims for treatment—diagnosis, number of visits, type of services provided and/or how long the client is expected to continue in treatment .... ____		____
6. Other (specify clearly)_____		
_____ .... ____		____
7. Other (specify clearly)_____		
_____ .... ____		____

This consent is subject to revocation by the client at any time. This consent shall have a duration no longer than that reasonably necessary to effectuate the purpose for which it is given and as specifically provided hereinafter in this part. (In order for this release to be valid, one column must be checked for each of the following conditions.)

Yes   No

____   ____   This consent will be in effect until the client has completed the clinical assessment and evaluation of alcohol-related dysfunction requested by the client's attorney, the courts. If treatment is recommended and the client seeks treatment with the program, then this consent will be in effect until the completion of the recommended treatment program.

Yes   No

____   ____   This consent will be in effect until 30 days after the client's last
date of service with the program.

____   ____   This consent will be in effect until_____.

Client's Signature: _____ Date: _____

Witness: _____ Date: _____

Signature of a person authorized to sign in lieu of the client:

_____

APPENDIX 2: Consent for Request of Information

WRITTEN CONSENT FOR RELEASE OF INFORMATION SIGNED BY THE CLIENT. (If other than client indicate below the relationship to the client and the reason for other than the client's signature).

RE: _____

DATE OF BIRTH: _____

MOTHER'S MAIDEN NAME: _____

SOCIAL SECURITY #:_____

I give my permission to:_____
(Name of person, organization or agency)

Address: _____
(Street)   (City)   (State)   (Zip)

To release the following information to the _____.
(name and address of the treatment program)

This information is needed to aid in the clinical treatment and evaluation of this person as a client in the program. The specific type of information requested is as follows:

	Yes	No
Admission and Discharge Summary	____	____
Use of Medications	____	____
Blood chemistry profiles	____	____
Information regarding drinking driving charge (DUI) date and blood alcohol level	____	____
Results of psychological testing	____	____
Results of neurological work-up and/or EEG	____	____
Social/drinking history	____	____
Clinical Summary of treatment	____	____
Other specify)_____	____	____

This consent is subject to revocation by the client at any time and, unless an earlier date is specified, it expires 90 days after it is signed.

Client's Signature: _____ Date: _____

Witness: _____ Date: _____

APPENDIX 3: Court Order of Disclosure (Under §2.63 and §2.64 of 42 CFR Part 2, Subpart E)

I. In accordance with _____
(the appropriate drug or alcohol statutory citation to the

_____
U.S. code[1])
and _____
(the pertinent sections of the regulations—e.g., Subpart E or 42 CFR Part 2)
_____ ;
this court finds:

(a) that the record shows good cause (as required in §2.64(d)) for the disclosure of certain objective data (limitations set in §2.63(a)) specified below, pertaining to John Doe (pseudonym used in accordance with the intent of §2.64(a) and (g)(3)) for the purpose of _____

_____ ;

(b) _____
(the specific facts necessitating disclosure)

_____
outweigh the possible injury to the patient, etc. (following language set forth in §2.64(d) and the authorizing statute): _____

_____ ;
and outweighs the following adverse effect upon the successful treatment or rehabilitation of the patient, etc. (following language set forth in §2.64(f)):

_____

_____ ;

(c) further, that disclosure will benefit the patient as follows:

_____ ;
or that disclosure will benefit the effectiveness of the treatment program or other program similarly situated as follows: _____

_____ .

II. It is therefore ordered that _____
(the program and/or name(s) of responsible

_____
program staff)

_____
is (are) authorized, in accordance with §2.61 of 42 CFR Part 2, and

_____
(the appropriate U.S. Code citation)
to disclose to this court and/or to the following named parties who have a need to know this information:

_____

_____ ;
the following limited information: _____

[1]42 U.S.C. 4582 for disclosures of alcohol abuse patient records; 21 U.S.C. 1175 for disclosures of drug-abuse patient records.

essential to fulfill the above-described objective(s). These persons may not redisclose the information or may redisclose the information only as follows:

_____

_____ .

    To the extent the disclosed information is to be retained by the court, in accordance with §2.64(g)(3), it will be kept in a sealed record.[2]

    (Optional.) Except pursuant to a court authorizing order issued in accordance with §2.65, no information disclosed pursuant to this order may be used to initiate or substantiate any criminal charges against a patient or to conduct any investigation of a patient.

[2]See also confidentiality provisions of §2.66(c).

SOURCE: From "Confidentiality of alcohol and drug abuse patient records and child abuse and neglect reporting," Joint Policy Statement by the Alcohol, Drug Abuse, and Mental Health Administration, and National Center on Child Abuse and Neglect (both of the Department of Health, Education and Welfare), February, 1978.

APPENDIX 4: Informed Consent—Client Admission Policy

    The following information is to explain one of the program's admission requirements. Please read this form carefully. Any questions you may have will be answered.

    At times, some clients drive to the program while they are legally intoxicated (greater than or equal to .10% blood alcohol concentration). By law, drunk driving is a misdemeanor. Besides being a crime, driving under the influence of alcohol (greater than or equal to .10%) is potentially a danger to yourself and others.

    If we suspect a client of driving to the program while legally intoxicated, we will administer a breath alcohol test to determine the exact blood alcohol level. If the blood alcohol level is greater than or equal to .10%, then the program staff will ask that person not to drive until his/her blood alcohol level is less than .10% or that he/she seek alternative means of transportation.

    If you insist on driving when legally drunk, then the program staff will have to take the following steps:

1. Inform you that you are about to commit, at least, a misdemeanor, and that since the staff has knowledge that a crime is about to be committed, we are obligated by law to contact the police or similar law enforcement officers.
2. We will then tell the police that you re suspected of being legally intoxicated and you are leaving our parking lot and are driving in the direction of

_____

3. If you are referred by the courts, probation or parole officers, or similar law enforcement agencies, driving away from the program while legally intoxicated will result in immediate termination from the treatment program.

    While this program policy applies to only a few clients a year, we must inform all clients seeking admission to the program of the policy. Please be assured that the staff will seek alternative means of transportation for all willing clients who drive to the program when legally under the influence of alcohol.

Check either (a) or (b) below:
_____ a. I have read the consent form. All my questions have been answered, and I freely and voluntarily seek admission to the program.
_____ b. the material contained in this consent form has been explained to me orally. All my questions have been answered and I freely and voluntarily seek admission to the program.

Date	Signature of Client
Date	Signature of Witness

APPENDIX 5: Research Project Consent

Program Name _____S. No.: _____

To: *PERSONS WHO AGREE TO PARTICIPATE IN THIS PROJECT:*
The following information is provided to inform you about this project and your particiption in it. Please read this form carefully. Any questions that you may have about the procedures in this study will be answered. Please feel free to ask any questions you may have about this study and/or the information given below.

1. THE PROCEDURES TO BE FOLLOWED IN THIS PROJECT, THE APPROXIMATE DURATION OF THE PROJECT, AND THE PURPOSES OF THIS PROJECT ARE DESCRIBED BELOW:

Any information we gather will be kept confidential and will not affect your treatment in any way; we will not identify you by name. If you choose to volunteer, you may withdraw your consent to participate at any time throughout the study.

The purpose of this project is to learn more about the effectiveness of alcohol treatment programs and approaches. Therefore, we are interested in following up and evaluating individuals who are participating in alcohol treatment programs, to determine the effectiveness of the various types of treatment approaches and services. We will gather this information first by asking you questions about your use of alcohol and other drugs and how it has affected other areas of your life (e.g., jobs, family, physical health, etc). This information will be collected today in a pretreatment interview lasting one to two hours. At this time, we will also ask you to take a breath test to determine if there is any alcohol in your bloodstream. The reason for this breath test is that we do not want to interview people who are drinking, as it sometimes affects the answers they give to various questions.

To determine your progress after you enter the treatment program and how it relates to the type of therapy services you receive, we will be maintaining contact with you for approximately the next twelve to eighteen months. During this period we will be askng you to give us information about your use of alcohol and other drugs and other aspects of your life — job, health, family relations, social and recreational activities, alcohol- and drug-related arrests and hospitalizations. This information will be sought through follow-up contacts. The follow-up interviewer will usually be the person who is interviewing you today. Follow-up contacts will be made either by telephone, by mail, or as a short personal interview, and will occur every one to two months. Three or six times throughout the follow-up period we will ask you to take a breath test to determine if you have any alcohol in your bloodstream. These results, along with other information, will never be reported to anyone else or any other agency. The follow-up information will be coded by number and in no way tied to your identity. These breath tests will be similar to the one we will be giving you today.

As part of this project, we also want to know how other people who know you think the treatment program is affecting you. Therefore, we will ask you for the names of some collateral sources—friends, spouse, employer, relatives, etc.—with whom we can talk about your progress and who can provide us with some information about your use of alcohol and other drugs and other areas of your life health. These questions are like the questions we will be asking you when we contact you. In addition, we will be obtaining records from various agencies with which you may have had contact or which may be able to supply us with additional information (driver records, hospital and arrest records, etc.). This information is to help us evaluate the effectiveness of the treatment program and your progress as an individual in this program. As with all data collected in this project, these data will be coded and your identity kept confidential.

2. YOUR RIGHTS AND/OR PRIVACY WILL BE MAINTAINED IN THE FOLLOWING MANNER:

Confidentiality will be protected at all times in accord with the Department of Health, Education and Welfare federal confidentiality guidelines for clients in alcohol and drug treatment programs. *All information will be coded by number rather than by name.* This information will be seen only by the people directly involved in the conduct of this study. A master code sheet will be kept under lock and key until the study is completed, at which time this code sheet will be destroyed. Any information used in our scientific reports will be based on groups of people, so that a particular individual could not be identified.

3. THE DISCOMFORTS, INCONVENIENCES, AND/OR RISKS THAT CAN BE REASONABLY EXPECTED ARE:

The main risk is that your identity and facts about your life will be known to the interviewer. However, we will take all possible precautions to ensure your privacy and confidentiality; these precautions are stated in Item 2. Another possible risk is that some people may become embarrassed when questioned about their past behavior. We will try to prevent this by using only people who volunteer to participate. Also, you are free to withdraw from participation at any time if you experience any unpleasant effects.

4. THE ASPECTS OF THESE PROCEDURES THAT WOULD NOT BE INCLUDED EXCEPT FOR THE CONDUCT OF THIS STUDY:

All procedures described in Item #1 are for the purposes of this project.

5. THE BENEFITS TO SCIENCE AND TO MANKIND THAT ARE SOUGHT IN THIS PROJECT ARE:

This information will help us to evaluate the effectiveness of our current treatment programs. Additionally, this information will help us and other alcohol treatment programs design and implement future alcohol treatment and evaluation programs. Your cooperation in this project is extremely valuable in aiding us to understand and help other people with problems similar to yours.

6. a. ALTERNATIVE PROCEDURES THAT MIGHT BE ADVANTA-
   GEOUS.
   b. REASONS FOR NOT USING THEM IN THIS PROJECT.
   None.

NOTE: YOU ARE FREE TO WITHDRAW THIS CONSENT AND TO DIS-
       CONTINUE PARTICIPATION IN THIS PROJECT AT ANY TIME.

STATEMENT BY PERSON AGREEING TO PARTICIPATE IN THIS PROJECT:

_____ a. I have read this Consent Form. All my questions have been answered, and I freely and voluntarily choose to participate. I understand that I may withdraw at any time. I agree to participate as a volunteer in this program.

_____ b. The material contained in this Consent Form has been explained to me orally. All my questions have been answered and I freely and voluntarily choose to participate as a volunteer in this program.

_____	_____
Date	Signature of Client
_____	_____
Date	Signature of Witness

CHAPTER 10

Extending Client Rights to Narcotic Addicts

Edward J. Callahan
Richard A. Rawson

Introduction

AT THE HEIGHT of the social upheaval of the 1960s perhaps no individual was feared as much as the "junkie"—the heroin addict, the criminal. Identified with stories of extensive and violent crime, the heroin addict has been viewed more mythically than realistically in the United States. While mental health professionals are aware that the public image of the addict does not accurately describe individuals who are addicted to heroin, this image of the addict still interferes with the protection of addicts' rights in treatment. This is especially true since in no other area of behavior is there more confusion over whether an individual is to be punished by the court system or treated. In addition, many of the relevant legal concepts have no operational definitions.

The purpose of this chapter will be to explore the influences that work against protection of addicts' rights in treatment and to suggest appropriate protective procedures for use in preserving these rights. Making such treatment effective is difficult because it often requires cooperative interaction with the criminal justice system while keeping pure the treatment goal of client advocacy with clients who sometimes behave obnoxiously.

In order to reach the goal of establishing guidelines for protecting the rights of the addict-client, we will review the history of drug use and abuse first culturally and then legally. This legal history will lead into an exploration of treatment philosophies and environments, both prison- and community-based. In the context of community-based services we will then examine client rights and the most serious threats to them. Finally, future legal and treatment developments will be considered. In order to understand the present and the future, it is first necessary to understand the past.

Drug Use: A Historical Perspective

People in all environments and eras have used naturally growing or easily derived chemicals to alter their behaviors and perceptions: psilocybin, peyote, cannabis, opiates, and alcohol. Sulkunen (1976) points out that the chemicals selected for use by a culture are those that appear naturally in that environment.

Generally, areas that have long histories of using particular substances develop cultural rituals that protect against the abuse of these substances; for example, Sulkunen points out that wine is not abused in Jewish culture due to its long history of ritual use. Drug abuse appears to become a problem when (1) a new chemical is introduced to a culture (e.g., coffee in medieval Europe), (2) members of a culture are introduced to a new environment that sanctions the use of other chemicals (American GIs in Vietnam), and (3) the amount of environmental stress increases (postindustrialization increases in alcoholism). (See Callahan and Rawson [1980] and Callahan, Price, and Dahlkoetter [1980] for more detailed presentations of these arguments.) Further, it has been argued that laws against drug use actually work against the culture's establishing protective rituals around the use of the substances (Zinberg, Jacobson, & Harding, 1975). For example, it could be argued that marijuana will present much less a threat to society once laws against its use are abandoned and cultural limits develop naturally.

Heroin has a reputation in the United States as an evil drug in the overall pharmacopoeia. This image has been achieved through extensive public relations efforts by the Drug Enforcement Agency and other government agencies rather than the chemical properties of the drug itself. Brecher (1969) points out that opiates comprise a class of drugs with a great many positive uses as medicine. In fact, he notes that opium was known in the 1700s as "GOM": "God's own medicine." Long-term addiction appears to be a great deal safer physiologically than addiction to alcohol—i.e., there are fewer adverse side effects to taking heroin regularly than in regular excessive consumption of alcohol. The dangers to the user appear to accrue from problems in acquiring the drug, the unavailability of legal, clean syringes, and the fact that purity of the drug is extremely variable across street dealers and drug shipments (Brecher, 1969).

Narcotics were used regularly and safely in the United States in the late 1800s. The typical heroin user at that point was likely to be a postmenopausal woman taking the opiate to deal with a variety of physical and psychological symptoms. With increased opium smoking in the Chinese labor community in San Francisco, fear began to develop about opiates as alien drugs and the first local statues against opium use appeared. Later, the United States saw favorable economic advantages—

(such as open trade in the East)—if opiates could be banned on a world-wide basis (Platt & Labate, 1973), and called an international conference to ban narcotics trading. In order not to look foolish going into such a conference, the federal government passed the first in a series of internal laws prohibiting opiates. These laws brought about an evolution both of behaviors required to maintain heroin use, and in the identity of the addict.

THE CRIMINALIZATION OF HEROIN USE

Over the course of the eighty-plus years of heroin-control laws in this country, the behaviors required to sustain addiction have changed. Earlier, in the late 1800s, narcotics addiction could be maintained for pennies a day by buying over-the-counter medications from drug stores, grocery stores, or even the colorful traveling medicine show (Platt & Labate, 1976). Later, despite passage of the Harrison Act in 1914, narcotics were still readily available with a prescription from a physician. However, with a later Supreme Court interpretation of the Harrison Act, availability from physicians lessened and narcotics became available only from special clinics. Finally, that avenue too was removed; with the end of freely available narcotics, underworld sales became profitable for the first time. As a result of this change in the availability of narcotics, the most common 1890s user—the postmenopausal woman—gradually decreased her habit. Her place as consumer was taken by various thrill seekers and increasing numbers of inner-city dwellers, mainly racial minorities. Only the cultural revolution of the 1960s brought large numbers of white faces back into heroin usage; possibly the presence of those same white faces is responsible for the gradual lessening of penalties for minor drug usage and the increased availability of treatment funds.

Today's addict is likely to be a member of a racial minority living in a large city. Availability of narcotics then, has consistently been the critical factor in determining who the users will be (Callahan & Rawson 1980). The evolution of the legal penalties for heroin use has changed the face of the user from postmenopausal woman to minority criminal. What do these role and identity changes imply?

The Roles of Client-Addict and Clinician-Jailer

Zimbardo and his colleagues have done a series of interesting studies in which asking students to role-play prisoners and guards brought about dramatic changes in their behavior (e.g., Haney, Banks & Zimbardo,

1973). Taking the role of the guard or prisoner brought the behavior of the students in line with the kinds of behavior that often occur in the prison situation: prisoners engaging in lying and stealing behavior and guards engaging in verbal and physical abuse of the prisoners in their care. Thus it seems likely that the addict and the professional can also be trapped by the role society has laid out for them. Quijano and Logsdon (1978) note the danger that befalls psychologists working in prison settings: Their roles are rigidified by the categorization system of the prison. Over time, psychologists learn to treat trustees in one manner and maximum security prisoners in a quite different manner. Similar dangers no doubt exist in providing outpatient counseling. In either case, the role of therapist suffers, and the therapist is less effective.

Many of the problems that Zimbardo and his colleagues noted involved denying rights to those "in trouble with the law." Addicts are automatically in trouble with the law; their behavior is controlled in part by the requirements for procuring heroin. Through peer training, they are more likely to be skilled in antisocial and manipulative behaviors. This legal status has created a unique treatment status for the addict.

Let us now look at some of the implications of this legal status for the clinician, both philosophically and practically.

THE ROLE OF THE CRIMINAL JUSTICE SYSTEM

In order to achieve a good perspective on how the relationship between the clinician and the criminal justice system can develop, it is critical for the clinician to understand the responsibilities of those working in criminal justice. These responsibilities have been stated succinctly by Newman:

> Judges, probation officers and parole officers have a primary obligation to protect society at large, and in exercising this obligation they must place consideration of the community's well being above all others. They cannot, and should not, have their roles redefined as therapists, any more than physicians should attempt to make decisions regarding the need for incarceration of criminals. (1974)

It should be clear from this statement that judges who are skeptical of diversion programs and treatment placement of addicts can be seen as merely carrying out their legal responsibility. It is the judge's duty to carry out the proper legal response to the addict's set of criminal behaviors, not to provide treatment. Similarly, Newman argues that probation and parole officers have an obligation to police the behavior of those under their surveillance and incarcerate anyone whose behavior violates the stated norms for his or her release.

Newman's stand represents a clear division of treatment from the criminal justice system. Such a stand has a great deal of merit. However, treatment did not develop from such an ideal model. We will now turn to a brief review of how treatment did develop.

TREATMENT ENVIRONMENT OF THE ADDICT

Until the 1960s the two most advanced treatment centers for addicts in the United States were located in Lexington, Kentucky and Fort Worth, Texas; both were housed in prisons. The close relationship of prison and treatment began in these programs and continued with the development of large-scale civil-commitment programs in California and New York State.

The philosophy supporting this combination of treatment and incarceration holds that even if treatment proves ineffective at least inmates cannot commit further crimes while imprisoned. As Jaffe (1978) points out, the lines between treatment and punishment have been further blurred by the actions of those in the criminal justice system who subscribe to the view that the addict is "sick"—i.e., diseased by opiate dependence. Thus, the diseased addict needs treatment rather than punishment. This view has placed many addicts in compulsory treatment instead of prison. This has also resulted in the hard-core user being diverted from prison for treatment with the nonaddicted user being sent to prison. On occasion, individuals have deliberately become addicted before going to trial in order to be eligible for diversion rather than prison. This legally created path of least resistance may sometimes also contribute to training younger users as addicts by allowing more socialization into the addict community through shared treatment time.

A corollary treatment philosophy has also developed: Because of an aberrant "addictive personality" all heroin users (and other drug users) need treatment. Within this philosphy all drug users (even recreational marijuana smokers) can be treated for their diseased personality instead of being held responsible for behavior that violates the law. This cooperative effort between the courts and treatment authorities can be seen as distorting the goals of the criminal justice system, which imply punishment.

Ironically, though, some of the most successful treatment of addicts has taken place in an atmosphere of respectful cooperation between treatment providers and courts. As we will see, heroin addicts appear to "clean up" best with some court contingencies. In fact, an argument can be made that the best treatment in changing behavior outside prison invokes some of the realities of the court system.

PHILOSOPHY OF AN APPLIED BEHAVIOR ANALYSIS IN THE COMMUNITY

One of the most perplexing questions facing clinical psychology has been how to change behavior thoroughly enough in the therapeutic setting so that it will also be changed in the client's natural environment. One innovative solution to this problem has been to work in the natural environment in the first place in order to avoid the need to generalize skills across settings. Tharp and Wetzel (1969) first employed this approach, with predelinquent youths in Arizona, and the same premise has been employed in two fairly successful heroin addiction programs (Boudin, Valentine, Ingraham, Brantley, Ruiz, Smith, Catlin, & Regan, 1977; Callahan & Rawson, 1980).

Successful behavior change in the natural environment requires skillful use of all available sources of control in concert. This, however, may mean that the behavior-change agent will either be a probation or parole officer or else use the powers of community agencies and the court system to punish the drug taking of the client. Several examples of the successful use of this approach now appear in the literature (Boudin *et al.*, 1977; Callahan *et al.*, 1980; Callahan, Rawson, Arias, Glazer, Liberman, & McCleaver, in press; Rawson, Callahan, Glazer, & Liberman, in press).

The one drawback to this approach is that the rights of the client can be lost in the rush to treatment. Many are now pointing out that clients have a right to refuse as well as be given treatment (McGough & Carmichael, 1977). Even when the client freely chooses to enter treatment, information obtained in the treatment process could conceivably be used to prosecute the client. Finally, the goals of treatment and of the court system may be similar, but they may not view behavior occurring in pursuit of goals in the same way. For example, if a program is interested in reducing a client's use of heroin and increasing competing activities, an occasional "dirty" urine sample may not be seen as a major problem. But, in California, if that dirty urine is reported in court the client is immediately liable to a minimum ninety-day jail sentence.

The issue, then, is a serious one. In order to help a client stop heroin use and establish a new lifestyle, the mental health agency may need the most powerful contingencies it can obtain. Strong rewards for stopping heroin use might be offered; strong punishment for addiction might also be arranged. Those contingencies can often best be obtained by working closely with the community, court, and probation-parole systems. Thus, the effective clinician often needs to deal with these agencies, to allow as much effective control of behavior as possible while still ensuring the rights of the client.

The cooperation of other agencies will also be crucial if a community-based shaping procedure is to be used to rehabilitate the drug addict. One powerful agency is the local vocational rehabilitation agency. While such agencies are charged with rehabilitating offenders, they are also evaluated in terms of their efficacy with regard to prospective employers, for whom they provide services. Since many heroin addicts have very poor job histories and are also quite likely to relapse, many agencies are reluctant to provide them with vocational training. This, of course, is a "Catch-22" position for both the mental health worker and the addict: The possession of job skills is the best predictor of successful outcome in the treatment of heroin addiction, yet heroin addiction is a stigma that prevents many addicts from obtaining job training and employment. One way around this problem is to allow addict-clients into job training only when they have developed a record of clean urine samples. A less satisfactory tactic which local agencies might suggest would be to guarantee access to urine records. This might prevent such an agency the embarrassment of sending a client to a job site when he or she was starting to use heroin again. A more acceptable alternative may be to agree to notify vocational rehabilitation of any problem with clients' status in treatment—e.g., if they are put on probation or suspended from treatment. Then the agency can make services contingent on good client status rather than urine samples per se. In each of these instances the addict-client has the right to refuse access to his or her treatment urine records, and even to knowledge that he or she is in treatment. However, each of the community agencies also has the right to refuse services to the addict or, in the case of the courts, to refuse to allow the addict to remain on the streets or, with probation-parole, to require extensive urine testing on their own. In each instance, the addict will have to make a decision based on the best information available. Thus the clinician is in the position of seeking two goals: (1) to advocate the client's rights *and* (2) to engineer the environment to help the client behave responsibly.

Practical Applications of Client Rights

With those goals in mind we will now turn to an examination of a series of practical issues for the clinician to consider: general legal issues, the voluntary nature of treatment, informed consent, confidentiality (for both voluntary and involuntary clients), and the rights of prisoners.

GENERAL LEGAL ISSUES

Many of the clients seen in drug treatment facilities have a variety of complex legal problems with which to deal, only some of which may result from heroin-related arrests. For this reason, Uelman and Eldridge

(1977) suggest that law-school practicum sites be developed at treatment facilities. This would not only provide law students with ample practice but aid the addict-clients as well.

In addition, it is critical for the clinician to avoid giving legal advice. Instead, it is worthwhile for treatment agencies to pursue law student placements or at least develop cordial relationships with the local public defenders office and legal aid programs, as recommended by Dubin, Buxton and Haller (1977). Areas in which these individuals are likely to have needed expertise include local and federal drug-possession statutes, sale and use laws, diversion policies, and the policies of local probation and parole officers.

One important aspect of local laws and policies is the procedures for the use of diversion programs. Diversion programs allow first (and sometimes repeating) offenders to avoid jail by seeking treatment. Procedure for diversion vary widely by state and even by county: For instance, although in California a person convicted of first-time heroin use is eligible for diversion to treatment, some counties encourage this policy while others avoid it. In fact, within a county two judges may have conflicting practices. When diversion is allowed, prosecution or sentencing is suspended while the client has the opportunity to be "rehabilitated," although it is not clear what constitutes "rehabilitation." If rehabilitation is to involve accepting treatment by a clinician, the relationship of the clinician to the legal authorities must be made clear. Is information to be passed back and forth regarding client progress? Are court penalties or rewards to be provided?

Finally, it is important to know the local policies of probation and parole. If a client is not allowed to use opiates, will a urine sample dirty with cocaine or a barbiturate subject the client to prosecution? If so, will the client's probation be revoked? What consequences will be reported marijuana use bring? Another critical local policy concerns overdoses. Do particular hospitals notify police of all overdoses? Certainly the primary responsibility of the clinician is to gain medical treatment for the client; however, it may be important for client and clinician to be aware of the legal ramifications of emergency treatment as well. However, the clinician cannot afford to aid the client in active circumvention of the law. It is thus important for the clinician to be aware of the local legal situation.

Several important legal issues with which the clinician must deal are discussed in the following sections.

THE VOLUNTARY NATURE OF TREATMENT

One of the most important federal laws on drug abuse is that any agency receiving funds from the Department of Health and Human

Services can accept only voluntary clients into treatment. Although the basic principle is stated clearly, its implementation can be confusing. It is clear, however, that "voluntary" does not imply a total absence of external pressure from the legal system or anywhere else in life. The key to the concept of voluntary presentation for treatment is that the client must be offered a set of viable choices. Thus, an arrested addict can voluntarily elect to enter a treatment program as an alternative to imprisonment. However, a person cannot be *sentenced* to be treated in a particular drug treatment program, nor can participation in one particular program be made a condition of probation or parole.

Even though it can smack of coercion, the relationship between the addict and the clinician must be a truly voluntary partnership. As defined by Newman,

> voluntary treatment describes a therapeutic relationship in which the primary responsibility of the clinician is to the patient. In an involuntary treatment setting, the clinician's primary responsibility is to some third party. An obligation to report patient attendance, progress or termination to an outside individual or agency defines the relationship as involuntary even if the patient is induced to sign, in advance, open-ended authorizations for such reports. (1974)

Since the clinician's primary obligation is to his or her client, careful consideration should be given to the kind of treatment offered to or imposed upon the client. For example, a client cannot be forced to enroll in a methadone maintenance program. However, due to the fact that methadone maintenance is the major treatment modality for opiate addiction there may be few or even no other alternatives, especially on an outpatient basis. Thus, some clients who are not long-term addicts sometimes choose to become long-term methadone maintenance clients in order to remain in the community. This presents a serious ethical dilemma to the staff of such a program.

Methadone maintenance is not the only treatment modality that must be considered with great care for the heroin addict. For example, aversion therapy procedures have sometimes been used with substance abusers without prior consent. For example, by pairing scoline (succinylchloline, a respiratory paralysis agent) with alcohol ingestion, attempts have been made to treat alcoholism (Clancy, Vanderhoof, & Campbell, 1967). Treatment of such great potential abuse might best be avoided with clients who are under strong influence from outside sources to seek and maintain treatment.

Even with less extreme treatment methodologies, the client-clinician relationship must be the primary source of goals set for treatment. If a client wishes to set a goal to achieve controlled use of opiates, the clinician is faced with three possible courses of action: (1) Dissuade the client, (2) accept the client's goal, or (3) refuse to treat the client. If the latter option is elected, the clinician's obligation is to help the client seek other treatment. However, in no case should a clinician agree to work with a client if they cannot agree on goals.

INFORMED CONSENT

In order to ensure that the client knows what is to be provided in treatment, informed consent is necessary. Informed consent has been interpreted by Sadoff (1974) to mean that the therapist must inform the prospective client about the therapeutic procedures he or she will receive if electing to undergo treatment, what the goals of this therapy will be, what its potential risks and benefits might be, and what—in detail—will happen to him or her if consent for treatment is given. In addition, Sadoff points out that the mental health practitioner must delineate the limits of confidentiality in each case. That, of course, will be determined by the legal status of the client. In addition, Scott (1977) points out that the clinician must point out to the prospective client that he or she has the right to refuse treatment as well. A sample script for informed consent is appended to this chapter (see Appendix 1).

Two points are salient here. First, many addicted clients asking for information about a prospective program will be under the influence of narcotics or other chemicals. In this case, it is unwise to have an informed consent form signed unless the same form is to be reviewed and resigned when the client is no longer under the influence of the drug. This precaution is suggested since it is not uncommon for clients to be unable to remember what they have said or heard when under the influence of heroin. In addition, it is possible that a document signed under the influence of opiates would not be valid in court.

Second, as previously mentioned, many courts will send a client to a treatment program as an alternative to jail. While this implies that the addict is being given a choice (jail versus treatment), it is possible that another court would find this a case of coercion. Providing a client with two courses of action one of which is obviously distasteful may be seen as eliminating any free choice. In order to avoid being a party to this ethical dilemma, the present authors accept referrals into treatment from the court system only if these clients are offered the option of seeking an alternative treatment placement if unsatisfied by the referral to our program (the Heroin Antagonist and Learning Therapy Project [HALT]). The treatment options of the client—including the right to leave treatment—are a critical part of the procedure of supplying full informed consent to the client.

Another aspect of informed consent is providing clients with information on the extent to which their involvement and progress in treatment are protected by confidentiality. Guidelines for confidentiality differ depending on whether treatment has been sentenced or not. Let us examine confidentiality first for the voluntary client.

CONFIDENTIALITY FOR THE VOLUNTARY CLIENT

The right of the addict-client to maintain anonymity of any sort derives from the client-physician privilege. Although this privilege is not one of the basic four privileges set out by common law—husband-wife, informer-government, attorney-client, and juror-juror (Weissman, 1976)— it has, however, been legislated into existence in most states. The amount of confidentiality privilege and responsibility accorded treatment personnel varies according to professional role and to local and federal statutes. When one statute is more rigorous in protecting confidentiality, it holds sway. Generally, physicians are accorded the most protection, psychologists the next most, and nonpsychologist therapists the least. Again, however, this privilege will vary according to state law and local legal precedents. West Virginia, for example, does not recognize any privileged communication between clients and psychologists.

Weissman (1976) provides detailed information on the interpretation of the two most critical federal statutes that control the confidentiality limits of drug-abuse treatment personnel: Section 408 of the Drug Abuse Office and Treatment Act of 1972 (P. L. 92-255) for drug abuse personnel; and the Comprehensive Alcohol Abuse and Alcoholism Prevention, Treatment, and Rehabilitation Act of 1974 (P. L. 93-282) for alcoholism treatment personnel.

These laws provide basic protection for all communication between treatment personnel and their clients except (1) when prior written consent for release has been obtained, and (2) without prior written consent in the cases of (a) a bona fide medical emergency, (b) scientific research, audits, and program evaluation, and (c) authorization by a show-cause court hearing where the public good is involved.

Interestingly, Weissman interprets these regulations as applying even to special probation and parole treatment units, so that these offices cannot use urine specimens or information provided them in the course of treatment to prosecute one of their treatment clients.

While these confidentiality rules hold for the client who comes voluntarily for treatment, other considerations hold for the client who comes into treatment under court order.

CONFIDENTIALITY FOR COURT-ORDERED CLIENTS

In the case of court-mandated treatment, full or partial information can be shared with the courts according to how much information the client agrees to give up. According to Weissman, several components are necessary for release of information:

1. name of client
2. name or position of person to receive information
3. name or position of person to relay information from program
4. purpose of disclosure of information
5. extent of information to be released
6. statement the consent can be revoked
7. date consent form is signed
8. signature of parent or guardian and client
9. signature of witness

A sample form derived from Weissman's suggestions is found in Appendix 2 at the end of this chapter. These consent forms would remain in effect for sixty days or until substantial change has occurred in the client's status (e.g., dismissal of court charges, acquittal, execution of sentence, or placement of formal charges). However, the court-mandated client cannot unilaterally revoke his consent for release of information.

Several legal issues remain unresolved regarding release of information. The first is that technically a client cannot be assumed to be giving informed consent to release of information if he or she does not know the contents of that information (Joling, 1974). While the right to confidentiality would obviously be violated in the instance in which an existing record is released without a client being aware of its contents, it is not known how this consent would affect a case in which a client agrees to give up information that does not yet exist (e.g., the results of urine tests scheduled to be taken during the next 60 days). Until contrary opinion is provided by legislation or the courts, programs and therapists can be asked by the courts to gain their clients' permission to release information not yet collected.

There are other known limitations to confidentiality, however, which can be considered at this point. In general, all information about a client and his or her behavior in a treatment program is confidential if there has not been a properly executed release of information. However, this does not prevent communication among personnel within a treatment program (Weissman, 1976). As in the rights of other mental health clients, it is not legal to even reveal that a certain person is a client under treatment, unless the client releases that information to the inquiring party. In fact, if a client commits a crime on the grounds against a staff member or another patient or against property, the criminal charges brought against the client cannot involve the revelation that he or she is under treatment. The code (Drug Abuse Office and Treatment Act of 1972) provides a fine of up to five hundred dollars for a first offense and one of no more than five thousand dollars for a second or subsequent offense. It is not clear how frequently this law has been utilized (implementation of a suit for grievances is the responsibility of the wronged client).

REPORTS TO THE COURT

Although the courts ask whether an addict has been "rehabilitated," the answer to that question is really beyond the capability of treatment personnel. Such an answer implies a change of state from addict to non-addict, and human behavior ordinarily does not change in such an all-or-none manner. But, instead of saying a client is "cured," a program can describe the client's behavior in treatment objectively.

The usual court letters provided by that HALT Project—of which the authors are a part—are intended to be as objectively verifiable as possible. The number of urine tests scheduled and their results are reported if the client's consent has been given. The number of therapy sessions scheduled and held is reported, again given the client's permission. Other program behaviors—such as calls to the project reporting data or efforts made to obtain or fulfill a job—would also be reported. No overall prediction of "cure" or "failure" is made; instead observable behavior is reported in detail. The courts appear favorably disposed to this system, and no client has ever asked to withold information from the courts. In the event of termination of a client from the program, a letter stating only this information is sent to the courts or to probation, depending on the source of initial referral. In addition, no further verbal information is shared on suspended or terminated clients unless a release of information has been signed. This agreement also appears acceptable to the other agencies, since it was stated before treatment began.

RIGHTS OF THE PRISONER: RIGHTS OF THE ADDICT-CLIENT?

While certain state and federal statutes address themselves directly to the rights of the addict-client, other rights are merely implied by, for example, what the court system has determined to be the rights of the prisoner. In this section we will briefly review these rights and consider their extension to the rights of client-addict in prison. As Ziegenfuss and Gaughan-Fickes (1976) have pointed out, there is a possibility that some of the internal policies of therapeutic communities and other drug rehabilitation programs may violate some of the basic rights that are now afforded any prisoner.

The most basic of prisoner rights pointed out by Ziegenfuss and Gaughan-Fickes are

1. the right to communicate and correspond with others (defined by *Morales* v. *Schmidt,* 1972),
2. the right to free speech,
3. the right to be free from cruel and unusual punishment (*Prison Reform Association* v. *Sharkley,* 1972),
4. the right to uncensored reading material unless there is a clear and present danger (*Jackson* v. *Bishop,* 1968), and
5. the right to due process in disciplinary hearings (*Wolff* v. *McDonnell,* 1974).

Possible violations of these rights might include various intensive punishments inflicted by some drug programs to bring about attitude change—viz., standing with nose and toes against the wall for an hour at a time (cruel and unusual punishment), elimination of patient correspondence (right to communicate), "hair cuts" or verbal dressings-down in which the addict-client is not allowed to defend himself or herself (due process), and so on. In each of these instances, Zeigenfuss and Gaughan-Fickes point out that a therapeutic community may well be in violation of clients' basic constitutional rights. Adoption of these procedures in a community mental health center might prove equally tenuous.

In summary then, an addict-client's rights cannot be less than those of a prisoner.

Narcotics Addiction in the Future

Narcotics addiction has been likened to an epidemic disease in this country. As such,

> it is public health dogma that no widespread human disease is ever brought under control by treatment of afflicted individuals. . . . Every plague affecting mankind has been controlled when discovery of the cause led to taking effective steps to remove it. This process is primary prevention. (Kessler & Albee, 1975, p. 557)

Primary prevention here can take two forms: (1) decriminalizing use of controlled substances—i.e., removing the legal penalty (Kurzman & Magelli, 1977), while examining the abuse of other drugs such as caffeine and nicotine more rationally (Bourne, 1977); (2) focusing on changing the societal strains that result in addictive behaviors for impoverished and minority members (Callahan & Rawson, 1980). The latter approach may be critical—according to Bayer (1978—since simple decriminalization ignores the social inequity underlying the behavior. Roffman (1977) points out that drug law changes may carry unexpected effects; he advocates careful consideration of the possible impact of such changes, just as with environmental policy changes.

In any event, drastic legal changes do not appear likely for a long time. However, gradual changes in the consciousness of the American people on the subject of drugs such as tobacco, nicotine, and tranquilizers may lead us to a more rational consideration of all drugs. For example, as Uelman and Wolf (1977) point out, a mother may now be held responsible for child abuse if she takes harmful drugs knowingly and voluntarily while pregnant. Thus, three main currents appear: (1) a questioning of the assumed "inherency of evil" in narcotics and necessity for drug-controlling legislation, (2) a liberalizing influence suggesting that narcotics and other drugs mask social problems such as poverty, lack of vocational skills, and education, and (3) a concurrent toughening of attitudes against unnecessary use of any drug, legal or illegal. How these currents will flow together to form future laws and attitudes remains to be seen. It is certain, however, that clinicians will need to work conscientiously to protect the rights of addict-clients for a long time to come.

References

American Psychological Association. *Casebook on Ethical Standards of Psychologists.* Washington, D.C.: Author, 1967.

BAYER, R. Heroin decriminalization and the ideology of tolerance: A critical review. *Law and Society,* 1978, *12,* 301–318.

BOUDIN, H. M., VALENTINE, V. E., INGRAHAM, R. D., BRANTLEY, J. M., RUIZ, M. R., SMITH, G. G., CATLIN, R. P., & REGAN, E. J. Contingency contracting with drug abusers in the natural environment. *The International Journal of the Addictions,* 1977, *12,* 1–16.

BOURNE, P. G. Drug abuse in the United States: A public policy analysis. *Contemporary Drug Problems,* 1977, *6,* 473–477.

BRECHER, E. M. *Licit and illicit drugs.* Boston: Little, Brown & Co., 1972.

CALLAHAN, E. J., PRICE, K., & DAHLKOETTER, J. Drug abuse. In R. Daitzman (Ed.), *Clinical behavior modification and therapy.* New York: Garland Press, 1980, pp. 175–248.

CALLAHAN, E. J., & RAWSON, R. A. Behavioral assessment of narcotic addiction and treatment outcome. In L. C. Sobell and M. B. Sobell (Eds.), *Treatment Outcome Evaluation in Alcohol and Drug Abuse.* New York: Plenum Press, 1980, pp. 77–92.

CALLAHAN, E. J., RAWSON, R. A., ARIAS, R. J., GLAZER, M. A., LIBERMAN, R. P., & McCLEAVER, B. A. Treatment of heroin addiction: Naltrexone alone and with behavior therapy. *International Journal of the Addictions,* in press.

CLANCY, J., VANDERHOOF, E., & CAMPBELL, P. Evaluation of an aversive technique as a treatment of alcoholism. *Quarterly Journal of Studies on Alcoholism*, 1967, *28*, 476–485.

DUBIN, L. A., BUXTON, M., & HALLER, L. Improving the relationship between mental health workers and lawyers. *Research Communications in Psychology, Psychiatry and Behavior*, 1977, *2*, 27–42.

HANEY, C., BANKS, C., & ZIMBARDO, P. G. Interpersonal prison. *International Journal of Criminology*, 1973, *1*, 69–67.

Jackson v. *Bishop*, 268 F. Supp. 804 (E. D. Ark. 1967); aff'd, 404 F.2d 571 (8th Cir. 1968).

JAFFE, J. H. The Swinging pendulum: The treatment of drug users in America. In R. L. DuPont, A. Goldstein, and J. O'Donnell (Eds.), Handbook of drug abuse. Washington, D.C.: U.S. Government Printing Office, 1978.

JOLING, R. J. Informed consent, confidentiality and privilege in psychiatry: Legal implications. *Bulletin of the American Academy of Psychiatry and the Law*, 1974, *2*, 107–110.

KESSLER, M., & ALBEE, G. W. Primary prevention. *Annual Review of Psychology*, 1975, *26*, 557.

KURZMAN, M. G., & MAGELLI, H. Decriminalizing possession of all controlled substances: An idea whose time has come. *Contemporary Drug Problems*, 1977, *6*, 245–259.

MCGOUGH, L. C., & CARMICHAEL, W. C. The right to treatment and the right to refuse treatment. *American Journal of Orthopsychiatry*, 1977, *47*, 307–320.

Morales v. *Schmidt*, 340 Fed. Supp. 544, 1972.

NEWMAN, R. G. Involuntary treatment of drug addiction. In P. G. Bourne (Ed.), *Addiction*. New York: Academic Press, 1974.

PLATT, J. J., & LABATE, C. *Heroin addiction*. New York: Wiley, 1976.

Prison Reform Association v. *Sharkley*, 347 Fed. Supp. 1234, 1972.

QUIJANO, W. Y., & LOGSDON, S. A. Some issues in the practice of correctional psychology in the context of security. *Professional Psychology*, 1978, *9*, 228–239.

RAWSON, R. A., CALLAHAN, E. J., GLAZER, M. A., & LIBERMAN, R. P. Behavior therapy versus naltrexone for heroin addiction. In N. Krasnegor (Ed.), *Behavioral treatment of the addictions*. Washington, D.C.: NIDA, in press. (Research Monograph)

ROFFMAN, R. A. Borrowing from the National Environmental Policy Act: A model for accountable drug abuse policy making. *Contemporary Drug Problems*, 1977, *6*, 373–395.

SADOFF, R. L. Informed consent, confidentiality in psychiatry: *Bulletin of the American Academy of Psychiatry and the Law*, 1974, *2*, 101–106.

SCOTT, E. P. The right to refuse treatment: A developing concept. *Hospital and Community Psychiatry*, 1977, *28*, 372.

SULKUNEN, P. Production, consumption and recent changes of consumption of alcoholic beverages. *British Journal of the Addictions*, 1976, *71*, 3–11.

THARP, R., & WETZEL, J. *Behavior modification in the natural environment*. New York: Academic Press, 1969.

UELMAN, G. F., & ELDRIDGE, J. W. Providing legal services to the addict: An experimental law school clinical program. *Contemporary Drug Problems,* 1977, *6,* 3–16.

UELMAN, G. F., & WOLF, J. E. Memorandum of law: Reyes v. Superior Court of State of California. *Contemporary Drug Problems,* 1977, *6,* 197–229.

WEISSMAN, J. C. The criminal justice practitioner's guide to the new federal alcohol and drug abuse confidentiality regulation. *Federal Probation,* 1976, *40,* 11–20.

WEISSMAN, J. C. The New York drug law evaluation: Further comment. *Contemporary Drug Problems,* 1977, *6,* 261–266.

Wolff v. *McDonnell,* 418 U.S. 539, 71 Ohio Op. 2d 336, 41 L. Ed. 2d 935, 94S. Ct. 2936 1974).

ZIEGENFUSS, J. T., & GAUGHAN-FICKES. Alternatives to prison programs—and client civil rights: A question. *Contemporary Drug Problems,* 1976, *5,* 207–217.

ZINBERG, N. E., JACOBSON, R., & HARDING, W. Sanctions and rituals as a basis for drug abuse prevention. *American Journal of Drug and Alcohol Abuse,* 1975, *2,* 165–179.

APPENDIX 1: HALT Project—Initial Explanation of Program

The Heroin Antagonist and Learning Therapy (HALT) Project is a heroin addiction treatment and research center which recently opened in Ventura, California. HALT has been funded for three years by the National Institute of Drug Abuse (NIDA) to provide two new treatment approaches for heroin addiction in Ventura County.

The two types of therapy use a narcotic antagonist (*naltrexone*) and behavior therapy respectively. These therapies will be provided to three groups of clients. One group of clients will receive the naltrexone, the effect of which is to block the "high" that a person experiences from shooting heroin. *Naltrexone cannot produce a high itself and is not addicting.* Naltrexone will not kill the urge to shoot heroine but will prevent the high usually produced by heroin. Over time, the urge to "shoot up" should decrease in strength, since the behaviors associated with heroin use no longer lead to the reward of a high. Prior research has found that naltrexone has very few side effects and produces no physiological or psychological dependence. *Taking naltrexone while any narcotics are in the body results in immediate and violent withdrawal.*

A second group of clients will receive behavior or *social learning* therapy. As part of this treatment, some extremely successful and powerful therapy techniques will be made available to the clients. These techniques are based on the fact that heroin use involves a collection of learned behaviors. The focus of this therapy, then, is to help the client abandon behaviors associated with heroin use and learn new, more productive behaviors. In particular, some techniques will teach the client ways of controlling the heroin urge (e.g., covert sensitization), while other techniques will teach the client ways to be more successful in dealing with their lives without using heroin (personal effectiveness training and contingency contracting). In addition, other forms of learning therapy will assist the client in dealing with such areas as marital difficulties, problems with family members, or problems in getting and holding a job.

The third group of clients will receive a combination of the naltrexone therapy and the learning therapy. Clients in all three categories will receive assistance in obtaining and maintaining employment, employment training, or further education. In addition, the project will assist all clients with legal problems regarding probation, parole, or impending court cases.

Several further points need to be made. First, due to the fact that HALT is in part a research program, the assignment of clients to therapy groups will be done randomly. Prior research has suggested that both treatment approaches should provide a good deal of success; there is no evidence that either treatment is superior to the other. The staff of HALT have been extensively trained in all components of the therapies being used. Second, although the HALT is an outpatient program with no residential facilities, it will be necessary for all clients to go through the fourteen-day detoxification program at Camarillo State Hospital. Third, the program is voluntary; at any time during the course of the therapy the client has the right to terminate his or her involvement and seek other referrals. Fourth, while it will not be possible for the client to select which treatment group to join, he or she will have a voice in selecting the specific aspects of treatment. Fifth, complete confidentiality will be guaranteed to the client on all aspects of the program.

Since the HALT is a federally funded program, there will be no charge for any of the services provided to the sixty addicts who will be treated. However, at the present time the Food and Drug Administration (FDA) has not approved the use of naltrexone with women. For this reason, only men will be treated as part of the research component of this project. In addition, the project plans to focus on those men between the ages of eighteen and twenty-five. While these restrictions do reduce the number of men over the age of twenty-five and women that can be admitted to the program, it may in some instances be possible to admit people in these categories.

APPENDIX 2: Informed Consent—Description of Client Rights and Risks in the HALT Project

I am aware that this is a clinical research study directed by Richard A. Rawson, Ph.D. and Robert P. Liberman, M.D. The purpose of the study is to evaluate the possible effectiveness of *naltrexone* (a narcotic antagonist) and *behavior therapy* in the treatment of heroin addiction.

I am further aware that:

1. Naltrexone is a narcotic antagonist, a drug which blocks the effects of heroin and other opiate drugs such as methadone and morphine, yet is not addicting.

2. If I take naltrexone within seventy-two hours of narcotic use, I will experience immediate narcotic withdrawal and become very ill.

3. Naltrexone is still an experimental drug and has not yet been approved for widespread use by the Food & Drug Administration.

4. If I volunteer for this project, I will be placed randomly (by chance) into one of four groups:

    a. High Intervention (behavior therapy); *mobile* dispensing of naltrexone.

    b. High Intervention (behavior therapy); *HALT* dispensing of naltrexone.

    c. Low Intervention; *mobile* dispensing of naltrexone.

    d. Low Intervention; *HALT* dispensing of naltrexone.

5. The behavior therapy of the High Intervention program will consist, in part, of:

    a. Strengthening Therapy

    b. Life Management Training

    c. Vocational Preparation and Placement

In addition, other behavior therapies will be provided for other specific clinical problems that either exist or arise.

6. If assigned to one of the Low Intervention groups, I am aware that treatment will consist of receiving daily 50 mg doses of naltrexone for one week; followed by a naltrexone schedule of two 100 mg doses and one 150 mg dose per week for the next six months. I further understand that my dose will be reduced in graduated amounts for two months following completion of the period described previously. In addition, I understand that personal and family counseling, as well

as assistance with welfare, employment, and legal agencies will be available if I need such services.

7. If I am in the group receiving a combination of the two interventions, treatment will consist of behavior therapy plus treatment with naltrexone as described above.

8. I know I am expected to stay in treatment for at least nine months; however, I am also aware that I may withdraw from treatment at any time without prejudice.

9. During the time that I am involved in this study I will be required to undergo various medical tests and to answer questions about myself and my experiences with whichever treatment I am receiving. I realize that these procedures are necessary for HALT to make sure that naltrexone is not harmful, and to determine how useful the treatments are in helping people like myself stay off heroin.

10. I will be required to give urine samples several times per week (collected under supervision).

11. The medical tests which I will undergo include physical examination, laboratory tests of blood samples, heart monitoring (EKG), and chest X-rays.

12. I have been told that naltrexone has been tested in animals and in humans and that it appears to be a relatively safe drug with no known serious effects.

13. I am aware that no one can entirely foresee the possible harmful effects of an experimental drug. There may be side effects or toxic effects of which the National Institute on Drug Abuse (NIDA) is not aware. Therefore, while HALT and NIDA believe that the risks to my health are minimal, they cannot be entirely sure of the eventual consequences of participation in the study. HALT has informed me of the following risks and discomfort which might be experienced by persons participating in this study:

   a. The side effects *sometimes* experienced by people who take naltrexone may include mild stomach cramps, nausea, and irritability. These symptoms are usually mild and tend to disappear after several days of continued use of the drug.
   b. The doses of naltrexone used in the study will block the effects of a moderate dose of heroin from twenty-four to seventy-two hours. Any attempt to overcome the blockade by shooting large doses of narcotics could be very dangerous and *could cause an overdose!*
   c. Naltrexone has been reported to cause a slight rise in blood pressure when people first begin taking it. This rise usually returns to normal after a few days of taking the drug; at present, this does not seem likely to be harmful to my health.
   d. Naltrexone will cause severe withdrawal if taken by persons who have used narcotic drugs within seventy-two hours.
   e. The medical tests required in this study involve taking small samples of blood by venipuncture (placing a needle into a vein). The risks of sampling blood in this way are extremely low in a medical facility with clean techniques. Potential complications of this procedure include pain, bleeding, bruising, light-headedness, fainting, and, in rare instances, infection.

14. I am aware that HALT cannot guarantee that I will receive any benefits from participation in this study other than those which I would get by being a part of any regular treatment program.

15. I have been informed that the results from the testing of naltrexone and reports on behavior therapy with people like myself make HALT think that these techniques may be very useful to addicted people.

16. I know that I am under no obligation to participate in this study.

17. I am aware that I may withdraw from this study and stop taking naltrexone at any time without penalty. My participation in this project is completely voluntary.

18. I know that if I choose not to be a part of this project the following treatment programs are available to me in this area:
   a. Young Adult Drug Counseling Service
   b. Ventura County Methadone Maintenance
   c. Hacienda House (formally DAPC)
   d. Ventura County General Hospital (Emergency Medical Services)
   e. Moorpark Drop-in Center
   f. Interface Community
   g. Teen Challenge
   h. Narcotics Anonymous

19. I know that if the procedures used in the program are to be changed I will be informed and asked to sign a new informed consent form.

20. I have been told that all the information collected on me in this study is confidential and will not be identified with me outside this project unless so agreed specifically by me, in writing, unless required by law.

21. The HALT Project will only contact a third party (i.e., employer, wife, family member, parole or probation officer) to obtain data for a follow-up study on me with my permission on a separate sheet.

Follow-up data may consist of HALT seeking information from employers on work attendance, work habits, and performance; from family and friends on attitude since treatment, changes in my lifestyle, and personal relationships. Parole and/or probation status will be investigated, and I will be interviewed by a HALT follow-up investigator concerning my life and activities after treatment at HALT.

22. I am aware that if I do things which are harmful to the HALT Project or harm other individuals associated with this project I will be discharged from treatment.

23. I know that I may inquire about any aspect of the program, the drug, or the behavioral therapy now or at any time during treatment. (Dr. _____ can be contacted at _____ and Dr. _____ at _____.)

I am fully conversant in the English language. I have read and I understand the above description of this program, and all my questions at this time have been answered satisfactorily. I hereby agree to participate in the HALT Project.

Date: _____   Signature:_____
                                                    Client

I have explained each paragraph of this form to the satisfaction of the above-named client.

                               Signature:_____
                                                    Witness

APPENDIX 3: Release of Information Form

I, _____, hereby authorize the staff of the HALT Program to release information about my:

    1. _____
    2. _____
    3. _____
    4. _____

to _____ of _____ .
      (individual)   (agency)

I realize that the purpose of this release of information is to allow successful treatment.

    I am also aware that I can revoke this release at any time. This release covers the time from _____ to _____ , inclusive.

_____   _____
       Date   Signature of Client

                             _____
                             Signature of Guardian

                             _____
                             Signature of Witness

CHAPTER 11

Rights, Risks, and Responsibilities in the Use of Self-Help Psychotherapy

Manuel Barrera, Jr.
Gerald M. Rosen
Russell E. Glasgow

IN HIS 1969 PRESIDENTIAL ADDRESS to the American Psychological Association, George Miller (1969) admonished psychologists to actively contribute their knowledge and skills to resolve the very real and pressing problems that people experience. He suggested that, rather than being confined to scientific settings, psychology be "given away" to the public as a way of promoting human welfare. Although there is much more that psychologists and other mental health professionals could be doing, they have made some clear attempts to share their knowledge with the public. A principle means for sharing information has been through the distribution of self-help materials that are designed to guide individuals in solving problems, acquiring new information, or changing behaviors.

Particularly when expressed in such altruistic terms as "giving psychology away," the efforts by professionals to develop and market self-help treatments can be perceived as a constructive and professionally responsible approach to assisting others in improving their own lives. But despite the possible benefits of self-help therapies, it is important to consider the potential risks to self-help consumers. Are there potential dangers for those who use self-help psychotherapies? What actions can professionals take to maximize the gains and minimize the risks to consumers?

Concern about the risks of therapy and the responsibility of professionals to protect consumers are not unique to do-it-yourself therapies. Chapters in this volume collectively illustrate general concerns about the protection of mental health and education consumers. But because self-help psychotherapies can involve limited face-to-face contact—or none at all—between professional and consumer, several issues warrant special consideration.

Definition and Scope of Self-Help Psychotherapies

For the purposes of this chapter, "self-help psychotherapy" will refer to procedures that assist consumers in making self-directed changes in the relative absence of therapist supervision. Self-help therapies most typically consist of books and other written materials, but they also appear in the form of audio- and videotape programs.[1]

Self-help approaches are certainly not new. Books have long been available to instruct the public in the popular therapies of the day. Ellis notes, "Cognitive and cognitive-behavior therapies such as RET, have been very widely used as modes of unsupervised self-help treatment for thousands of years" (1978, p. 5). Among the historical examples of self-help books, Ellis cites the Bible, Koran, and other religious works which have strived to create changes in the attitudes and behaviors of their readers. Self-help books more clearly related to mental health were published as early as the turn of the century (Crane, 1905; and Dumont, 1913). In the more recent past, there have been prominent examples of books that have had a major impact on public thinking (e.g., Peale, 1956; Spock, 1946).

Literally hundreds of self-help therapies exist. Kimbrell (1975) has noted that over 100 books on weight control are on the market, a single publisher (Wilshire Book Company) lists 160 titles related to self-improvement, and over 200 books are available on child care alone (Clarke-Stewart, 1978). The scope of clinical problems addressed by self-help media is extensive, and includes many of the problems that are presented to professional therapists. Similarly, self-help is certainly not confined to any particular theoretical orientation or school of therapy. A full range of therapeutic approaches from psychoanalysis to behavior modification is represented.

Even though there has been a proliferation of self-help therapies, there has been a conspicuous lack of systematic evaluation, either before or after the programs are marketed (Bernal & North, 1978; Clarke-Stewart, 1978; Glasgow & Rosen, 1978, in press; McMahon & Forehand, in press). Glasgow and Rosen are following their first review of self-help be-

---

[1] Because this chapter is primarily concerned with professional responsibilities in developing self-help psychotherapies, it will not be directly concerned with self-help organizations that emphasize mutual aid among nonprofessional consumers (e.g., Alcoholics Anonymous). These organizations will be considered relevant here only if they incorporate the use of self-help materials, such as those of Stuart (1977) in his work with Weight Watchers.

havior therapy manuals (1978) with a second review, two years later (in press). In the first interview the ratio of evaluative studies to manuals was 86 percent; this figure dropped to 59 percent for new manuals covered in the second review. Seemingly, as the number of self-help psychotherapies increases, consumers are faced with the increased availability of untested materials and procedures.

Benefits from Self-Help Psychotherapies

In order to put the subsequent discussion of dangers and needed safeguards into proper perspective, the benefits that potentially result from self-help psychotherapies deserve acknowledgment. The possible advantages offered by self-help therapies make it worthwhile to consider ways of reducing the risks to consumers through responsible professional action.

EXPANDING THE RANGE OF SERVICES

Perhaps the most positive attribute of self-help therapies is that they expand the provision of clinical services by allowing consumers to "self-direct" their own treatment under varying levels of professional supervision (Glasgow & Rosen, 1978). There are numerous examples of how therapists might economically monitor ongoing self-help therapies with telephone contacts (Kahn & Baker, 1968; Phillips, Johnson, & Geyer, 1972; Rosen, Glasgow & Barrera, 1976; Zeiss, 1978), written communications (Bastien & Jacobs, 1974; Marston, Marston, & Ross, 1977), infrequent sessions (Glasgow, 1978), or group supervision (Barrera, 1979; Hagen, 1974; Miller, 1977).

The reduced contact with professionals that results from self-help methods has several implications for expanding services. First, because of fewer required contacts with each client, therapists can conceivably redistribute their time in order to serve more clients. Second, self-help treatments can reach individuals who live in areas where clinicians are scarce. Recent evidence suggests that mental health professionals are clustered in affluent urban centers and are relatively absent in less affluent rural areas (Richards & Gottredson, 1978). Until professionals become more equitably distributed, consumers might profitably use self-help materials on their own or with the occasional long-distance supervision of therapists. A third application of self-help therapies calls for clients to use these approaches for problems particularly suitable for self-directed change, while devoting time with therapists to confronting issues less amenable to self-help. Finally, with reduced therapist contact comes the possibility of decreased costs, so that therapy will be within financial reach of more consumers.

EDUCATING CONSUMERS
ABOUT PSYCHOTHERAPY

In addition to changing problematic behaviors and attitudes, self-help psychotherapies can also serve an educational function. For individuals who know little about psychotherapy, the explicit descriptions of treatment procedures that are often contained in self-help therapies are ideally suited to structuring expectations for prospective clients. Structuring the expectation of clients prior to their entry into psychotherapy has been found to have beneficial effects on participation in treatment and its outcome (Hoehn-Saric, Frank, Imber, Nash, Stone, & Battle, 1964). For several years Patterson and his colleagues have used programmed texts, such as *Living with Children* (Patterson & Gullion, 1968) and *Families* (Patterson, 1971), to teach parents the basic principles of child management before having them work intensively with therapists (Patterson, Reid, Jones, & Conger, 1975). Marks points out to prospective readers of his book on fear reduction that "severe problems are best handled by professional therapists, but you can help them help you if you understand your difficulty a bit better and get some idea of how to cope with it" (1978, pp. x–xi).

Evidence that self-instructional materials can have beneficial effects on subsequent therapy has been provided by Parrino (1971). In this study subjects who used programmed texts to learn relevant pretherapy information responded significantly better to behavioral treatment for snake phobia than those control subjects who either read irrelevant information or received no pretherapy preparation.

In a somewhat different vein, self-help therapies have been used in formal courses to teach students the principles of behavior change. More specifically, there have been several college-level courses in which students learned behavior therapy techniques by conducting their own self-modification projects (Barrera & Glasgow, 1976; McGahie & Menges, 1975; Reppucci & Baker, 1969).

MAINTAINING TREATMENT EFFECTS

There has been some suggestion that self-help psychotherapies aid consumers in achieving long-lasting treatment gains that are resistant to relapse. After completing therapist-administered treatment, clients might receive self-help materials to assist them in continuing therapy procedures or serve as a reference for reinstituting treatment as needed. Miller (1977) reports a study in which clients received a self-help manual for the control of problem drinking, following their involvement in therapist-directed treatment. Although the beneficial effects of using the manual were relatively small, the results suggested that self-help psychotherapy may be an economical method of improving maintenance.

Even when not used subsequent to therapist-administered treatment, self-help approaches are thought to enhance maintenance effects by increasing self-attributions for change. Stuart (1977) briefly reviewed the argument, based on attribution theory (Davison & Valins, 1969), that behavior changes are more likely to be maintained if attributed to self-mastery than to factors outside an individual's control. To the extent that self-help therapies cultivate belief in self-control they could sustain treatment effects beyond those achieved with therapist-administered psychotherapy. More data are needed, however, to substantiate this claim.

PREVENTING THE DEVELOPMENT OF PROBLEMS

Christensen, Miller, and Muñoz (1978) have discussed self-help therapies' potential utility not only in treatment and maintenance but in the prevention of mental health problems. Prevention can be conceptualized as including efforts to prevent both the disorder's initial occurrence and a mild disorder from becoming even more severe (Cowen, 1973). Many of the self-help books that attempt to teach parenting skills to parents of "normal" children and much of the popular literature on nutrition and exercise represent approaches for promoting healthy lifestyles that are intended to prevent problems from initially developing. Other self-help psychotherapies are designed to appeal to individuals who have recognized at least the beginning signs of a problem they desire to better understand or change.

Clark and his colleagues (Clark, Green, Macrae, McNees, Davis, & Risley, 1977) report the development of self-help materials that illustrate the combination of both prevention approaches. Their advice protocol was written specifically to help normal families reduce the problems they experience with their children on shopping trips. Within this context they also included procedures for promoting positive interactions between parents and their children to make these trips both pleasurable and educational.

SUMMARY

Although many of the potential benefits of self-help are still speculative and without extensive empirical validation, they show a substantial promise for prevention, treatment, and maintenance. At a time when direct clinical services are often costly and scarce, do-it-yourself therapies represent a branch of mental health technology that could provide inexpensive, accessible methods of making self-improvements (Lanyon & Johnson, in press). In many ways the time seems right for self-help therapies. People are already accustomed to consulting do-it-yourself books for making home improvements, repairing valuable possessions, and growing their own food. As people stock their homes with technological hardware, such as audio-cassette players, videotape units, and even computers, there is every likelihood that self-help will increasingly be available through a variety of media. The numerous beneficial applications of self-help psychotherapies provide sufficient justification for professionals to continue to develop, evaluate, and improve the products they offer consumers.

The Risks of Self-Help Psychotherapies

Despite the unique contributions that self-help can make, our enthusiasm for these approaches should be tempered by a critical appraisal of the concomitant dangers that might be involved in their use. There is a propensity for professionals to adopt the mind-set that while at least some clients will derive substantial benefit from treatment, others will at worst merely fail to change at all. It is difficult to consider the possibility that some will actually become *worse* as a result of our hard work and well-intentionel efforts. By now, however, most therapists are at least somewhat aware that psychotherapy can produce not only positive and neutral effects, but "deterioration effects" as well (Bergin, 1971; Stuart, 1970). Extrapolating from the results of therapist-directed psychotherapy leads us to the disconcerting realization that some enlisting the aid of self-help therapies in the hope of making improvements might actually experience unanticipated, undesirable effects. In order to inform consumers of potential dangers and to embark on steps to maximize the safety of self-help approaches, it is obviously important to delineate the risks involved in their use.

IMPROPER ASSESSMENT

The first stage of traditional psychotherapy ideally involves a thorough assessment of the client's skills, deficits, and self-defined treatment goals. In most cases the clinician attempts to determine (sequentially) whether psychotherapy is appropriate for the client, what target problems are in need of modification, and which treatment methods are likely to achieve the desired objectives. The vast literature on clinical assessment attests to the complexity of these tasks. Yet in those self-help therapies that do not include initial evaluations by professionals, consumers are expected to conduct the same sequence of assessment and decision making that a trained clinician would conduct. Not only is self-assessment one of the most difficult tasks that faces the self-help consumer, it is one that contains substantial risks that could result from faulty evaluations and errant decisions.

Two basic errors can be made by those deciding to pursue self-help therapy. Although it can be argued that there is always room for improvement, some might diagnose themselves as "sick" when there is little objective evidence for this judgment. In these cases, some self-help therapies may simply aid and abet the consumer in maintaining his or her self-label rather than leading to the abandonment of it. When self-help materials do not contain procedures for preventing self-identified false positives, consumers invest needless time and energy in attempts at self-change and risk the adverse consequences of sustained labels of abnormality.

A second and perhaps more dangerous outcome of faulty initial self-assessment occurs when consumers treat themselves for conditions that are inappropriate for self-help, either because of the severity of the problem or because nonpsychological treatment methods are needed. When applied inappropriately in these ways, not only is self-help likely to be unsuccessful, there is the real danger that its use will result in the postponement of proper professional care. Consider, for example, problems such as tension headache or sexual dysfunction, in which the possible contribution of organic conditions should be adequately assessed. Relying exclusively on self-help psychotherapies could prevent professional treatment and contribute to mounting severity of the problem.

Determining whether a self-help approach is appropriate may often depend on a rather precise specification of the problem, particularly as the effectiveness of a program becomes established for a certain problem and client population. For example, a self-help book might be effective for certain phobias, but ineffective for generalized anxiety or recalcitrant fears such as agoraphobia. A set of materials might be appropriate for reactive depression, but not for the depressive phase of manic-depressive disorders.

Pinpointing problem areas also involves the determination of just who has the problem, who should be involved in treatment, and who might be effected by the therapy procedures. Professionals can recognize the importance of *objectivity* in conducting broad-based assessments of clients' intrapersonal characteristics as well as their social and physical environments. Yet it is also apparent that distorted perceptions, preoccupations with the self, and impairments in judgment are frequently at the core of the problems that clients bring to therapy and can lead to inappropriate self-assessment. As examples of one extreme, we are reminded of clients who seek individual therapy out of self-blame for their sexual inadequacies, depression, marital distress, or child management problems when others reasonably share in the responsibility for making necessary changes. A risk of self-assessment is a perpetuation of a "blame-the-victim" orientation (Ryan, 1971) when treatment might more appropriately focus on environmental agents, actively including them within a comprehensive treatment plan. At the other extreme, some self-help therapies have been developed to assist the consumer in changing the behavior of another individual (e.g., child management books). In cases where the self-help consumer behaves as a "therapist" for others, the negative consequences of faulty assessment are extended to people other than the actual self-help user.

RISKS IN PRESCRIBING TREATMENT METHODS

Once it has been determined that a self-help approach is appropriate, and a target problem has been identified, the consumer is faced with the selection of suitable treatment materials. Often a number of self-help therapies representing different therapeutic approaches exist for a given clinical problem. How is the consumer to select from among the available programs? To facilitate educated comparison shopping, information concerning each program's efficacy and potential risks should be readily accessible. However, as topical reviews of self-help therapies have noted, there is a marked lack of evaluative research on most available programs (Clarke-Stewart, 1978; Glasgow & Rosen, 1978, in press; McMahon & Forehand, in press). Since it is unlikely that many consumers scrutinize the professional literature in order to select a self-help therapy, they often run the risk of selecting untested programs of questionable effectiveness.

Even after a particular self-help therapy has been selected, the task of choosing among alternative approaches is still not over for the consumer. In recognition of the complexity of many clinical disorders, writers frequently include descriptions of a variety of techniques, each of which addresses a distinct facet of a larger syndrome or constellation of problems. Books on parenting, weight control, smoking reduction, and other multifaceted problems often include a "Chinese menu" of techniques that requires the reader to exercise judgment in making appropriate selections. Currently there is a clear shortage of research findings that could aid consumers in identifying specific techniques that would optimally match their presenting problems. Because even in therapist-administered treatment it is unclear which therapist, client, and treatment conditions combine to form effective treatment (Bergin &

Strupp, 1972), it is likely in self-help therapy that the problem of creating the best fit between consumers and techniques will be a persistent one.

THE RISK OF FAILURE

Over the years there has been a considerable amount of controversy regarding the effectiveness of psychotherapy (Eysenck, 1952, 1972; Luborsky, 1954, 1972). A few forms of psychotherapy can boast impressive success rates with certain client populations, but there are no guarantees for success attached to most treatments. Just as we can expect that some clients who receive therapist-directed psychotherapy will fail, we can also safely predict that some self-help consumers will be unsuccessful in their efforts at self-improvement. Whereas in therapist-directed treatment a professional is available to make necessary referrals or other recommendations in the event of failure, failure of self-help efforts will of course occur in the relative absence of therapist supervision; it is therefore particularly important to consider its ramifications and contributing factors.

As discussed earlier in the chapter, successful self-help is believed to lead to greater maintenance than therapist-directed treatment because it enhances self-perceptions of competency and control over behavior. Extending this argument, we might predict that unsuccessful self-help will carry a relatively greater risk of impaired self-perceptions of worth and efficacy. It would also be important to determine if failure at self-help discourages consumers from consulting with mental health professionals or attempting other self-help approaches.

What factors contribute to the failure of self-help therapies? As previously discussed, clients' assessment of targets for change and selection of appropriate treatment programs are key initial tasks that influence the potential success of self-help. However, beyond these initial phases the failure of many consumers to complete their programs is a prominent problem. Difficulties with noncompliance have been noted with self-directed procedures to treat fear reduction (Barrera & Rosen, 1977; Marshall, Presse, & Andrews, 1976; Rosen, Glasgow, & Barrera, 1976), sexual dysfunction (Zeiss, 1978), weight control (Hanson, Borden, Hall, & Hall, 1976), and study behavior (Beneke & Harris, 1972). Treatment procedures have little chance of benefiting consumers unless they can be successfully completed.

For some treatment methods, early termination may create problems that are more severe than those existing prior to treatment. Consider, for example, child management procedures that instruct parents in extinguishing their children's negative behaviors. Increases in negative behaviors have been typically observed shortly after the initiation of extinction procedures, and termination of therapy at the point of heightened disruptive behavior would serve to exacerbate an already undesirable condition.

Related to the problem of clients prematurely terminating self-help therapy is that of them incorrectly implementing prescribed treatment procedures. Despite the pains taken by program developers to clearly specify instructions, there is little assurance that therapy regimens will be followed as described. Because self-help therapies differ substantially in complexity and clarity, they might also differ in their potential for intentional or unintentional client noncompliance. Furthermore, self-help therapies seem to vary in the degree of risk they present as a result of deviations from the prescribed procedures. For example, deviations from a self-help approach to child management advocating the exclusive use of positive contingencies for desirable behavior might present fewer risks than deviations from one calling for punishment of undesirable behavior. Similarly, if people are going to make mistakes or improvise on treatment procedures, a program instructing readers in desensitization procedures emphasizing gradual approach of fear-eliciting stimuli might be less dangerous than one based on flooding procedures.

SUMMARY

The preceding sections have described the risks that consumers potentially encounter in determining the appropriateness of self-help therapy, assessing targets for change, selecting treatment methods, and implementing therapeutic procedures. Often the tasks of self-help, while complex and demanding, are as yet unsubstantiated by research. Consumers are asked to make judgments and follow procedures that challenge even experienced therapists. These conditions and the ever-present potential for human error make the pursuit of self-help a risky enterprise.

There are other possible dangers that might result from the use of self-help therapies, which could have been discussed here. But rather than delineate everything that could conceivably go wrong with self-help, an attempt has been made here to draw attention to risks that have major negative consequences or are frequently present among existing programs. In light of the extant risks, there are compelling reasons for professionals to consider guidelines for developing self-help programs perhaps more rigorous in some respects than those for traditional psychotherapy. The concern expressed by Clark *et al.* (1977) for self-help parenting manuals should be more generally applied to other forms of self-help:

> For popular dissemination, such advice "packages" need to be evaluated more thoroughly than procedures disseminated through professionals to

ensure that . . . the advice as presented would be understood, followed, and not misused by parents. (p. 606)

Professional Responsibilities

When discussing the responsibilities of those who develop and market self-help therapies, it is important to keep in mind that self-help programs flourish even without the assistance of mental health professionals. But although professionals are not entirely responsible for the activities of the self-help industry, they can make valuable contributions to the improvement of self-help, including protection of the safety of consumers.

Despite the long involvement of professionals in the production of self-help therapies, they have not established specific standards guiding the development and marketing of self-help products. Instead, monetary contingencies and the decisions of publishers heavily influence which self-help programs are to be developed and distributed to the public. The role of professional organizations in regulating self-help is controversial (Goldiamond, 1976; Rosen, 1976, 1977), and it may prove difficult to achieve a consensus regarding acceptable practices. But even in the absence of specific standards for the development of self-help therapies, it is still possible to examine the extent to which existing ethical standards address the issues related to self-help.

ETHICAL STANDARDS AND PROFESSIONAL RESPONSIBILITIES

Although psychologists represent only one group of mental health professionals, they illustrate the role of professionals generally in the development of responsible self-help approaches. Consider, for example, those sections from the current *Ethical Standards of Psychologists* (APA, 1977) that are applicable to self-help. The Preamble states that psychologists are "committed to increasing knowledge of human behavior and of people's understanding of themselves and others and to the utilization of such knowledge for the promotion of human welfare." Principle 1 alerts psychologists to their social responsibility in affecting the lives of others and to the need to maintain the highest standards of their profession. Principle 2 states that psychologists should "only provide services, use techniques, or offer opinions as professionals that meet recognized standards." Principle 4 requires psychologists to take into account the limitations and uncertainties of current knowledge and techniques, and to ensure that their public statements present information that is scientifically accurate and acceptable.

In 1978 the American Psychological Association created the Task

Force on Self-Help Therapies[2] to consider the applicability of its ethical standards to "do-it-yourself" treatments. This task force paraphrased the above-cited principles in the following manner:

> Self-help therapies can help people to understand themselves and they may provide one of the most effective instructional modalities for promoting human welfare (Preamble). However, psychologists bear heavy professional responsibilities in developing such programs. This is particularly the case in light of the influence that psychologists may have on the behavior of others (Principle 1). Accordingly, self-help therapies that are developed by psychologists should meet recognized standards, as is the case for all therapeutic modalities (Principle 2). The development of self-help therapies should not be compromised by financial pressures or other factors (Principle 1). Public statements, announcements, and promotional activities pertaining to a commercially published self-help therapy should be informative. Sensationalism is to be avoided in such statements. The limitations as well as the benefits of a self-help therapy should be clearly stated (Principle 4).

A visit to a local bookstore will suffice to demonstrate the extent to which these ethical standards are being violated. The titles of books and the promotional claims that accompany them are frequently in violation of Principle 4. In many cases, one cannot help but feel that professional responsibility has given way to financial pressures. Certainly, the titles of self-help programs and promotional claims have not been kept within the bounds of existing data. Consider, for example, the Mahoneys' statement, "We remain a long way from any semblance of justification of complacency in weight regulation; significant poundage losses are still in the minority and long-term maintenance has remained unexamined" (Mahoney & Mahoney, 1976, p. 30). Yet, as Franks and Wilson note in their *Annual Review of Behavior Therapy*, "the same year these very same authors published a book entitled *Permanent Weight Control*" (1978, p. 656). Extravagent claims do a disservice to the public by fostering unrealistic expectations; and these claims do a disservice to professionals as well by discrediting through association those who responsibly develop self-help therapies.

RECOMMENDATIONS FOR PROFESSIONAL ACTION

There are several ways in which professionals can contribute to the development of self-help psychotherapies in order to protect consumers from potential dangers.

---

[2] The APA Task Force on Self-Help Therapies consists of Manuel Barrera, Jr. Cyril Franks, Herbert Freudenberger, Russell Glasgow, Susan Gilmore, Edward Lichtenstein, Peter Nathan, and Gerald Rosen (chair). At the time of this writing the recommendations made by the task force are still under review.

1. Professionals could promote the systematic development of effective self-help procedures by establishing standards similar to those that guide the developers of psychological tests. The involvement of responsible professional organizations could provide needed leadership in establishing these guidelines. Such a recognized set of standards would be a principle vehicle for drawing attention to the potential risks of self-help. The guidelines would also clarify methodological issues and suggest directions for developing programs to minimize risks.

Some of the raw materials for these standards already exist in the literature. Methodological considerations for evaluating programs have been previously discussed (Glasgow & Rosen, 1978, in press). In addition, Clark, Risley, and others have outlined a model for the step-by-step creation of self-help materials that can serve as a valuable guide to other professionals (Clark et al., 1977; Risley, Clark, & Cataldo, 1976). There is certainly ample room for supplementing the existing literature with examples of adequately developed self-help programs. Establishing guidelines would, one hopes, stimulate research on difficult problems—such as noncompliance and inadequate self-assessment methods—that present possible risks.

2. In addition to developing safe, effective treatment procedures, professionals have a responsibility to inform consumers of the potential benefits and risks of self-help programs. A standard set of information could accompany instructional materials developed by professionals. Books could contain a fact sheet explaining the extent to which and conditions under which the program had been evaluated, recommended uses of the program, reading level of the instructions, and realistic expectations regarding outcome. As program evaluations are conducted, consumers could be provided with evaluation results having implications for the use of the materials. For example, findings from a study by Zeiss (1978) led to the following caution to readers in Zeiss and Zeiss's self-help program for premature ejaculation:

> Research we have done with an earlier version of this program suggests that couples can successfully treat their own premature ejaculation difficulties, but it also indicates that couples have a lot of difficulty following through with the program on their own. In our research, minimal contact with a therapist averaging only 6 minutes a week makes a tremendous difference in couples' abilities to complete treatment. . . . You may wish to make similar arrangements for yourselves. (1978, pp. 36–37)

Appropriate cautions should routinely accompany self-help materials.

3. Professionals could participate in more broadly educating the public in the use of self-help therapies. A pamphlet could be developed describing the numerous self-help therapies now available. Realistic expectations in light of sensationalized claims would be discussed. The options of using self-help materials with or without therapist supervision would be considered. Activities of organizations such as the Committee on Public Information of the American Academy of Pediatrics and the National Self-Help Clearinghouse exemplify possible roles for professionals in educating consumers.

SUMMARY

When professionals accept the responsibilities and rewards that come from developing self-help therapies, they also accept the responsibility for protecting consumers against the potential risks. Existing ethical standards already provide professionals with considerable direction for making significant contributions to the self-help arena. Specific standards for guiding the creation and careful evaluation of self-help therapies might do even more to encourage professionals to maximize both the safety and efficacy of their programs. Finally, by informing consumers of the potential risks and benefits of self-help, professionals will increase the ability of consumers to make educated decisions regarding use of self-help psychotherapies.

References

American Psychological Association. *Ethical standards of psychologists.* Washington, D.C.: Author, 1977.

BARRERA, M., JR. An evaluation of a brief group therapy for depression. *Journal of Consulting and Clinical Psychology,* 1979, *47,* 413–415.

BARRERA, M., JR., & GLASGOW, R. E. Design and evaluation of a personalized instruction course in behavioral self-control. *Teaching of Psychology,* 1976, *3,* 81–84.

BARRERA, M., JR., & ROSEN, G. M. Detrimental effects of a self-reward contracting program on subjects' involvement in self-administered desensitization. *Journal of Consulting and Clinical Psychology,* 1977, *45,* 1180–1181.

BASTIEN, S., & JACOBS, A. Dear Sheila: An experimental study of the effectiveness of written communications as a form of psychotherapy. *Journal of Consulting and Clinical Psychology,* 1974, *42,* 151.

BENEKE, W. M., & HARRIS, M. B. Teaching self-control of study behavior. *Behaviour Research and Therapy,* 1972, *10,* 35–41.

BERGIN, A. E. The evaluation of therapeutic outcomes. In A. E. Bergin, & S. L. Garfield (Eds.), *Handbook of psychotherapy and behavior change: An empirical analysis.* New York: Wiley, 1971.

BERGIN, A. E., & STRUPP, H. H. *Changing frontiers in the science of psychotherapy.* Chicago: Aldine-Atherton, 1972.

BERNAL, M. E., & NORTH, J. A. A survey of parent training manuals. *Journal of Applied Behavior Analysis*, 1978, *11*, 533–544.

CHRISTENSEN, A., MILLER, W. R., & MUNOZ, R. F. Paraprofessionals, partners, peers, paraphernalia, and print: Expanding mental health service delivery. *Professional Psychology*, 1978, *2*, 249–270.

CLARK, H. B., GREENE, B. F., MACRAE, J. W., McNESS, M. P., DAVIS, J. L., & RISLEY, T. R. A parent advice package for family shopping trips: Development and evaluation. *Journal of Applied Behavior Analysis*, 1977, *10*, 605–624.

CLARKE-STEWART, K. A. Popular primers for parents. *American Psychologist*, 1978, *33*, 359–369.

COWEN, E. L. Social and community interventions. *Annual Review of Psychology*, 1973, *24*, 423–472.

CRANE, A. M. *Right and wrong thinking and their results.* Boston: Lothrop, Lee & Shepard Co., 1905.

DAVISON, G. C., & VALINS, S. Maintenance of self-attributed behavior change. *Journal of Personality and Social Psychology*, 1969, *11*, 25–33.

DUMONT, T. Q. *The art and science of personal magnetism.* Chicago: Advance Thought Publishing Co., 1913.

ELLIS, A. Rational-emotive therapy and self-help therapy. *Rational Living*, 1978, *13*, 1–6.

EYSENCK, H. J. The effects of psychotherapy: An evaluation. *Journal of Consulting Psychology*, 1952, *16*, 319–324.

EYSENCK, H. J. A note on "Factors influencing the outcome of psychotherapy." *Psychological Bulletin*, 1972, *78*, 403–405.

FRANKS, C. M., & WILSON, G. T. (Eds.). *Annual review of behavior therapy: Theory and practice* (1977, Vol. 5). New York: Brunner/Mazel, 1978.

GLASGOW, R. E. Effects of a self-control manual, rapid smoking, and amount of therapist contact on smoking reduction. *Journal of Consulting and Clinical Psychology*, 1978, *46*, 1439–1447.

GLASGOW, R. E., & ROSEN, G. M. Behavioral bibliotherapy: A review of self-help behavior therapy manuals. *Psychological Bulletin*, 1978, *85*, 1–23.

GLASGOW, R. E., & ROSEN, G. M. Self-help behavior therapy manuals: Recent developments and clinical usage. *Clinical Behavior Therapy Review*, in press.

GOLDIAMOND, I. Singling out self-administered behavior therapies for professional overview. *American Psychologist*, 1976, *31*, 142–147.

HAGEN, R. L. Group therapy vs. bibliotherapy in weight reduction. *Behavior Therapy*, 1974, *5*, 222–234.

HANSON, R. W., BORDEN, B. L., HALL, S. M., & HALL, R. G. Use of programmed instruction in teaching self-management skills to overweight adults. *Behavior Therapy*, 1976, *7*, 366–373.

HOEHN-SARIC, R., FRANK, J. D., IMBER, S. D., NASH, E. H., STONE, A. R., & BATTLE, C. C. Systematic preparation of patients for psychotherapy—I: Effects of therapy behavior and outcome. *Journal of Psychiatric Research*, 1964, *2*, 267–281.

KAHN, M., & BAKER, B. Desensitization with minimal therapist contact. *Journal of Abnormal Psychology*, 1968, *73*, 198–200.

KIMBRELL, G. M. Note: Diet dilettantism. *Psychological Record*, 1975, *25*, 273–274.

LANYON, R. I., & JOHNSON, J. H. Technology in mental health: A conceptual overview. In J. B. Sidowski, J. H. Johnson, & T. A. Williams (Eds.), *Technology in mental health care delivery systems*. New York: Erlbaum/Ablex, in press.

LUBORSKY, L. A note on Eysenck's article, "The effects of psychotherapy: An evaluation." *British Journal of Psychology*, 1954, *45*, 129–131.

LUBORSKY, L. Another reply to Eysenck. *Psychological Bulletin*, 1972, *78*, 406–408.

MAHONEY, M. J., & MAHONEY, K. Treatment of obesity: A clinical exploration. In B. J. Williams, S. Martin, & J. Foreyt (Eds.), *Obesity: Behavioral approaches to dietary management*. New York: Brunner/Mazel, 1976.

MARKS, I. M. *Living with fear: Understanding and coping with anxiety*. New York: McGraw-Hill, 1978.

MARSHALL, W. L., PRESSE, L., & ANDREWS, W. R. A self-administered program for public-speaking anxiety. *Behaviour Research and Therapy*, 1976, *14*, 33–40.

MARSTON, A. R., MARSTON, M. R., & ROSS, J. A correspondence course behavioral program for weight reduction. *Obesity and Bariatric Medicine*, 1977, *6*, 140–147.

McGAGHIE, W. C., & MENGES, R. J. Assessing self-directed learning.. *Teaching of Psychology*, 1975, *2*, 56–59.

McMAHON, R. J., & FOREHAND, R. Self-help behavior therapies and parent training. In B. B. Lahey & A. E. Kazdin (Eds.), *Advances in clinical child psychology* (Vol. 3). New York: Plenum, in press.

MILLER, G. A. Psychology as a means of promoting human welfare. *American Psychologist*, 1969, *24*, 1063–1075.

MILLER, W. R. Behavioral self-control training in the treatment of problem drinkers. In R. B. Stuart (Ed.), *Behavioral self-management: Strategies, techniques, and outcome*. New York: Brunner/Mazel, 1977.

PARRINO, J. J. Effect of pretherapy information on learning in psychotherapy. *Journal of Abnormal Psychology*, 1971, *77*, 17–24.

PATTERSON, G. R. *Families*. Champaign, Ill.: Research Press, 1971.

PATTERSON, G. R., & GULLION, M. E. *Living with children*. Champaign, Ill.: Research Press, 1968.

PATTERSON, G. R., REID, J. B., JONES, R. R., & CONGER, R. E. *A social learning approach to family interventions: Families with aggressive children* (Vol. 1). Eugene, Oregon: Castalia Publishing Co., 1975.

PEALE, N. V. *The power of positive thinking*. New York: Prentice-Hall, 1956.

PHILLIPS, R. E., JOHNSON, G. D., & GEYER, A. Self-administered systematic desensitization. *Behavior Research and Therapy*, 1972, *10*, 93–96.

REPUCCI, N. D., & BAKER, B. L. Self-desensitization: Implications for treatment and teaching. In R. D. Rubin & C. M. Franks (Eds.), *Advances in behavior therapy.* New York: Academic Press, 1969.

RICHARDS, J. M., JR., & GOTTREDSON, G. D. Geographic distribution of U.S. psychologists: A human ecological analysis. *American Psychologist,* 1978, *33,* 1–9.

RISLEY, T. R., CLARK, H. B., & CATALDO, M. F. Behavior technology for the normal, middle-class family. In E. J. Mash, L. A. Hamerlynck, & L. C. Handy (Eds.), *Behavior modification and families.* New York: Brunner/Mazel, 1976.

ROSEN, G. M. The development and use of nonprescription behavior therapies. *American Psychologist,* 1976, *31,* 139–141.

ROSEN, G. M. Nonprescription behavior therapies and other self-help treatments: A reply to Goldiamond. *American Psychologist,* 1977, *32,* 178–179.

ROSEN, G. M., GLASGOW, R. E., & BARRERA, M., JR. A controlled study to assess the clinical efficacy of totally self-administered systematic desensitization. *Journal of Consulting and Clinical Psychology,* 1976, *44,* 208–217.

RYAN, W. *Blaming the victim.* New York: Random House, 1971.

SPOCK, B. *The common sense book of baby and child care.* New York: Duell, Sloane, & Pierce, 1946.

STUART, R. B. Self-help group approaches to self-management. In R. B. Stuart (Ed.), *Behavioral self-management: Strategies, techniques, and outcomes.* New York: Brunner/Mazel, 1977.

STUART, R. B. *Trick or treatment: How and when psychotherapy fails.* Champaign, Ill.: Research Press, 1970.

ZEISS, R. A. Self-directed treatment for premature ejaculation. *Journal of Consulting and Clinical Psychology,* 1978, *46,* 1234–1241.

ZEISS, R. A., & ZEISS, A. *Prolong your pleasure.* New York: Pocket Books, 1978.

PART III

Safeguarding Institutionalized Clientele

In this section, authors continue to describe systems for preserving the rights of various client populations, giving special attention to rights issues specific to the settings in which services are provided. As Martin cautioned in the book's keynote chapter, certain treatment settings may threaten life, liberty, or property to the extent that due process is required before any deprivation. In addition, he summarized several cases indicating that the courts are beginning to critically examine the restrictions and limitations characteristic of many settings providing mental health, educational, and/or health care services.

For example, Martin noted that beginning with the *Wyatt* vs. *Stickney* case, courts have established certain minimal standards for treatment settings, such as adequate diets, opportunity to privacy, and opportunity to interact with others. In meeting these standards, practitioners must in effect "guarantee" unconditionally many items which they may have previously "dispensed" contingent upon behavior. Therefore, with changing legislation and with the restrictiveness characteristic of many treatment settings, the message of the authors in this section takes on special significance.

In the section's first chapter, Dineen and Sowers consider the rights of the developmentally disabled in vocational settings. After discussing the substance of the Rehabilitation Act of 1973 and its impact on the developmentally disabled, the authors list client rights that must be identified and preserved in vocational training programs. Then they describe specific strategies for providing effective training in these settings while safeguarding the rights of the mentally retarded client. The chapter concludes with a stimulating discussion of such "future issues" in vocational training as the recommendation that more training programs adopt the standards of the Commission on Accreditation of Rehabilitation Facilities (CARF) and that the training available in sheltered workshops be made more intensive.

Timbers, Jones, and Davis address the protection of the rights of children in group-home settings. The authors note that, since children are removed from "parental protection" for placement in the group-home setting, the group home becomes obliged "to protect the civil and human rights" of the child and "assumes the place or role of the child's natural parent as well as that parent's rights, duties, and responsibilities with respect to the child." The authors first examine the risks to which youth in group-home settings are exposed. They proceed with a description of a comprehensive system for protecting the rights of group-home residents. In their discussion, Timbers and his colleagues make a strong argument in favor of well-designed program evaluation systems indicating their agreement with other contributing authors that "the adequacy of any approach to safeguarding rights will invariably go hand in hand with the overall quality of the treatment program provided."

The next three chapters in this section concern the rights of individuals receiving services in medical and health care settings. For example, Creer and Renne offer the technology currently in use at the National Asthma Center in Denver, Colorado, as an example of how the rights of chronically ill children can be preserved while receiving services in a residential treatment and medical research center. After examining some of the legal and ethical issues that arise in providing treatment for and conducting research with chronically ill youngsters, the authors present specific procedures for protecting the child's rights from preadmission to follow-up. The authors also provide a valuable discussion of recent regulations governing research with children (Federal Register, January 1978), relating these regulations to the special needs of chronically ill children and the special problems associated with serving these children in a residential medical research setting.

Cataldo and Ventura address the rights of clients receiving services in acute-care hospitals. The authors provide discussion and examples of behavioral procedures which are employed to ensure client rights. They also describe an institution-wide program for establishing and maintaining staff procedures to protect client rights. Such a program has been employed at the Hopkins Medical Institutions. The major goals described are to protect client rights, ensure quality care, and ensure that the medical benefits afforded a patient in a large hospital are not at the expense of the patient's rights.

Protecting the rights of nursing home residents is the topic of the next chapter by Edwards and Sheldon-Wildgen. The authors begin by examining the placement of the elderly in nursing homes, including a discussion of the different means of involuntary commitment and the rights of the elderly individual in this process. The authors proceed with a discussion of a resident's rights within the nursing home facility and present specific procedures that nursing home administrators should employ to ensure that the rights are protected. The final section of the chapter is devoted to a discussion of procedures for restoring the rights of the nursing home client and a recommendation to develop alternatives to nursing home care, e.g., community-based programs. As Edwards and Sheldon-Wildgen observe: "The rights of the elderly must be restored. Growing old in America should not be . . . a time when all is lost including one's dignity, self-respect, and happiness."

Favell, Favell, and Risley address the rights of clients in mental retardation facilities, beginning their discussion with a consideration of the human and legal rights that are often denied or abridged in these settings. The authors describe four approaches to client advocacy in residential settings, including in-house advocates, regulatory agencies or certifying groups, courts, and quality assurance systems. After identifying the advantages and disadvantages of each approach, the authors recommend quality assurance as the most desirable system for ensuring client rights in mental retardation settings. In the remainder of the chapter, Favell et al. describe the essential components of an effective quality assurance system, one that has as its primary effect that "clients begin to receive habilitative training and quality care that include a concern for clients as people."

The final two chapters in this section are concerned with treatment settings that have received the special attention of the courts and consumer advocates in recent years: the psychiatric hospital and the prison. Hasazi, Surles, and Hannah begin their discussion of client rights in the adult psychiatric hospital with an examination of the different factors that have contributed to the increased interest of courts and state legislators in mental health settings and the resultant developments in mental health legislation. The authors note that "client rights are best safeguarded when the efforts of the hospital are complemented by an active public law system, responsible mental health advocacy, and legislative reform." After considering the client's procedural and substantive rights, Hasazi et al. conclude with a helpful checklist that summarizes specific procedural safeguards for ensuring client rights in the psychiatric hospital setting.

Crow's chapter on the rights of prisoners begins with a discussion of litigation dealing with prisoners' rights. The author then focuses on the right of offenders to rehabilitation, i.e., "a rehabilitative purpose is or ought to be implicit in every sentence of an offender unless ordered otherwise by the sentencing court." However, Crow notes that although such provisions are set forth in many state statutes, there has been limited attention given to the achievement of this goal. In the concluding section of his chapter, the author addresses the role of the prison administrator in assuring that the rights of the prisoner are protected.

The reader will note that the central theme that emerged in the previous section of the book is also apparent in the chapters in this section. Specifically, to reiterate the statement by Timbers et al. in this section, they note that "the adequacy of any approach to safeguarding rights will invariably go hand in hand with the overall quality of the treatment program provided." The authors in this section are therefore united in their recommendation that service providers establish program evaluation, accountability, and quality assurance procedures to ensure the effectiveness and appropriateness of services delivered and to preserve the rights of the client in the process.

CHAPTER 12

Client Rights of the Developmentally Disabled in Vocational Settings

John P. Dineen
Jo-Ann Sowers

AMERICA IS A COUNTRY rich in the tradition of protecting freedoms. Though the range of rights and protections was initially quite narrow, the nation's growth has been paralleled with a broadening interest in extending equality to more segments of society. The physically and mentally handicapped, long a silent and ignored minority, have in the 1970s emerged as the focus of increasing attention as they and their advocates demand an end to discrimination in practices governing employment, education, housing, and services. Although possibly the least assertive among the handicapped, the mentally retarded have nevertheless won increasing rights to humane and "effective" treatment. Still, the gap between the rights legally guaranteed and those actually respected remains embarrassingly large. In this chapter, the authors will suggest practical procedures for professionals in vocational settings who must deal with the difficulties faced by the handicapped, especially the mentally retarded, as they exercise their right to pursue a career and a full and normal life.

The Right to Work

One right few would argue with is the freedom to pursue employment appropriate to one's interests and abilities. For most Americans employment remains a key to independence in adult life, and over the years various minorities have contested discriminatory practices in hiring and promotion. The Rehabilitation Act of 1973 addresses two issues relevant to employment for the handicapped. Section 503 of the act requires affirmative-action hiring practices for the handicapped by a large propor-

tion of private employers, while Section 501 directs federal agencies to
to set up similar affirmative action plans. Section 504 requires, among
other issues, an end to the exclusion of handicapped children and
adults on the basis of their handicap from schools receiving federal
funds.[1] Superficially, it would seem that this act covers discriminatory
practices that previously prevented the handicapped from either acquiring a job or receiving the educational training necessary to prepare for
a vocation. Regrettably, the law's effect has been uneven among the
various handicaps.

EDUCATIONAL OPPORTUNITIES

Section 504's mandate for educational opportunities provides an apt
example of the act's inconsistent effect. It requires that all entrance examinations and practices after admission be modified to the extent that a
person's handicap not prevent him or her from gaining access to the
classroom, participating in classroom activities, taking tests, and so on,
but it does not require that every curriculum offering be appropriate for
every disability or that curriculum be added to accommodate a particular
disability. Most persons with physical and sensory handicaps are usually
able to find an area of study at a community college, university, or vocational technical program that they are both interested in and capable of
doing (with some relatively minor modifications by the program). Unfortunately, because of the nature of their disability and the type of modifications that would have to be made, the retarded are unable to do the same.
For Section 504 to have a clear effect in ending educational discrimination against the mentally retarded, it would be necessary for educational
institutions to implement curriculum offerings appropriately adjusted to
meet the needs of the mentally handicapped. For example, secondary education programs develop skills in areas such as auto mechanics, electronics
assembly, and food service that could be modified for the mentally handicapped.

---

[1] Portions of the texts of Sections 503 and 504 of this act (29 U.S.C. Sections 793-794)
read as follows: "Any contract in excess of $2,500 entered into by any Federal de-
partment or agency for the procurement of personal property and nonpersonal
services (including construction) for the United States shall contain a provision requiring that, in employing persons to carry out such contract the party contracting
with the United States shall take affirmative action to employ and advance in employment qualified, handicapped individuals" (Section 503, "Employment Under
Federal Contracts"). "No otherwise qualified, handicapped individual in the United
States . . . shall, solely by reason of his handicap, be excluded from the participation in, be denied the benefits of, or be subjected to discrimination under any program or activity receiving Federal financial assistance" (Section 504, "Non-Discrimina-
tion Under Federal Grants").

The Education of All Handicapped Children Act of 1975, P. L. 94-142, establishes that all people who are age-eligible (under twenty-one) must be provided with the "most appropriate" education in public schools. While this much-needed law may promote educational practices for children that will enhance the employment prospect of the handicapped in the future, its effects will not be felt by the retarded adult who is no longer eligible.

PLACEMENT AGENCIES: NOT FOR THE RETARDED PERSON?

Although the retarded adult has little opportunity to prepare for work in educational settings, Sections 501 and 503 of the Rehabilitation Act still protect his or her right to apply for jobs. Since many retarded people lack the skills necessary to successfully pursue job leads, placement agencies for the handicapped exist to provide an intermediary between the client and employer. Little objective data regarding the effectiveness of these agencies exists, but typically they provide some assistance in selecting appropriate vocational areas, matching job openings with the client's interests, and providing follow-up services once the client is employed. For many handicapped individuals these services are sufficient to result in the relatively speedy acquisition of jobs, but for the retarded the services may lack components essential to adequately preparing for and subsequently maintaining employment. While handicapped individuals with physical limitations must learn to compensate for their deficits, their ability to acquire new job skills is unimpaired. However, the retarded by definition learn slowly, often requiring weeks or months to learn a sequence of tasks, specific job skills, and acceptable rates of work. Without prior preparation their chance of retraining a job is often minimal, which means that some sort of training before work is obtained may be necessary. On-the-job training, though often not offered by placement agencies, may be a critical part of successful placement of the mentally retarded. Also, more extensive follow-up services are needed for the mentally handicapped than for the physically handicapped, since the transition into employment requires a *generalization* of skills and behaviors beyond the ability of many moderately and severely retarded individuals. Further, since follow-up services typically include only brief in-person checks at work, the possibility of the agency becoming sensitive to abusive employer practices is greatly decreased. This can be a danger for the newly employed retarded person whose ability to defend himself or herself against exploitive demands by co-workers or supervisors is frequently minimal. And when an agency offers only short-term follow-up services (e.g., three months), possible changes in job conditions may again effect the retarded more dramatically than those with other handicaps. For example, after six months of successful employment a retarded worker might be presented with new machinery to work with. The handicapped worker may require a longer time than normal to learn the task and thus be in danger of losing his or her job. Most placement agencies are not set up to provide needed long-term follow-up services for their handicapped clients.

SHELTERED WORKSHOPS: POSSIBLY TOO SHELTERED?

For reasons indicated above, among literally millions of retarded adults the most viable choice for those who wish to prepare for a job or have secure employment is to enter a sheltered workshop or development center. Two recent surveys (Department of Labor, 1977; Greenleigh Associates, 1975) of sheltered workshops and developmental centers give a clear picture of the current state of this art. There are approximately three thousand workshops and developmental centers, with approximately five hundred thousand persons served per year. The majority of workshops serve a variety of handicapped people, including the mentally ill, the physically disabled, and the retarded. The work performed by clients is usually obtained through contracts with local industries to perform production services such as assembling or packaging components. Greenleigh Associates reports that these jobs are "generally so low skilled, tedious, unrewarding and unremunerative that they are seldom found in the competitive sector. . . . Thus, it can be seen that sheltered workshop clients are relegated to a secondary labor market status." This conclusion is substantiated by the wage-earning figures for workshop clients. One-half of regular workshops had average client earnings of slightly over three thousand dollars per year, while one-tenth earned less than one thousand.

Related to the workshop role as a habilitation facility, the surveys reveal that approximately 13 percent of the persons in a workshop are placed in competitive employment yearly, and the vast majority of those placed have been in the workshop less than one year. The longer a person stayed in a workshop the less the probability that he or she would be placed. This suggests that possibly those being placed are the least trained but most capable persons, while the less capable remain indefinitely in the workshop, a hypothesis supported by the estimate that only about seven thousand dollars is spent annually on professional staff. The majority of workshop staff is clerical and production-oriented with little or no professional training, which may explain why the highest wage earners of the clients in a workshop are those who have been there less than one year, whereas those who have been in the workshop the longest earned the least amount.

All of these facts lend credence to the idea that workshops are not providing either the optimal place for retarded persons to work or a very effective place for them to be habilitated. As places to work, they are essentially institutions where only other handicapped people work, the work is repetitous and menial, the wages are meager, low expectations of performance prevail, and inappropriate social behavior is tolerated. As a habilitation facility little quality training is provided, and accountability, objective goal setting, and data collection requirements are either inadequate or nonexistent.

Placement services by workshops vary widely in quality and scope, but frequently resemble those offered by the placement agencies. Although one basic difference between the two is that workshops offer some training, the dissimilarity between skills taught in-house and those expected on the job would lead one to believe that on-the-job training and follow-up are as vitally necessary for workshop graduates as for those placed by agencies. As with the agencies, workshops may offer only short-term follow-up services that include little if any on-the-job training ("OJT") and advocacy protection. These services might be adequate for those clients with relatively minor handicaps placed by workshops into competitive employment, but probably will be inadequate for more disabled individuals, whose placement into competitive employment will increasingly be the focus of workshop efforts. They will thus need more sophisticated placement services.

REHABILITATION INDUSTRY CERTIFICATION

In the early 1970s the rehabilitation industry began to search for ways to become accountable to the consumers of its services. One result was the formation of the Commission on Accreditation of Rehabilitation Facilities (CARF) in 1973. Accreditation is now offered to sheltered workshops and other rehabilitation facilities that meet standards regarding record-keeping, client confidentiality, fiscal management, physical facilities, services, personnel, and administration. Site visits occur on a yearly or once-every-three-years basis (depending on the number of concerns regarding the facilities' operations). Unfortunately, many state developmental or vocational rehabilitation agencies do not encourage sheltered workshops to have CARF inspections. Another qualification is that the CARF standards must be fairly general in order to cover a wide variety of rehabilitation facilities; thus little specific advice can be offered for developing effective treatment procedures that both respect client rights and promote habilitation.

Suggested Guidelines for Safeguarding Client Rights

Nowhere is there a clear definition of those rights that should be assured a retarded adult who enters a vocational training program, whether it be a sheltered workshop, a developmental center, job training, or a placement service. In response to this obvious need the authors propose the following list of rights, which most professionals would agree should be accorded.

Clients have the right to

1. training in the most normal and least restrictive environment possible,
2. work that is as normal as possible and has the potential to prepare the person for a job in the competitive market,
3. evaluation by measurement tools that are appropriate for retarded persons and for the skills to be taught,
4. the highest quality training possible by qualified professionals,
5. opportunities to function at the highest level possible,
6. information about new and modified goals of training,
7. reports of one's progress,
8. individualized attention and training,
9. assurance that trainers are held accountable for positive, negative, or lack of effects of training,
10. confidential treatment of personal records, both past and present,
11. job placement when the person has completed training, rather than being held in the program,
12. placement in a job closely similar to what the person was trained to do, has demonstrated the ability to do, and has expressed an interest in doing,
13. on-the-job training sufficient to establish acceptable work rates, task completion times, and independence,
14. follow-up services sufficient to assure quick intervention on problems that could lead to job dismissal, for a period of at least one year,
15. advocacy assistance on the job, and
16. the opportunity to make informed decisions regarding acceptance or rejection of a potential job.

PROGRAM DEVELOPMENT

It is clear from the Department of Labor ("DOL," 1977) and Greenleigh (1975) reports that the typical sheltered workshop fails to protect our first two proposed rights. These are probably the most important for the overall assurance that retarded persons in vocational programs receive the best possible training and have the greatest opportunity for vocational normalization. Unfortunately, these two are also probably the most difficult for existing sheltered workshops to assure because of established organizational structures that inherently do not lend themselves to the provision of a normal environment and work training having the potential to prepare the person for job placement in the competitive market.

Options for New Programs.   There are several options available to the professional interested in providing vocational training for the mentally retarded such that the first two rights are assured. For those planning a new program, the strongest suggestion is to avoid the contract work system. Instead, an attempt should be made to follow four basic program development steps. The first step is to identify specific jobs for which to provide training by surveying the community in which the clients reside, finding out which jobs have a great deal of similarity from one setting to the next, a fairly high availability, and the possibility of being handled acceptably by the retarded. Such a survey would insure that clients will be receiving training in jobs in which they can potentially be placed.

The second step is to locate a training site. The most critical point to remember in selecting a training site is the importance of finding one as similar as possible to those places where the client may eventually be placed. For example, if food service jobs such as dishwashing and table busing are going to be the ones trained for, the training site should be a restaurant or cafeteria. Some programs that have trained for food service jobs have actually bought small restaurants, while others have utilized existing facilities in schools, hospitals, or other large institutions. This step, of course, assures that the clients will have an opportunity to work in a very normal environment in the presence of many nonhandicapped persons and with social, survival, and vocational requirements very similar to those needed when placed in a job.

The third step in setting up a new program is to observe and collect data on the competitive jobs that have been selected for training, in order to determine exactly what tasks are required, how they are done, and the speed requirements for each. These same tasks, task completion procedures, and speed requirements should then be incorporated into the training program. For example, if it were found that most janitors have to mop floors in a forty-by-twenty-foot area in approximately ten minutes, then the janitor trainees in the training program will be required eventually to meet this same criterion. As Wolf (1978) has eloquently pointed out, this type of social validity procedure ensures that the skills selected are those that are required and viewed as necessary by the "real" world—i.e., employers. It ensures that the goals set for training are not arbitrarily determined by a group of rehabilitation specialists whose knowledge of a particular industry and its demands is limited, but rather by objectively obtaining a picture of the job as it actually exists.

The fourth step is to determine what other behaviors and skills in addition to specific task performance and work rates are necessary for job success. This again is a social validity procedure ensuring that the skills selected are those that are required in competitive employment. For example, the Food Service Vocational Training Program (FSVTP) at the University of Washington (Sowers, Thompson, & Connis, 1978) has found that the following skills are necessary for job success in the food service industry: independence (the ability to complete each task correctly and on time without the need for instruction or prompting), staying on task, good grooming, time management (performing certain behaviors at designated times), and instruction following. The program also found that some of the skills *not* required by the majority of food service jobs are the ability to read, to write, to count, to do math, and to tell time. By identifying which skills are necessary and which are not, training becomes much more efficient. Many workshops spend a great deal of time during the day attempting to teach time telling, money counting, reading, and similar skills, instead of focusing on those necessary for work. Retarded persons should have the opportunity to acquire these skills, but the role of the vocational program should be job preparation. In other words, if job placement is not dependent upon the surveyed skills, they should not be taught during the time devoted to vocational training. It is clearly not normal to be taking a large portion of the day off from work to go to class. These skills can be taught after work in the late afternoon or at night by some other agency.

Options for Existing Programs. For those professionals who do not have the luxury of being in a position to begin a new training program, but rather are operating within an established sheltered workshop which they would like to make more normal for the clients and providing of opportunities to move into competitive jobs, there are several options. The first is to set up an extension of the workshop out in the community, using the steps described above. The FSVTP (Sowers et al., 1978) assisted a sheltered workshop in the Seattle area in setting up a food service training program at a private hospital a few miles from the workshop. Several clients from the workshop received training supervised by workshop staff on a daily basis. A second, less desirable option is to find jobs in the community that can be taught in the workshop, and set aside a portion of the workshop for training on these jobs instead of contract work.

The authors are not attempting to suggest that all retarded persons are capable of working independently in competitive industry. Many of the persons in workshops today are so mentally handicapped that they will always need some special supervision and allowance for their decreased abilities. The challenge to the rehabilitation profession today, however, is to find ways to integrate these persons with normal workers and into normal environments, rather than being satisfied to allow them to spend the majority of their day in a segregated, non-normal environment.

Another approach to integrating retarded persons into normal environments is the "enclave" concept; this entails placing several handicapped persons into a commercial work site with special supervision. If a group of severely retarded persons can sit in a workshop putting together gizmos, it seems clear that they could put the same gizmos together in an actual factory, where they would have the opportunity to work in a normal environment, interact with normal co-workers, and have the dignity of working in a real factory.

Thus far, this chapter has emphasized general program organization and development. The remainder will detail specific procedures that can be used by any program to ensure client rights, regardless of its basic organization and orientation.

ADMISSIONS PROCEDURES

Vocational educators and researchers have directed a great deal of time and effort for many years toward developing predictive measures. Their goal has been to develop both written and performance test batteries that can be administered quickly and inexpensively and will predict how a person will function in any one of a number of professions. The positive aspect of this approach is to see to it that persons choose the correct vocational area before spending a lot of time and money for training, ensuring that persons not capable of certain professions do not needlessly use the limited money and space available for education and rehabilitation programs. Unfortunately for the retarded— who have few prior-developed basic skills, lack academic skills, and have slow learning rates—these tests have often functioned to screen them out of programs or at least to markedly decrease expectations for their success. Consequently, it would be to the advantage of these clients for training programs to use an evaluation system that directly measures a person's performance on the specific job being trained for *after* sufficient time has been provided for training. Retarded persons who have little past training or work experience should be given a minimum of two months of training in a program before a decision is made whether he or she will benefit from it or not. In this way, the program can assume the client is being provided the right to demonstrate his or her ability to work when appropriate training is provided and evaluation is made directly of the skills that will be required in the program and on the job.

One of the major difficulties in ensuring a retarded adult's rights becomes obvious during the admission process. The problem is that, despite having the same legal rights as a nonhandicapped adult (unless the parent or other person has obtained legal guardianship), he or she may have decreased decision-making abilities. Often, well-meaning adults have appropriately or inappropriately usurped some or all of the client's decision-making responsibilities, and thus will strongly influence both admissions and subsequent training decisions. A far too typical scene shows the retarded applicant turning to the parent each time a question is posed and refusing to answer until getting some sign from the parent. A large number of these persons, of course, do need an advocate. In fact, a parent willing to act as an advocate is an important tool for assuring that the client's rights are protected. The problem comes in trying to make sure that the client has the opportunity to make as many decisions as he or she is capable of making and in using the advocate to assist the client with the remainder. Clearly this is no easy task, but several procedures are available to a program that aid in protecting client rights.

The admissions interview is extremely important to ensuring that both the applicant and critical others have a clear understanding of the program. This allows them to decide based on an objective program description whether they wish to participate, and enhances later co-operation when the person does join the program. A program representative should describe the program in detail to them in language that the retarded person is best able to understand. Important inclusions are the amount of money the person will earn during training, probable training duration, training procedures that will be used, a realistic appraisal of inherent dangers if the person is placed in a competitive job (e.g., moving around the community independently), absenteeism policies, loss of social security benefits after placement, probable earnings on the job, a realistic description of the type of work the person will be trained for (including likelihood of evening and weekend hours and job advancement) and program termination policy. Another important item to be discussed during this meeting is that of alternative programs available in the community. This is important to ensuring that the person can make an informed choice regarding the services that best meet his or her own needs and wants. After the interview all persons should be shown the site of training sessions, be allowed to observe, and be encouraged to ask questions.

In addition to the verbal description and tour of the program two other procedures can be of assistance in clarifying the program for applicants and critical others. The first is the use of a small handbook that clearly and simply describes the program and its goals, procedures, and policies. This is especially helpful for parents or advocates as a clarification of any ambiguities in the verbal interview and for reference after the beginning of training. The second procedure is a short slide presentation describing what happens to a client in the program. This is particularly helpful for the retarded client who has a difficult time picturing what something is going to be like, given only a verbal description.

TRAINING AND EVALUATION PROCEDURES

Individual Training. Perhaps the most important right that any client in a program should be accorded is the right to be treated as an individual. Clients come to programs with different performance levels and rates of learning and unique behavior deficits and problems. In order to ensure that these are taken into account, an individual program plan ("IPP") should be devised and utilized. Using IPPs a supervisor is required to set individual goals for each trainee, and specify individual intervention plans using procedures the supervisor feels will be most effective for the particular trainee. The written IPP form used by a program should require clear specification of all long- and short-term goals, behavioral definition of the targeted behaviors, exact data collection and intervention procedures, and plans for programming maintenance and generalization. In order to ensure that IPPs are appropriately and effectively implemented, certain rules regarding their use should be devised. Included in these rules should be the stipulation that an IPP must be written if routine data collection shows little or no progress being made by a trainee in some area, or if a unique behavior problem arises and persists. The training should not begin until the IPP form has been completed and baseline data collected, reviewed, and discussed by the entire staff.

The written IPP system and rules for use ensure three things: (1) The trainers will actively provide training and continuously work toward progress and movement by each client. (2) The data indicated objectively the existence of a problem. (3) The procedures used will be ethically appropriate and clinically sound.

Standard Training Goals. Although individualization is of exceptional importance, people often overlook the importance of having standard goals. In order for a client to be ready for job placement, he or she must be able to perform certain skills and forms of behavior at acceptable levels. Criteria for these skills and behaviors are those that were determined through the survey during the program development stage. For example, before clients training to be dishwashers can be placed, they must be able to complete 90–100 percent of the assigned tasks correctly within the time limits each day, work without assistance for 90–100 percent of the tasks each day, come to work 100 percent of the time, and so on.

These standard goals for all program trainees enhance client rights in three ways. First, the goals are sufficiently clearly stated that the trainees, parents, critical others, and funding and accreditation agencies know exactly what the program is working toward with each client and what must be accomplished for placement to occur. Thus the program can be held accountable by the consumers. Second, by setting the same long-term standardized goals for everyone, the trainers will more likely make concerted efforts to move all trainees toward them regardless of entrance functioning level. Third, based on these standard goals, appropriate and specific evaluation and assessment tools can be devised. Instead of using general trait evaluations, which often are poor indicators of progress over time, assessment measures can be made to indicate specific progress toward each of the established goals. The combined use of standard behavior goals and individual program plans as training objectives ensures both accountability and individualization of treatment.

Another critical way to ensure accountability is, of course, data collection. Unfortunately, in many workshops where the emphasis is still only on production rates any additional data collection is sometimes seen as only more paperwork. However, as pointed out above, data should be collected daily for both the standard behaviors—such as task completion and independence—and on-task behavior and, in order to insure consistency, standard data-collection forms should be devised that include the trainer's name, client's name, and date. This provides a permanent record verifying that data collection did in fact take place on a specified date, along with the observer's identity.

All intervention-change decisions by the trainer-supervisors should be based on the data. The decision to discontinue training in order to place the trainee on a job or to terminate him or her from the program should also be based on this data. Weekly staff meetings should be held, at which the trainer-supervisor describes the previous week's data for each trainee and proposes any program changes or new IPPs. All of these procedures promote trainee-related decisions based on objective information, rather than subjective impressions. The trainer-supervisor cannot simply say to a parent or funding agency, "I really feel that Sam has made progress since I began working with him." The hard truth regarding the trainer's successes or failures will be clearly shown by the data. The staff meetings are of particular importance because of the great influence that professional peer pressure can have. Here the staff can offer reinforcement for necessary client behavior changes—however small—censorship for lack of progress due to inadequate changes, and suggestions for improvement in the future.

In order to assure that critical others in the client's life have an opportunity to hold the program accountable, monthly meetings with parents and advocates and bimonthly meetings with funding agencies are suggested to ensure discussion and review of the client's data, progress, and problems. The use of graphs as a visual representation of a client's progress for nonprofessionals and the client are extremely important. By carefully and thoroughly explaining the exact purpose of each graph—defining each line, line direction, and symbol—the trainer can facilitate a good understanding by any interested person—including the trainee—of progress being made. The use of graphs, with care taken to make the trainee and critical others capable of understanding them clearly, is an important means to further promote trainer and program accountability, thereby protecting the client right to quality and appropriate training.

Most-Normal Training Procedures. There are two major ways in which client rights in training can be abused. The first is the lack—sometimes the total absence—of active intervention to benefit a trainee. This has been the emphasis of the discussion thus far—how to ensure that such training does occur. The second major way in which client rights can be abused in training is the use of procedures that are not only ineffective but actually detrimental to client progress, have the potential to create negative emotional side-effects, or simply are not the most normal that could be utilized. The discussion here will focus on how to ensure that the training procedures utilized are the most normal possible, effective, and not conducive to negative emotional side-effects.

There are many intervention procedures that have been shown by researchers to be extremely powerful and effective in changing behaviors. These procedures include token economies, over-correction, contingent food and other tangible reinforcers, and home report cards. These procedures are of course not the most normal available to a trainer. The most normal training procedure is probably social instruction. Social instruction includes a clear definition of the correct and incorrect behavior, a rationale for why the "correct" behavior is important, complete instructions and a demonstration on how to perform it, praise for correct and appropriate behaviors, and feedback for incorrect and inappropriate behaviors. In order to assure that each client has an opportunity to perform the required behaviors correctly under the most normal circumstances, social instruction should always be utilized first, systematically, and consistently. Social instruction also has the advantage over more intensive and complex procedures of being the easiest to withdraw while still obtaining maintenance of behavior. Although the more complex procedures are extremely effective, they require much more sophisticated and time-consuming fading schedules.

Understanding the Training.   One of the most important aspects of social instruction from a client-rights point of view is the use of the rationale: Even when the more intensive procedures are instituted, an attempt should still be made to give a rationale for performing or not performing a behavior. Some examples of rationales are "It's important that you work fast, because when you get a job you will have to move fast to get your work done" and "If you hit people when you get a job, you will be fired." Encouraging trainer-supervisors to give rationales to clients also encourages them to think of and treat clients as persons who in fact deserve to be given an explanation of the things asked of them as well as procedures done to them. It is very easy for nonhandicapped persons, even professionals (sometimes professionals especially), to simply take the attitude toward the retarded, "I know what's best for you" and assume that the retarded person has no interest in, no need to know, and no ability to understand rationales. The requirement of a rationale serves as a preventive measure to this attitude on the part of trainer-supervisors.

Two other, similar procedures can be used to further enhance the client right to know about and understand one's individual program. The first requires the trainer to explain carefully an intervention program and its consequences before it begins. This is especially important when the more intensive procedures are used. For instance, if the plan is to place a client into time-out whenever screaming is exhibited, the client should be told beforehand exactly what the unwanted behavior is and what will happen if it does occur. The second procedure is to go over the data on a routine basis with the client, discussing progress or the lack of it, and asking for input by the client into future program planning.

Negative Consequences.   Although social instruction and positive reinforcement programs should always be attempted first, there are situations in which negative consequences are necessary in order to change behaviors. Certain precautions should be taken, of course, to ensure that they are used appropriately without abusing the client's rights. The first and simplest procedure is to insist that negative consequences be used only in conjunction with positive consequences. So, for example, if verbal reprimands are given for inappropriate behavior, verbal praise must be programmed for appropriate behavior. Another procedure involves putting the IPP system into effect. All procedures, especially those that include negative consequences, should be carefully and precisely written up, fully reviewed, and critically discussed by the staff. Parents and advocates should be informed and their approval received with that of the client, who should be allowed to give input. If the client feels that the consequences are too harsh and wants to be given an additional opportunity to change without the program, the trainer should work out a time-limit agreement with the client to do this. All these procedures serve to ensure that the persons with a vested interest in the client have an opportunity to review the appropriateness of the negative procedures, make alternative suggestions, and give final approval.

Self-monitoring. As stated previously, one of the most difficult problems in assuring client rights for retarded persons is their dependency on others due to their decreased intellectual ability (often due itself to others' reinforcement of this dependency). This will continue to be a problem for the retarded client when placed in a job in competitive industry, and will leave the person open to potential abuse by employers and co-workers. Vocational training programs should attempt to provide some training that will assist the client to become more independent and learn to control his or her own behavior. One extremely successful procedure is the training of self-monitoring. For a variety of skills and behaviors such as grooming, time management, task completion, and task change, the trainee can in fact be taught to evaluate and record his or her own behavior. By learning to self-monitor, the trainee learns to control his or her own behavior and thus increases greatly the chances that maintenance will occur on the job once the training program no longer is there to provide assistance and feedback. In essence, the client will no longer be reliant on the assistance of others. Although this may be one of the more difficult ways to go about trying to protect client rights, it is also probably the most useful. If the controlling power is turned over to the client, the likelihood that his or her rights will be abused is less.

Termination Before Graduation. As previously noted, to ensure that all clients have the right to opportunities to perform to the best of their ability, at least two months of training and evaluation should be done before a decision is made regarding their appropriateness for a program. At the end of the two-month period each case should be carefully reviewed. No standard cutoff point should be established for this decision; rather, the individual amount of improvement should be considered. For instance, the program should not state that all trainees must have reached at least a 50 percent level of competence on all behaviors in order to remain in the program. One trainee may have started at 15 percent and improved to 40 percent, while another started at 45 percent and reached the 50 percent criterion. With a rigid 50 percent criterion the second trainee would be retained and the first would not, although the first was showing much greater improvement and, from the trend of the data, should eventually actually bypass the second trainee. With this population, which has a slow learning rate and often little experience with structured programs, it is suggested that unless both the performance level and the learning rate are minimal clients be given an additional few months. If it becomes clear that the client has little chance of bene-fiting from the program, or if his or her exhibition of violent behavior or repeated absenteeism has not responded to treatment, all critical persons (including the client) should meet. The difficulties, possible solutions, and alternative programs should be thoroughly discussed. If the client and critical others still want to try to remain in the program, a trial extension period should be arranged. At the meeting a written contract should be made that specifies exactly what the client must have done, along with what the parents and critical others must have done by the end of the trial period in order to remain in the program. All parties should sign the contract. At the end of the contract period another meeting should be held to discuss progress since the agreement. If the agreed-upon goals have not been reached, the trainee should be termi-nated when the most suitable alternative program has been identified. The program staff should actively assist the client in finding such a program.

MOVING INTO COMPETITIVE EMPLOYMENT

The transition from job training to actual employment is especially difficult for moderately and severely retarded workers with slow learn-ing rates and high resistance to change. This phase therefore appears to offer a potential for great abuse of client rights. For example, many vocational programs make a sharp distinction between training and place-ment, which may mean having placement staff with little knowledge of training procedures and training staff unsophisticated in the demands of the actual jobs they train clients to acquire. As pointed out earlier, workshops may train for jobs that do not exist in the community. Once on the job, a retarded person may be less able to defend himself or herself against exploitive demands by co-workers and supervisors than would most other new workers. Simply by being labeled as retarded, the person may evoke unwarranted and inappropriate responses from co-workers whose knowledge of the developmentally disabled is minimal. Finally, without assistance in learning new tasks, the retarded person can quickly fail at a job he or she could otherwise eventually perform with ease.

Job Development. Several procedures are available that will not only provide excellent treatment but respect the rights of clients through-out the placement process. First, potential placement sites should be identified long before a given client is adjudged job ready, to allow for an active exchange of information between program representatives and the employer. This allows each side to formulate and answer questions regarding the appropriateness of hiring a program graduate, the education of the employer about retardation, and the functional observation of potential jobs before an opening occurs in order to make a task analysis. Actual observation by the placement staff will enhance the usual well-intended, but often useless, job descriptions with objective information regarding task-change times, work rates, necessary skills, and the all-too-frequently differing expectations of on-line supervisors and managers.

When an opening occurs in a business, information on the position should be shared with trainers to help them make a determination of its appropriateness for any of the current job-ready clients. Being able to compare expected job demands with client training data is another advantage of having training skills that directly relate to actual jobs, and of course serves to protect the client from inappropriate placement in a job whose requirements would require an excessive amount of on-the-job training. Other considerations for the staff might include specific client limitations—e.g., "cannot reach racks located higher than six feet three inches," public transportation accessibility to the job site, the availability of health benefits (which may be quite important to a client without other access to medical care), the potential of physical danger to the client posed by late working hours in rough neighborhoods, and insecure hours or shaky job security.

Accepting a Job Offer. The client recommended by the staff for a job opening deserves the right to make an informed decision regarding the acceptance of a job. A danger in placing moderately and severely mentally retarded people in jobs is that they frequently are unable to ask even basic questions about the job and thus are easily ignored in the placement process. A retarded person should be given the opportunity to visit the job site, talk to the supervisor, and watch the present employee perform the work.

The traditional job interview, consisting only of an oral question-and-answer session, may screen out those handicapped individuals whose ability to communicate in an interview situation is far below their ability to perform the job under consideration. For the retarded person, it may be desirable to perform one or more of the tasks required by the employer as part of the "interview," thus allowing the client to evaluate the job demands just as the employer evaluates his or her performance. Another possible means of clearly demonstrating the client's capabilities is to videotape his or her work at the training site for viewing by the employer.

This procedure for job development respects both the client's and the employer's right to make informed decisions regarding the offering and acceptance of a job. Ideally, neither would be "surprised" by the other when the client begins the job. It also ensures that the positions offered program graduates require skills and abilities appropriate to the client's level of functioning.

On-the-Job Training. When a client is hired, it ought to be his or her right to receive follow-up training adequate to establish acceptable work rates, task completion times, and independence. This may include social instruction, public transportation training, job restructuring to exclude tasks easily handled by other employees (such as ordering supplies), individual behavior change programs for specific social or vocational behaviors, co-worker education, illustrating task changes with pictorial cues, and assistance with the work itself. Data should be taken on task completion, speed, and independence and then shared with the client, the parents or guardians, and the supervisor. The data not only documents the extent to which the client is handling the work—which can be useful to the client if the employer changes his or her mind about retaining the retarded worker—but it can serve to detect subtle client progress and educate the employer about objective methods of evaluating an employee, and, in the case of an inappropriate dismissal of the client, can be very useful in subsequent legal proceedings.

Although some employers express a preference for training the client themselves, difficulties in establishing consistent task sequences, breaking a job up into small, understandable steps, and coping with the client's slow acquistion rate make such efforts risky with moderately and severely retarded adults. It is recommended that OJT begin with the whole of the client's working shift in order to ensure that every portion of the working day is clearly understood both by trainer and client. The eventual decision to reduce the level of OJT should be based on the client data, which is sensitive to increasing amounts of independence in performing the job.

Finally, training programs should consider guaranteeing that the job will be completed each day to the employer's satisfaction. This places the contingency on the placement person to provide rapid and practical training for the client or do the work himself or herself. It also would keep the placement staff in touch with realistic job demands, which can in turn be relayed to the staff trainers.

Long-Term Follow-up. Long-term data collection can take several forms, but should always be sensitive to the variables that appear related to job loss in general. This will allow follow-up staff to monitor client behaviors that serve as early indicators of trouble and to intervene before a problem reaches a critical stage. Four areas of behavior on the job that seem to be related to job retention include the quantity and quality of job performance, the client's behavior in interpersonal situations, the client's worker characteristics—such as showing up for work on time, working under pressure, working without excessive direct supervision, and showing enthusiasm for work—and personal appearance.

As with the objective data, the evaluation also will document a client's satisfactory job performance, which can be potentially useful in legal proceedings should the client lose his or her job due to blatantly discriminatory practices. When the employer is well aware that the client's progress as an employee is being carefully monitored, and has ample opportunity to discuss problems with the follow-up staff, he or she may be less likely to fire the client outright without consulting the staff than if no contact were made.

Job Loss. Although it has not been listed as one of the client rights proposed by the authors, the concept of automatic retraining after job failure is quite appropriate for the mentally retarded individual, who can be expected to have a difficult time adjusting to the numerous variables commonly encountered in competitive employment. For example, data from the FSVTP (Sowers et al., 1978) placement staff suggest that a client's likelihood of retaining a second, third, or even fourth job is higher than with his or her first competitive position.

Future Issues

Institutional programs of vocational habilitation will in all probability change as dramatically in the coming decade as they did in the early 1970s. The examination of treatment focus and procedures, as exemplified in this chapter, should gain momentum as professionals begin questioning the effectiveness of existing vocational programs and designing new ones. Certainly one step toward ensuring client rights would be the adoption of the CARF standards by an increasing number of habilitation agencies. State vocational rehabilitation ("VR") agencies electing to purchase services from only those habilitation programs that meet CARF standards can hasten the process. At the same time, the standards themselves may become more explicit in outlining treatment procedures to enhance client rights.

One result would be a shift from extended sheltered employment to intensive training programs oriented toward competitive employment—necessitating a change in policy by state VR agencies.

Currently between five and seven thousand dollars is spent to maintain an individual in a sheltered workshop for two years. In an intensive training program that same amount of money may be more quickly spent, in a six-month training and a three-month placement and follow-up period. Of course, the client who moves to competitive employment eventually begins to pay back the cost of training through taxes, and ideally requires little or no maintenance expense. State VR agencies will have to become willing to put their money "up front" to fund these programs; this will require a reorganization of funding patterns. At the same time, longer periods of follow-up funding may become necessary as more severely disabled individuals are placed into jobs.

Up to this point we have discussed program policy as if under the assumption that vocational programs will gladly adopt changes in training focus and procedure demonstrated to be effective by researchers. Unfortunately, however, major social change often requires litigation or legislation. The Rehabilitation Act of 1973 certainly offered the potential of ending many discriminatory employment practices (Gilhool, 1976), but still needs to be tested in the courts before its usefulness for the retarded can be established. So far, no successful cases regarding employment discrimination against retarded people have been brought under its Section 503 (Mental Retardation Law Reporter; Amicus). For educational opportunities to become accessible to the retarded adult, the intent of its Section 504 will also have to be tested in the courts. It is the authors' opinion, based on discussions with lawyers and Department of Civil Rights personnel, that a retarded person who sues a vocational technical school on the basis that it refused to make a curriculum offering accessible would have little chance of winning.

Summary

It is a revealing and important point that this chapter the first attempt to deal in depth with client-rights issues as they relate to the vocational training and placement of the retarded adult. Until very recently this was simply not an issue. Why? Certainly not because client rights were being adequately protected, but rather because the general public, parents, advocates, clients, and professionals alike assumed that retarded adults were incapable of being highly productive vocationally and competitively employed. As with blacks, women, and those with physical and sensory handicaps, only when they began to demonstrate their ability to perform at levels equal to those of whites, males, and the nonhandicapped did rights become an issue. Retarded adults are just beginning to show that with appropriate training they too are capable of high levels of performance. Consequently, their right to receive adequate training and placement is now becoming of increased importance to all persons involved in the field of vocational habilitation.

References

Amicus. South Bend, Ind.: National Center for Law and the Handicapped (Bureau of Education for the Handicapped, Office of Education, U.S. Department of Health, Education and Welfare), & Developmental Disabilities Office (Office of Human Development, U.S. Department of Health, Education and Welfare), 1979.

BELLAMY, T., PETERSON, L., & CLOSE, D. Habilitation of the severely and profoundly retarded: Illustration of competence. *Education & Training of the Mentally Retarded,* 1975, *10,* 174–186.

Department of Labor. *Sheltered workshop study* (Vol. 1). Workshop survey prepared by Whitehead, C. W. Washington, D.C.: U.S. Department of Labor, 1977.

GILHOOL, T. K. The right to community services. In M. Kindred, J. Cohen, D. Penrod, & T. Shaffer (Eds.), *The mentally retarded citizen and the law: The President's Committee on Mental Retardation.* New York: Free Press, 1976.

GOLD, M. W. Vocational training. In J. Wortis (Ed.), *Mental retardation and developmental disabilities: An annual review* (Vol. 7). New York: Brunner/Mazel, 1975, pp. 254–264.

Greenleigh Associates. *The role of the sheltered workshops in the rehabilitation of the severely retarded* (Vol. 1). Executive summary. New York: Greenleigh Associates, Inc., 1975.

Mental Retardation Law Reporter. American Bar Association, Commission on the Mentally Disabled, 1979.

SOWERS, J., THOMPSON, L. E., & CONNIS, R. T. The Food Service Vocational Training Program: A model for training and placement of the mentally retarded. In G. T. Bellamy & G. O'Connor (Eds.), *Vocational habilitation of the developmentally disabled: Contemporary service strategies.* Baltimore: University Park Press, 1979.

WOLF, M. M. Social validity: The case for subjective measurement, or how applied behavior analysis is finding its heart. *Journal of Applied Behavior Analysis,* 1978, *11,* 203–214.

CHAPTER 13

Safeguarding the Rights of Children and Youth in Group-Home Treatment Settings

Gary D. Timbers
Robert J. Jones
Jerry L. Davis

Introduction

COMMUNITY-BASED GROUP HOMES are emerging as the intervention of choice for a broad category of children whose emotional and behavioral problems are serious enough to require active residential treatment outside their family households but not sufficiently serious to warrant incarceration or other institutionalization. Children currently receiving group-home treatment across the nation tend to require remediation for emotional disturbance, delinquent and predelinquent behavior, various kinds and degrees of learning disability, or mild mental or cultural retardation. As a class, they typically enter group homes with persistent histories of maladjustment at home and at school, truancy, academic failure, and running-away behavior and may as a result have been adjudicated as status offenders. In addition, many have committed illegal acts such as shoplifting, assault, or breaking and entering, which have resulted in charges of delinquency.

□ The authors wish to acknowledge the assistance of Elizabeth Jameson and Loren Warboys of the Juvenile Justice Legal Advocacy Project in San Francisco in the planning and review of this chapter.

The preparation of this manuscript was supported, in part, by Grant No. MH 32854–02 from the National Institute of Mental Health (Center for Studies of Crime and Delinquency—Saleem Shah, Chief), Department of Health, Education, and Welfare. The Bringing It All Back Home Project also receives support from the State of North Carolina Division of Mental Health and Mental Retardation Services and from Title XX of the Social Security Act of 1974.

RESPONSIBILITY FOR THE PROTECTION
OF CHILDREN'S RIGHTS

For purposes of this discussion, the most important thing that group-home residents have in common is that they have been removed for a period of time from that ill-defined umbrella of protection provided by their parents and natural homes. While this umbrella of parental protection is in practice more a conventional expectation of our society than a uniform reality, it nevertheless constitutes the basis upon which child service agencies such as group homes become obliged to protect the civil and human rights of the children in their charge. Common law has for centuries viewed a child's natural parents as the primary instrument of that child's protection and welfare until he or she reaches the age of legal majority. The moment a minor is removed, for whatever reason or purpose, from the supervision and care of his or her natural family and remanded to the custody of an agency or organization, that agency or organization assumes legal responsibility for the care and protection of the child's rights. Under the doctrines of *in loco parentis* (in the place of a parent) and *parens patriae* (the state's sovereign power of guardianship over persons under disability), the service agency or organization assumes the place or role of the child's natural parent as well as that parent's rights, duties, and responsibilities with respect to the child. The intent of these doctrines applies in the case of children irrespective of the reason for removal from parental care—i.e., whether the assumption of custody by the state was precipitated by the child's behavior, the behavior of the child's parents, or the physical absence of the child's parents. With respect to children removed from their parents' care because of parental behavior or absence, it was held in *Inmates of Boys' Training School (BTS)* v. *Affleck* that

> children who are committed to BTS because they are dependent or have been neglected by their parents are confined on what must be pure *parens patriae* theory. They are at BTS because of their parents' actions, not their own. To cause them to suffer deprivations under law because of their status is constitutionally forbidden. [364 F. Supp. 1354 (D.R.I. 1972)]

In the case of children whose own delinquent or antisocial behavior has led to their removal from their natural parents, the same doctrine requires consideration of the interests of both child and society, as in *Kent* v. *United States*:

> *Parens patriae* requires that the juvenile court do what is best for the child's care and rehabilitation so long as this disposition provides adequate protection for society. . . . But it is clear that society can be protected without departing from civilized standards for the prompt and adequate care of disturbed children. [130 U.S. App. D.C., 343, 401 F. 2d 408, 411–412 (1968)]

Thus, there are existing legal imperatives that demand the responsible care and protection of children whose supervision has been removed from their parents and assumed by the state. In some instances the machinery works quite well. But, as is often the case with such litigation, it has been a long time in coming, and its intent is often more certain than is its practice. The subtle fallibilities of the system as it is currently applied—and thus the actual risks that children in group homes and other residential treatment facilities continue to face—may be best understood against the background of the development of what has been called the "child-saving movement." It was this movement that spawned, among other things, the first underpinnings of our present juvenile justice system. The passage of the first juvenile court statute in Illinois in 1899 was among the earliest instances of growing general concern that children under majority age who are offensive to society ought to be treated differently than adult criminals. While the intent of this new thinking about the treatment of minor offenders was certainly benevolent (see discussion in Platt, 1969), history has shown that the social-legal realities that grew out of that thinking had mixed implications for the children whom it would affect.

The Illinois initiative was intuitively attractive to other states caught up in the child-saving movement, and many of them modeled their own juvenile laws after the Illinois statute (Lerman, 1971). The humanitarian thrust of these new legal proscriptions was that perhaps some manner of court intervention other than rote punishment might be applied to offending juveniles, such that the progression to adult criminality might be short-circuited. As Shah (1975) has pointed out, this new approach to juvenile offenders seemed to obviate the usual necessity for legal safeguards, inasmuch as it was to be remediative and therapeutic rather than punitive. This presumably reasonable aspect of the developing juvenile justice system was one of two subtle facets that were fated to subsequently receive stern criticism. The other was the related and equally reasonable view that, since the new system was to be rehabilitative and nonpunitive, why not also broaden somewhat the category of offensive behaviors that would be subject to the new methods of treatment? Thus, in one well-intentioned and initially well-received humanitarian stroke, minor members of society were made vulnerable to state intervention for various age-related status offenses and were deprived of due process of law for both status offenses and delinquent acts. The problem, of course, was that the architects of the juvenile justice system could not know what shape the new alternative treatment modes would take, and could not ensure that they would be free of punitive concomitants. The tragedy is that it took society more than half a century to formally acknowledge the inherent shortcomings of this system. During that time it became gradually apparent that preexisting notions about criminal disposition and corrections would undermine the intent of the original juvenile court statutes. That incarceration must be a necessary element in the disposition of any lawbreaker, whether the proposed treatment be·rehabilitative or punitive, was evidenced in the widespread appearance of reform schools that ominously resembled prisons in structure, security orientation, and remote geographic placement. Children were no longer put in jails with adults to await disposition, but the detention homes where they were placed had bars and guards. This is not to say that the aspirations of the child-savers had altogether been lost sight of; rather, the manner of the implementation of those aspirations was weakening the resulting product.

Finally, in the mid-sixties, formal recognition of the magnitude of this discrepancy between the early ideals of the formulators of the juvenile court system and the injustice of the process that actually evolved occurred in the form of two related court decisions. In the first (*Kent* v. *United States*), Justice Fortas commented, as part of the majority opinion,

> There is evidence, in fact, that there may be grounds for concern that the child (socio-legally) receives the worst of both worlds: that he gets neither the protection accorded to adults nor the solicitous care and regenerative treatment postulated for children.

In a later but similar decision, *In re Gault*, Justice Fortas, as part of the majority opinion of the same court, characterized the care of the incarcerated status offender thus:

> Instead of a mother and father and sisters and brothers and friends and classmates, his world is peopled by guards, custodians, state employees, and "delinquents" confined with him for anything from waywardness to rape and homicide. [387 U.S. 1 (1967)]

The irony of these and subsequent rulings is apparent, and has been aptly put by Shah (1975): "The courts had to finally intervene to save the child(ren) from the consequences of the child-saving movement."

THE NATURE OF RISK IN THE GROUP-HOME ENVIRONMENT

The idea of community-centered treatment for dependent, emotionally disturbed, predelinquent, or delinquent children is not new. During the entire period between the conception of the juvenile court system and the present, a menagerie of remediative intervention strategies have been attempted which have shared a focal interest in keeping the child in his or her community.

It is quite probable that many such programs were conceived out of undefined but growing discontent with the shape that the juvenile justice system was taking, particularly with its institutional aspect. One approach to child care and treatment that has survived from among these community-based strategies is the group home. A group home is typically considered to be a home-like structure serving from five to nine clients and located in or near a community.

In terms of the degree and number of potential risks to which their youthful residents are inherently exposed, group homes probably fall somewhere between community mental health services offering outpatient counseling to children (see Chapter 2 of this book) and more restrictive or remote institutional environments such as detention centers and training or reform schools. This is simply because the group home is intermediate between these other treatment modes with respect to both proximity or accessibility of the child to his or her parents and the dimension of intrinsic restrictiveness.

Technically, even in a group home, the potential for compromising children's constitutional rights is always present. If, for example, it can later be demonstrated that a less restrictive treatment alternative would have been sufficient to address a particular child's behavioral and emotional difficulties, that child's abiding right to "least restrictive" treatment would have been undermined at the time of admission to a group home. During residence and treatment in a group home, both coarse and subtle abrogations of children's physical, psychological, educational, and other rights can occur on almost a moment-to-moment basis. Even a child's discharge from a group home can under certain circumstances constitute a breach of his or her rights. In actual practice, however, it has been the experience of the authors that abuses of children and their rights in group homes are not commonplace, and when they do occur are rarely flagrant and almost never truly malicious. That same experience indicates that professionals involved in the implementation and operation of group homes are by and large sincerely concerned with the welfare and rights of the children in their care.

This is not to suggest that children's rights are at present adequately protected in group home environments. They are not. No particular intervention method or configuration can guarantee the effective protection of children's rights. Group homes are not excepted from this, and in fact the rights of some children in some group homes require substantially more protection than they now have. The point—one that will be reflected throughout this chapter—is that human rights protection in any treatment context is a matter more of information than motivation. When children's rights are threatened in a group home, it is generally because someone did not "know any better": Someone was unfamiliar with existing, applicable case law, was insensitive (for lack of information) to ethical considerations that case law has not yet addressed, or, more typically, was inappropriately selected or trained for a direct care position (both, again, for lack of basic information of technology). We commend the enterprise of community leaders who press for the installation of group homes, albeit with a certain awareness that some bases will not initially be covered. It is in the nature of complex societies that events do not always occur in their ideal order. It is our hope, however, that the information in this chapter will help address the issues associated with the protection of children's rights as effectively as possible, given the legal and ideological guidance that is currently available.

PURPOSE AND PERSPECTIVE

This chapter will attempt to accomplish three major objectives. First, it will help the reader identify the major categories and sources of risks to which the youthful residents of group homes may be exposed. This will be approached by way of a review of existing case law that can be brought to bear directly upon the issues involved in the protection of the rights of children in community-based group homes. The review will enumerate the minimum standards presently prescribed by law regarding children's rights in residential treatment programs, and will attempt to familiarize the reader with the legal authority from which each standard derives. This aspect of the discussion will also address the important issue of children's right to treatment.

Second, a comprehensive system for protecting the rights of group-home residents will be presented. This protection system is intended not only to satisfy minimum legal standards but, if applied fully and conscientiously, to go well beyond current legal requirements toward an ethically and morally ideal technology for ensuring children's civil and human rights. Detailed instruction will be offered in this section for implementing and sustaining the individual elements or strategies that constitute the protection system. Protection of children's rights as they relate to research, as well as to treatment per se, will also be addressed.

While the recommendations to be offered have been formulated for application in *any* group home, independent of its orientation to treatment, the third major objective here will be to communicate throughout the authors' firm conviction that the adequacy of any approach to safeguarding children's rights will invariably go hand-in-hand with the overall quality of the treatment program provided. Irrespective, again, of the treatment philosophy adopted by a given group home, the effective protection of children's rights will prove almost impossible to accomplish in the context of a poorly conceived, weakly administered, asystematic, or loosely monitored group-home treatment program. Conversely, those elements of treatment that seem to define and characterize sound, healthy, systematic group-home programs, tend almost intrinsically to involve sensitivity to the rights of their youthful clients.

Most of the specific recommendations to follow are based on procedures currently in use at the Bringing It All Back Home (BIABH) project. The BIABH project is a region-wide services delivery program that provides residential youth treatment in communities throughout the western region of North Carolina. The project is composed of a central professional staff which provides training, consultation, and evaluation services to the treatment staffs of nine group homes serving a twelve-county area. Each of the homes operates autonomously under the direction of a community-comprised, nonprofit corporation. The project represents one of the nation's largest independent applications of the Teaching-Family Treatment Model (Maloney, Timbers, & Maloney, 1977). The original intent of the Teaching-Family model was to foster the provision of high-quality residential, community-based, family-style treatment based on social learning theory and operant principles for emotionally disturbed, predelinquent, or delinquent boys and girls (Phillips, Phillips, Fixsen, & Wolf, 1974). Each group home is staffed by a carefully selected and trained married couple who are called teaching-parents and are the principals in the administration of the treatment program. They are assisted by part-time alternates. The homes serve five to six youths each on a twenty-four-hour basis, although allowing weekend (and progressively longer) visits by the children to their natural homes is part of the remediation approach. In addition to their intensive contact with the youths in their homes, the teaching-parents work closely with each child's parents, teachers, court counselors, or other agency professionals to ensure a comprehensive and coordinated approach to his or her needs.

The Teaching-Family Treatment Model has four defining elements or components: an emphasis on *remediation through teaching and counseling,* a behaviorally based *motivation system* to support the teaching effort, *self-government* by the youths in the home, and a general orientation toward *family-style living.* This treatment package is focused on the goal of successful return by each youth to his or her natural home. The teaching-parents are the nexus of their treatment programs. They are also the key and the primary instrument in the protection of rights of the children in their charge.

These specifics are offered not as a recommendation of the Teaching-Family treatment approach (although we do recommend it) but rather to share with the reader the perspective from which the preparation of this chapter has been approached. While occasional reference to the actual utility of a specific policy or practice at the project site will be made, all suggestions have been formulated for use in group-home programs representing a broad range in treatment orientation, scope, sophistication, and funding resources.

Legal Overview

Most court cases and statutory enactments concerning the rights of children have originated from litigation directed at institutions for delinquent, mentally ill, or retarded children and adolescents. This body of case law is, nevertheless, directly applicable to group homes. This extrapolation is based on the similarities not of the facilities but rather of the youths they serve. The commonality is that it is state action that results in clients' placement in the institutions and that typically state action is also involved in the placement of children in group homes. State action may include state or local agency placement of a child as well as court disposition. In addition, the use of state or local funds to support the placement—even though it may have been initiated by parents—should be considered as state action (*Gary W.* v. *State of La.,* 437 F. Supp. 1209 [1976]). For the group home where no state action is involved (e.g., funded through contributions, with placement made exclusively by parents), it would still be advisable to follow the recommendations in this chapter. In the latter type of program case law involving right to treatment would not be applicable, but the penal laws of the state would apply, covering such acts as child abuse and assault. Also applicable would be the licensing regulations of the state.

BASIC RIGHTS

"Basic rights" is a term used here to cover a wide variety of client rights that can best be defined as minimum requirements for a child living in a facility. These basic rights should not be considered "privileges" to be provided or removed contingent upon appropriate or inappropriate behavior.

In *Inmates of Boys' Training School* v. *Affleck,* it was held that juveniles cannot be held in any facility without their being provided the following:

- a room equipped with lighting sufficient for reading until 10:00 P.M. (authors' opinion is that bedtime is changeable based on age of youth and morning activities)
- sufficient clothing to meet seasonal needs
- mattresses, pillows, and bedding—which must be changed once a week—including blankets, sheets, and pillowcases

- personal hygiene supplies, including soap, toothpaste, towels, toilet paper, and a toothbrush
- a daily change of undergarments and socks
- minimum writing materials—i.e., pen, pencil, paper, and envelopes
- prescription eyeglasses, if needed
- access to books, periodicals, and other reading materials
- daily showers
- access to medical facilities and nursing services
- general correspondence privileges

Numerous other basic rights have been established by court action, and they are summarized below:

Religion. Children confined in institutions should have opportunities to exercise the religious freedom guaranteed by the First Amendment. This includes the client's right to both attend or refuse to attend religious services.

Food. Three nutritious meals a day should be provided.

Mail. Children have the right to receive and send mail. Outgoing mail should not be tampered with or censored. Incoming mail can be inspected in the presence of the child for contraband. Censorship of incoming mail can only be condoned if it is done for a specified period of time and for the purpose of preventing serious harm to the child. Such mail not delivered to the addressee should be returned to the sender with a letter of explanation.

Education. Education must be provided to children who are within the age limits covered by compulsory school attendance laws. This is an important consideration for group homes that do not utilize public schools. Group homes utilizing public schools should be aware of the *Education for All Handicapped Children Act* (P. L. 94-142), which directs that all handicapped children have available to them a free, appropriate education emphasizing special educational and related services designed to meet their unique needs. Group homes should take whatever course of action (various actions are defined in the law) is most appropriate on behalf of group-home clients, to ensure that public schools are providing them with an appropriate education.

Visitation by Parents. Parents (excepting parents whose parental rights have been terminated by the courts) and foster parents have the right to visit their children, and children have the right to be visited by their parents or foster parents. Telephone communication between parent and child should also be permitted.

Visitation by Attorney. A child should have unrestricted access to his or her attorney.

Privacy and Possessions. Clients should be able to retain personal property—excepting, of course, materials that are inconsistent with the child's treatment (e.g., contraband, weapons, drugs, etc.).

Exercise. Adequate opportunities for exercise should be provided.

Interaction with Members of the Opposite Sex. Under appropriate supervision, children should be provided with opportunities for interaction with members of the opposite sex, except where for specific reasons a child's treatment may be hindered by such contact.

Clearly defined and written policies—and supervision to ensure that the policies are carried out—provide the best way to guarantee that the basic rights described above are not violated.

BEHAVIOR CONTROL PROCEDURES

More problematic are those actions taken by group-home staff in the face of various child behavior problems. Some of the more serious problem behaviors that can occur in the group home are physical or verbal aggression against staff or other residents, property damage, self-inflicted injury, refusal to comply with house rules, and running away. In addition, failure to provide basic living conditions may be a passive act of omission.

Confronted with client acts of defiance or aggression, group home staff must be very cautious in their choice and use of alternative procedures. In terms of behavior management, treatment is best directed at prevention rather than remediation. (Dealing with defiant and aggressive behavior will be addressed in greater detail under "Treatment-Staff Training," p. 263.)

Many behavior control procedures are unnecessarily restrictive, and constitute cruel and unusual punishment (in violation of the Eighth Amendment) or curtail personal freedom without due process (in violation of the Fourteenth Amendment). The courts have established that when children are placed outside the home through the judiciary process, the purpose of such placement must be for treatment—not punishment. This is succinctly stated in *Inmates of Boys' Training School* v. *Affleck*:

The constitutional validity of present procedural safeguards in juvenile adjudications, which do not embrace all of the rigorous safeguards of criminal court adjudications, appears to rest on the adherence of the juvenile justice system to rehabilitative rather than penal goals.

Rehabilitation, then, is the interest which the state had defined as being the purpose of confinement of juveniles. Due process in the adjudicative stages of the juvenile justice system has been defined differently from due process in the criminal justice system because the goal of the juvenile justice system, rehabilitation, differs from the goals of the criminal system, which include punishment, deterrence and retribution. Thus, due process in the juvenile justice system requires that the post-adjudicative stage of institutionalization further the goal of rehabilitation.

Corporal Punishment. Corporal punishment—or any actions generally described as causing physical pain or discomfort—have been found unacceptable by the courts. See *Gary W.* v. *State of Louisiana, Morales* v. *Turman* (364 F. Supp. 166 [E.D. Tex. 1973]), and *Nelson* v. *Heyne* (Civ. No. 72-S-98 [N.D. Ind., filed Feb. 1, 1976]). In addition, corporal punishment is prohibited in many states either by law or licensing regulations. Even where corporal punishment is permitted by state law, group homes and their staff still may be held liable in money damages for any injuries inflicted.

Seclusion, Locked Time-Out, Isolation. These terms describe slightly different procedures. However, there are only a few ways in which any of them can be implemented in the group-home setting. Such procedures usually involve restricting a child to a locked barren room, bedroom, or closet. Case law is very clear that seclusion, isolation, or time-out cannot be used as punishment. The only legally acceptable occasion for using these procedures is when their use is based on substantial evidence that the juveniles *constitute an immediate threat to the physical well-being of themselves or others.*

The use of these procedures must be approached very cautiously, as suggested by the court in *Morales* v. *Turman.*

> Experts were unanimous in their opinion that solitary confinement of a child in a small cell is an extreme measure that should be used only in emergency situations to calm uncontrollably violent behavior, and should not last longer than necessary to calm the child. . . . The child should not be left entirely alone for long periods. . . . Prolonged confinement of a child to a single building can be harmful unless the child is receiving a great deal of attention during the time of confinement. Experiments in sensory deprivation have shown that the absence of many and varied stimuli may have a serious detrimental effect upon the mental health of a child.

In *Gary W.* v. *State of Louisiana,* the court further held that locked time-out is not acceptable, and listed the following guidelines for the use of time-out:

No child shall be placed alone in a locked room either as punishment or for any other purpose. Legitimate "time out" procedures may be used under close and direct professional supervision.

These standards shall apply to "time out" procedures.

- They are to be imposed only when less restrictive measures are not feasible;
- Placement shall be in an unlocked room with a staff member constantly nearby in a place where the staff member can supervise the child;
- The child shall have access to bathroom facilities as needed;
- The period of isolation or segregation shall not exceed 12 hours unless renewed by a qualified professional;
- Except in an emergency situation in which it is likely that a child would harm himself or others, the decision to place a child in "time out" shall be made pursuant to a written order by a qualified professional. . . . Any such order must specify the terms and conditions of "time out" and the rationale for the decision; and
- Emergency use of "time out" shall be authorized only by the superintendent . . . and shall be limited to a period of not more than one hour.

It is the authors' opinion that seclusion, locked time-out, and isolation should be considered only if the client demonstrates volatility. If they are used, carefully written procedures should govern their use, and written documentation should be maintained. It should be borne in mind that one of the advantages of a group home is that family-style living can be approximated; if group homes use time-out, seclusion, or isolation rooms, they may take on an institutional character, thus defeating much of the purpose and philosophy of the community-based group home program.

Physical Restraint. Physical restraint can take two forms: restraint by mechanical apparatus and restraint by a staff member physically holding the child. The latter is acceptable when a child is violent and in danger of harming himself or herself or others. This form of restraint should be used only if less restrictive alternative techniques have been tried and have failed. Mechanical restraints in group homes are not recommended.

Food Restriction. A child is entitled to three nutritious meals a day. These meals should not be awarded as privileges. Not allowing a child three meals a day would constitute a violation of his or her rights.

Forced Work. Make-work—in which nothing is accomplished by the work (e.g., moving rocks from one place to another)—was found to be cruel and unusual punishment in *Morales* v. *Turman.* Limits should be placed on the amounts of work done by a child, since the Thirteenth Amendment against involuntary servitude does apply here. This ban would include work done for staff members if no compensation is provided. However, as directed in *Gary W.* v. *State of Louisiana,*

> a child may be required to perform without compensation such housekeeping tasks as would be performed by a child in a natural home, foster home, or group home, provided that nothing in the child's individual treatment plan forbids such work.

Forced Medication.   Psychotropic medication can only be prescribed by a physician and should be administered by either a physician or qualified nurse. Medication administered as punishment is unlawful.

Unusual Practices.   A number of exotic practices have been brought to the attention of the courts. For example, to prevent running away children's clothing has been removed or, as a form of discipline, a technique known as "hair dance" has been used, in which staff pull children's hair or drag them around by their hair. Verbal abuse, in which staff or other children swear or verbally humiliate to child, has occurred in some settings. As a form of discipline or to force compliance, children have been required to "take care" of another child—which invites physical or verbal abuse. These have all been found legally unacceptable, while often presented under the guise of treatment, they are intolerable and certainly violate the rights of children.

RIGHT TO TREATMENT

Quid pro Quo

> When the state chooses, for the most humane motives, to offer or require institutional confinement of a person, it must consider means that are capable of achieving its purposes that are least stifling to personal liberty, and it must offer a therapeutic consideration, a *quid pro quo,* for the deprivation. [*Gary W.* v. *State of Louisiana*]

The significance of *quid pro quo* (literally, "something for something") here is that by sending a child to a group home the state requires that child to give up that measure of freedom associated with living with his or her natural family, and in return the state must provide something. That "something" is treatment. The right to treatment under such circumstances has been established by the courts as a constitutional right.

The courts have found it easiest to recognize when treatment is not occurring; they have found it more problematic to specify what treatment is. Nevertheless, the courts have dictated certain standards for institutions that can also be applied to group homes. The remainder of this section will review some of these standards, but it should be remembered that there is no absolute or court-established form for correct treatment.

Least Restrictive Alternative. Community-based group homes have become increasingly popular as the courts have embraced the concept of "least restrictive treatment." This concept or principle is best interpreted to mean that a child, within the limits of availability and his or her special needs and problems, must be treated in that environment that most closely resembles the inherent freedom, flexibility, and surroundings associated with the natural home. Whereas the courts have viewed large regional institutions as substantially restrictive, the community-based group home has—for good reason—been considered much less so. The recent deinstitutionalization movement regarding the delinquent, mentally ill, and mentally retarded has followed this principle of the right to treatment in the least restrictive environment. Thus, the group home can, by its very nature, typically meet the client's right to treatment in the least restrictive environment vis-à-vis institutions. However, group homes must avoid referrals that might best be served in an even less restrictive setting. The standard test for this is to see if all less restrictive approaches have been considered and found to be unacceptable.

The least restrictive alternative can also mean the least drastic or disruptive means to achieve treatment. For example, positive approaches to treatment must be attempted before physical restraint or other more restrictive procedures can be used.

Individual Treatment Plans. Proper treatment for children must be provided on an individual basis. Both the need for individual treatment and the expectations of treatment are eloquently stated in *Gary W.* v. *State of Louisiana.*

> The constitutional right to treatment is a right to a program of treatment that affords the individual a reasonable chance to acquire and maintain those life skills that enable him to cope as effectively as his own capacities permit with the demands of his own person and of his own environment and to raise the level of his physical, mental and social efficiency.

Staff Selection, Training, and Development. Inherent in the right to treatment is the implication that appropriately selected and trained staff are necessary to carry out a treatment program. Furthermore, these staff must be sufficient in number to adequately meet treatment and child care needs. See *Morales* v. *Turman* and *Martella* v. *Kelley* (349 F. Supp. [1972]) for further discussion.

Treatment Program. As mentioned above, the courts have never hesitated in determining when a treatment program is nonexistent;

they have been adamant in supporting the right to treatment and therefore the need for a treatment program. But *what treatment is* has been left to the child care experts. The following questions should be considered by the group home director in reviewing or developing a treatment program:

1. Is the program individualized to meet the needs of individual children, or are all children subject to identical regimens? Are there individually devised treatment goals for each child?
2. Are staff members sufficiently qualified and trained to carry out the treatment program? Are staff prepared to meet emergency situations that might occur?
3. Is the focus of the program on the child's return to his or her natural or foster home or to self-sufficiency? Or is it, on the other hand, on a successful adaptation by the child to the requirements of group home living, which may be unrelated to the goal of return?
4. Is there a system of supervision that ensures that the treatment program is being carried out as intended?
5. Is there provision for periodic external evaluation of the program?
6. Is there a vehicle by which the implementation of program policies and procedures is meaningfully documented?

A System for Protecting the Rights of Group-Home Residents

PRELIMINARY CONSIDERATIONS

No one intentionally designs a program to violate children's rights. However, it is during the planning stage that several critical decisions are made that have a significant impact on the extent and quality of children's protection as well as their treatment. Insufficient or conceptually weak plans also can result in later, sometimes serious, violations of children's rights. A fairly firm position on three crucial, related issues should ideally be established prior to the development of staffing, training, and evaluation strategies, and certainly before the group home begins admitting children.

The first of these issues is a determination of the *target population* to be served by the group home. This should include specification of age and sex of children, number of children to be served at one time, and the range of behavioral and emotional problems that the program will be expected to handle. These considerations should form the basis for admissions guidelines. The greatest danger here is the risk of making the guidelines too broad. For example, placing an eight-year-old truant in a home with a sixteen-year-old who has been adjuged committing drug possession puts the eight-year-old at measurable risk.

The second consideration is the identification of *treatment goals.* These general objectives should be directly related to the problems commonly exhibited by the target population. This is not to say that individual treatment goals are unnecessary; individual goal planning should proceed when children are admitted for treatment. But in the planning stage a program must have an overall idea of treatment goals that will be applicable to a majority of the population.

Closely related to the selection of treatment goals is the third issue, the selection or specification of the focal elements of the *treatment program.* Ideally, a treatment program would be selected that has demonstrated effectiveness in addressing and accomplishing the treatment goals for the target population. Some psychological theories sound attractive, but their practical application to actual client problems falls far short of the successful resolution of targeted problems. When this occurs, children's right to treatment is thrust into jeopardy.

If these issues have been resolved thoughtfully and in advance, the way is paved for the final preparatory task that should precede actual program implementation. This is the development, in writing, of a *working policy manual.* Written policies are critical. Minimally, a policy manual should include personnel guidelines, job descriptions, fiscal guidelines, treatment policies (covering acceptable and unacceptable procedures), confidentiality guidelines, and guidelines covering informed consent. Also specified in the policy manual should be the proposed content of client records, including, at the least, copies of medical examinations, social history, psychological evaluation, treatment plans, progress notes, and special incident reports. The policy manual should also list procedures required for compliance with state licensing regulations. Failure of the group home to comply with fire safety, sanitation, and state-imposed program guidelines can result in the violation of client rights. It is imperative that staff be aware of group home policies; the safest way to transmit this information is through written materials. Preservice training (see pp. 263–265 ff. below) affords an excellent opportunity to present and elaborate on the more critical aspects of the policy manual.

SELECTION OF TREATMENT STAFF

Perhaps the single most important factor in safeguarding client rights involves the selection of direct-care staff. This is particularily true in programs that utilize direct-care staff as primary therapists. However,

even in homes where direct-care staff have little treatment responsibility, they still spend a great deal of time alone with the clients. As
such, they are in a position to have a direct impact on the clients' lives
and protect or infringe on their rights. Staff implementation errors
within a program, not the program per se, most commonly account for
violations of client rights.

At first glance it appears that selection of direct-care staff follows
the typical hiring process and includes the development of a job description, advertising, interviewing, and checking of personal and professional references. But the literature offers little if any guidance as
to exactly what constitutes a good group home worker. Experience
indicates that there appear to be generic qualities that such workers
seem to share. Some of these are (1) a fondness and genuine concern
for youths, (2) the personal stability to maintain control of their own
emotions while under pressure, (3) patience, (4) the ability to accept
and work with the youths even when they, the youths, are having
problems, and (5) the ability to exercise sound judgment and behave
with maturity. Beyond these general qualities, other factors that should
be assessed prior to selection will be based on the specific requirements
of the job itself as well as any existing state regulations such as educational requirements.

Due to the subtle and often ambiguous nature of these necessary staff
characteristics, the task of assessing their presence becomes difficult and
demands a great deal of creativity and individualization. Traditionally,
interviewers have relied heavily on open-ended questions about various
issues involved in group home operations. Such questions, if carefully
phrased so that the applicant must make assumptions in order to fill in
information gaps and worded so that "right" answers are not readily
apparent, can yield valuable information along a number of important
dimensions. For example, an applicant applying for a primary therapeutic position in which youth advocacy is important might be asked to
respond to the following hypothetical situation:

> Kerry's main problem has been tantrumming and running away. Since she
> came to your home, she has only run once and has made good progress in
> school. After this runaway incident, she was warned by the authorities that
> she would go to a lock-up facility if any more problems arose. Last weekend,
> however, she not only ran but left the home cursing you and the home.
> Now you and Kerry are in court and the judge thinks she should go to the
> secure facility. He asks for your opinion. What would you say?

While the answer to this question will provide a direct indication of
the degree of the applicant's tendency to advocate for a youth's return
to the group home, it is also likely to provide information in areas such
as (1) the tendency to be positive and focus on progress rather than on

continuing problems, (2) tendencies to take youth behaviors personally, (3) confidence in dealing with clients' problems, (4) tactfulness, (5) ability to articulate views, and (6) compatibility with the treatment philosophy.

The following question might also yield information on multiple aspects:

> When James came into your group home, he had not been in school in four months. It is a requirement in the group home that the youths attend school. After being in the home one month, James brings home a report card with one D, one B, and the rest Cs. How would you respond to him after looking at the card?

Careful attention to which of the grades applicants mention first, where they place their emphasis, their level of enthusiasm, and so on, should reveal, among other things, (1) whether they tend to be positive, (2) how accepting and supportive of the clients they are likely to be, (3) how enthusiastic they tend to be about clients' progress, and (4) whether they are likely to set unrealistic expectations for clients. While the specifics of the questioning will depend on the information desired, this quasi-projective approach can lead to an efficient and accurate assessment of the characteristics necessary for quality in service delivery.

Finally, since these applicants will have direct contact with the children if hired, careful checking of their personal and professional references should be done as standard practice.

TRAINING OF TREATMENT STAFF

High quality preservice training of treatment staff is essential to the protection of children's rights for several reasons. The first relates to a common characteristic of group home residents. In addition to individual problems stemming from emotional disturbance, learning disability, or retardation, most group home clients share persistent histories of defiant and unmanageable behavior. Treatment staff who for want of adequate preparation through training lack the ability to effectively control problem behavior using appropriate, established procedures will tend to readily resort to punitive, possibly abusive, or even illegal alternatives. Second, new and untrained staff members will invariably encounter almost systematic "victimization" at the hands of group home residents, even if the problems and behavior of the resident population had recently been under control. Most children will seize upon such an opportunity to resurrect their presenting problem behaviors; the frequency of limit-testing among all the youths will escalate predictably and almost immediately. If not corrected, this circumstance will become progressively more frustrating and explosive, will seriously interrupt the previous progress of the youths in the program, and may precipitate the premature and unnecessary removal of some clients from treatment. Third, inadequate preservice training will also, for the reasons just discussed, foster treatment staff "burn-out," thus establishing an unfortunate cycle of ineffective intervention and accelerated staff turnover. Finally, as has been previously emphasized, children enter group homes with an abiding right to treatment above and beyond the responsible management of their antisocial behavior. It is the effective application of specific procedures acquired through high-quality preservice staff training that most directly guarantees this right to treatment.

The scope and content of the preservice training required will be largely determined by the sophistication of treatment responsibilities to be assumed by the staff, client characteristics and needs, and the intent or goals of treatment. Most programs should, however, include at least the following topical areas: (1) The treatment philosophy must be addressed in specific procedural terms. (2) There should be detailed description of program components as well as of how they will be applied to meet the needs of individual clients. (3) There should be a complete explanation of staff members' duties and responsibilities (including specific program policies and procedures) and the relationship of their jobs to the overall delivery of therapeutic services. (4) Clients' rights should be enumerated and defined and the legal and ethical responsibilities of staff regarding those rights presented. (5) Perhaps most important, training should provide the staff member with a realistic perception of the kinds of situation likely to be encountered, and with a repertoire of procedures for dealing effectively with this range of anticipated client problems.

Regarding the process of training, many of these topical areas can be effectively presented using a standard classroom instructional format (i.e., lecture, discussion, question-and-answer, etc.). However, the authors strongly recommend an alternative approach to teaching those specialized skills that the trainees will be expected to use in their direct, treatment-related interactions with clients. These are the skills that staff will be exercising in order to effect in the youths in their charge new learning and the remediation of presenting problems. These competencies represent the very core of high-quality treatment; the trainees must be trained to mastery, and that mastery must be demonstrated. We have found that this is best accomplished through a combination of behavior simulation by a trainer and subsequent skill rehearsal, eventually to the level of near-perfection, by the trainee. Initial simulations are addressed to positive, preventive teaching techniques. When these are mastered, simulations are then centered on those problems that characterize the particular youths to be served and are best ordered for training purposes from minor or routine problems (e.g., ignoring instructions, modest limit-testing, etc.) to more serious or difficult-to-control ones (e.g., verbal threats, open defiance, physical aggression, etc.). An instructional episode progresses as follows: First, effective and ethically acceptable intervention procedures are explained and demonstrated to the trainee. A trainer then models a youth behavior problem, and the trainee attempts to manage that problem using the new procedures or skills. Finally the trainer, trainee, and other trainees present review the trainee's performance. This sequence is repeated until the trainee demonstrates near-perfect mastery of the required skills. Training then proceeds with the simulation of a more serious or disruptive problem.

Experience has shown this behavior-simulation–skill-rehearsal approach to be optimally effective in establishing an effective intervention repertoire among direct-care staff for group homes. As applied to the problem of aggression, for example, preservice training incorporating this appoach would establish (by demonstration) a trainee's ability to implement (1) effective ways to prevent aggression by recognizing and dealing with the types of behavior pattern, both verbal and nonverbal, that lead to aggression, (2) specific procedures for teaching behaviors that are incompatible with aggression, (3) specific nonabusive techniques for dealing with overt aggression, and (4), if restrictive procedures are necessary, specific policies and procedures to be followed in both obtaining any necessary authorization to use the techniques and subsequent documentation and review of their use.

In-Service Training. Some form of training must follow preservice training. If not, staff performance often deteriorates as staff begin to look for "short cuts," forget certain basic aspects of preservice training, and become frustrated. Even though this may happen unintentionally, violation of client rights, by staff either failing to provide treatment or using abusive procedures, can occur.

In-service training can be both simple to implement and very beneficial to the staff members involved. In-service training sessions can be used to trouble-shoot as regards previously trained-for treatment procedures, describing new treatment techniques, and provide updated information on legal and ethical issues. If staff from more than one home attend in-service training, mutual problem solving among staffs is encouraged. In any case, staff morale can be boosted by in-service training.

Treatment Staff Consultation. On-site consultation can effectively deal with much of the staff performance attenuation described above and also offer many of the same benefits as in-service training. But it affords an additional protection of client rights that can only be achieved through direct observation of staff implementation of the treatment program in the group home setting. On-site observation allows for a review of staff ability to implement various treatment procedures. Further, progress of clients toward specified treatment goals can be monitored. In-home consultants can also provide much-needed moral support to the group home staff. Finally, periodic observation and supervision by persons external to the day-to-day program operation can prevent the group home from becoming a closed system impervious to outside review and comment—and therefore more prone to violating client rights.

In addition to periodic on-site visits, providing direct-care staff with twenty-four-hour-a-day access to a knowledgeable and supportive external information source can prove invaluable in safeguarding client rights. This service can be provided, usually via telephone, by various professionals (e.g., a program consultant, supervisor, or staff psychologist) and can thus be quite cost-efficient. Regardless of cost, the benefits, both to clients and direct-care staff, are immense. First, such consultation allows the staff to receive advice when it is needed most—either in a crisis situation or as one is developing. By providing acceptable alternatives, the consultant can often help the staff successfully prevent or interrupt a crisis. Second, by encouraging staff to call whenever questions arise, staff implementation errors—which could result in serious problems—may be avoided. Third, the simple fact that assistance and support are readily available often instills staff with the confidence to utilize established procedures in dealing with difficult clients. Further, this service can provide needed moral support at the very time staff may be frustrated or doubting their own abilities, thereby alleviating some of the major sources of staff "burn-out."

PLANNING INDIVIDUAL TREATMENT

A valuable safeguard of a child's right to treatment in a group home is the individual treatment plan. A successfully constructed and appropriately monitored treatment plan can serve as an effective guide for the child's progress through the program.

Although intake procedures differ greatly among facilities, staff should always be trained to use all sources of input in developing treatment plans. The following questions should be asked of both the referring agent and the parents (if available):

1. In specific terms, what are the reasons for the referral?
2. What difficulties does the child have in the school, home, community, and peer group?
3. What behavioral and emotional improvements are expected as a result of the treatment program?

Client input into treatment planning is also desirable, subject of course to the ability of the youth in question. Involvement can make the youth aware of the treatment goals, lead to greater youth investment in the treatment program, and allow the treatment plan to reflect goals spontaneously specified by the youth.

Monitoring the implementation of the treatment plan by observation is vital, and will save the process from an otherwise certain destiny as "just more paperwork." The treatment program should be directed at the client goals, and *in vivo* monitoring will help ensure that this is accomplished. The treatment goals may also be used as a standard against which to measure actual client progress. It is recommended that observable standards of performance be used rather than written progress reports will both weaken the monitoring process and preclude adequate documentation of progress (that is, one piece of paper—progress notes—will be offered to document another piece of paper—the treatment plan!).

CONFIDENTIALITY

It is the group-home staff's responsibility to assure the confidentiality of all client records. The release of client information to unauthorized individuals violates the rights of the child, and if the child is harmed because of the release the group home will be subject to civil damages. The group home can protect the confidentiality of client records by

1. safeguarding records against loss, defacement, tampering, or use by unauthorized persons;
2. having written policies that require the consent of the consumer's guardian prior to release of information to authorized individuals;
3. having written policies and staff training that emphasize the importance of not releasing or discussing confidential client information with unauthorized persons; and
4. following the guidelines provided by each state regarding the type of person who can have access to records, and the procedures (e.g., forms, verification) to be employed as safeguards.

INFORMED CONSENT

Unfortunately, documentation of informed client consent has come to be viewed by many service providers and other professionals (especially applied researchers) as a vehicle more for their own protection than for the protection of clients and research subjects. Properly devised and managed informed consent procedures will serve to protect both the client and the service provider–researcher. In the group home environment, informed consent strategies are used in two ways. As regards the first, all group homes should have standard procedures for adequately informing the child client and his or her parents or guardian regarding the parameters of the child's residence and treatment in the group home. This informed consent to treatment becomes vital when real choices concerning the kind and duration of treatment are to be made. As for the second, those group homes in which children, by virtue of their residence in the facility, are candidates for research or experimentation must also solicit the informed consent to participate in such research from the child and his or her parents or guardian. Since these two kinds of informed consent serve different purposes, they will be treated separately.

Informed Consent to Treatment. The primary purpose of informed consent to treatment is to ensure that the child and his or her parents or guardian (1) understand why the child is a candidate for group-home placement, (2) understand the nature of the child's participation in every aspect of the treatment program, (3) understand the nature and extent of any risks or discomforts that might accrue to the child's residency and involvement in the program, (4) are aware of the anticipated benefits of the program to the child (but are also aware that such benefits cannot be guaranteed), (5) understand what, if any, alternatives to group home placement are available to the child, and (6), given the understanding, consent in writing to the child's participation in the program as described.

Note that the relationship to the child of the person or persons whose consent is formally solicited will vary with the case. For example, neither the consent of the child nor that of his or her parents would be required for a child whose placement in a particular group home had been ordered by juvenile court. If, however, the effort to place the child in the group home had been initiated by the parents, then only their permission or consent would be required to admit that child. (While the child's consent might be requested, it would not be required if the parents consented to treatment.) Finally, if the decision to seek group home placement had been arrived at with complete mutuality by the child and his or her parents—i.e., if the child were actually offered a real choice in the matter—then consent would be solicited from the child as well as the parents. In any case, the child should be present and fully understand all information exchanged as part of the informed consent process, whether or not the child's formal consent is to be solicited.

Ideally, the emphasis with informed consent to treatment should be on "informed" rather than "consent." The point of the whole process is to be certain that everyone who will be directly affected by the child's entry into treatment understands what is happening, why it is happening, and what to expect. While no single approach to informed consent to treatment will meet the specific requirements of all group-home programs, the following suggestions may prove useful:

1. Focus the entire process on information exchange, and probe for evidence that the information presented is actually understood by all principals.
2. Construct an informed consent document that is complete enough to adequately describe the treatment program but is also readable and fairly brief. (BIABH once designed an informed consent statement that discussed ·virtually every detail of our treatment program. We asked an attorney to review the thirty-page statement to determine if it would protect us in the event of a lawsuit. His response was "Of course not; no *reasonable man* could be expected to wade through the damned thing.")
3. Use the informed consent document as a basis from which to converse with the child and parents about the issues involved. Read through the document with them and encourage them to interrupt to ask any questions they might have.
4. Ask the child or the parents to describe impressions of the program to you; this will help determine the adequacy of their understanding of the information presented to them and will identify and correct any areas of uncertainty or misunderstanding on their part.
5. Finally, it is advisable to give a signed copy of the informed consent document to each person whose signature appears on it, along with the name and phone number of a responsible professional who can be contacted if concerns over its content or the child's care or treatment arise later.

There are two other areas related to informed consent where agreement must be reached between parent or guardian and the group home at the time of admission. These are whether group home staff can authorize routine or emergency medical treatment, and parental responsibilities during the course of treatment.

Informed Consent to Research Participation. Two practical tasks should be undertaken prior to the development of specific informed consent guidelines for use in the group-home setting. First, the prospective researcher should acquaint himself or herself with current legal and ethical considerations bearing on research with human subjects generally.[1] Second, the special fragilities of group-home residents must be

---

[1] Martin and Kelty, in Chapters 1 and 20 respectively in this book, offer general and informative discussions of legal and other issues that must be considered in any research involving human participants. Martin's review of regulations recently proposed by the National Commission for the Protection of Human Subjects in Biomedical and Behavioral Research will prove particularly useful. As a supplement to these proposed regulations, we would strongly recommend *Ethical Principles in the Conduct of Research With Human Participants,* published in 1973 by the American Psychological Association.

carefully considered before a decision is made to use them as subjects of research. They have special emotional and behavioral vulnerabilities, have been removed from the abiding protection of their natural families, and represent to some extent a captive population. In short, these children have already found themselves in harm's way. The point is that the researcher should take great care to avoid experimentation with group-home residents done purely for reasons involving his or her own convenience. In general, if adult subjects can satisfy the requirements of proposed research as well as children, adults should be used. Similarly, if children in an environment less restrictive than the group home can meet research requirements, it would be wise to approach them rather than group-home residents. Another way of putting this is that any research involving children in group homes should be addressed either to some defining characteristic of this special population of children or to some aspect of the group-home environment or treatment program.

Having thus arrived at a considered decision to conduct research requiring the participation of group home youths, the researcher must now contemplate the question of their protection. As with any research involving human subjects, it is absolutely necessary that prospective participants in group home research be fully informed as to the requirements of their participation, the general purpose of the research, any possible risks or discomforts that they might experience as a result of participation, and the voluntary nature of their participation in the research. Unlike consent to treatment, consent to participation in research must always be solicited in writing from the child as well as from the parents or guardian.

Regarding the process for establishing informed consent to participation in research, the following steps are suggested in addition to those recommended above for consent to treatment.

1. Discuss the importance to the child of your efforts to ensure the confidentiality of data you hope to collect from him or her, and describe the procedures by which you are prepared to guarantee that confidentiality.
2. Arrange, if possible, for the child to actually experience some representative aspects of the research. If, for instance, the research involves a series of experimental trials, put the child through a simulated trial. Or, if survey research is planned, read some representative questions from the survey instrument to the child. This should be done in the presence of parents or guardian if their formal consent is to be solicited.
3. Be certain that the child and the parents understand that the child's participation in research *is not a condition of treatment;* include this point in the informed consent document.

4. Finally, take advantage of any human-rights protection review facility at your disposal. Most research is sponsored by a college, university, or other institution, most of which are now required to review the procedures to be used for the protection of the human rights of subjects participating in the research they sponsor. Have the institutional review committee of the organization sponsoring your research carefully review your informed consent procedures and documents. (They may even be prepared to help you develop these strategies and materials.) Also, include in your informed consent document the name and phone number of the chairperson of this committee, with an invitation for the child or parents to contact this individual directly if any problems or concerns arise in connection with the child's participation in the study.

EVALUATION OF STAFF PERFORMANCE

Concept of Consumer Evaluation. Let us assume that the operator of a hypothetical group home has adopted the major children's rights protection procedures suggested so far. Policy has been established and set down in a manual. Effective staff selection procedures have been implemented, and treatment staff receive good quality preservice training and participate in an ongoing program of in-service training and individual consultation. Individual treatment planning and behavioral record-keeping are proceeding properly and systematically, the confidentiality of all client records is being maintained, and effective procedures are being implemented for establishing informed consent to treatment and research participation. Let us further assume that all of these elements of the child protection system are being undertaken conscientiously and that the total package is smoothly working as intended. Are these efforts in unison sufficient to ensure the rights of the children served by the program? They are not, and the reason is simple: All of the aforementioned measures are essentially internal. In combination, these necessary procedures have carried the protection process as far as it can be carried within the circle of people who conceived and implemented the program. What is missing is accountability to—and completion of the feedback loop from—the varied community of individuals whose needs are, one hopes, served by the program.

There are various individuals whose proximity to the group home and density of contact with it qualifies them to make responsible judgments regarding its general effectiveness in meeting the goals of the children it serves while protecting their rights. Among the direct consumer groups whose periodic input may be valuable to the group-home operator are: agency and court professionals who refer youth to the program (e.g., social services caseworkers, mental health counselors, court counselors, probation officers, etc.), all teachers and other school professionals having contact with the youths from the group home, all members of the group-home's board of directors, the parents of the youths in the program, and, most important of all, the youths themselves. Note that these individuals as a group share a special perspective on the functioning of the group home. Unlike the group-home operator and his or her training, consultation, and treatment staff—the service providers—the group-home's consumers are the recipients of its services whose investment in the quality of the program is personal rather than proprietary. They are thus in a perfect position to offer objective input, critical as well as positive, on the state of the program without risk of damning themselves or their own efforts. For this reason the independent consumer evaluation occupies an important place in any child client protection system. It is, typically, the only vehicle for assessing the condition of the group home that is not confounded by the proprietary interests of the group home's operational or management team.

Evaluation: Process and Procedures.   Every group home's unique configuration and circumstances will dictate the final form of its evaluation process. Evaluation scope, frequency, and various details of method will hinge upon the purpose of the particular group home, its population, and its resources. The recommendations to follow are based on a consumer evaluation format that has proved successful at BIABH over the past six years (see Fields, Maloney, Maloney, Timbers, & Jones, 1976). This evaluation format is in turn based upon—but not identical to—the Teaching-Family evaluation approach developed at the original Achievement Place Project (see Phillips, Phillips, Fixsen, & Wolf, 1974). This discussion will focus on those elements of the evaluation process that are fundamental in the protection of children's rights. Individual programs may adapt the resulting evaluation systems to suit their unique needs.

Key Requirements of an Effective Consumer Evaluation.   The first step in preparing an effective program of independent evaluation is to determine who the relevant consumers of the program are. Some guidance on this has already been offered here. The next step is to determine what information these consumers can provide that will assist the program in meeting its treatment objectives and adequately protecting the rights of its clients. Next, a method for soliciting this information from the consumers must be devised. Finally, a strategy must be constructed for meaningfully assembling the information gathered and communicating it to the group-home's management and treatment staff. The following specific suggestions are offered toward meeting these requirements:

1. The information-gathering process should focus on the performance of those group-home staff members (the treatment staff) who have direct and primary responsibility for the children in the program and for the remediation of their presenting problems. At BIABH the teaching-parents constitute the treatment team. In other group homes the treatment team will include house-parents or their equivalent, alternate direct-care and treatment providers, and other professionals such as psychologists and counselors (who provide intervention or therapy in—perhaps as an integral part of—the group home program). Secondarily, information should be solicited regarding the parameters of the program itself, independent of the treatment team's administration of it. This will help consumer respondents separate their concerns about the treatment philosophy of the program from their concerns and comments about the treatment team's application of it per se.

2. Most consumer input can be most efficiently collected through the mails, by use of a "consumer feedback questionnaire." The comments of agency and court professionals, school personnel, members of the board of directors, and parents can be gathered in this fashion. Comments and input from youths in the group home, however, are best solicited using an interview format.

3. Ultimately, the content of the questions addressed to consumers (by mail or interview) will determine the practical utility of the evaluation enterprise. Excepting the youths themselves, consumers should respond to succinctly phrased questions concerning such things as their familiarity or frequency of contact with the program and its treatment staff, their satisfaction with the degree of cooperation that they receive from the treatment staff, the degree to which they feel the treatment staff's efforts have been demonstrably effective in helping the youths reach their treatment goals, and so on. A rating-scale format may prove useful in quantifying consumer responses to such questions. The format used at BIABH permits consumers to rate their degree of satisfaction for each question area on a seven-point scale, the extreme values of which are "completely satisfied" and "completely dissatisfied." In addition, consumers are encouraged to offer their spontaneous comments and observations following each question.

4. It is essential to the validity of the consumer evaluation process that consumers' anonymity be protected, at least vis-à-vis the treatment staff whose performance they are being asked to evaluate. Although it is useful to have consumers identified on the questionnaires they return (so that individuals not responding to the questionnaires may be prompted), all identifying information should be eliminated at the time the consumer data are being assembled for presentation to the treatment team.

5. Ideally, consumer information should be collected and analyzed by someone who is familiar with the group-home's treatment policies but does not have a proprietary investment in them. (If this evaluation

function must of necessity be performed by the program director or other training or consultation staff members, particular care should be taken to ensure that the evaluation procedures are vigorously objective and that the anonymity of consumer respondents is guaranteed.) Larger group-home projects, such as BIABH, may enjoy the luxury of an on-staff evaluation expert or team. This person or team initiates the evaluations, analyzes and assembles the data from the evaluation, prepares an evaluation report for the treatment team which includes all evaluation data and specific recommendations to the staff for remedying any problems that the evaluation has revealed, and is available for a conference with the treatment team after it has had an opportunity to digest the evaluation report.

In combination with the independent consumer evaluation just discussed, it is strongly urged that all group home evaluations include an on-site observational visit by an evaluator trained in the specifics of the treatment program as well as in current performance-evaluation methods. A "professional in-home evaluation visit" is a key part of all evaluations conducted by BIABH and other group home sites using the Teaching-Family treatment model. This visit is typically scheduled to begin in the late afternoon, allowing the evaluator or evaluators to spend an entire evening observing the treatment team, the youths, and the interaction between the two. A fairly elaborate rating system—using the previously mentioned seven-point satisfaction rating scale—is used to record the observations and responses of the professional evaluators.

Every effort is made to make the evaluation visit as casual and comfortable as possible for the youths and the treatment staff. Private interviews with each youth in the program are conducted as part of the visit. For purposes of protecting the rights of these youths, this youth evaluation is probably the single most important component of the entire evaluation process. It represents the one opportunity many children will have to articulate any discontent they may have with the treatment team, the program itself, and with life in general in the group home. As with the other consumers, the validity of the youth responses will depend upon absolute protection of their anonymity in the later communication of their input to the treatment team. The interview format used at BIABH includes a written questionnaire—again incorporating the seven-point satisfaction rating scale—which the evaluator reads through with each youth, followed by a period of conversation during which the youth is prompted to express any and all feelings, good or bad, about every aspect of his or her treatment in the group home. All data from the professional in-home evaluation visit, including youth ratings and comments, are included in the aforementioned evaluation report.

In terms of the frequency of such evaluations for group homes, we recommend a minimum of one thorough evaluation per year. In addition, any areas of an evaluation that pointed to performance deficiencies on the part of the treatment team should be reevaluated after steps have been taken to correct these deficiencies. Subsequent reevaluation should be performed until all aspects of treatment staff performance are in line with the quality standards of the program.

If the key elements of the evaluation process are designed and implemented carefully, most abuses of children, both subtle and serious, will find their way into the data produced by it. If, for example, the children in a group home are being clothed or fed inadequately, various consumers will comment on that fact. If the children's right to treatment is being breached by inadequate or ineffective intervention by the treatment team, the professional in-home evaluation visit will reveal the deficiency. And if real abuses to the children are being perpetrated by the treatment team, these youths will have an opportunity to discuss them confidentially with a caring and nonjudgmental adult as part of the youth evaluation visit. The complete evaluation process represents an independent assessment of the group-home program and the performance of its direct-care and treatment staff. Its usefulness lies not only in its effectiveness in guaranteeing the rights of the group-home residents, but also in its utility as an important in-service training tool for treatment staff and its administrative value toward overall program quality control.

Summary and Conclusion

Residents of community-based group-home programs are especially vulnerable to threats against their civil and human rights because they are children, they have special emotional and behavioral problems, they have been removed from the moment-to-moment care and protection of their natural families, and no comprehensive technology now exists to guarantee their protection. The present chapter does not purport to offer such a comprehensive technology. It has, however, attempted to identify those aspects of group-home services delivery that are most likely to compromise children's rights and outline a system of practical strategies by which potential abuses and injustices in the group home environment can be substantially minimized. If we have additionally made some contribution toward the development of the urgently needed larger technology for the protection of children's rights, so much the better.

Needless to say, children in all group homes must be afforded the basic rights enumerated above in the legal overview. The system of protection described subsequently is intended to significantly exceed these minimum legal standards. Following the premise that both effective resident protection and treatment quality are functionally inseparable, the protection system will serve in a general way as a guide to good-quality group-home treatment. Many of its specific components are elaborate, and all are to some extent time consuming. It has been suggested that the group-home operator endeavor to (1) *understand the applicable laws* and stay current on local regulations and restrictions, (2) develop a *program policy manual* that specifies, on paper, all procedures and policies guiding the program's operation, (3) adopt a *systematic treatment* program that attends to the *treatment goals* established for the home's *target population,* (4) *select treatment staff carefully,* hiring the best people he or she can find and afford, (5) prepare this treatment staff for specific problems as well as routine responsibilities through a vigorous program of *preservice* and *in-service training* and monitor resulting staff performance through *regular professional consultation,* (6) adopt and use an effective program of *informed consent, individual treatment planning, records review,* and *guaranteed confidentiality,* and (7) devise a system for periodic staff *performance evaluation* by the actual consumers—including the youths themselves—of services offered by the program. This package of strategies applied as a system represents an energetic undertaking.

No two group-home programs will assemble precisely the same combination of safeguard methods. Even within BIABH each individual group home enjoys, and occasionally suffers from, its own idiosyncracies. All group homes, however, have policies (whether crudely or carefully formulated), staffing methods, a treatment program of some description, some system of record-keeping, and all provide for some form of preparation (training) and evaluation of treatment staff. We implore readers to carefully examine these core elements of their own group-home enterprises and consider the various ways recommended here for deriving the most child-protection potential from each element. How far the recommendations can be carried out in individual programs will vary with their needs and resources. Each program must respond to its own special circumstances, as it considers and develops a system that protects children's rights and freedoms.

References

Ethical principles in the conduct of research with human participants. Washington, D.C.: American Psychological Association, 1973.

FIELDS, S., MALONEY, D. M., MALONEY, K. B., TIMBERS, G. D., & JONES, R. J. Evaluating the satisfaction of consumer groups involved with group home care for adolescents. *Western Carolina Center Papers and Reports,* 1976, *6,* (No. 4).

LERMAN, P. Delinquents without crimes: The American approach to juvenile status offenses. *Transaction/Society,* July–August 1971, pp. 257–286.

MALONEY, D. M., TIMBERS, G. D., & MALONEY, K. B. BIABH Project: Regional adaptation of the Teaching-Family Model group home for adolescents. *Child Welfare*, 1977, *56* (No. 1), 787–796.

PHILLIPS, E. L., PHILLIPS, E. A., FIXSEN, D. L., & WOLF, M. M. *The teaching family handbook.* Lawrence: The University of Kansas Press, 1974.

PLATT, A. M. *The child savers: The invention of delinquency.* Chicago: University of Chicago Press, 1969.

SHAH, S. A. Juvenile delinquency: A national perspective. In J. L. Khanna (Ed.), *New treatment approaches to juvenile delinquency.* Springfield, Ill.: Charles C Thomas, 1975.

CHAPTER 14

The Rights of Chronically Ill Children in Residential Programs

Thomas L. Creer
Charles M. Renne

RESIDENTIAL FACILITIES for the treatment and rehabilitation of chronically ill children have unique characteristics that tend in turn to produce special problems associated with efforts to protect client rights. For example, in these settings patients often experience independently administered treatment programs simultaneously. This usually involves medical treatment and a behavior rehabilitation program, each originating from spearate units of the facility and employing staff from different disciplines. Problems arise in communication between the staffs conducting the programs, which can detrimentally influence the coordination of these treatments for the patients, and ultimately the patients themselves. Patients may simply become lost in a mass of confusion and neglect.

Under such conditions the ability of a facility to adequately monitor and sufficiently protect the rights of its residents is open to serious doubt. It is true that residential facilities are subject to a plethora of laws and regulations. On one hand they are expected to comply with principles governing all hospitals and health care facilities; this involves adherence to federal and state decrees as well as guidelines proposed by such regulatory agencies as the Joint Commission on the Accreditation of Hospitals (JCAH). Compliance with these principles ensures not only that ethical and legal standards become an integral part of the day-to-day operation of these facilities, but that fees required for maintenance of the organizations, particularly third-party payments, can be obtained.

On the other hand, residential facilities are also subject to state and federal regulations governing the institutionalization of children that present yet another set of principles to guide their daily operations.

278

Hence, institutions for chronically ill children must adhere to regulations promulgated by agencies ranging from JCAH to the Federal Drug Administration, from state and city health departments to local school districts.

Still, even with these regulations and the scrutiny they invite, the protection of human rights all too often depends upon the individuals employed by the institutions—their whim, chance knowledge, or awareness of the rights issues involved in specific situations. Under such circumstances serious infractions are bound to occur, albeit often unintentionally. In the interest of achieving timely patient disposition decisions and safeguarding patient rights, it behooves these facilities to build into their organizational structures routines and procedures for increasing staff awareness of rights issues and insuring that treatment needs are met without violation of these rights. In other words, they must initiate procedures that will aid not only in the detection of rights violations but in the active pursuit of preservation of these rights as well.

The National Asthma Center at Denver, Colorado, may be considered a prototype of the residential health care facility described above. Fortunately, early experiences there led to a recognition of the potential confusion and problems that the setting could pose for its patients. Subsequently, a technology was developed and implemented that promoted care and protection of patients while averting much of the confusion and disorder that otherwise might have prevailed.

This discourse will focus on some of the legal and ethical issues that arise in both the treatment of chronically ill youngsters and research conducted with them in a residential facility. Ethical and legal guidelines governing the operation of such a facility also will be reviewed. Finally, a technology currently in use at the National Asthma Center will be offered as a model in the hope that at least some of the properties it possesses might be adapted for use by other health care facilities in the interest of safeguarding the rights of their patients.

Protecting the Rights of Patients in the Pursuit of Health

The goals of treatment and rehabilitation at the National Asthma Center have been delineated in detail elsewhere (Chai & Newcomb, 1973; Creer, Renne, & Christian, 1976). Briefly, the major aims are to establish control over asthma so that the children can live normal, active lives, remove asthma from the center of patient and family activities, help youngsters acquire self-monitoring and self-help skills, decrease or eliminate behavioral excesses, correct behavioral deficits, and mainstream all patients into family and community activities once they are discharged.

One rationale underlying these goals is that all children have a right to live as normal a life as is permitted by their illnesses; this implies that children must undergo the process of becoming responsible for themselves and less dependent upon others. A correlate of this rationale is the belief that children should be held accountable for their actions and self-sufficiency and responsibility can be taught via well-designed environmental programs based on social learning principles and procedures. To be effective then, treatment and rehabilitation programs for chronically ill children should remove impediments to their evolution toward independence and actively provide them with the opportunity to develop responsible behavior.

Programs openly espousing such treatment goals and their underlying rationale have taken a significant first step toward protecting human rights, especially the right to treatment, since subscribing to these goals alone places client rights at the very fulcrum of their programs. Although the treatment programs of most residential facilities are guided at least implicitly by similar goals, all too often the objectives remain unwritten or even unspecified. As a result, those working within the programs easily lose sight of these goals and the principles emanating from them, which should underlie and direct their practices. This results in an inconsistent program at best.

When treatment goals and their underlying rationale are specified and made public, it becomes more likely that a goal-oriented program will evolve along established ethical and legal guidelines, with a more active pursuit on the part of staff of meeting stated objectives. A by-product of such an effort, should be the achievement of better compliance with those laws and regulations governing the rights of patients imposed by outside agencies.

Even with the most worthwhile, publicly stated treatment goals neatly tied into a treatment program, placing the responsibility for human rights protection solely on the operation of the treatment program is an uncertain and usually insufficient means of preserving patient rights. It is equally important that protective monitoring, preventive, and redressing procedures be built into all aspects of a facility's involvement with clients.

Residential facilities are often legally required to obtain power-of-attorney for their residents. By so doing, institutions assume legal responsibility for the protection of their residents' health, welfare, and legal rights. This legal responsibility is in effect a mandate dictating that precautions be built into treatment programs to ensure the protection of patients and their rights.

The technology described below emphasizes various strategies utilized in protecting the rights of patients at each phase of their involvement with the residential treatment facility at the National Asthma Center:

preadmission, admission, treatment and rehabilitation, discharge, and follow-up.

PREADMISSION

The preadmission phase starts with an inquiry from parents, legal guardians, or professionals interested in admitting the patient. The admission office forwards them a description of the facility, the treatment rationale, and the residential and hospital programs, including rules and regulations governing discipline, parental visits, and so on. In addition, they are sent an outline of the eligibility requirements for admission (see sample, "Admission Criteria and Initial Processing Letter," p. 282) and the conditions under which patients remain in residence following admission. Finally, they receive an explanation of the facility's legal and ethical responsibilities to patients and their families. The latter reflect suggestions made by an institutional legal committee composed of attorneys responsible to the facility's board of trustees. An accompanying power-of-attorney document expresses succinctly the extent of this responsibility. At every step of the way, a concerted effort is made to help potential applicants make what is for them the correct determination regarding the question whether to seek admission.

Admission procedures hinge upon the supposition that parents or legal guardians have the basic responsibility for deciding whether children require admission to a residential program. The health of the children must be at the core of their decision. Nonetheless, the importance of involving children in this determination must not be overlooked, with the amount of input from them corresponding to age and level of maturity. Older children, in particular, must play an active role in this decision-making process. Preadmission instructions should emphasize the importance of preparing youngsters for their impending separation from home. With children in their teens, it is best to contact them directly to determine their willingness to be admitted for treatment and rehabilitation. Any reluctance on their part, or any evidence from the application materials of insufficient preparation, should be brought to the attention of parents or those professionals assisting the parents in processing the application. Admission dates are then set when both children and their parents accept the need for the residential program. This ensures that the basic desires of both children and parents are honored.

However, admission into a residential treatment and rehabilitation program at this point should not be automatic. All applicants should be screened. Usually this is done by an admissions committee, on the basis of information provided in application materials. Commonly, these materials

Admission Criteria and Initial Processing Letter

Re:_____

Dear _____ ,

The information below will help you to determine whether or not the application for the admission of the above-named child should be pursued. If the applicant appears to meet our basic admission requirements as determined from this letter, then more detailed information, on which our decision regarding admission will be based, will be requested. We wish to spare parents time and expense in completing our numerous and detailed admission forms in those cases where it is obvious that the child cannot be accepted for admission to this facility. Therefore, we ask that the following items be given careful consideration:

1. That the illness be persistent and difficult to manage within the home environment.
2. That the child, at the time of admission, be at least 6 years of age or eligible for admission into the first grade, but not over 15 years of age.
3. That the child *must* attend the nearby public school.
4. That "special" continuous supervision on a one-to-one basis or a highly structured and controlled environment is not available and that 16–24 children reside in cottages under the supervision of only one child-care worker at any one time (one child-care worker per 16–24 children). Therefore, if a child presents *behavior* problems that require special supervision or environmental management (e.g., continuous disruptive behavior requiring *excessive* staff attentiona and which would be detrimental to the adjustment or rehabilitation of other children in the cottage; sociopathic or antisocial behavior; violent behvior; suicidal behavior, etc.), then he/she may not be eligible for admission, or for continuing in the program should these events occur following admission to the facility. Behaviorally, the child should be capable of being left unsupervised (in or outside of the cottage; on the way to school, etc.) for at least 15 to 30 minutes when not having asthma.

Given the above conditions and your knowledge of this child, do you want to pursue the admission? Whatever your decision is on this matter, please check the appropriate space below, sign your name in the space provided and return this letter to us.

Yes_____   No_____

_____
(Signature and title of party completing form)

The Admissions Committee will act immediately on the basis of the information provided in this brief report. Should you wish to pursue admission, all necessary admission forms will be sent to all appropriate parties for completion. When all the admission materials have been completed and returned, the Admissions Committee will then make the final determination as to the child's eligibility for admission.

If you have questions regarding this form or any aspects of our facility or its admission policies, please do not hesitate to contact me.

Sincerely yours,

include a medical report, a social history, various behavior and problem checklists completed by parents, and an academic-progress and behavioral-adjustment report from school. Completed materials are confidential, accessible only to the admissions committee. The information is maintained in locked file cabinets and becomes part of the patient's personal confidential treatment file upon admission.

Occasional considerations may arise that supersede the right to treatment as defined by admission to the facility. Acceptance into the program is based upon factors influencing both the short- and long-term interests of the child and other residents with whom he or she will live. Also, the physical environment as well as the thrust of the rehabilitation program itself may impose limits on the type of child that can be accepted into the program. Youngsters who pose a danger to themselves or others and who are repeatedly socially disruptive, not responsible to routine behavior-management contingencies, too immature for separation from their parents, or adamant in their refusal to enter the program might not be admitted. However, because of the danger of misinformation and error associated with information in the records, it is best to be lenient in assessing admission eligibility, in order that treatment will not be unjustly withheld.

Where uncertainty exists as to potential adverse effects of admission, patients are admitted on a trial basis. In these cases, the trial condition is stipulated in acceptance letters to parents and children, along with an explanation of the basis for such a decision. Essentially, the trial designation alerts staff involved with these patients to the need for special attention in assisting them to adapt to the separation and the rehabilitation and treatment program. Trial admission patients are given priority for medical investigation, in the event that they cannot be retained in residence for the full term. Fortunately, the majority of youngsters initially accepted on a trial basis successfully adapt to the program.

Parents of children not admitted into the program are assisted by the admissions committee in finding alternative treatment sources in the home community or, if necessary, elsewhere.

ADMISSION

Children and their parents or guardians meet with various staff members immediately upon arriving at the facility. The patient representative reviews patient rights, and identifies members of the staff responsible for the care and treatment of the youngster. A Staff Identification Form, given to both children and their parents, identifies the administrator and the supervisors of each service, and contains instructions indicating who should be contacted for specific concerns arising over the course of the program. The patient representative ensures that

Staff Identification Form

To make it easy for you to obtain answers to any question that may arise while _____ is in residence, a list of staff persons is provided below. It would be best to contact the person who is most likely to possess the information you seek.

   I.   *Clinical Services:*

      A.   The Child-Care Workers for _____ cottage (Ext. _____) are _____ , _____ , and _____ . They should be consulted regarding:

          1. The day-to-day management of the cottage, including concerns about personal grooming, care of personal belongings, clothing needs, etc.

          2. Requesting and arranging phone calls and writing home.

          3. The monthly allowance account.

          4. Sending food and other items.

      B.   The physician is _____ (Ext. _____), and should be consulted for:

          1. All medical matters, including the treatment of asthma and other illnesses, immunizations, medications, and hospitalizations.

          2. Medical reports and medical history.

          3. Questions about the relationship between asthma and owning pets, diet, etc.

      C.   The psychologist is _____ (Ext. _____). Contact the psychologist regarding:

          1. Psychological and behavioral adjustment, including homesickness, behavior problems, complaints of unhappiness, school adjustment, etc.

          2. Psychological treatment, discipline or behavioral management, family counseling, child and parent training, etc.

          3. The kind of information to be conveyed to the child in correspondence or via telephone, or concerns over the content of letters sent home.

          4. Psychosocial history and psychological reports or investigative procedures.

 II.   *Patient Representative:* Contact the patient representative (Ext. _____) for any concerns related to the rights of the child and/or the family. The patient representative, _____ , serves as a special advocate for all children in residence, and will directly investigate any situation in which the rights of children or families are threatened.

III.   *Supervisory Personnel:*

      A.   _____ is the supervisor of the residential program responsible for the performance of Child-Care Workers, night attendants, and the recreation/tutoring staff. The following matters should be directed to this office (Ext. _____):

          1. Problems left unresolved with the residential staff.

          2. Requests for visits.

      B.   _____ is chief of Clinical Psychology. This office (Ext. _____) should be contacted for any unresolved concerns about the child's psychological treatment or well-being.

C. _____ is Head of Hospital Services, and should be consulted (Ext. _____) for any unresolved matters pertaining to the child's medical treatment and well-being.

IV. *Administrator:* _____ is responsible for the overall administration of the facility, and can be contacted (Ext. _____) for such matters as maintenance, housekeeping, and any concerns over issues or procedures which cut across all functions and departments of the facility.

While it would be helpful to us and efficient for you to take up matters directly with specific staff members as designated above, the list is not intended to constrain you from contacting any staff person you may want to talk to directly about any matter.

My office (Ext. _____) will, of course, always be of help in any way possible.

Sincerely,

Director, Behavior Science Division

both parents and children understand their basic rights and procedures for addressing any concerns over possible violations of these rights.

Child-care workers outline the daily routine procedures, and acquaint parents and their children with the facility. The Group Living supervisor describes the general residential program, including policy regarding visitations, telephone contacts, participation in recreation activities, monitoring strategies employed in the cottages, and discipline procedures. Parents or guardians may sign documents at this time giving permission for their child to visit with persons whom the parents designate—e.g., relatives or friends of the family—or for the child's inclusion in irregularly held activities that may involve some attendant risk—e.g., skiing.

A clinical psychologist discusses specific behavioral management and rehabilitation programs with parents, and prepares them for the impending separation and their possible emotional reactions to it. When indicated, parents are encouraged to seek and accept professional counseling within their home communities. Individualized intervention programs may be prescribed for families, specific goals for rehabilitation described, and an approximate timetable for treatment and discharge provided.

The psychologist also discusses with each family the procedures for safeguarding confidentiality, reminding children that parents have a right to be informed of treatment progress via medical and behavioral reports. Children are told that the content of their private discussions with the psychologist is confidential and will not be divulged in reports without their consent. The only exceptions to such confidentiality center around issues that may place the patient or others in jeopardy. For example, misuse of prescribed medication may be reported to the physician, since such information is crucial to the overall treatment and ultimate welfare of the child. Even in such instances, however, the issues would be discussed first with the youngster before the information is conveyed to others.

TREATMENT AND REHABILITATION

A primary aim of the treatment and rehabilitation program is to maintain responsiveness to the needs of patients. The effort begins with in-service training immediately upon employing a new staff member. Employee orientation includes discussing patient rights and staff responsibility to safeguard these rights. They also learn procedures to be followed in the event that questions related to possible violation of patient rights arise.

All patients attend regular classrooms in nearby public schools. Close staff contact is maintained with personnel in these schools so that the children attend at minimal risk to their health. Attendance in regular classrooms ensures youngsters of their right to instruction in the mainstream of education. This is an attempt to adhere to written standards governing the education of children marked by society as suffering a physical handicap.

Required peer review conferences help physicians to follow a child's medical treatment and adhere to investigative procedures closely. The treatment of patients and progress made in bringing their asthma under control, their need for hospitalization, and the length of their stay in the hospital unit are topics regularly covered in weekly medical peer review meetings. Consulting specialists confer with the medical staff on a routine basis, not only when medical problems arise that do not fall within specialty areas of the facility's staff. Staff physicians send periodic reports to parents and referring physicians concerning treatment regimens, number of hospitalizations, and any other conditions warranting medical attention. Legal guidelines concerning confidentiality are strictly followed in keeping parents and their designated professional contacts apprised of the children's medical progress and welfare.

After an initial three-day stint in the hospital unit—a time devoted to evaluation—children are discharged to the residential rehabilitation units. They are assigned to a cottage according to age and sex. The units are staffed by child-care workers, night attendants, and psychologists. Along with the physician, these staff members work together as a team directly responsible for the care, welfare, and rehabilitation of the children in their respective cottages. They attempt to meet this responsibility through management of the general residential program, specific cottage-behavioral programs, and individualized intervention programs, and by ensuring that the children's needs are met by others involved, such as teachers, tutors, recreation staff, and so on.

Residential units all subscribe to cottage behavioral programs to assist in the behavior management and rehabilitation of the children within the units. Forerunners of the current programs have been described elsewhere (Christian, 1974; Renne, Henry, Pisarowicz, Weidell, & Bailey, 1975). Generally, the programs emphasize increasing children's positive, appropriate behaviors by granting privileges, with some attention given to decreasing their inappropriate responses by withholding these same privileges. Privileges are usually extra activities or reinforcers not routinely experienced in the residential setting, such as staying up past the regular bedtime. When aversive procedures are necessary, there is a concerted effort to use the least restrictive of several potentially effective procedures, and to apply them only on an individual—rather than a group—basis. Aversive consequences, along with the inappropriate behaviors they follow, have been delineated in the program descriptions; all children are made aware of them during their admission preparation and later orientation to the cottage routine. These contingencies are initiated only upon completion of the orientation phase, so that children are certain to have knowledge of them before they are applied.

The cottage behavioral programs are flexible and accommodate wide variations in age and skills. One important aspect of the programs is the step-level concept they embrace: Placement at successively higher achievement levels within the programs is contingent upon children meeting specific behavioral criteria for independence and maturity, with the goal of moving them toward the more "mature" levels at a pace consonant with their current abilities and readiness to assume greater personal responsibility. At the advanced levels there is less staff monitoring and less direct involvement in behavioral management. Behavioral contracting as a management technique is used extensively with patients at these higher levels, accompanied by greater input from them into decisions affecting their treatment and rehabilitation.

Precautions have been taken to protect human rights in the course of administering both the cottage behavioral programs and the general residential program. The programs were reviewed first by members of the facility's legal committee and then by a judge, to ascertain whether there are any actual or potential violations of patient rights. According to the recommendations of these professionals, changes were made when necessary. The programs are reviewed periodically by the Behavior Science Peer Review Committee to ensure that subsequent changes made by the teams are not in violation of human rights and that programs continue to further the rehabilitation of the residents. Specialized psychological services—provided for individual children at the facility and that fall outside the cottage programs—also are scrutinized routinely for potential infractions of patient rights.

The organization of the staff, the structure of the program, and the routine operation procedures combine to provide a system of continuous checks on the effectiveness and appropriateness of the rehabilitation program. Personnel working directly with the children are supervised by an experienced professional from their respective departments—e.g., Group Living, Clinical Psychology, and Hospital Services. Each department is represented on a Clinical Coordinating Committee which facilitates the interdisciplinary aspects of the clinical operations. This committee arbitrates differences that arise among staff members on issues affecting the treatment of patients, and provides a means for resolving staff differences with respect to disposition of patients. The committee establishes policies guiding the general clinical operating procedures and periodically reviews them in terms of their current necessity, value, and effectiveness.

The two weekly peer review meetings held by the physicians and psychologists respectively, have proved to be effective as a means of monitoring the clinical programs. They make certain that patients receive competent treatment and that consultation is sought for problems lying outside the competencies of the staff. Equally important is their ensuring that a child's right to treatment is fulfilled.

Several strategies have been built into the program as routine operating procedures to help protect patients and their rights. Children newly admitted into the cottages are assigned immediately to one of three child-care workers in the cottage as a primary contact. These "contact" counselors (Burns & Brown, 1979), along with the psychologist, have direct responsibility for their patients' overall rehabilitation program. This function requires that they be knowledgeable at all times of their patients' status within the program, so that they may serve as advocates for them. The contact counselors pay extra attention to their contact patients' safety, protection, rehabilitation progress, and need for specialized programs, and to whether other staff are meeting their responsibilities to the children. For example, the contact counselors work closely with the team psychologists in the design and implementation of special intervention programs required by their patients; in addition, they must serve as advocates by pursuing the initiation and completion of such services.

Another strategy routinely employed is the random selection of patients by the clinical supervisor for presentation at the clinical psychology peer review meeting. Here patient records are examined, with special attention directed to their completeness in listing patient needs, program implementation dates, ethical considerations in selecting and implementing programs, and progress of patients undergoing individualized intervention programs. The clinical psychologists are held accountable for the behavioral rehabilitation of the children, including the aspect of seeing that their rights are protected.

Assessment is an indispensable tool in both the rehabilitation of patients and the safeguarding of their rights. It is a continuous process, beginning with preadmission and continuing through the follow-up phase. During the rehabilitation phase a daily behavior checklist, the Comprehensive Problem Behavior Survey (Renne & Christian, 1975)—a narrative record composed daily by child-care workers—and a nighttime behavior checklist completed by night attendants are key elements in the assessment effort. From these sources, problem behaviors are targeted for change, and the results of behavior change programs continuously charted. The Behavior Science Patient Progress Record, kept in the file of each patient, helps track a child's progress through the program. It lists all routine procedures along with the dates they were initiated and

Behavior Science Patient Progress Record

Name: _____   Admitted: _____

Cottage: _____   Discharged: _____

General Program	Date Begun	Date Completed	Comments
Verification Interview (P) Beh. Analysis Int. (P) Precipitant Interview (C) Beh. Analysis Int. (C) Building Orientation Educational Program Self Medication Parent Education			

Reports	Date Completed	Date	Peer Reviews Comments
Initial Interim Interim Interim Discharge			

SPECIFIC PROBLEM AREAS			
Description	Intervention Begun	Intervention Terminated	Comments (Results)

completed. Areas requiring specialized intervention are recorded on the form, with dates of initiation and completion of the intervention. For other than routine interventions, informed consent is obtained from children and parents; the consent to treatment is then included with the Progress Record.

Complaints regarding possible violations of rights may come to the attention of the patient representative from children themselves, staff members, parents or acquaintances of the patients, and routine checks made by the patient representative, who has access to both the records of patients and the clinical and peer review meetings. Regardless of the source or nature of a complaint, an incident report is filed by the patient representative. This report states the official complaint and describes the situation and circumstances surrounding the incident in question. The names of all principals involved and their specific actions, dates, times, and deviations from routine procedure are included. Recommendations follow providing a course of action to be taken by the administration and clinical staff. The report is processed through an administrative assistant, who together with the patient representative attempts to redress any violations and take measures to prevent a reoccurrence of the event. If the conclusions of the report are questioned, the matter is then referred to the Institutional Review Board for a second opinion and recommendations.

The patient representative works independently of the administration and clinical staff, thereby remaining in a position to process incident reports in an unbiased manner.

DISCHARGE

Readiness for discharge is determined by the clinical team. Discharge clearance forms, signed by the psychologists and the physicians, are processed upon completion of the medical and behavioral programs. The clearance forms can be initiated by any team member, but one dissenting opinion is enough to impede discharge. Where agreement cannot be reached among the staff persons involved, the issue is brought before the departmental peer review committees. Should agreement not be forthcoming from this strategy, the issue is referred to the Clinical Coordinating Committee for a final decision on the matter.

All premature discharges—e.g., disciplinary discharges—are discussed at the psychology peer review meeting with the patient representative and team psychologists to be certain that such discharges are justified.

Sometime during the course of the children's tenure at the facility (usually at discharge) families undergo an extensive training program. This program teaches them about asthma, its management, and the extent of their and their children's responsibility for maintaining the treatment routine after discharge. Most often this involves a structured routine developed at the facility which is to be implemented within the home.

Reports summarizing current treatments and providing recommendations for continued medical care are sent home with all discharged patients, along with two weeks' worth of medication.

FOLLOW-UP

Contact is maintained with the families by the psychologists and physicians for several weeks following discharge. This is done to discern whether the children's newly acquired behaviors generalize to the home environments and asthma remains under control. Information from a formal assessment package, completed one year post-discharge, is compared with preadmission information to assess overall treatment effectiveness. This follow-up contact places the facility in a position to continue rendering some assistance, aid in securing professional help from the patient's community, or recommend readmission in the event of a breakdown in asthma control, thereby maximizing efforts to both safeguard and advance patients' right to effective treatment.

Research

Considerable research, much of it funded by pharmaceutical firms, occurs in institutions for chronically ill children. The settings offer an ideal environment in which to conduct research, for several reasons: First, there is usually a homogeneous population of patients with respect to a given illness or affliction. This eliminates the need to ferret subjects out of the general population. Second, experimental control can be established in such settings, thereby improving the reliability and validity of any research findings. Finally, a particular population of patients in a health care setting represents those for whom the greatest benefit can be anticipated with the introduction of a particular therapeutic technique. Humane factors, combined with a potential economic benefit to a sponsoring organization, make this a significant consideration.

Special ethical and legal questions arise, however, in conducting research with chronically ill children in a residential setting. First, because the patients are at the facility, they constitute what might be considered a captive population; their physical condition makes them vulnerable to exploitation. Second, questions can be raised as to whether adequate consent can be obtained from subjects in such a setting. As will be noted shortly, this is a critical point in regulating research with human subjects. Finally, there are indications that the lure of research support sometimes can lead to unethical and illegal responding on the part of investigators. For example, a 1973 survey of drug research indicated that up to 32 percent of the studies contained falsified data (Wade, 1973). Considering the potential for abuse, ethical and legal safeguards are a necessity.

In 1974, P. L. 93-348 created the National Commission for the Protection of Human Subjects of Biomedical and Behavioral Research. One charge of the commission was to study the nature of research with children, the purposes of such research, steps necessary to protect children as subjects, and requirements for the informed consent of children and their parents or guardians. As a consequence of such inquiry, recommendations have been made to the Secretary of Health, Education, and Welfare regarding policies to define circumstances under which research with and for children is appropriate. Recent regulations offered by the commission provide a framework for the discussion that follows.

GUIDELINES FOR RESEARCH WITH CHRONICALLY ILL CHILDREN

Regulations to govern research with children were proposed recently by the commission (National Commission, January 1978). The commission suggested several recommendations in this report; they were later discussed and in most instances adopted by the commission (National Commission, July 1978). The relevance of several of the recommendations presented by the commission, as they relate to chronically ill children, is discussed below.

Recommendation 1. This points out that while research is important to the health and well-being of all children, such investigation must be conducted in an ethical manner. As the commission notes, children deserve the best care that society can provide.

The commission's stand is of significance to chronically ill children, since only by their serving in research studies can innovative methods evolve for the diagnosis and treatment of their physical condition. As a result, thousands of such youngsters are currently involved in studies that will ultimately benefit countless other patients, both young and old. For example, many youngsters are currently receiving medications that, because intensive investigation is required by the Federal Drug Administration, will be available to other patients only after such research is completed. As noted earlier, however, the potential exploitation of these children makes it imperative that any research adhere to the remaining recommendations of the commission.

Recommendation 2. This sets forth general conditions for conducting research with children. Specifically, it is recommended that such investigation proceed only when an institutional review board ("IRB") has determined that (1) the research is scientifically sound and significant, (2) where appropriate, studies have first been conducted on animals, adult humans, or older children prior to involving infants, (3) risks are minimized by employing the safest procedures consistent with sound research design and using clinically tested diagnostic or treatment procedures whenever feasible, (4) adequate provisions are made to protect the privacy of children and their parents and maintain the confidentiality of data, (5) subjects are selected in an equitable manner, and (6) the conditions of all applicable subsequent recommendations are met. The statements embodied in this recommendation may appear self-evident, but two clauses, 1 and 5, merit a brief discussion.

With regard to clause (1), emphasizing *scientifically* sound and significant research, the commission reaffirmed its position in the following manner:

> Respect for human subjects requires the use of sound methodology appropriate to the discipline. The time and inconvenience requested of subjects should be justified by the soundness of the research and its design, even if no more than minimal risk is involved. In addition, research involving children should satisfy a standard of scientific significance, since these subjects are less capable than adults of determining for themselves whether to participate. [National Commission, January 1978, p. 1086]

At first glance, it might appear that this would be one of the easier points to resolve, but that is not the case. A number of problems arise: First, who is to decide whether research is scientifically sound? An IRB is charged with making this decision, but it may not be an easy task, depending upon the composition of a particular board. If, for example, a board is composed of a spectrum of representatives from the community—e.g., clergymen, housewives, teachers, lawyers—the group may be incapable of deciding whether a particular proposal is scientifically sound. In such a case, the IRB might seek advice from scientists not involved with the project. This step is recommended by the commission (e.g., National Commission, November 1973, January 1978) and represents the best approach to managing ethical and legal issues within an institution: having an IRB composed of community members who can solicit whatever scientific advice they require.

Unfortunately, however, few IRBs operate in this manner. In the first place, they rarely contain a number of divergent voices, but usually consist of a group of scientists many of whom are deciding upon the ethical and legal merits of their own research, several administrators from the facility where the research is being conducted, and a token clergyman. Under these circumstances, the following tableau occurs at many IRB meetings: The scientists argue among themselves about the scientific worth of the proposal—mainly resorting to esoteric reasoning that has nothing to do with ethical or legal questions—the administrators seemingly daydream about how they can spend the indirect costs generated by the proposed research, and the clergyman muses as to how he ever allowed himself to be appointed to the IRB in the first place! The end result is that the function of the group is forgotten—i.e., whether or not ethical or legal questions arise over the study. There is a remedy for such a state: A committee of scientists can debate the scientific value of a study *before* forwarding the protocol to an IRB for ethical clearance. In this manner an IRB, ideally comprised of several representatives from the local community, can concentrate on ethical and legal issues raised by the proposal.

A related question arises at this point: What defines significant research? This is a more complex question than might initially be assumed. On one hand there are many scientists who view any study they conduct as significant, simply because they are scientists. To raise a question about the significance of their work is tantamount to denying the worth of science. The unwary person who asks such a question, particularly if a lay person, may trigger a long polemic about the history of science and its demigod figures. The same scientists also show a proclivity to regarding research as significant simply if it is supported, regardless of the reasons the funding organization has supplied the money.

On the other hand, increasing attention is being focused toward ensuring that a research project with human subjects is clinically relevant (Creer, 1978; Kazdin & Wilson, 1978). This posits that it is not enough to obtain findings that may be statistically significant; rather, it must be demonstrated that any results benefit the subjects involved and, potentially, other humans. This theme of clinical significance is interwoven throughout proclamations issued by the National Commission, and presents a challenge to any IRB.

In clause 5, dealing with selection of subjects, the commission noted;

> Subjects should be selected in an equitable manner, avoiding overutilization of any one group of children based solely upon administrative convenience or availability of a population living in conditions of social or economic deprivation. The burdens of participation in research should be equitably distributed among the segments of our society, no matter how large or small these burdens may be. [National Commission, January 1978, p. 1086]

In principle, there would be few arguments with this sentiment. In the reality of residential facilities for chronically ill children, however, the recommendation is sometimes forgotten. Youngsters in these institutions are often involved in research projects, because—as noted at the outset—they reside in environments that are considered natural breeding grounds for research. Furthermore, some children participate in more studies than do others residing in the same residential facility, often because of the requirements of investigators. For example, a youngster whose condition is considered severe may be more likely to be selected for a study than a child suffering from a milder form of the illness. It is not uncommon that, over a period of time, one youngster will participate in several studies, and a second child not be involved in any research. A number of factors contribute to this state, including the aims of the investigator, the reasons the research was funded, and—to be candid—administrative convenience.

There is a way to promote equalization of participation in research among residents at a health care facility: This entails that the IRB periodically review the history of research participation for all youngsters at a residential facility, to determine whether overselection is occurring. Appropriate action can then be taken by the IRB if such is the case.

Recommendation 3. Research not involving greater than minimal risk to children may be conducted or supported provided an IRB has determined that (1) the conditions set forth in Recommendation 2 have been met, and (2) adequate consent has been obtained from both the children and their parents.

There is no consensus of agreement as to what constitutes "risk" in studies with human subjects. Barber (1976) has been particularly vociferous on this point: He mailed a questionnaire outlining six simulated research proposals, similar to those that might be reviewed by an IRB, to investigators in hospitals and research centers. The survey was answered by 293 respondents who, according to Barber, constituted a nationally representative sample of all such institutions. Generally, those completing the questionnaire were active researchers and members of their institution's IRB. The results can be illustrated by one of the six protocols and the responses obtained by Barber. This protocol proposed that the thymus gland, a component of the immunological system, be removed unnecessarily from a random sample of children undergoing heart surgery. The aim of the operation was to learn the effect of the thymectomy on the survival of an experimental skin graft made at the same time. Barber reported that a pattern emerged in the responses to this and the other protocols: In the case of the high-risk thymectomy, 72 percent of the respondents said the project should not be approved no matter how high the probability that it would establish the efficacy of thymectomy in promoting transplant survival. However, 28 percent of the respondents said they would approve the experiment, and of those 6 percent said they would approve even if the chance of significant results was no better than 10 percent! The conclusion voiced by Barber and his colleagues was "Whereas the majority of the investigators were what we called 'strict' with regard to balancing risks against benefits, a significant minority were 'permissive,' that is, they were much more willing to accept an unsatisfactory risk-benefit ratio" (1976, p. 27). It is the permissive investigator who poses a problem to an institutional review board.

Recommendation 4. Where more than minimal risk is possible in research investigating either an intervention procedure that may directly benefit individual subjects or a monitoring system for the well-being of subjects, such research may be conducted or supported provided that an IRB has determined that (1) any risk is justified by the anticipated benefit to subjects, (2) the relation of benefit to risk is as favorable to the subjects as that presented by alternative approaches, (3) conditions set forth in Recommendation 2 are met, and (4) adequate provisions for consent of both children and parents are made.

Review boards of institutions for chronically ill children are repeatedly presented research protocols in which greater than minimal risk is a possibility; a decision must be made whether the benefit-risk ratio warrants proceeding with the study. In most cases where an intervention procedure is to be introduced, it is usually anticipated that youngsters selected for the study will benefit from application of the method. It is also recognized, furthermore, that such innovative treatment procedures develop because of weaknesses in currently used procedures. Under these circumstances, there is usually a favorable relation of benefit to risk.

Possible risks that may occur with use of a different monitoring system are also considered by review boards. A common example will illustrate the role of an IRB: It is important to know how quickly medications are absorbed into the bloodstream, and to study this problem blood may be periodically drawn from a group of subjects. A question then arises as to the best way to obtain blood samples from subjects. One hand method is to draw blood in the usual way by needle and syringe. There is attendant discomfort to this procedure, particularly when repeated a number of times over a brief period of time. Another method involves the investigator inserting a catheter in a subject's vein. This reduces the discomfort, but the risks inherent in using the procedure exceed those that might be anticipated by drawing blood in the traditional manner. It may be the duty of the IRB to determine whether benefit to the subjects—e.g., less discomfort—outweighs risk—e.g., the catheter becoming loose.

Recommendation 5. Research where more than minimal risk to children is presented—either by an intervention that lacks the prospects of direct benefit for a subject or a monitoring system not required for the well-being of subjects—may be conducted or supported provided an IRB has determined that (1) such risk presents only a minor increase over minimal risk, (2) the intervention or monitoring procedure offers subjects experiences that are reasonably commensurate with those occurring in their actual or expected medical, psychological, or social situations, and is likely to yield generalizable knowledge about the subjects' disorder or condition, (3) the anticipated knowledge is of importance for understanding or ameliorating the subjects' disorder or condition, (4) the conditions of Recommendation 2 are met, and (5) proper consent is obtained from both the children and their parents.

What is meant by "minimal risk" merits a brief discussion. In deciding whether the degree of risk justifies a study, the National Commission has suggested that an IRB consider four criteria: First, a common-sense estimation of the risk is a major guideline. It is probable that a broadly constituted review board might be more capable of such judgment than an IRB composed only of scientists and administrators. Second, an estimate based upon the investigator's experience with similar interventions or procedures is useful. Here, the IRB should consider not only a particular investigator's personal background with the procedure, but the risk other scientists have encountered or suggested. Third, any available information about the procedure should be presented to the review board. This posits that the investigator is familiar with the published literature about the procedure he or she wishes to use in the study. Fourth, the situation of the proposed subjects must be taken into account. With children in a facility for the chronically ill, the question must always be raised whether the youngsters would be exposed to such risks if they were not in the facility.

Recommendation 6. The IRB must determine, in addition to the other duties, that adequate provisions are made for (1) soliciting the assent of the children (when capable) and the permission of their parents or guardians, and, when appropriate, (2) monitoring the solicitation of assent and permission, and involving at least one parent or guardian in the conduct of the research. The commission emphatically states, "A child's objections to participate in research should be binding unless the intervention holds out a prospect of direct benefit that is important to the health or well-being of the children and is available only in the context of the research" (National Commission, July 1978, p. 961).

Earlier herein it was noted that there are questions whether adequate consent can be obtained from children, especially those in a medical environment. The pros and cons of this debate are cogently summarized by Ramsey (1970). The commission has been concerned with this, and has suggested conditions that should exist for children to participate in research. Those that pertain to children institutionalized because of a chronic illness are outlined below.

First, the commission repeatedly voices the opinion that the assent of children should be required when they are seven years old or older. ("Assent" is used rather than "consent" by the commission, to distinguish a child's agreement from a legally valid consent). They believe that children of seven years or older are generally capable of understanding the procedures and general purposes of research and of indicating their wishes regarding participation. Parental consent is suggested to be sufficient for children below seven or those so incapacitated that they cannot be reasonably consulted. (The IRB determines the children's capability of assenting.)

It is repeatedly reaffirmed by the commission that the child's assent to participation in research is more important than the permission granted by his or her parents. However, if the research involves an intervention that might significantly benefit the health and well-being of a youngster, and that intervention is available only in a research context, the objections of a small child may be overridden. Accessibility to a new medication is an illustration of this; again, there is a possibility that such a situation might arise in a residential facility for chronically ill children.

Second, "parental permission" implies a collective judgment on the part of a family living in a reasonably normal setting that a child can participate in a study. The permission of both parents should be documented, if at all possible. It may be difficult, if not impossible, for a review board at a residential setting to make a determination that parental consent reflects a family consensus; logistically, it is frequently difficult to obtain written documentation from both parents, particularly in light of today's soaring divorce rate. Nevertheless, the commissions' suggestions here are fair and prudent.

Third, a review board should assure that the children selected as subjects in medical settings experience good relationships with the parents or guardians and their physician; in institutional settings, the IRB should further ensure that the children are receiving care in supportive environments. To assist the review board in this regard, someone —such as a member of the child's treatment team—may be asked to serve as consultants.

Fourth, the commission suggests that small children or infants participate in research only in the presence of their parents. This permits parents to be sufficiently involved in the research to understand its effects on their children and intervene if necessary.

Finally, the commission suggests that, in the case of disagreement between a child and his or her parents, the IRB appoint a third party to mediate the matter with all concerned and be present during the consent process. The role of the third party can be expanded so that this person becomes an advocate for the youngster in all decision making regarding the child's participation in research. This seems especially important when the child is living away from his or her home, as in a residential environment for chronically ill children. Someone such as a child-care worker should be available at all times to guarantee that the youngster's rights are protected; a child advocate, appointed by the institution's IRB, is perfect for this niche.

In concluding this discussion of chronically ill children and their rights, it is suggested that researchers and IRBs involve, as much as possible, a youngster's treatment team in research decisions. For example, the teams can recommend those children most apt to benefit from participation in a study, or, once a youngster becomes a subject, can serve an advocacy function with respect to the child's participation. Such a process increases the probability that the subject will benefit from sharing in research and that his or her rights will be protected.

Summary

This chapter has highlighted legal and ethical issues that arise in a residential facility for chronically ill children. We would like to share three final impressions with the reader: First, there has been a revolution in concern over legal and ethical issues surrounding chronically ill children. Whereas a decade ago a physician or researcher would have readily initiated a treatment procedure for a child, the same professional would today hesitate in order to consider whether there could conceivably be a violation of the youngster's rights. Second, what are considered the rights of children—especially in a health care facility—are constantly being honed and reshaped. Such a process becomes apparent if one reviews the many regulations and proclamations issued by the National Commission for the Protection of Human Subjects of Biomedical and Behavioral Research during its short life-span between its creation in 1974 and its statutory demise in October 1978. As a consequence, the programs of most residential treatment programs are in a state of constant scrutiny and revision. Finally, there is considerable confusion among staff members of residential institutions for chronically ill youngsters as to what exactly the rights of their patients are.

A revolution begins with the stating of a problem; a definitive framework for managing the problem emerges from the revolution. At the moment, the framework for ensuring the rights of chronically ill children in residential facilities is still in the throes of creation.

References

BARBER, B. The ethics of experimentation with human subjects. *Scientific American*, 1976, *234*, 25–31.

BURNS, K., & BROWN, T. The contact counselor and behavioral goals contracting: Means of individualizing treatment within a cottage program. *CARIH Research Bulletin*, 1979, *9* (No. 1).

CHAI, H., & NEWCOMB, R. W. Pharmacologic management of childhood asthma. *American Journal of Diseases of Children*, 1973, *125*, 757–765.

CHRISTIAN, W. P. A step-level program in behavioral management in a residential treatment setting. *CARIH Research Bulletin*, 1974, *4* (No. 3).

CREER, T. L. Asthma: Psychological aspects and management. In E. Middleton, Jr., C. E. Reed, & E. F. Ellis (Eds.), *Allergy: Principles and practice*. St. Louis: C. V. Mosby Co., 1978.

CREER, T. L., RENNE, C. M., & CHRISTIAN, W. P. Behavioral contributions to rehabilitation and childhood asthma. *Rehabilitation Literature*, 1976, *37*, 226–232, 247.

KAZDIN, A. E., & WILSON, G. T. Criteria for evaluating psychotherapy. *Archives of General Psychiatry*, 1978, *34*, 407–416.

National Commission for the Protection of Human Subjects of Biomedical and Behavioral Research. Protection of human subjects: Policies and procedures. *Federal Register*, November 16, 1973, *38* (No. 221).

National Commission for the Protection of Human Subjects of Biomedical and Behavioral Research. Protection of human subjects: Research involving children. *Federal Register*, July 21, 1978, *43* (No. 141).

National Commission for the Protection of Human Subjects of Biomedical and Behavioral Research. Research involving children: Report and recommendations. *Federal Register*, January 13, 1978, *43* (No. 9).

RAMSEY, P. *The patient as person.* New Haven: Yale University Press, 1970.

RENNE, C. M., & CHRISTIAN, W. P. *The comprehensive problem behavior survey.* Denver: National Asthma Center, 1975.

RENNE, C. M., HENRY, L. PISAROWICZ, P., WEIDELL, L., & BAILEY, C. The Chapter House Cottage behavior management program. *CARIH Research Bulletin*, 1975, *5* (No. 1).

WADE, N. Physicians who falsify drug data. *Science*, 1973, *180*, 1038.

CHAPTER 15

Patient Rights in Acute-Care Hospitals

Michael F. Cataldo
Michael G. Ventura

THIS CHAPTER IS about patient rights in acute-care hospitals.[1] As can be judged from the names of at least some of the contributors to this book, patient rights are viewed herein, in part, from the perspective afforded by behavioral science—and the present chapter will be no exception. While there are many features of acute-care hospitals that are similar to other settings in which client rights are an important concern (e.g., schools, institutions for the handicapped, facilities for the chronically disabled and aged, etc.), there are also many areas of difference. The population served is obviously different, as are the staff problems, financial constraints, and legal mandates which impinge upon and influence the functioning of acute-care facilities.

This chapter will also concern itself with an often-voiced criticism of behavioral approaches—that is, that behavioral approaches tend to

[1] We have chosen the term "patient," as opposed to "client," in discussing these issues of rights because it is appropriate for hospital-based programs. We also should like to point out that the American-usage definition for these words shows "patient" to be a more favorable term. According to *Webster's New World Dictionary of the American Language* (World Publishing Co.) the definition of "client" and its derivation mean "one leaning on another for protection," and, formerly, "a person dependent on another as for protection or patronage." In modern usage, it means "customer." "Patient," on the other hand, is derived from the Latin word for passion and has the meaning of "suffering and forbearance" but not necessarily dependency.

□ The authors would like to thank Mrs. Lois Biddle for her assistance in assembling materials for preparation of the risk prevention aspects of this chapter and Robert Cuilla for his work on the staff-compliance project at the Kennedy Institute.

Preparation of this material was supported in part by Grant 917 from the Maternal and Child Health Service and is part of a collaborative effort of the Law Office of the Johns Hopkins University Hospital, the Department of Behavioral Psychology of the John F. Kennedy Institute, and the Behavioral Medicine Program of the Johns Hopkins University School of Medicine.

be well researched but singularly limited with regard to the scale of their application, being usually implemented with a small group for the purpose of a demonstration study. Accordingly, this chapter will present not only a discussion and an example of procedures by which behavioral approaches can be employed to ensure components of patient rights, but will also describe an institution-wide program for establishing and maintaining staff procedures to protect patient rights. This program, instituted at the Johns Hopkins University medical institutions over the past three years, will be presented in detail, including those aspects of it that should have general application to other institutions and hospitals.

Patient Rights

The issue of patient rights, at least in acute-care hospitals, can be considered as two distinctly separate questions: (1) What are patient rights? and (2) How are they to be ensured? With regard to the first question, one point of view is that patient rights, like other human rights, are based not on human behavior—nor on the law, nor finances, nor politics. This view would hold that human rights are abstractions of ideals inherent to man's nature, are a part of man's natural inheritance, and as such come from the belief that there are natural limits to government because we are subject to higher laws than those of man (cf. Wood, 1977). An alternative, more behavioral approach, to this notion (cf. Skinner, 1974) is that the concept of human rights proceeds from cultural practices, not biological inheritance or god-given beneficence. Regardless of how one views the basis for this concept, clearly human rights can be influenced by the law, financial policies, and policies of government. Further, the actions of one individual or set of individuals toward another can ensure or violate human rights, and this clearly describes human behavior and a situation that behavioral science can address. Yet, as Wood (1977) has stated, from the point of view of the law, human (and therefore, patient) rights are "legally defined classes of individually reinforcing events and behaviors, and the state has the power to restrict or deny them as a means of meeting its own, presumably group, goals. The legal regulatory mechanism, due process, is a cultural practice whose purpose is the weighing of these sometimes conflicting interests" (pp. 106–107). Thus, in discussing patient rights let us assume that such rights are immutable abstractions, subject in practice to both the legal exercise of due process and the conduct of human behavior, and at the very least influenced by financial, political, and a host of other contingencies.

Factors Influencing Patient Rights

QUALITY OF CARE

An interest in contributing to the reduction of human suffering is often a factor that motivates professionals to enter the field of health care. Procedures that lead to the development and maintenance of improved patient care, including patient rights, should therefore be of immediate interest to health care professionals. Unfortunately, procedures leading to improvements in quality of care often have to compete with the practical realities of a hospital system. Thus, the idealized aspirations of clinicians and scientists alike—often well founded in empirical fact—are often never realized. On occasion, concern for improving the quality of care combined with legal precedent and financial necessity provides a sufficient impetus for significant and long-lasting changes in acute-care hospital practices.

LEGAL PRECEDENT

Malpractice. From the perspective of the medical profession, malpractice might be better termed errors of omission or of medical-professional judgment. However, for the purposes of this paper "malpractice" will be used in its legal sense. Malpractice litigation is based upon the premise that a patient's right to reasonable medical care has been violated. Reasonable medical care is judged to be determined by what is the common procedure or recommendation in similar cases. This judgment is a professional one based upon what other physicians would do in similar circumstances. For this reason, in medical malpractice cases the testimony of medical experts is often required in order to render a judgment.

Judgments rendered in favor of the plaintiff have resulted in increasing financial awards. In fact, the average medical malpractice award has doubled over the past six years. The average award in 1970 was $14,281, as compared to $27,708 in 1976. This increase in the size of malpractice awards is twice the rate of general inflation. In a recent HEW study based upon a survey of 84 percent of malpractice claims closed by private insurance carriers, 93 percent of the malpractice awards resulted in payments of more than $500 to the injured party. Analyses based upon the severity of injury related to medical malpractice indicate three distinct categories and amounts of awards: insignificant or temporary injury, resulting in an average award of $7,563; permanent or total injuries, for which the average award was $145,275; and injury resulting in death for which the average award was $57,468. Interestingly, only 6 percent of claims were disposed of as the result of a court verdict. In contrast, 53 percent of the cases surveyed in the study resulted in payments after a suit was filed but before the trial had begun, and 37 percent were settled without the plaintiff even having filed suit.

Analysis by hospital size, geographic area, medical sub-specialty, and other factors reveals that large hospitals were more often involved than small; claims most often occurred in the northwestern part of the United States; claims were most often filed against neurosurgeons, orthopedic surgeons, and plastic surgeons; and the percentage of claims was highest for surgical errors (33 percent) and institutional errors (32 percent). Data on claims also indicate that injuries to patients most often occurred in the operating room (42 percent), with the second most frequent site being the patient's hospital room (24 percent).

As impressive as these statistics are (cf. *Modern Health Care,* 1979), medical malpractice is a difficult and expensive legal process. Litigation requires much research into the medical aspects of the case and the testimony of numerous expert medical witnesses. For this reason—and despite the documented, sizeable awards by the courts—few attorneys wish to handle medical malpractice cases. However, recent suits centering not on negligence in medical or surgical treatment procedures but rather on negligence in regard to informed consent for such procedures have made the preparation and conduct of litigation much simpler.

Informed Consent. The issues involved in informed consent litigation over the past ten years can be abstracted in the following ten points (references are to the relevant litigation):

1. The fountainhead of the informed consent doctrine is the patient's right to exercise control over his or her own body (*Schloendorff* v. *Society of New York Hospital,* 1914).
2. The doctrine takes full account of the fact that the patient depends completely on the physician for information on which he or she(the patient) makes decisions (*Cobbs* v. *Grant,* 1972).
3. A physician cannot properly undertake to perform therapy without the prior consent of his patient (*Mohr* v. *Williams,* 1905; *McClees* v. *Cohen,* 1930, regarding consent to operative procedures.)
4. In order for the patient's consent to be effective, it must have been "informed" in that the patient received a fair and reasonable explanation (*Kenny* v. *Lockwood,* 1931).
5. The doctrine of informed consent imposes on the physician the duty to explain the procedure and to warn the patient of risks

so that the patient can make an intelligent and informed choice (*Salgo* v. *Stanford University Board of Trustees,* 1957)

6. The doctrine requires the physician to reveal the nature of the ailment, nature of the proposed treatment, the probability of success, alternatives, and risks (*Natanson* v. *Kline,* 1960; *Scaria* v. *St. Paul Fire & Marine Ins. Co.,* 1975, regarding medical malpractice.)

7. The law does not allow a physician to substitute his judgment for that of the patient in the matter of consent to treatment (*Collins* v. *Itoh,* 1972).

8. With regard to the use of a standard consent form, unless a person has been adequately apprised of risks and alternatives any consent given is necessarily ineffectual (*Pegram* v. *Sisco,* 1976). Authorization by such an inadequate consent form is simply one additional piece of evidence. (*Garone* v. *Roberts' Technical & Trade School,* 1975).

9. The informed consent doctrine is properly cast as a tort action for negligence, as opposed to battery or assault (*Cobbs* v. *Grant,* 1972; *Downer* v. *Veilleux,* 1974; *Trogun* v. *Fruchtman,* 1973), except that surgery performed without a patient's informed consent is a technical battery (*Shetter* v. *Rochelle,* 1965, 1966).

10. Beyond these general principles, there is considerable disagreement on (1) whether the duty to warn should be based on a professional or general-reasonableness standard of care, (2) whether expert testimony is required to prove standard of care, (3) the appropriate test for proving causal connection between failure to disclose and any resulting injury or damages, and (4) how one determines that consent is truly informed (legal versus behavioral methods).

A most important aspect of informed consent litigation is that it is not necessarily as difficult to prepare as medical malpractice litigation. Recent court decisions on informed consent litigation have not applied professional-standard-of-care considerations, but instead employed a general or lay standard of reasonableness set by law and independent of medical custom. This means that expert testimony by medical experts is not necessary for settling the issue of negligence in obtaining informed consent—rather, only evidence as to whether the patient was truly informed. These precedents, based upon a general standard for informed consent, protect the patient against a possible conspiracy of silence by physicians (should it ever exist in a court case), and also make cases easier to try, even by attorneys not particularly well versed in medical law. This doctrine of informed consent also means that correctly performed medical procedures that result in harm to a patient, even though such harm is a known risk of the procedure and *not* the result of negligence on the physician's part in performing the procedure, can be just cause for compensation if the physician was negligent in informing the patient of the risks and alternatives. The case of *Sard* v. *Hardy*, originally decided in favor of the defendant and recently reversed by the Maryland Court of Special Appeals, serves as a good example.

The Case of Sard v. Hardy. In an opinion rendered by Judge J. Levine, the central issue in the appeals case was whether the appellants, Mr. and Mrs. D. P. Sard, Jr., had presented legally sufficient evidence to permit a jury to decide whether appellee, Dr. E. D. Hardy—a physician specializing in obstetrics and gynecology—had been negligent in failing to advise the Sards that the sterilization procedure, a tubal ligation, that he performed on Mrs. Sard might not succeed in preventing future pregnancies, and failing to disclose alternative means of achieving the desired result. Briefly, the facts of the case are that Mrs. Sard became pregnant for the first time in 1965, at which time she developed eclampsia (occurrence of convulsions because of hypertension due to pregnancy), necessitating premature delivery by Caesarean section to save the lives of mother and child; yet the child was dead at birth. Mrs. Sard's first contact with Dr. Hardy was in 1966 in regard to her second pregnancy, which was delivered successfully by Caesarean section. Later in 1967, Mrs. Sard became pregnant for the third time, and discussed with the appellee, who was supervising her prenatal care, the possibility of sterilization after delivery. The factors surrounding this decision were that Dr. Hardy had gone on record as indicating that future pregnancies would endanger her life, and that for this reason he recommended sterilization. Mrs. Sard testified that the appellee had informed her that women usually do not have more than three Caesarean deliveries. Further, Mrs. Sard and her husband felt that they could not afford any more children. Also, according to her testimony the appellee had offered her three options: sterilization, oral contraception, or an IUD. Neither Mr. or Mrs. Sard had been informed that a vasectomy was an option, nor that the tubal ligation procedure that was eventually performed (a Madlener technique having a 2 percent risk of failure when performed at the time of the Caesarean) had anything other than a 100 percent probability of preventing pregnancy, nor that the procedure would have had a greater chance of success if performed at a time other than that of Caesarean birth, nor that alternative tubal ligation procedures have substantially lower failure rates under similar circumstances (e.g., the Uchida and Irving methods, having less than .1 percent risk of failure).

Mr. Sard, whose testimony revealed he was functionally illiterate, had been asked to sign a consent form for the sterilization of his wife, which he did. Only ten to fifteen minutes before being wheeled into the delivery room for the Caesarean delivery and tubal ligation, Mrs. Sard was given the same form to sign, which she did without reading it.

Three years after the delivery of her second healthy child and the performance of the tubal ligation, and despite the assurances of the appellee that she was sterile, Mrs. Sard became pregnant for the fourth time, delivering her third healthy child by uneventful Caesarean section.

While the original decision in this case was in favor of the defendant, Dr. Hardy, it was later overturned by a court of special appeals. This higher court ruled that sufficient evidence had been presented by the Sards to permit a decision in their favor. One significant point about this case is that while eight causes of action were set forth against Dr. Hardy, the judgment rested only on the issue of informed consent. Specifically, Count 1 charged appellee with negligence in the performance of the sterilization; Count 2 asserted a claim under the informed consent doctrine; Count 3 related to negligence following the operation; Counts 4, 5, and 6 sought damages in regard to the first three counts; Count 7 charged breach of express warranty; and Count 8 sought damages for that breach. The appellants dropped the negligence claims, and the appeals court judged that although there was not sufficient evidence to demonstrate a breach of express warranty, there was sufficient evidence on the informed consent count.

Thus, while the treatment procedure in this example may have been performed as competently as possible and the unfortunate sequelae been well within the limits of acceptable risk, because the patient had not been informed of this risk and the alternative procedures, the courts judged that the patient had been wronged.

FINANCIAL NECESSITY

For a number of reasons, not the least of which is the increase in successful malpractice litigation, the cost of malpractice insurance has recently risen dramatically. As an example, complete coverage for the hospital and all physicians at the Johns Hopkins University medical institutions rose approximately 2500 percent between 1961 and 1976. In one year, 1976–1977, this rate increased another 190 percent.

The result of such increases in malpractice insurance has been that some institutions (including Hopkins) have chosen to become self-insured; others have chosen other modes of coverage, such as captive insurance companies, offshore companies, or cooperative associations with other hospitals. In such situations the contingencies shift. Previously, the insurance companies assumed the risk of payments resulting from major litigation against a medical institution, for which service a fee was paid by the institution. The contingency for the institution was on paying the premium to avoid the risk. In a self-insured status, where the institution must make payment for any justifiable claims of negligence, the contingency is on reducing the risk of negligence.

Previous to the adoption of a self-insured status by a medical institution, avoiding negligent practices that would violate a patient's right to competent treatment, informed consent, and so on was motivated primarily by the institution's wish to provide quality care. Once an institution has assumed a self-insured status, ensuring patient rights and avoiding practices with high risk for negligence become matters not only of quality care but of survival as an institution.

SUMMARY

The first of two questions raised earlier in this chapter was, What are patient rights? From the above discussion, they can be considered as immutable abstractions that can be influenced by circumstances, including legal and financial factors. In the case of acute-care hospitals, the rights to competent medical care and to exercise control over the types of procedure performed (including none) both have a history in legal precedent. Further, the financial necessity that medical institutions become self-insured presents an additional and most potent motivation for protecting patient rights. All of which sets the stage for the second question: How are patient rights to be ensured?

Ensuring Patient Rights

Specifying patient rights does not ensure them. Neither does the passage of regulations or laws. All of these activities, however, are likely to change the behavior of treatment staff to some extent and decrease the likelihood that patient rights will be violated—which, of course, is the desired outcome. In this regard—changing staff behavior—the field of behavioral science may have some distinct contributions to offer. The area of behavioral science that has been involved in the experimental analysis of behavior especially has a good deal to offer. Specifically, this area of science has demonstrated principles related to the very precise control of behavior and the application of these principles to very practical situations in a variety of settings. The procedures demonstrated in these settings have often gone beyond merely informing staff of requirements, to include demonstrating how conditions can be established in which staff will reliably carry out required procedures. In this sense, such behavioral procedures link the issue of specifying patient rights to that of staff compliance with procedures that protect these rights. Many aspects pertinent to patient rights in acute-care hospital settings are similar to those behavior change procedures well documented in other settings. To the extent that this is so, consideration about patient rights and strategies for dealing with them will be equally applicable.

PROCEDURES TO CHANGE STAFF BEHAVIOR

Over the past decade, the behavioral literature has demonstrated successful procedures to evaluate and maintain staff performance. Target populations in this research literature have included classroom teachers and high school athletes (Hart, Reynolds, Baer, Brawley, & Harris, 1968; McKenzie & Rushall, 1974), mental health practitioners (Paul, McInnis, & Mariotto, 1973), paraprofessional tutors (Barnard, Christophersen, & Wolf, 1974), psychiatric aides (Pomerleau, Bobrone, & Smith, 1973), and hospital personnel (Gardner, Brust, & Watson, 1970; Johnson & Ferryman, 1969).

The primary focus of procedures across staffs and settings has been the provision of information on responsibilities and feedback on performance. Staff-management procedures have traditionally included the presentation of memorandums delineating the expectations of administration and senior staff, and the provision of in-service training workshops designed to educate staff (Foster, 1970). However, in motivating staff to initiate ward activities, memos and workshops have been found to be inferior to the public posting of performance feedback and an activities schedule (Quilitch, 1975). This may be because memos and workshops do not impose any particular consequence on staff behavior, they merely describe job requirements. Performance feedback, on the other hand, changes as a function of staff behavior, thus providing differential consequences for compliance or noncompliance. In some cases performance feedback has been sufficient to increase and maintain staff compliance (Panyan, Boozer, & Morris, 1970; Welsch, Ludwig, Radicker, & Krapfl, 1973). In other instances additional consequences have been added to provide more potent feedback and effect staff compliance. These additional consequences have included the use of commerical training stamps (Brocker, Morgan, & Grabowski, 1972), tokens exchangeable for cash (Pommer & Streedbeck, 1974), and a performance lottery (Iwata, Bailey, Brown, Foshee, & Alpern, 1976).

This literature can be characterized as identifying procedures successful with paraprofessional staff and with behaviors directly related to therapeutic goals. However, the protection of patient rights to a very great extent involves the behavior of professional staff—often professional staff at the very highest level. Also, procedures necessary for ensuring patient rights are often not immediately or directly relevant to improvements in therapeutic outcomes. In this regard, a recent study conducted at the John F. Kennedy Institute has shown that procedures very similar to those reported can be effective also in changing professional staff performance of behaviors required by the institution but not necessarily or immediately related to therapeutic outcome (Cataldo & Russo, 1979). In this study four staff requirements were monitored over a forty-five-week period. These requirements were (1) posting and updating of daily staff schedules, (2) posting and updating of daily treatment data on each patient, (3) attendance and presentation of treatment cases at required staff meetings, and (4) the completion of required reports for medical records. During baseline, the performance of these requirements was only monitored; each requirement was characterized by low or variable levels of compliance. However, using a multiple baseline design across categories of requirements demonstrated that an intervention procedure of weekly public posting of individual and group data on compliance is sufficient to get all staff to maintain high levels of compliance. Posting and updating of their schedules by the staff increased from 11 to 86 percent; posting data on patient treatment programs increased from 51 to 92 percent; attendance and presentation criteria at meetings increased from 62 to 85 percent; and the timely completion of reports changed from 67 to 85 percent.

PROCEDURES TO CHANGE STAFF BEHAVIOR ON AN INSTITUTION-WIDE SCALE: THE HOPKINS RISK PREVENTION PROGRAM

While these procedures offer evidence that methods exist for improving staff compliance with administrative requirements similar to those requirements necessary for protecting patient rights, they have neither done so on a scale large enough for application to an institution-wide program, nor have they specifically targeted the many aspects of staff accountability necessary to ensure patient rights. Yet programs at acute-care hospitals have for some time been concerned with patient rights. These programs have been characterized as "risk prevention"—preventing (or at least reducing) the risk that a patient's rights will be violated. As with the analysis of an individual's behavior in designing a behavior change program, the institution must undergo a similar analysis, and procedures must be employed that both improve compliance and provide self-corrective feedback. Such a program is exemplified by that initiated at the Johns Hopkins University medical institutions.

The Hopkins Professional Liability Risk Prevention Program is based on the notion that such a program developed within an institution with high standards of care and active educational programs must focus in part on the deficiencies in the system. A review of losses in liability claims and of high-risk incidents shows that the occasional serious occurrence can be very costly, and that such occurrences are usually preventable, often have a recurring pattern, and either reflect a deterioration in adherence to an existing policy or the need for an improved policy. Accordingly, unfavorable therapeutic outcomes must be carefully scrutinized, and approaches developed to prevent their recurrence. Practices that are at risk must be modified. Documentation of care must be recorded diligently with legal implications in mind.

Development of a program such as this calls for a strengthening of preexisting, highly diverse, and reasonably effective institutional systems for maintaining patient safety and a high quality of patient care. At Hopkins this system has for many years depended upon the function of the Medical Board and its standing committees. In recent years, the addition of the Incident Review Committee has brought a litigation-prevention emphasis to this function. In addition, the creation of the Quality Assurance Committee has provided for review of professionals' credentials, systematic quality-of-care monitoring, and an element of improved coordination to the function of the system. This diverse activity has evolved slowly into an operational system that involves many individuals with needed special expertise. The program at the Johns Hopkins University medical institutions was designed to strengthen all parts of the system from the perspective of professional liability and prevention and management of risk. In order to understand the bases of this program, elements of the overall institution program should be reviewed.

Administrative Commitment. Since their inception, the Hopkins medical institutions have been dedicated to the provision of optimal medical care. Their bylaws stress compliance with well-established accepted practice, documentation of care provided and staff conduct, and the maintenance of high standards in medical educational programs in accordance with the policies of the Institutions.

Administrative accountability and control are the bases for a risk management program. The development and implementation of an ongoing systems approach of professional review, based on sound management concepts with the patient as the central focal point, are prerequisites dictated by the Hopkins administration for program design.

Data Base. The Hopkins Professional Liability Risk Prevention Program's data-based information system provides (1) the inventory and analysis of cumulative experience regarding all incidents, in particular and more specifically high-risk incidents, (2) the inventory and monitoring of high-risk policies and procedures, and (3) the inventory and monitoring of high-risk procedural skills as related to patient care.

This computerized data system takes inventory of incidents according to locality, type, participants, procedure deficit, contributory factors, patient care outcome, actions taken, and claims management outcome. Analysis of patterns in patient care and in policy and procedures can be monitored, and areas of deviation from established criteria identified. Quality control is established in the provision of schedules for recurrent monitoring of high-risk policies and procedures, problem policy reviews, and archiving results. Support is provided to the standing committees of the Medical Board in the form of monitored results, scheduled problem policy review, or scheduled monitoring of policy changes.

Committee Structure and Relationships. Elements of the Professional Liability Risk Prevention Program are structured to the perceived needs. Delegating authority, receiving and analyzing information, developing strategy, and monitoring of effectiveness are accommodated by a decision-making unit offering a forum for discussion and a wide range of disciplines and standing committees on which to draw. The Professional Liability Risk Prevention Office relates to the Medical Board and its standing committees by (1) maintaining the current direct reporting of the Incident Review Committee to the Medical Board and the Quality Assurance Committee and (2) overlapping membership on the other standing committees of the Medical Board. These standing committees and their function are listed below.

- *The Committee on Infection Control* makes recommendations to the Medical Board on development and surveillance of policies and practices associated with control and prophylaxis of infection acquired within the hospital.
- *The Safety Policy and Advisory Committee* makes recommendations to the Medical Board designed to produce safe characteristics and practices and eliminate—or reduce to the extent possible—hazards to patients, staff, and visitors.
- *The Quality Assurance Committee* evaluates the quality of medical care, documents findings, and makes recommendations to the Medical Board for improving quality of care. It reviews the Medical Staff credentials and makes recommendations to the Medical Board about appointments, reappointments, and privileges. It makes recommendations about continuing medical education. The committee routinely receives information from standing subcommittees, (1) the *Medical Audit Subcommittee*, which conducts retrospective audits of quality of care, (2) the *Utilization Review Subcommittee*, which measures and evaluates use of available facilities and services,

and (3) the *Incident Subcommittee* which investigates unusual occurrences in care of patients.

- *The Pharmacy and Therapeutics Committee* is responsible for the development and surveillance of policies and procedures relating to use of drugs, maintenance of the hospital's drug formulary, and education of physicians, nurses, and students on matters pertaining to the use of drugs.

Communication System Between Hospital and Patient: Department of Patient Relations. An important factor in a risk prevention program is the patient representative. The use of this ombudsman to communicate with patients affords other hospital personnel the opportunity of knowing how the patient perceives the atmosphere in which care is given. With the patient representative acting as a liaison between the patient, the institution, and the community, the patient can seek solutions to his or her problems and concerns on a neutral level.

The Department of Patient Relations at Johns Hopkins University Hospital is a direct arm of administration, and is comprised of patient representatives (seven in number), interpreters, a host or hostess, a librarian, and the information receptionists who man the information desks. The patient representatives are assigned to particular buildings, and they visit the new admissions, interpreting as needed the policies, procedures, and services available for patients, families, and visitors. They revisit those with unmet needs or problems, documenting anything out of the ordinary or serious in nature and forwarding that information to the director's office. Normally, the patient representatives respond to the needs of the patients, since the intention and aim is to resolve problems while they are still small. Patient representatives provide specific channels through which patients can seek solutions to their problems, concerns, and unmet needs. The Department of Patient Relations is in a position to "humanize" the red tape and be sensitive to problems with potential legal implications.

The director's office serves as a center for all letters of complaint/compliment/special problems and special requests addressed to the president, executive director, or trustees of the Johns Hopkins University Hospital. All complaints and special problems are investigated and responded to as quickly as possible. Copies of them are forwarded to the appropriate department—as well as the Legal Department—for their input and action. Corrective action, as required, is implemented with the department involved. The original complaint is filed after the action is completed. Complimentary letters received by the president, executive director, or trustees are also responded to and copies are forwarded to the appropriate department, or employees' personnel files.

The Department of Patient Relations is the referral center for all special problems and requests that cannot be resolved by other hospital departments, the important thing here being that there be a rapid response to all telephone and written requests received by this office. If it is necessary for subsequent responses, a "tickler" file keeps that system in order.

The patient representative's office helps families with housing and travel arrangements and also makes appointments for interpreters.

The very active Patients' Free Library is supported by the Women's Board but managed by one of the Patient Relations Staff. In conjunction with volunteers, who take book carts to the floors, the librarian prepares brief, summary book-report lists that are distributed on the floors to assist patients in requesting books from the library.

All Patient Relations departmental activity is described in a monthly report for the administrator of the hospital, the assistant directors of each of the various buildings and the managers of the service organizations. This allows the Department of Patient Relations to research procedural problems that cause complaints with that department or service, and then rectify them.

Claims Management. A claims management system involves claims filed, litigation in progress, reserves posted, settlements and judgments paid, and proper financial management of professional liability reserve funds. The handling of potential liability is based on the concept of immediate, open, and honest discussion of incidents with those involved and fair compensation for hospital-acquired injuries. Cases of relative severity are reported directly to the Law Office by phone or letter. A representative of the Law Office becomes involved in those cases having the potential for liability, and investigation and further discussion with patient or family become the responsibility of this designated person. The decision whether compensation is advisable is addressed at the policy-making level, and, when warranted, reserves are set aside. Authority for decisions regarding compensation of a lesser nature—e.g., waiver of charges for treatment or waiver of the entire bill for services— is delegated to the hospital attorney. When necessitated, medico-legal sessions with the involved physician are held in an effort to determine the hospital's position and develop legal strategies. In this sense the hospital attorney is in the position to direct both the Risk Prevention Program and the Legal Office. The ability to have one individual monitor and direct the functions of both these complementary entities is an essential key to the success of the entire hospital effort in this area.

Committee Monitoring. The Joint Committee on Professional Liability meets on a bimonthly or quarterly basis, depending on the need to review the performance of the Professional Liability Risk Prevention Program and the departmental risk prevention programs.

GENERAL CONSIDERATION FOR AN
INSTITUTION-WIDE PROGRAM
TO ENSURE PATIENT RIGHTS

Clearly, the Hopkins model is extensive and thorough, although specific to the design of that particular medical institution. Certain general principles can be used from this one example for application in other hospitals. Some relate to critical aspects that are surely essential to any successful program, and others are less important but enable a program to be conducted more easily and effectively.

The first to be discussed here is also the first to be considered in beginning a program—that such a program must have support from the very highest levels of authority. This is necessary because, as with any new program, there will be resistance to change. When the change is in the behavior of all medical staff (no matter how senior) the resistance is likely to be greater than any program director and staff can surmount. In the case of Hopkins, the program had immediate support from the Director of the Johns Hopkins University Hospital (Robert Heyssel) and the Dean of the Medical Faculty (Richard Ross). In fact, this high level of administration had initiated a risk prevention program a few years previous to its becoming a financial necessity, not in anticipation of high malpractice insurance but for it to serve as a model for ensuring quality of care. Without such support similar programs have a very low probability of success.

A second critical feature is the manner by which the program is established. The experts on how to carry out effective treatment procedures, reduce risk, and ensure patient rights are the same individuals charged with successfully carrying out the procedures—the hospital staff and faculty. In order to be effectively implemented, the program should be designed by them. Of course, sufficient and frequent promptings to address the problems and detail risk-prevention procedures will be necessary. However, a risk prevention program staff is much more likely to be successful if it prompts and facilitates the work of staff in the various hospital departments, rather than developing and specifying the necessary procedures itself.

Thus, to initially establish a program, high-level administrative support provides motivation and serves as a mandate for its creation, while the risk prevention program's staff facilitates the activities of direct-care staff and faculty in specifying the particulars of the program.

The specification and continued refinement of procedures is accomplished by dividing the areas needing attention into distinct committees. In the case of the Hopkins example, these include the Committee on Infection Control, the Safety Policy and Advisory Committee, the Medical Audit Subcommittee, and so on. This allows a clear division of responsibility to those individuals most knowledgeable about the area. The risk

prevention staff's relationship to those committees is, again, to facilitate
their efforts by bringing to their attention problems to be considered and
making sure that there is a flow of information between committees, so
that committees' efforts can be integrated.

As in any good behavior-change program, adherence to risk prevention procedures must be monitored. Specification of the procedures does
not necessarily mean that they will be followed. Therefore, an essential
role for the risk prevention program is to monitor adherence by checking
records, having close contact with patients and staff, and following up on
all incidents. The obvious outgrowth of this consideration is the use of
a data system on problems and incidents. A data system permits not only
identification of potential problem areas but also assessment of the effectiveness of the program. In the case of the Hopkins risk prevention
program, while it has not been in effect long enough for expected long-
term outcomes to be realized, in the year-and-one-half of its existence
incident reports provided to risk prevention staff have increased five-fold
over previous periods and there has not been one surprise claim by a
patient.

An interesting feature to consider is the use of the patient ombudsman
strategy as detailed in the Hopkins program. This permits the better
collection of data on incidents and provides an early warning of potential claims, but, most important, better serves the patient by providing personnel who are solely responsible for seeing to it his or her problems and needs are adequately met.

The success of any program is dependent upon the staff. With regard to staff for a risk prevention program, certain types of individual
may be more successful than others. Staff often have no product at the
end of the day, but rather progress toward a long-term goal; therefore,
they should be screened as to what types of job they have had previously, and whether they would find this new job satisfying. Since a
risk prevention program staff member must have considerable knowledge
of medicine, nurses make excellent candidates, particularly those with
administrative nursing experience, such as nursing supervisors or nurses
connected with PSRO reviews. Nurses bring to the job familiarity with
hospital routine, a knowledge of medicine, and insight into patients.

The last feature to consider is of primary importance throughout
every stage of the program—that is, the philosophy of the program.
Prevention—by protecting patient rights and ensuring quality care—is
the key. The purpose of such a program is not to make sure there are no
patient claims, but rather to honestly evaluate potential risk situations
and institute procedures that reduce this risk. Such a program can then
readily differentiate between an honest error and negligence. In a
similar fashion, it can serve to protect the physician by being equally
sensitive in identifying a patient who wishes to sue for reasons other
than negligence.

The larger the size of a hospital, the more people forget or do not even know to whom to go about actual or potential problems. The risk prevention program outlined above provides a structure to ensure that the medical benefits afforded a patient in a large hospital not be given at the expense of his or her rights.

References

BARNARD, J. D., CHRISTOPHERSEN, E. R., & WOLF, M. M. Supervising parapro-fessional tutors in a remedial reading program. *Journal of Applied Behavior Analysis,* 1974, *7,* 481.

BROCKER, W. A., MORGAN, D. G., & GRABOWSKI, J. G. Development and mainten-ance of a behavior modification repertoire of cottage attendants through TV feedback. *American Journal of Mental Deficiency,* 1972, *2,* 128–136.

CATALDO, M. F., & RUSSO, D. C. Developmentally disabled in the community: Behavioral/medical considerations. In L. A. Hamerlynck, P. O. Davidson & F. W. Clark (Eds.), *History and future of behavior modification for the developmentally disabled: Programmatic and methodological issues.* New York:Brunner/Mazel, 1979.

Cobbs v. *Grant,* 8 Cal.3d 229, 104 Cal. Rpter. 505, 502 P.2d 1, 9 (1972).

Collins v. *Itoh,* 160 Mont. 461, 503 P.2d 36, 40 (1972).

Downer v. *Veilleux,* 322 A.2d 82, 89–90 (Me. 1974).

FOSTER, R. Here's how in-service education works. *Modern Hospital,* October 1970, pp. 95–98.

GARDNER, J. M., BRUST, D. J., & WATSON, L. J. A scale to measure skill in ap-plying behavior modification techniques to the mentally retarded. *American Journal of Mental Deficiency,* 1970, *5,* 633–636.

Garone v. *Roberts' Technical & Trade School,* 47 App. Div.2d 306, 366 N.Y.S.2d 129, 133 (1975).

HART, B. M., REYNOLDS, N. J., BAER, D. M., BRAWLEY, E. R., & HARRIS, F. R. Effect of contingent and non-contingent social reinforcement on the coopera-tive play of a preschool child. *Journal of Applied Behavior Analysis,* 1968, *1,* 73–76.

IWATA, B. A., BAILEY, J. S., BROWN, K. M., FOSHEE, T. J., & ALPERN, M. A per-formance-based lottery to improve residential care and training by institu-tional staff. *Journal of Applied Behavior Analysis,* 1976, *9,* 417–431.

JOHNSON, D., & FERRYMAN, Z. In-service training for the non-professional in a mental retardation center. *Mental Retardation,* 1969, *7,* 10–13.

Kenny v. *Lockwood,* [1932] 1 D.L.R. 507, 520 (Ont. 1931).

McClees v. *Cohen,* 158 Md. 60, 62–63, 148 A. 124 (1930).

McKENZIE, T. L., & RUSHALL, B. S. Effects of self-recording on attendance and performance in a competitive swimming training environment. *Journal of Applied Behavior Analysis,* 1974, *7,* 199–206.

Modern Health Care. Malpractice awards double in size. May 1979, p. 34.

Mohr v. *Williams,* 95 Minn. 261, 104 N.W. 12, 15 (1905).

Natanson v. *Kline,* 186 Kan. 393, 350 P.2d 1093, 1106; 187 Kan. 186, 354 P.2d 670 (1960).

PANYAN, M., BOOZER, H., & MORRIS, N. Feedback to attendants as a reinforcer for applying operant techniques. *Journal of Applied Behavior Analysis,* 1970, *3,* 1–4.

PAUL, G. L., McINNIS, T. L., & MARIOTTO, M. J. Objective performance outcomes associated with two approaches to training mental health technicians in milieu and social learning programs. *Journal of Abnormal Psychology,* 1973, *82,* 523–532.

Pegram v. *Sisco,* 406 F. Supp. 776, 779 (W.D. Ark.), *aff'd,* 547 F.2d 1172 (8th Cir. 1976).

POMERLEAU, O. F., BOBRONE, P. H., & SMITH, R. H. Rewarding psychiatric aides for the behavioral improvements of assigned patients. *Journal of Applied Behavior Analysis,* 1973, *6,* 383–390.

POMMER, D. A., & STREEDBECK, D. Motivating staff performance in an operant learning program for children. *Journal of Applied Behavior Analysis,* 1974, *7,* 217–221.

QUILITCH, H. R. A comparison of three staff-management procedures. *Journal of Applied Behavior Analysis,* 1975, *8,* 59–66.

Salgo v. *Stanford University Board of Trustees,* 154 Cal. App.2d 560, 317 P.2d 170, 181 (1957).

Sard v. *Hardy,* 34 Md. App. 217, 367 A.2d 525 (1976); 34 Md. App. 231 & 235 (1977).

Scaria v. *St. Paul Fire & Marine Ins. Co.,* 68 Wis.2d 1, 227 N.W.2d 647, 654 (1975).

Schloendorff v. *Society of New York Hospital,* 211 N.Y. 125, 105 N.E. 92, 93 (1914).

Shetter v. *Rochelle,* 2 Ariz. App. 358, 409 P.2d 74, 82 (1965); 2 Ariz. App. 607, 411 P.2d 45 (1966).

SKINNER, B. F. *About behaviorism.* New York: Knopf, 1974.

Trogun v. *Fruchtman,* 58 Wis.2d 596, 207 N.W.2d 297, 311–13 (1973).

WELSCH, W., LUDWIG, C., RADICKER, J., & KRAPFL, J. Effects of feedback on daily completion of behavior modification projects. *Mental Retardation,* 1973, *11,* 24–27.

WOOD, W. S. Behavior modification and civil rights. In J. E. Krapfl & E. A. Vargas (Eds.), *Behaviorism and ethics.* Kalamazoo, Mich.: Behaviordelia, 1977.

CHAPTER 16

Providing Nursing Home Residents' Rights

K. Anthony Edwards
Jan Sheldon-Wildgen

THE NUMBER OF ELDERLY AMERICANS increases yearly, with approximately ten percent of the population at present over the age of sixty-five. It is estimated that in 1980, there were over 40 million persons in America of sixty-five years of age or older (Porzio, 1976). In spite of these increasing numbers, the elderly are living in a society that emphasizes physical fitness, beauty, intelligence, wit, agility, and, primarily, *youth*.

Those who differ from the norm (e.g., the mentally retarded or ill) are often segregated, usually under the theory that special care and treatment are needed. Institutions house those whom society believes cannot adequately care for themselves or should not, for one reason or another, be allowed to live independently in the community. For decades Americans chose to ignore those whom they had no contact with. Therefore, commitment to residential institutions and the conditions of these facilities were not challenged or even considered.

An abrupt change in this attitude was witnessed in the past decade. Advocate groups began protesting involuntary commitment that so frequently and easily took place. Then, the kinds of living conditions the committed were forced to reside in and the types of treatment, or lack thereof, that they were receiving were also held questionable (see, e.g., *Rouse* v. *Cameron*, 1966; *Wyatt* v. *Stickney*, 1972; *New York State Association for Retarded Children, Inc.* v. *Rockefeller*, 1973; *Donaldson* v. *O'Connor*, 1975). Lawsuits in the mental health area became numerous and soon cases in other areas were being heard, including institutions for juvenile offenders (e.g., *Morales* v. *Turman*, 1973) and prisoners (e.g., *Clonce* v. *Richardson*, 1974). Standards for living conditions, treatment,

□ The research for this chapter was supported in part by Program Project Grant HD 00870 from the National Institute of Child Health and Human Development. The authors wish to gratefully acknowledge the many contributions to this chapter made by Dr. Todd R. Risley.

319

services, and patient rights were first promulgated by the courts (the first and most noteworthy being those mandated by Judge Johnson in *Wyatt v. Stickney*, 1972), with Congress (Developmentally Disabled Assistance and Bill of Rights Act, 1975) and state legislatures (e.g., Kansas Statutes Annotated, 1976b) quickly following suit. More recently, courts have addressed community facilities for the mentally retarded and ill, and have required that minimum standards be followed and basic rights provided (e.g., *Brewster* v. *Dukakis*, 1978; *Wuori* v. *Zitnay*, 1978).

The basis for most cases that were brought in the mental health field involved the fact that the majority of residents in the facilities were involuntarily committed (see, e.g., *Wyatt* v. *Stickney,* 1972). Since these persons had not broken any laws requiring incarceration, the courts found that the justification (or *quid pro quo*) for depriving them of liberty is that the state provide adequate care and treatment; otherwise, their basic rights under the Fifth and Fourteenth Amendments are being violated. One could argue that under the Fifth and Fourteenth Amendments, which require equal protection, voluntary patients in the same institutions should receive the same rights. The courts, however, have shied away from cases involving private facilities and voluntary residents, presumably under the theory that a person who voluntarily chooses to reside in a facility can choose the type of institution desired, and, if the care or treatment offered is unpleasant, is free to leave at any time. More recently, the courts have begun addressing the issue of the right to commit another individual (usually a relative) to an institution without a hearing. Cases normally occur when a parent commits a child to an institution for the mentally retarded or ill (e.g., *Bartley* v. *Kremens*, 1975), but the issue is the same when a child seeks to commit an elderly parent. Thus, the right to force another to reside in a facility, other than the person's home, solely on the judgment of a relative, or persons contacted by the relative, is being challenged.

The elderly residing in nursing homes are often in a uniquely disadvantaged position. Although some have been through competency or commitment hearings and found to be "incompetent" or "in need of treatment," and placed in nursing homes, thus presumably being provided with "due process of law" before being deprived of their liberty, many others are placed in nursing homes without a hearing or adequate representation. Once in the "home," they are presumed to be voluntary residents and may leave at any time. Many of these "voluntary residents, however, are physically unable to leave. Although many may vocalize a desire to leave, they physically have no means to do so. There are also those who have been placed in nursing homes because they cannot totally care for themselves. Rather than being provided with services in the community in order to enable them to reside in their own homes, they are withdrawn from society and placed in nursing homes. Once residents are in a nursing home, the staff often assume major responsibility for their functioning, thus doing most things for them (e.g., feeding and dressing them). Often intended in the best interest of residents, this type of overprotective attitude can contribute to their deterioration after they are placed in the institution.

This chapter will examine the placement of the elderly in nursing homes and explore alternative methods of care that might be available and feasible. Additionally, the rights that should be provided for residents of nursing homes and some methods that can be used to ensure that these rights are enforced will be described.

Placement in Nursing Home Facilities

The right of the government to intervene in the lives of individuals who have not committed a criminal act has been based on the doctrine of *parens patriae* and/or the police power of the state. The doctrine of *parens patriae* comes from English law, which held that the king as "father of the country" was responsible for the care and custody of individuals who, because of age or mental ability, were unable to adequately care for themselves. In the United States today, "this function of the king has vested in the states, and each state is charged with the responsibility of caring for those who are incapable of looking after their own interests" (Blee & Sheldon-Wildgen, 1979, p. 105). There are other instances when an individual's irrational or, perhaps, dangerous behavior may require protection from that person. Under the state's police power—which allows the state to protect the public's safety, health, and morals—it may intervene and commit a person who is dangerous to society in order to protect the public. Although these two concepts (*parens patriae* and the state's police power) are different, both allow the state to place an elderly person in a mental institution or nursing home.

There are numerous situations in which someone should intervene in an elderly persons' life. In a recent article, Regan describes an example where the state, under the *parens patriae* doctrine, could, and probably should, intervene in order to provide care for a person.

> Mrs. D., an 82-year old woman, was starving to death in an old rowhouse in northwest Baltimore. She lay curled across the pink sheet of her double bed, legs pulled up and her hands clutched together below her cheek. Her skinny body was swamped in a puddle of brown and her sickly pink nightgown was stuck to the bed. Downstairs, the glass pane was missing from the front door so anyone could open it and enter. . . . Neighbors, numerous agencies, even a couple of relatives knew Mrs. D. was there, but they had no ability, authority, or inclination to do anything about it. Meals-on-Wheels,

Visiting Nurses, a Geriatric Evaluation Team from the Health Department had all come and gone. A daughter-in-law drew on Mrs. D.'s social security and pension checks and held her savings account, but she refused agency requests to help her mother-in-law. [1978, p. 250]

Although elderly persons frequently have been taken advantage of, there are instances in which society needs to be protected. Often, these situations involve an elderly individual who would be diagnosed as mentally ill. Thus, when elderly persons are threatening, for example, to harm their family, neighbors, or society at large, it may be necessary for the state to intervene and commit these individuals to a mental institution or nursing home.

Unfortunately, there are often cases where the family, with the aid of the state, seeks to commit an elderly individual to an institution or nursing home for reasons that fall neither under the *parens patriae* nor police-power doctrines. Rather than considering the best interests of the elderly person or society, family members will often consider only their own needs when asking that the state commit the person. Regan and Springer (1977) describe the case of Josiah Oakes, an elderly but otherwise stable individual, who became engaged to a young woman with a questionable reputation shortly after the death of his wife. Oakes's family had him committed to a Massachusetts institution, stating that he had hallucinations and was unable to take proper care of his business affairs. This case is not atypical. Often, there is no legitimate reason to confine an elderly person (i.e., the individual's own safety is not at risk nor is the individual a threat to society) other than the family's concern about their reputation, estate, or burden placed on them by the responsibility for care.

Whatever the reasons for placement in an institution or nursing home, when an elderly person is placed there against the person's will, it is referred to as an *"involuntary commitment."* Procedural safeguards must be provided those people involuntarily committed, since the Constitution requires that an individual's freedom cannot be curtailed without due process. But what about those individuals who "voluntarily" go to nursing homes at the urging of family, doctor, or social service agent or provider? Nursing homes largely are comprised of people who have not had hearings to determine whether they require placement in a nursing home; most people reside there because the family or social worker felt the move was best. Although labeled as voluntary residents, it is questionable whether their placement is truly voluntary, especially because many state that they do not want to live in a nursing home and would like to leave. Many elderly individuals, however, are physically unable to leave the nursing home, and a large number of others have no place to go, since their homes have often been sold. It may be that most nursing home residents are only assumed to be voluntary.

Actually, almost all are involuntarily committed and should either be provided procedural safeguards or allowed to live outside the nursing home. Since the Fifth and Fourteenth Amendments require that a person's liberty cannot be curtailed without due process of law, to place an elderly individual in a nursing home against that person's will would therefore violate his or her constitutional rights.

There are two primary types of proceeding that can be used to place an elderly individual in an institution or nursing home: civil commitment and guardianship action (Regan & Springer, 1977). The standards for civil commitment to an institution are vague, but normally the court attempts to determine whether the reason or need for the commitment and the dangerousness of the individual justify a denial of freedom (Blee & Sheldon-Wildgen, 1979). Unfortunately, the Supreme Court has failed to specifically identify the requirements necessary for involuntary confinement. It did state in the landmark decision, *Donaldson* v. *O'Connor* (1975), however, that a finding of mental illness alone does not justify the state's intervention if the individual involved is "dangerous to no one and [can] live safely in freedom" (*Donaldson* v. *O'Connor*, 1975, p. 575). Most states require that the person to be committed be mentally ill and in need of treatment. Courts have been requiring that the "in need of treatment" requirement be evidenced by an extreme likelihood that the unconfined individual will do immediate harm to oneself or others (Blee & Sheldon-Wildgen, 1979). More progressive courts require that the finding of dangerousness be based on a recent overt act, attempt, or threat to do harm (see *Lynch* v. *Baxley,* 1974; *Lessard* v. *Schmidt,* 1972).

One of the most important requirements in the civil commitment process is that the elderly individual be provided with procedural safeguards at a commitment hearing. These procedural safeguards should include (1) notice of the hearing prior to commitment, (2) the right to have counsel present at all stages of the commitment process, and the right to a court-appointed attorney if the individual does not have one, (3) the right to be present at the hearing, to testify, and to present and cross-examine witnesses, (4) the right to be free of any medication or therapy that would hinder the individual's judgment or ability to prepare for the hearing for at least forty-eight hours prior to the hearing, (5) the right to have a standard of proof required (either "clear and convincing proof" or "beyond a reasonable doubt") for determining that the person needs institutionalization, and (6) the right to a mandatory review of the individual's case (see, e.g., Kansas Statutes Annotated, 1976a).

Another legal method that can be used to involuntary commit an individual is a guardianship hearing. "Guardianship is a relationship, authorized by statute, between two individuals in which the guardian or conservator has the power to make and carry out legally binding decisions on behalf of the ward/conservatee who has been found to be incapable of responsible decision making" (Blee & Sheldon-Wildgen, 1979, p. 86). The guardian is given the power to make decisions regarding the personal aspects of the life of an individual (ward), including the person's residence or commitment to an institution; a conservator is responsible for handling the business and financial affairs of the individual (conservatee).

Since guardianship essentially involves removing a great amount of a person's decision-making power, it cannot be done without just reason and without following certain procedural requirements. Normally, any adult can make an application in court seeking guardianship for an elderly person. In order for a guardian to be appointed, however, a hearing is required, in which it must be determined that the elderly person is incapacitated and in need of a guardian. The elderly person has the right to be present at the hearing and to present evidence, and cross-examine witnesses. The major issue to be determined at the guardianship hearing is whether or not the elderly individual is incapacitated or incompetent. A court, in deciding that a person is incapacitated or incompetent, must find that the individual does not have the mental capacity to make or communicate decisions regarding the individual's person or estate. In an attempt to aid the court in making this crucial decision, physicians or psychiatrists perform mental examinations and report their findings (Blee & Sheldon-Wildgen, 1979).

Guardianship is a very restrictive process, and it should not be taken lightly since the consequences of it are drastic. An elderly person who is declared incapacitated or incompetent loses most of that individual's decision-making power and basically lives under the control of the guardian. In addition, in some states, a person who is declared incapacitated or incompetent loses many legal rights, including the right to marry, the right to enter into contractual agreements, the right to bring court actions, the right to consent to medical or treatment procedures, and even the right to vote.

Guardianship can present a serious problem for many elderly persons due to the "all-or-nothing" character of the procedure. Regan (1978) points out that many elderly individuals experience a gradual deterioration in their functional capacity rather than an abrupt cessation of all decision-making ability. Thus, a more flexible mechanism is needed, tailored to each individual's needs (Regan, 1978; Blee & Sheldon-Wildgen, 1979). Under a limited guardianship concept, a guardian should be appointed to be responsible only for those tasks that the elderly individual is totally incapable of performing. This procedure would allow elderly persons to retain decision-making control over those aspects of their lives for which they are able to make decisions.

Persons considering placing an elderly person in a nursing home need to be aware that they cannot unilaterally and legally place an individual in a nursing home against that person's will. People must also be cognizant that the commitment and guardianship proceedings themselves can have drastic and sometimes cruel effects on elderly people. Being determined mentally ill and in need of treatment or unable to make decisions about oneself is not a pleasant experience for anyone. If the person has the mental capacity to understand what these hearings are about, it will likely be a crushing blow to the person's dignity and self-concept. Thus, if an elderly person expresses a desire to live somewhere other than in a nursing home, alternatives should be explored.

In addition, nursing home administrators should be aware that an elderly person who does not want to remain in the nursing home and did not go through a commitment or guardianship hearing can file a law-suit against the facility for unlawful detention. Unlawful detention (false imprisonment) occurs whenever someone interferes with the personal freedom of an individual without legal authority. As Bund (1978) points out, actual force in detaining a person is not necessary, nor is it necessary to demonstrate that there was any ill-will or malice: "All that is required to establish a case is unlawful detention, which means detention against the will or consent of the patient" (p. 111). In cases where false imprisonment or unlawful detention is demonstrated, the elderly nursing home resident can be awarded monetary damages. This could be costly for a nursing home, especially if a class action is brought on behalf of all similarly situated residents in the nursing home. Thus, staff and administrators of nursing homes should establish procedures that allow residents to voice their desire to leave, should take whatever action is necessary to find appropriate placement for them. By seeking less restrictive alternatives to nursing home placement and concurrently providing residents with certain rights, more decision-making power, and more freedom it may be that fewer residents will desire to leave.

Residents' Rights Within Nursing Home Facilities

It was in the late 1960s and early 1970s that consumer and advocate groups made the public aware of the deplorable conditions that existed in many of the institutions and facilities where disabled individuals resided. It was clear that many residents were being abused, denied appropriate treatment, and essentially deprived of their personal rights and liberties. Courts, state legislatures, Congress, and governmental agencies began to establish minimum standards for institutions and enumerate basic rights that should be provided for all residents. Thus the 1970s may well be remembered as the decade of patient rights.

Nursing home facilities were not exempt from this public and governmental scrutiny. In 1974, the Department of Health, Education and Welfare developed a set of patient rights to be enforced in all skilled nursing facilities that participate in the Medicare or Medicaid programs (DHEW, 1978a). In 1976, a similar set of rights applicable to intermediate-care facilities were developed (DHEW, 1978b). A brief discussion of each right that should be provided for nursing home residents under these regulations is given below.

1. *The right to know of one's rights and responsibilities as a resident and rules and regulations about patient conduct and responsibilities.* These expectations should be clearly defined to each resident before admission or within five-work days after admission. Interpretative guidelines issued by HEW require that the facility's policies be written and presented in a language understandable to the resident. Thus, appropriate means should be utilized to inform any resident who is deaf, blind, or non–English speaking. Each resident competent to do so should sign a statement indicating that these regulations have been provided and verbally explained. Additionally, copies of residents' rights and responsibilities should be posted in an attempt to ensure that residents continue to know their rights.

2. *The right to know of services available within the facility and the related fees (especially when these services are not covered by the Title XIX program or the facility's per diem fee).* The interpretative guidelines indicate that professional services, supplies, and any recreational or personal-care services or items (e.g., laundry, cosmetics, beautician services, haircuts) are often available to residents. If they are not included in the per diem rate, this should be clearly indicated, with rates shown. This right implies that residents have been informed of available services, can physically use them, have free access to them, and have access to funds with which to use them. Unfortunately, many nursing homes have only vending machines available as a service exchanging money for goods, although some have a snack bar. But even here residents often do not know where the services are, and many of them are physically incapable of using them. Frequently, access to the services is limited implicitly—if not explicity—to staff and visitors. Many times, residents do not have access to money with which to use the services. Additionally, in cases where there may be minor dietary restrictions in effect for a resident, the patient may be warned against using the snack bar or even prevented from using it.

3. *The right to know one's own health and medical condition (unless medically contraindicated) and to be given an opportunity to participate*

in planning one's total care and treatment plan, in addition to the right to informed written consent before participating in experimental research. The resident's plan of care and treatment should be developed not solely by the physician or staff, but with the resident's participation. Residents must be fully informed of the conditions and available alternative courses of care and treatment, and their consequences Total resident care should include medical, nursing, nutritional, and rehabilitation and restorative therapies. In addition, written *informed consent* must be obtained from any resident being considered for participation in experimental research. Informed consent normally requires the following:

- a. a complete and honest explanation of the procedures to be followed
- b. a description of all attendant discomforts and risks
- c. a description of the expected benefits
- d. an offer to answer any questions the resident might have concerning the procedures (any questions should be completely and honestly answered)
- e. freedom to withdraw consent and stop participation at any time without having negative consequences imposed

4. *The right to the assurance that transfer or discharge is only for medical reasons, self-welfare, other's welfare, or nonpayment of charges with notice and documentation.* The HEW interpretative guidelines apply this protection to moves within an institution as well as outside it, in an attempt to provide a stable environment for the residents. Wilson (1978) notes that it is still unclear how much notice must be given before transferring a patient for nonpayment; she concludes that thirty days would be an appropriate amount of time. Unfortunately, the term "welfare" is vague and open to interpretation, but a nursing home should have documented and valid reasons before transferring a resident for the individual's or other residents' welfare.

5. *The right to be encouraged and assisted in exercising one's rights as a resident and citizen, and to accomplish this by having the right to voice grievances and recommend changes in policies and services to facility staff or to outside representatives, free from restraint, interference, coercion, discrimination, or reprisal.* The interpretative guidelines require the facility to inform residents of issues or pending decisions that affect them, and to solicit the resident's views prior to action. Interestingly enough, the guidelines further suggest that residents be involved in exercising their rights by having a resident council. This resident council—which is a form of self-government—would provide a forum for discussion of issues and serve as a method of communication between the resident body and the facility. Additionally, the guidelines require each facility to have a written policy for making and resolving grievances that ensures protection of residents from any form of reprisal or intimidation; written records should be kept of all grievances filed and actions taken. The facility should also provide residents with the names and addresses of local law enforcement personnel as another means of redress. The facility must assist residents in exercising their rights as citizens, including the rights to vote, marry, divorce, execute instruments, acquire and dispose of property, and worship as they desire.

6. *The right to manage one's personal financial affairs or be given at least a quarterly accounting of financial transactions made on the resident's behalf (should the facility accept the resident's written delegation of this responsibility to the facility for any period of time in conformance with state law).* The facility must additionally maintain records of residents' funds received by or deposited with the facility. If residents are able to manage their own financial affairs, it would be in their (and the facility's) best interest to do so.

7. *The right to be free from mental and physical abuse and chemical and physical restraints, except as authorized in writing by a physician for specified and limited periods of time, or when necessary to protect the patient from injury to oneself or others.* Each facility is required to have written policies and procedures governing the use of restraints, must specify which staff member may authorize the use of restraints, and clearly delineate the following:

   a. Orders indicate the specific reasons for the use of restraints;
   b. Their use is temporary and the resident will not be restrained for an indefinite amount of time;
   c. Orders for restraints shall not be enforced for longer than 12 hours, unless the resident's condition warrants;
   d. A resident placed in the restraint shall be checked at least every 30 minutes by appropriately trained staff and an account is kept of this surveillance;
   e. Reorders are issued *only* after a review of the resident's condition;
   f. Their use is not employed as punishment, for the convenience of the staff, or as a substitute for supervision;
   g. Mechanical restraints avoid physical injury to the resident and provide a minimum of discomfort;
   h. The opportunity for motion and exercise is provided for a period of not less than 10 minutes during each 2 hours in which restraints are employed, except at night; and
   i. The practice of locking residents in their rooms or using locked restraints also constitutes physical restraint and must be in conformance with the requirements contained in this standard. ["Interpretative Guidelines," (DHEW, 1978b)].

8. *The right to be assured confidential treatment of one's personal and medical records, and the right to approve or refuse their release to any individual outside the facility, except in the case of the transfer of a resident to another health care institution or as required by law or*

third-party payment contract. This guideline also applies to nursing staff. Nurse's stations are usually placed in strategic areas for rapid surveillance of patients and often are unattended. Care should be taken to ensure that a patient's medical records cannot be seen at one of these stations. Financial records and social service records are also protected under this right.

9. *The right to be treated with consideration, respect, and full recognition of one's dignity and individuality, including privacy in treatment and care of one's personal needs.* The guidelines emphasize that staff should "display respect for residents when speaking with, caring for, or talking about them as constant affirmation of their individuality and dignity as human beings." Additionally, in order for residents to retain their dignity, they should be allowed to exercise choice about what they will do in their daily living activities, and when, rather than be rigidly scheduled. The facility should elicit and respect resident's preferences about such things as menus, clothing, religious activities, friendships, activity programs, and entertainment.

One of the most important things a facility can do to help an elderly person maintain dignity is to respect the right to privacy when being treated or engaging in personal hygiene activities. Doors should be closed, curtains drawn, and only persons directly involved in the care of the resident present.

10. *The right not to be required to perform services for the facility that are not included for therapeutic purposes in one's plan of care.* As a protection against involuntary servitude (i.e., requiring the residents to involuntarily perform institutional maintenance–type behavior), the interpretative guidelines require that any services or labor done for the facility must be voluntary or therapeutic. If done strictly for therapeutic reasons, the activity must be "professionally developed and implemented," with clearly stated therapeutic goals that are measurable. A time-limit must be stated; a review is required at least quarterly. This prohibition should not be interpreted to mean that residents should not be allowed or encouraged to take care of their own personal daily activities—e.g., bathing, dressing, eating, making their own beds.

11. *The right to associate and communicate privately with persons of one's own choice, and send and receive personal mail unopened, unless medically contraindicated (as documented by one's physician in one's medical record).* The interpretative guidelines emphasize the need for residents to maintain contact with the community, and therefore visitors can be restricted by the facility only if

a. the resident refuses to see the visitor,
b. the resident's physician documents specific reasons why such a visit would be harmful to the resident's health, or

    c. the visitor's behavior is unreasonably disruptive of the functioning of the facility (this judgment must be made by the administrator and the reasons documented and kept on file).

There seem to be very few reasons for restricting the right to send or receive mail, or to hold telephone conversations. The interpretative guidelines require not only that telephones be available and accessible for private use but that the facility make it known that telephone communication is possible and assist those who need help in making phone calls. Additionally, assistance should be provided those who require help in reading and sending mail.

    12. *The right to meet with and participate in the activities of social, religious, and community groups at one's discretion, unless medically contraindicated (as documented by one's physician in one's medical record).* The interpretative guidelines require that facilities encourage and assist residents to engage in the desired activities both "in or outside of the facility." This, again, promotes the idea that nursing home residents should maintain their community ties. A resident always has the right to refuse to participate in any of these activities. Additionally, there are few medical reasons why one should not be allowed to engage in the activities of one's choice.

    13. *The right to retain and use one's personal clothing and possessions as space permits—unless to do so would infringe upon rights of other patients, and unless medically contraindicated (as documented by one's physician in one's medical record).* Wilson (1978) points out that the theft of residents' personal property is reported a prevalent problem throughout nursing homes. The interpretative guidelines address this issue by requiring each facility to provide secure storage and safe locations for personal property. Thus, a nursing home cannot relieve itself of total responsibility for resident's belongings.

    14. *A resident's right, if married, to be assured privacy for visits by one's spouse; if both are inpatients in the facility, they are permitted to share a room, unless medically contraindicated (as documented by the attending physician in the medical record).* Companionship is extremely critical for all persons, but especially the elderly. Visits from others should be encouraged, and the right to have private visits from members of either sex should be applicable for single, as well as married, persons.

    In cases where the resident (1) has been legally adjudged incompetent, (2) is found to be medically incapable of understanding these rights, or (3) exhibits a communication barrier, the first four rights listed above devolve to the resident's guardian, next of kin, sponsoring agency, or representative payer. The other rights remain with all residents independent of their mental state, subject to the specified qualifications.

ENFORCEMENT OF RESIDENTS' RIGHTS

Placement in a nursing home is obviously a change in lifestyle for almost any person. It need not, however, be a drastic change or a degrading, humiliating experience. Still, for many individuals, placement in a nursing home unfortunately signals "the end"; they are no longer capable of living independently or taking total responsibility for themselves. Although residents may need some type of help or care, many can live as productive and creative citizens with a bright outlook for the future. The rights enumerated above are required to ensure that each resident's stay in a nursing home not only be pleasant but also conducive to maintaining a self-sufficient and dignified style of life. It is critical that nursing homes actually provide residents with these rights; thus it is necessary to consider methods of ensuring that they are actually provided.

Wilson (1978) outlines different levels at which nursing home residents' rights can be enforced. The most obvious is the federal government's administrative enforcement system. The federal regional offices of Health Standards and Quality in the Health Care Financing Administration of HEW have ultimate responsibility for the enforcement of these rights. Federal surveyors, however, examine only approximately 3 percent of the nursing homes each year. Because the federal agency can monitor so few facilities each year, every state (usually the Health Department within the state) has been delegated the responsibility of providing more frequent checks and inspections and given the right to provide certification. Additionally, individual residents or consumer groups can make formal complaints about any denial of residents' rights. Regional HEW offices or the responsible state agency will investigate and verify complaints.

Unfortunately, many problems arise when the federal government attempts to actually ensure that rights are provided in the appropriate manner. When inspectors or surveyors visit a facility, they can look at records and determine if they are being kept correctly. Thus, they can easily determine if the facility has a written document outlining the residents' rights and responsibilities (DHEW, 1978a, [1]) or makes a quarterly accounting of financial transactions made on behalf of a resident (6). It is more difficult, however, to ensure that residents have been allowed to send mail (11), allowed to interact with community groups (12), or treated with dignity and respect (9). These types of rights, like others, do not produce "tangible" evidence that can be examined, and are therefore harder for the agency to enforce (Wilson, 1978).

Another problem involves the "complaint system," which allows an elderly resident or advocate to complain to HEW about any deprivation of rights. Unfortunately, few complaints are received. This may be because few people know about this mechanism, or that residents are not allowed to freely communicate with others. As Wilson (1978) suggests, residents should be informed that they may file complaints and instructed in how to do so, along with the description of their rights.

Finally, the federal administrative enforcement system is often weak due to inappropriate disciplinary tools (Wilson, 1978). If violations of residents' rights are found, the government can de-certify the facility. This is the only available penalty; since it is so severe, enforcement officials are reluctant to use it. Less severe consequences are needed in order that violations can be recognized and penalties implemented without the closing of the facility. One method suggested by Wilson (1978) is to issue citations and impose monetary fines (these fines could accrue to the residents). Additionally, a system could be developed to reduce the amount of Medicare or Medicaid that a facility could receive, according to the number of violations found. If these monies were to be reduced as a result of residents' rights violations, the facility would not be allowed to charge the residents personally in order to make up this deficit. In such situations the total amount of federal money could be reinstated when rights are provided. If a facility is found to have several violations of resident's rights, it should be closed.

In addition to enforcement through administrative channels, there could potentially be enforcement through private litigation. Obviously, if a resident is abused or denied the right to informed consent, a tort action may be brought. Likewise, a resident could sue under state law if the facility has not properly accounted for a resident's financial transactions. It is not clear, however, whether a private cause of action accrues to a resident "based on the federal patient's rights regulations *per se*" (Wilson, 1978, p. 260). Two recent cases cited by Wilson (*Stella Fuzie* v. *Manor Care, Inc.* [1977] and *Hazel Berry* v. *First Healthcare Corporation et al.* [1977]) indicate that courts are recognizing and enforcing the residents' bill of rights under private causes of action. Unfortunately, many elderly persons might be prevented from bringing a private cause of action because they lack the physical energy or ability to pursue a law-suit, are isolated from the community and legal counsel, or lack financial resources enabling them to hire an attorney (Wilson, 1978). The family, community advocates, or nursing home volunteers can assist in this endeavor by providing the emotional and financial encouragement and support for these elderly residents who have been denied rights. With close contact, advocates, volunteers, or family members can ensure that residents' rights are provided. They can contact the appropriate governmental agencies or attorneys (e.g., legal aid) when these rights are denied (see Kahana, 1973).

Most states have legislation requiring nursing homes to comply with rules and regulations that address the health, safety, nutrition, and sanitation of the nursing home residents (e.g., Kansas Statutes Annotated, 1978). If on inspection the home is found not to be in compliance with any of the rules or regulations, a correction order may be served on the license holder (administrator or owner). If deficiencies are not corrected, a citation is issued and may be publicly published. Civil penalties may be assessed—often as much as one hundred dollars per day—for noncompliance. If the home continues with its deficiencies, it can be closed.

Restoring Nursing Home Residents' Rights and Developing Alternatives to Nursing Home Care

Nursing home residents have a right to a quality of life that is pleasant, humane, legal, and ethical, as outlined in the above section. Additionally, nursing home residents should have a *right to habilitation,* which is a right to recover any skills that they may once have had in their repertoire but which, for one reason or another, they no longer exhibit but are capable of performing. Nursing home residents' rights can be restored in a variety of ways. One might think that the most obvious method is developing a monitoring system to ensure that the *quality of life* rights enumerated above are actually provided. That, however, connotes an adversarial system—a type of system that need not exist unless there is a blatant and intentional abuse of these rights. The *right to habilitation* is often denied, however, due to the good intentions of nursing home staff who seek to overprotect and "over-care" for residents, a lack of staff time to appropriately deliver services, or a lack of knowledge about efficient and effective organization and management systems. This section will describe how the *right to habilitation* can be denied through the benign efforts of staff in addition to outlining how systems can be developed to restore this right. Finally, alternatives to nursing home placement will be discussed.

THE INSTITUTIONALIZATION SYNDROME

Unlike many who are institutionalized (e.g., the autistic or mentally retarded), nearly all elderly nursing home occupants once exhibited the skills of most people who are capable of living independently and engaging in the autonomous activities of daily living. After living in an institution for a brief period of time, however, many residents no longer engage in self-sufficient behaviors, but begin behaving in ways characteristic of those who have lived in the institution over a longer interval (i.e., they become apathetic and refuse to properly care for themselves).

After behaving in these ways for a long period of time, it becomes difficult to behave in ways similar to the autonomous ones engaged in prior to coming to the nursing home.

One major problem that plagues nursing homes is that staff and volunteers often do too much for the residents. The staff, realizing that the elderly people will never become any younger, want to do as much as they can to make the elderly residents comfortable and happy; they thus do everything for them. Another factor is that it is often much faster for the staff to perform daily living tasks for the residents rather than allowing the residents to do it themselves. Miller provides some good examples of this type of situation:

> the use of a wheelchair to speed a resident to the dining room when the resident is ambulatory, albeit very slow; the feeding of a resident who could feed [himself or herself], but who is sloppy and very slow; the laying out of specific clothing for a resident who could and should decide . . . which items to wear; the cleaning of shelves, window-sill, etc., in the bedrooms of residents who could and perhaps should be encouraged to participate in straightening up their own living space. [1977, p. 32]

As more help is provided by staff, residents begin accepting progressively more help. The resident may eventually be viewed as "helpless," and much former self-care is provided by others. Once a great deal of help is "needed," a role in decision making about self-care is removed. This type of thinking escalates; as residents are more and more frequently viewed as helpless they are allowed to make progressively fewer decisions. Finally, the residents may not be trusted to be alone, and all but a small amount of privacy is lost.

It is therefore easy to see how the conditions of institutionalization can contribute to the dependent and "incompetent" status of nursing home residents. Improperly given assistance may produce further deterioration in self-help behavior, making the resident increasingly passive and dependent on the staff. Residents, for example, who self-feed but have poor manners are often served meals in their rooms. The staff's concern for maintaining pleasant dining conditions for other residents has the effect of removing the unpleasant diner from the "mainstream." And long periods of social isolation and withdrawal from participation with others appears to decrease the likelihood of social interaction or participation in the future. The whole process is often talked about as being "no one's fault"; it is just easier to "institutionalize" than to rehabilitate residents.

It should be emphasized that a nursing home resident should *never* be denied a pleasant, humane, or legally appropriate environment. Nor should any resident who is unable to care for himself or herself ever be denied the appropriate help. There are many good reasons, however, for encouraging self-care and permitting choices, thus contributing to the rehabilitation of patients. Therapeutic settings that promote self-care provide a more pleasant environment for patients and staff both. Many residents begin to interact more with one another socially, smile more, and appear healthier; they may even live longer. In these ways, residents can make the work of the staff easier by making the work environment more pleasant. Residents may begin to ask questions, suggest some startegies for therapy, and even assume more of their own care by participating in the activities of daily living. There is less care required from staff, and thus staff's load is lightened. The elderly persons are then legitimately called "residents" rather than "patients," and are more independent than dependent.

MISDIAGNOSING "SENILITY"

"Senility" is often defined by nursing home caretakers and administrators as the observed presence of (1) confusion, (2) incontinence, (3) inactivity, and (4) nonambulation. Often, however, these behaviors can be produced by environmental events rather than by the person's becoming senile. For example, confusion can be produced by drugs, food or water deprivation, or inactivity. Incontinence may be produced by dehydration, miscuing, or pain. Inactivity and nonambulation may occur when it becomes physically painful to move or embarrassing to be seen stumbling. Inactivity and nonambulation may be demonstrated by a resident also because everything is located within reach or there is nowhere to go. Additionally, movement may stop when it is seen as having no effect on the environment (e.g., wheeling to the administrator's office to request a telephone line and being ignored).

Residents in nursing homes have the right to educational assistance with the purpose of eliminating senility-like behaviors and restoring the former skills of bowel and bladder functioning, ambulation into alternative settings, and engagement with richer parts of the environment. Residents labeled as "senile" can be assisted at intervals timed to provide access to toilet facilities just prior to bowel and bladder functioning. This may be just before and after meals, with two-hour intervals between meals. While toileting assistance is being provided, the residents can be offered juice or water. Liquids are usually accepted if offered frequently enough. Given added opportunities to consume liquids, dehydration is less likely to occur. Ambulation training can be provided "incidentally" by assisting residents to the toilet and permitting them to self-help to the fullest of their ability. Thus, opportunities for guided assistance and reinforcement for ambulation can be provided. Being provided with opportunities to participate in recreational as well as daily living activities increases the resident's engagement with the environment. Since a lack of engagement is closely associated with debilitation, such opportunities should reduce the likelihood of confusion and inactivity.

In a study that demonstrated the effectiveness of changing staff behavior in order to eliminate "senile" types of behavior in residents, sixteen geriatric patients were examined in a 100-bed skilled-care facility; initial measures of dehydration showed that nearly half were dehydrated (Spangler, Edwards, & Risley, 1977). Most had "accidents" during each shift, and the majority were not engaged with the environment much of the time. Assistants were trained to systematically visit each resident's room with a cart equipped with at least two kinds of fruit juice and with diapers, linens, and a variety of recreational material. In less than two weeks of the systematic use of the cart, urinometer readings indicated lower dehydration; when liquids were offered from the cart, no residents were defined as "dehydrated." Incidents of soiling for thirteen of the sixteen residents were reduced; soiling incidents, recorded at the end of the shift when residents were assisted in use of the toilet, were halved. Finally, engagement with the environment was increased for all patients; an average increase of about 12 percent in frequency of engagement was recorded when recreational equipment was offered from the cart. Apparently many residents in nursing homes have "accidents" because they are not asked if they need to use the toilet; are dehydrated because they are not offered fluids; and are inactive because they are left with no materials to engage them.

In this study a more complete unit of basic care or assistance and checklists for subroutines such as stocking the cart, interacting with patients, use of the commode or bedpan, hand-washing, bedsore prevention and positioning the patient in bed, bed-making, changing and cleaning patients when accidents occur, taking acetest and clinitest measures, and catheter care were later added to basic procedures. Preliminary data indicated that with full use of the checklist, approximately twelve geriatric patients having varying infirmities could be provided with a wide range of care (from little to complete) by an aide and encouraged to self-care in intervals of less than two hours. Training in this pilot work involved two two-hour sessions consisting simply of the basic checklist being read to the aide as the aide progressed through the steps.

Final evaluation of these procedures will require training by feedback as the aide progresses through each step, until all steps are performed without error. Maintenance will be examined and ensured by brief but frequent evaluations at approximately two-week intervals. Retraining will be provided any time the aide shows less than criterion performance.

An administrator is obligated to generate training, supervision, and monitoring systems that will assist this class of nursing home residents to obtain self-care and self-help skills in toilet use, fluid intake, ambulation, and environmental engagement. The administrator also seems obliged to ensure that behavior is not reduced to dependency levels by training and supervising staff, and to monitor the system. Included in the system must be assurance that residents' skills will be graduated to the next highest level at opportune moments.

THE DEVELOPMENT OF ORGANIZATION AND MANAGEMENT SYSTEMS FOR NURSING HOMES

The rights of nursing home residents can be restored by developing organization and management systems that are effective, efficient, and humane (Risley & Edwards, 1978). Geriatric aides can be trained by competent training aides and monitored internally by the nursing staff members who act as supervisors and the whole system monitored externally by an agent of the administrator (consultant). Improving the efficiency of care routines, increasing their effectiveness, and increasing humaneness requires at least three phases.

First current operations of nursing homes must be observed. One nursing home could be selected to serve as a model and training site for all other nursing homes in the state or catchment area. Once selected as a model-training site, the nursing home's organization and management systems must be rearranged in such a manner that efficient and effective, yet humane, procedures focused on restoring self-care and self-help skills are clearly observable and measurable. There must be some clear supervisory systems and monitoring programs established. In addition, a quality-assurance system must ensure that patient outcomes are clearly positive. At this point, the nursing home can be used to define scales for Medicaid payment to other nursing homes contingent upon attaining a specified service delivery level. Medicaid payments can also be considered on the basis of restoration of self-care and self-help skills and the use of alternatives to nursing homes. The more capable the resident, the less direct care and the more relative monetary payoff there is to the facility.

Once the model-training facility is established, community citizens can be trained in the facility to care for their relatives in their own homes, nursing home aides can be trained to monitor the care given as "home health care" workers, and licensed nurses can be trained to perform as "visiting nurses" providing occasional nursing treatment and supervising the home health care services. The persons designated as external monitors can ensure that the routines as trained are maintained and that there is a continual assurance of quality.

Patients can then be brought to the nursing home during the day to participate in self-care and self-help rehabilitation programs and be taken home at night. Total "care" would entail about three to four hours per day as opposed to twenty-four-hours per day in the nursing home or sixteen hours per day at home. Residents requiring twenty-four-hours per day care in the nursing home can be taken out of the home during the day on activities-oriented programs designed to restore self-care and self-help skills. Thus, the nursing home would care for four classes of "patients": those requiring twenty-four-hour per day care and treatment, those requiring only day-care, those requiring night care and rehabilitative day activities, and those requiring home care accompanied by rehabilitation programs.

For patients in the home, prosthetic equipment can be "loaned" until no longer needed. Thus, a stock of prosthetic equipment (including handrails and wheelchairs) can be maintained and recycled at little replacement cost to the nursing home.

The first phase described above will be the most expensive, because it requires the establishment of a training site and the development of training programs and personnel. The second phase can begin repaying costs, because training is now directed toward the people whose lack of skills require nursing home services, and care for them can now take place in the home. The third phase should be the least expensive. Compared with the past, it should "provide" revenues; the physical plants have been established, the training and model site now provides the needed criteria levels, and the prosthetic equipment base has been established.

Two key concepts in developing a good nursing home model are *efficiency* and *effectiveness*. Efficiency reduces cost by promoting less movement in time—getting jobs done faster. Examples of this from some past work are (1) using a weighing system to take inventory on towels, linens, diapers, and so on was found to be much faster and even more accurate than counting, and (2) the use of a cart system, which aides used routinely to ask nonambulatory residents if they needed assistance to the toilet, to offer fluids, and to leave the patients with some recreational equipment. This routine reduced diaper usage, cutting costs considerably; ensured that patients were no longer dehydrated, in all probability extending their lives; and meant that residents were more active, making the environment more pleasant for staff as well as patients and relatives.

Effectiveness, however, may cost more because it may take more time. There are often ways, however, to reduce the time increase by becoming more efficient. For example, in a pilot study residents were assisted with meals by an aide trained with systematic procedures and an aide trained in the usual manner. It was found that the systematically trained aide required about 50 percent more time, but within a short time (three days) the residents were doing most of their own feeding, requiring little assistance, and other residents and relatives of residents were in agreement that the trained aide was more competent and more humane. With refinements, the trained aide could conceivably work with two patients at one time. This would require less time than before with two separate patients, thus being more efficient. An additional bonus is that eventually spoonfeeding would no longer be required with many patients. They could then be "graduated" to the dining room, where additional programs designed to maintain and train in self-care and self-help skills would continue.

THE DEVELOPMENT OF COMMUNITY ALTERNATIVES TO NURSING HOME CARE

Although much can be done to improve the type of care residents receive within nursing homes, thereby restoring many residents' rights, an elderly person has the right to live independently in the community if at all possible. The following section briefly outlines some programs that can be developed in and by the community to allow elderly people to live as independent and self-sufficient individuals.[1]

High-rise Apartments. The federal government provides for subsidized housing for the elderly under a Section 8 plan (U.S. Department of Housing and Urban Development). There has been an upper limit of $8,100 on the amount of income a person over age sixty-two can have and still be allowed to live in this type of housing. Occupants pay not more than 25 percent of their adjusted income; the federal government pays the remaining amount.

Many communities have utilized Section 8 funds to build high-rise apartment buildings for the elderly, and have found that there are economic as well as humane, reasons for doing so. Economically speaking, the government's contribution to the rent of an elderly person living in a "high-rise" is often much less than it would be to keep this same person in a nursing home. More important, perhaps, the elderly person living in a Section 8 high-rise maintains much independence and retains dignity. Since a portion of each individual's income goes to pay the rent, residents do not feel that they are totally "living off society." Addi-

[1] Many of the ideas for this section were obtained from a personal conversation with Mr. James E. Sheldon. Those interested in obtaining further information about these topics may contact Mr. Sheldon by writing to him at the following address: Community Coordinating Council of Independence, Inc., 700 North Fifth, Independence, Kansas 67301, or calling (316) 331-2764.

tionally, although residents live in separate apartments within the high-rise, they frequently interact by talking in the lounge, sharing meals, and participating together in craft and exercise classes, rummage and craft sales, games and tournaments, and potluck dinners. Companionship often increases, as does food intake, with many residents commenting that they feel "reborn."

It is hypothesized that one of the critical elements in making this type of program succeed is the employment of a couple that essentially manages the complex. Couples should take an active interest in residents' lives and should encourage and assist them in engaging in many activities. What may be needed in the future is the development of short training courses or workshops that can instruct couples in the skills needed to successfully operate such a high-rise program for the elderly. More important than good managerial skills are those interpersonal skills that indicate that the couple is sincerely interested in the well-being and happiness of the residents.

Congregate Eating Programs.   The Congregate Eating Program is a federally subsidized program operating under the Older Americans Act. This program provides five nutritious meals a week for persons over age sixty-two; they are required to pay either a nominal fee or nothing, according to their income. Normally, the government contracts with either a commercial food-service facility, a hospital, or a school, which then prepares and serves the meals. This program addresses itself to the nutritional needs of the elderly, who often when living alone find it difficult to prepare meals for themselves. Additionally, it provides elderly persons with the incentive to get out into the community and socially interact with others, thus providing companionship for those who might otherwise be lonely. For those individuals who are physically unable to leave their homes, the Meals-on-Wheels Program can provide the much-needed nutritional sustenance.

Taxi Service Program.   Another innovative program that has proved quite successful in smaller communities is the Taxi Service Program for the elderly, which can be federally subsidized with revenue-sharing money. In communities where there is no public transportation service available, the elderly are often handicapped because they cannot afford to take a taxi and are unable to drive themselves. They therefore remain at home, isolated from the community, or have to rely on others, which can become a degrading situation. In the subsidized taxi program, a city enters into an agreement with local taxi services whereby the elderly pay a nominal fee to use the taxi and the city pays the difference with federal money. This is often done by giving the elderly people coupons which they present to the taxi driver each time they use the taxi. The elderly person pays a small additional amount (e.g., forty cents), and then rides anywhere in the city. At the end of the month, the taxi company turns the coupons in to the city for reimbursement. This provides not only more business for the taxi companies but a great amount of independence for the elderly. Additionally, elderly individuals can maintain their dignity, since they no longer have to rely on, or ask favors from, others.

Senior Citizen Centers. Many communities have developed senior citizen centers where elderly persons can meet to play games, have covered-dish dinners, or merely interact with one another. The elderly in some communities have additionally developed social clubs (e.g., the Over 60 Club), which sometimes meet weekly in those centers. This provides a recreational service, in addition to allowing the elderly to get out into the community and interact socially.

The programs described above can be developed in any community; they need not be expensive for the community, because they utilize federal funds specially earmarked for the elderly. Often these programs and living arrangements can mean the difference between a person who remains active and alert and one who eventually becomes an invalid. Most important, these programs allow elderly individuals to live independently in the community and maintain their dignity and self-respect, which are necessary basic rights for all individuals.

Conclusion

Concern for the rights of all Americans is of great importance at the present time and is increasing rapidly. The issue of the rights of mental patients has attracted more attention than any other area of the law (Ennis & Emery, 1978), and the rights of hospital patients have been included in books sponsored by the American Civil Liberties Union (ACLU) (Annas, 1975). Most recently, a working paper dealing with protective services for the elderly was published by the U.S. Senate's Special Committee on Aging, the first volume addressing the rights of the elderly (Regan & Springer, 1977). Other authors have provided cogent discussions of the elderly in general (e.g., Butler, 1975). Fortunately, a complete volume addressing the rights of older persons has recently been published (Brown, 1979).

The elderly, especially those who reside in nursing homes, have specific rights that have often been illegally or unjustly removed from them. Although they are a "captive audience," they are not equivalent to prisoners in penal institutions nor are they members of an untrained population. These people have in nearly all instances once had the recognition of rights that the more "able-bodied" currently have. Removal of legal recognition of their rights simply makes them more vulnerable and their caregivers better protected from charges of inhumane acts.

The trends are toward more clearly defined rights for all populations, including geriatric patients. As the rights of other populations become more clearly delineated, nursing-home policy makers can better promote and provide policies, anticipating change based on legislation in other settings. If they do not, then expensive litigation will follow that can only be reflected back to the nursing home residents in terms of cost.

Service providers in nursing homes therefore have an obligation to provide appropriate, humane care and treatment for elderly residents. In order to adequately provide these rights, the following must be done: (1) provision of the nursing home with appropriate staff and equipment, (2) provision of training of staff to perform the services and maintain the equipment so that rights can actually be provided, and (3) maintenance of staff at a level such that outcomes are visible and rights fulfilled. Briefly stated, the setting, processes, and products that guarantee the fulfillment of rights for the elderly are essential.

Since we are dealing with human beings in dependent settings, it is the responsibility of individuals outside the nursing home system to ensure that residents retain their rights. Not only should geriatric aides as caregivers be accountable for their patients, nurses as supervisors accountable for their caregivers, and administrators (or consultants) accountable for their supervisors, but residents, relatives, and friends should serve as members of advocacy groups for assurance of quality of care and quality of life.

For maintenance of the quality of care (humaneness) it is imperative that consumers (residents and their relatives) continue to routinely evaluate the care given and that social validation for the programs is provided by residents' relatives and advocacy groups providing input through routine care reviews. Thus, provision of the care as viewed by the consumer provides for input from nonprofessionals who have interests other than research or cost. Although cost and research are certainly important, we cannot neglect the patients' care as viewed by them and their relatives; this ensures the longevity of programs that are less expensive and requires research into socially acceptable methods for reducing costs further. Additionally, supervisors (licensed nurses) need supervisory training, training personnel need to know how to train, and external monitors need to be positioned to prevent the system from drifting from patient concerns.

The rights of the elderly must be restored. Growing old in America should not be thought of as a time when all is lost, including one's dignity, self-respect, and happiness. Rather, the elderly should be treated with respect and provided with enough support to encourage independence. In summary, the following must be done: (1) Provide adequate staff training, appropriate supervisory training, mechanisms for monitoring training and supervision, and mechanisms for consumer evaluations, (2) continually record and frequently evaluate processes and outcomes, (3) generate self-government and self-improvement programs, (4) provide residents with an advocacy system consisting of relatives, friends, and themselves, and (5) develop community alternatives that encourage independent living.

References

ANNAS, G. J. *The rights of hospital patients.* New York: Avon Books, 1975.

Bartley v. *Kremens,* 402 F. Supp. 1039 (E.D. Pa. 1975).

BLEE, B., & SHELDON-WILDGEN, J. *Legal rights: A Kansas guide to developmental disabilities law.* Kansas City, Kans.: University of Kansas Medical Center Printing Service, 1979.

Brewster v. *Dukakis,* CA No. 76-4423-F (E.D. Mass. Dec. 6, 1978).

BROWN, R. N. *The rights of older persons.* New York: Avon, 1979.

BUND, E. Legal aspects of nursing home practice. In M. Mitchel (Ed.), *A practical guide to long term care and health services administration.* Greenvale, N.Y.: Panel Publishers, 1978, pp. 94–118.

BUTLER, R. N. *Why survive? Being old in America.* New York: Harper & Row, 1975.

Clonce v. *Richardson,* 379 F. Supp. 338 (W.D. Mo. 1974).

Department of Health, Education and Welfare. 42 Code of Federal Regulations §§ 405.1121(k): (1), (6), (9), (11), and (12) (1978a).

DHEW. 42 Code of Federal Regulations § 442.311 (1978b).

Developmentally Disabled Assistance and Bill of Rights Act, 42 United States Code § 6010 (Supp. 1975).

Donaldson v. *O'Connor,* 493 F.2d 507 (5th Cir. 1974); *aff'd,* 422 U.S. 563 (1975).

ENNIS, B. J., & EMERY, R. D. *The rights of mental patients.* New York: Avon, 1978.

Hazel Berry v. *First Healthcare Corporation et al.,* Civil No. 77-208 (D.C.N.H. 1977).

KAHANA, E. The humane treatment of old people in institutions. *The Gerontologist,* 1973, *13,* 282–289.

Kansas Statutes Annotated §§ 39–923 *et seq.* (Supp. 1978).

Kansas Statutes Annotated §§ 59-2901 *et seq.* (1976a).

Kansas Statutes Annotated §§ 59-2929 (1976b).

Lessard v. *Schmidt,* 349 F. Supp. 1078 (E.D. Wis. 1972); *vacated for entry of definitive decree,* 414 U.S. 473 (1974); *clarified,* 379 F. Supp. 1376 (E.D. Wis. 1974); *vacated on procedural grounds,* 421 U.S. 957 (1975).

Lynch v. *Baxley,* 386 F. Supp. (M.D. Ala. 1974).

MILLER, J. L. Obstacles to the realization of patient's rights. *Concern,* 1977, *4*(1), 28–34.

Morales v. *Turman,* 364 F. Supp. 166 (E.D. Tex. 1973).

New York State Association for Retarded Children, Inc. v. *Rockefeller,* 357 F. Supp. 752 (E.D. N.Y. 1973).

PORZIO, R. The aged and the law. *Vascular Surgery,* 1976, *27* (7), 222–230.

REGAN, J. J. Intervention through adult protective services programs. *The Gerontologist,* 1978, *18*, 250–254.

REGAN, J. J., & SPRINGER, G. *Protective services for the elderly.* Special Comm. on Aging, U.S. Senate, 95th Congress, 1st Session. Washington, D.C.: Government Printing Office, 1977.

RISLEY, T. R., & EDWARDS, K. A. Behavioral technology for nursing home care: Toward a system of nursing home organization and management. Paper presented at the Nova Behavioral Conference, Port St. Lucie, Florida, May 1978.

Rouse v. *Cameron,* 373 F.2d 451 (D.D. Cir. 1966).

SPANGLER, EDWARDS, K. A., & RISLEY, T. R. Behavioral care of non-ambulatory geriatric patients. Paper presented at the meeting of the Association for Advancement of Behavior Therapy, Atlanta, Georgia, May 1977.

Stella Fuzie v. *Manor Care, Inc.,* Civil No. C 77-265 (N.D. Ohio 1977).

WILSON, S. H. Nursing home patient's rights: Are they enforceable? *The Gerontologist,* 1978, *18*, 225–261.

Wuori v. *Zitnay,* No. 75–80-SD (D. Maine, July 14, 1978).

Wyatt v. *Stickney,* 325 F. Supp. 781; *aff'd on rehearing,* 334 F. Supp. 1341 (M.D. Ala. 1971); *aff'd on rehearing,* 344 F. Supp. 373; *aff'd in separate decision,* 344 F. Supp. 387 (M.D. Ala. 1972); *aff'd sub nom, Wyatt* v. *Aderholt,* 503 F.2d 1305 (5th Cir. 1974).

CHAPTER 17

A Quality-Assurance System for Ensuring Client Rights in Mental Retardation Facilities

James E. Favell
Judith E. Favell
Todd R. Risley

THE INFAMOUS NEGLECT and mistreatment of mentally retarded institutional residents have been well publicized (e.g., Blatt and Kaplan, 1966) and prosecuted (e.g., *N.Y.A.R.C.* v. *Rockefeller*, 1973) in recent years. Numerous cases of litigation (e.g., *Wyatt* v. *Stickney*, 1972; *Welsh* v. *Likens*, 1974) have called public attention to widespread and sometimes grotesque inadequacies in the health care, education, treatment, and living conditions that were presumed to be provided by public mental retardation facilities. Public facilities serving the retarded have been accused—and in some cases found guilty—of not only failing to provide adequate treatment (e.g., *Wyatt* v. *Stickney*, 1972) and education (e.g., *M.A.R.C.* v. *Maryland*, 1974), but also of violating the basic constitutional rights (e.g., the Eighth Amendment "Protection from Harm" cited *N.Y.A.R.C.* v. *Rockefeller*, 1973) of those they purport to serve.

This chapter will describe some of the major factors involved in institutional violations of rights, some of the more common and widespread attempts at protecting residents' rights, and, finally, some not-so-common approaches we have implemented over the past five years in two public residential facilities.

Some Problems

VIOLATION OF RIGHTS

A full discussion of the nature and extent of institutional threats to residents' rights is not possible or appropriate here. Many factors that contribute to rights violations are either intrinsic to the situation (e.g., residents' physical vulnerability) or involve external factors largely outside the control of the institution's own managers (e.g., capricious funding). Here we will concentrate on factors that we believe are subject to substantial control by procedures and systems that can be implemented by an institution's own management to improve both the treatment and protection of these institutionalized clients.

Partly because residents tend to be relatively unattractive and either socially unresponsive or—sometimes—physically violent, and because progress in habilitation tends to be very slow, there is little intrinsic reinforcement for staff interactions with residents. As a result, caregivers spend most of their time engaged in nonresident related activities—bed-making, floor-mopping, record-keeping, conversations with each other, and so on (Bensberg, 1974).

Even when staff are engaged in job-related activities, relatively little of their time is spent with residents, and even when they do interact with residents the interactions are usually nonsocial (e.g., Blindert, 1975; Harmatz, 1973). As a result, the developmental gains that might be produced by the relatively higher rates of social interaction that would occur in a "normal" social environment do not occur for the retarded in institutions. Moreover, residents' environments often are not only deficient in the number and quality of social interactions that might directly *produce* some amount of behavioral development, but are also lacking in the quantity and quality of interactions necessary to *maintain* gains that might have been produced outside the living environment (e.g., in school). Thus gains made through special remedial efforts are transitory, because the residents' overall environment fails to support the maintenance of such improvements. After remedial efforts are discontinued or shifted to a different topic, previous gains disappear, resulting in spurts of development across different areas but an overall stagnant level of development, because the individual developmental gains are not cumulative. Supporting this point, Keith and Lange (1974) found that over 40 percent of the behaviors acquired by residents in one institution-wide program were lost within three to twenty-six months following their acquisition.

Even basic care (e.g., bathing, feeding, etc.) is often inconsistent and rushed to the point of being unpleasant or even dangerous. Not only does this rush endanger residents (a substantial portion of institutional deaths are caused by aspirating food) and deprive them of some of the few institutional opportunities for sensual gratification, it also deprives them of important natural opportunities for learning and maintaining self-help skills (Hart & Risley, 1975). Even opportunities for self-entertainment are limited, with much of the residents' time spent in barren rooms without toys or other entertainment materials. When staff do respond to residents, it is frequently with a negative response ("Stop that." "Sit down and be quiet." etc.), with most of the residents' appropriate behavior—or approximations of appropriate behavior—going unnoticed or—sometimes—punished. Even the common courtesies shown normal infants, such as talking to them about what is happening is ignored. The implicit assumption seems to be "Oh, he wouldn't understand if I told him, so why bother?" As a result, the opportunities for residents to learn word associations are minimal, and the assumption becomes a self-fulfilling prophecy.

In addition to numerous forms of neglect there are varying forms of active abuse, ranging from relatively mild verbal abuse—such as derogatory or profane language directed at a resident—to physical injury from mechanical restraints, beatings, etc. Although such abuse sometimes has darker motives, it is frequently a well-intentioned but naive attempt to deal with serious behavior problems.

CONTRIBUTING FACTORS TO NEGLECT AND ABUSE OF RESIDENTS

There are numerous characteristics of caregivers, supervisors, managers, and "the system" that contribute to the neglect and abuse of residents.

Policies and procedures are frequently unwritten and established, maintained, and modified through word-of-mouth and rumor mechanisms rather than formal, written, officially sanctioned communications.

Staff turnover is frequently high, and new staff usually require considerable on-the-job training before being able to perform the job satisfactorily. This means that a significant number of the caregivers are either performing duties they have not yet been trained to do or are in classroom training, where they provide no service at all. In-service training is often slow and inefficient, relying on didactic classroom teaching rather than "hands-on" practical instruction. Staff are taken away from their duties for in-service training on a schedule that is convenient for instructors but independent of, and sometimes in conflict with, the schedule of peak demands for resident care. Also, graduation from a training class frequently is based on the number of hours a caregiver has attended class rather than on competency-based examinations. Didactic training frequently focuses on theory and philosophy, with too little attention given to practical information. Thus new caregivers arrive in a cottage, fresh from classroom training, only to be "retrained" by veteran caregivers in "how things really work," which often includes a strong "non-work ethic" with ongoing peer pressure not to be an "over-achiever."

Departmental empires enforce rigid job descriptions for different paraprofessional "specialists," making cooperation between staff difficult and creating inefficiency as one class of staff sits waiting for another to rush through work with the residents so that they can begin work while the others in turn relax.

First-line supervisors typically have numerous jobs—timekeeping, dispensing medicines, bookkeeping, etc.—that take them away from the employees they are supposed to supervise. They have frequently been selected for supervisory work based on good previous performance as caregivers. But the skills needed to be a good supervisor are quite different from those (as caregiver) on which their promotion was based. Usually there is minimal formal training, if any, in how to be a supervisor. Without such training—and because most are under the social influence of the caregivers from whose ranks they came—many supervisors find it easier to do the staff's work themselves rather than get staff to do it.

Feedback to caregivers from supervisors and administrators, when it occurs, is often based on the more immediately visble performance products, such as ward cleanliness and tidiness, than the more subtle dimension of residents' developmental gains. Feedback on staff performance typically occurs in time of crisis—accidents to residents, complaints from relatives, low ratings from inspectors, etc. Thus, feedback is typically infrequent, negative, and unrelated to the quantity and quality of staff interactions with residents.

Some Popular Solutions

LITIGATION

Over the past several years, a variety of class action suits have been filed on behalf of institutional residents being denied their rights to treatment, education, protection from harm, and so on. Rulings have generally favored the plaintiffs, and the publicity of these cases has no doubt increased the general awareness of residents' rights. Some decrees have specified standards in areas where there previously were none (e.g., staffing ratios in *Wyatt* v. *Stickney,* 1972), and such standards have been used by managers in evaluating their own facility's services and in supporting requests for additional resources. But legal remedies are painfully slow and expensive: The 1972 *Wyatt* v. *Stickney* case has been appealed and upheld, but seven years after the initial ruling monitors of the institutions involved still report serious abridgments of rights. Moreover, although such cases specify the rights to be protected, provide motivation for protection (by specifying aversive consequences for future violations), and to some extent specify the resources necessary for protection, they do not provide the defendants with a technology for effectively managing the resources to accomplish the goals.

LICENSING AND ACCREDITATION

Medicaid is a major source of funds for operating institutions. This legislation (Title XIX of the Social Security Act) specifies standards for protecting client rights, procedures for monitoring compliance with the standards, and, to a limited extent, the resources needed. It also provides motivation by making large amounts of federal money contingent on compliance.

But there are two serious problems with these monitoring procedures: First, monitoring is frequently done by another agency of the state, which stands to lose large amounts of federal money if a facility is not certified. This conflict-of-interest situation cannot help but cause leniency in the enforcement of standards. Second, monitoring tends to occur in the form of very overt inspections, announced in advance. The result may be the institutions get ready and put on a good show for the few days of annual inspection, and what the monitors see is an atypically good situation (e.g., Bible & Snead, 1976).

The Accreditation Council for Services for Mentally Retarded and Other Developmentally Disabled Persons (ACMR/DD) provides monitoring by outside inspectors. However, their monitoring is neither universal nor totally independent, since agencies voluntarily request and pay for ACMR/DD inspections. As with Title XIX monitoring, ACMR/DD inspections are announced in advance.

INCREASED SPENDING

Throughout the recent legal and socio-political efforts on behalf of the retarded, a strong theme has been "The staffing in our institutions is often insufficient in quantity and quality to provide adequate services." That this has been proved true in some cases, and probably will be in others yet to be adjudicated, is reflected in the explicit specification of numbers and qualifications of staff in court decrees (e.g., *Wyatt* v. *Stickney*, 1972) and accreditation standards (e.g., Joint Commission on Accreditation of Hospitals, 1978). While it is undeniably true in many cases that institutional staff are insufficient in quantity and quality to provide even minimally adequate services, there is another theme present in recent literature which warns that although increased staff training and numbers may be *necessary* in some cases, they are in general *not sufficient* to solve the problem of inadequate services.

Relevant to the concern about *inadequately trained* staff, Bensberg (1974), in reviewing previous work by himself and others, concluded that relatively few deficiencies in staff performance are attributable to insufficient staff training. He suggests that the majority of errors in staff performance must be solved, not by additional staff training, but rather by improvements in staff organization, supervision, and environmental design. This conclusion is supported by Keith (1972) who points out that training staff in habilitation skills is fruitless without an environment arranged to *maintain* the performance of the staff's skills.

Regarding the tactic of increasing the *quantity* of staff, it has been observed (e.g., Blindert, 1975) that increasing the number of staff is likely to result not in more staff interactions with residents, but rather in more "leisure-time" activities (e.g., increased "off-task" conversation between staff members). Twardosz, Haskins, Cataldo, and Risley (in press) have found that increases in the number of staff can, in the absence of good organization and supervision, actually decrease each staff member's interactions with residents. Bensberg (1974) has reported that in one survey of four institutions (Bensberg & Barnett, 1966) an average of 30 percent of the caregivers' time was spent in "personal leisure time activities" such as reading and sleeping. In combination, the preceding findings are disturbing because they suggest that (1) much of current staff resources are being wasted due to improper utilization and (2) additional staff resources—as are being required by court rulings and accreditation standards—may simply add to existing waste rather than improve services to residents.

HUMAN RIGHTS COMMITTEES AND ADVOCACY

Some institutions have developed "human-rights committees," usually composed of volunteers from the surrounding community, and some have hired in-house "resident advocates," who review, investigate, and make recommendations to management on various issues concerning residents' rights. Usually, the focus is on identifying rights violations and exerting pressure for immediate correction, rather than in-depth analysis of the underlying causes of the problem. Thus, an advocate may discover a case of child abuse and be satisfied with the dismissal of the staff who committed the abuse; but it is the administration's responsibility to examine the underlying causes (e.g., inadequate staff training or supervision), which without correction would lead to similar problems in the future.

Use of human-rights committees and resident advocates has an advantage over accreditation and licensing inspectors in that their monitoring can be more nearly continuous and they can usually spend more time investigating specific cases. A major dilemma, however, concerns their motivation: To the extent that they might be totally on a volunteer basis, the amount of time and effort put into their work will usually be less than what would be expected from paid employees; but to the extent that management provides extrinsic incentives (e.g., salaries), independence and objectivity are threatened.

SUMMARY

Although each has its limitations, the preceding approaches have their place in a total solution to the problem of protecting institutional residents' rights. As a group they can be seen as means of identifying problems and providing the motivation and raw materials for solving them. But abuse and neglect have continued in some cases, not for lack of raw materials or motivation to provide protection, but for lack of a blueprint and technology for motivated managers to use in transforming the raw materials into an efficient, high-quality, humane service for the education, treatment, and care of handicapped persons.

A Quality Assurance System

Our work on "institutional reform" has been largely based on research done by the Living Environments Group at the University of Kansas, directed by Todd R. Risley.[1] In particular, we have drawn from research on the organization and management of infant and toddler daycare (Herbert-Jackson, O'Brien, Porterfield, & Risley, 1977; O'Brien, Porterfield, Herbert-Jackson, & Risley, 1979). We began in 1975 by totally reforming a ward of profoundly retarded nonambulatory residents at the Western Carolina Center. Since then, we have replicated our nonambulatory model at the Eastern Oregon Hospital and Training Center, and have developed fundamentally similar, though somewhat less detailed, quality maintenance systems throughout both facilities' retardation services.

Because our work with the nonambulatory residents has been more adequately detailed, it will be used to exemplify the concepts and principles involved in our quality assurance system.

The basic ingredients of our staff training and quality maintenance

[1] This program is being developed jointly by the Western Carolina Center, under the direction of J. Iverson Riddle, and the Living Environments Group of the University of Kansas, under the direction of Todd R. Risley. This research is supported by NICHD Grant #1 ROI HD 10853, under the direction of James E. Favell.

systems are (1) a set of detailed, comprehensive, easy-to-read procedures manuals, describing all the important aspects of the ward's organization and operation, (2) an on-site supervisor with formally specified supervisory responsibilities, and (3) an external monitor, who does not work directly with the staff but drops in periodically to take formal evaluative measures of overall performance and give feedback to the supervisor on the quality of his or her program.

POLICY AND PROCEDURES MANUALS

We have found it important to have policies and procedures stated in easy-to-read manuals that are readily accessible to staff. Without such manuals, policies and procedures are distorted as they pass from generation to generation of new caregivers and supervisors. By having such information available in writing, the supervisor is spared a great expense in time of having to explain everything orally.

TRAINING NEW CAREGIVERS

The first step in the training of new employees is for them to read the policy and procedures manual. Next, trainees observe regular staff performing the activities they are trying to learn, and ask questions to clarify details of the procedures. When they think they understand how to perform the job, the supervisor gives them the opportunity to try it. While they are practicing, the supervisor watches and gives feedback on performance.

To be sure that new employees learn every important detail of the specified job, supervisor uses checklists to focus the attention of both trainee and supervisor on all the important aspects. Each checklist is composed of questions (usually in yes/no answer form) derived from the procedures manual. We have found that without this kind of detailed specification of procedures supervisors and their employees tend to focus on some aspects of the routine while neglecting or forgetting others. An example of such a checklist is shown in Figure 1.

New employees are considered to be trained or certified on a routine only when they can perform it with a 100 percent score on the checklist. Substandard scores indicate a need for rereading the manual or additional observation and practice with feedback from the supervisor.

In this way new employees are trained to perform each of the many "routine" activities—feeding, bathing, diapering, cleaning, etc.—in the precise and efficient way necessary for an optimally effective and efficient overall ward operation.

Staff Observed: _____

Observer: _____

Date: _____

Training: Watch new staff member conduct one complete bath.

Monitoring: Observe a different staff member each week, watching each caregiver once a month.

Scoring: Criterion = 100% "yes" (or n.a.). Procedures must be done in the listed sequence to be scored "yes."

Routing: 1. Supervisor immediately gives completed checklist to staff for initialing.
2. Staff initials and returns to Supervisor.
3. Supervisor gives completed checklists to External Monitor weekly.

		Circle One
1.	Did the staff member wash her own hands before contacting the resident?	Yes No
2.	Were all of the materials assembled within reach of the bath tub before the resident was brought to the area? (Once the resident was on the netting he/she was never left alone.)	Yes No
3.	Did the staff member explain to the resident that he/she was going to take a bath?	Yes No
4.	Were the resident's dirty clothes and diaper placed in the proper receptacles? (Check that socks and polyester fabrics were put in separate bags and that no diapers were put in clothes hamper.)	Yes No
5.	Did the staff brush the resident's teeth and rinse his/her mouth with the mouthwash solution?	Yes No
6.	Was resident's hair washed (if indicated on bath chart)?	Yes No
7.	Did the staff clean hair, face, and body in that order?	Yes No
8.	Was special soap or lotion used (if indicated on bathing chart)?	Yes No
9.	Did the staff dry the resident and lie the resident on the towel?	Yes No
10.	Was deodorant applied?	Yes No
11.	Did the staff conduct and record a health check?	Yes No
12.	Was the resident's hair brushed?	Yes No
13.	Was the resident taken to the appropriate activity, play, or feeding?	Yes No
14.	Did the staff record appropriately on the master schedule board, bathing charts, and health chart?	Yes No
15.	Check the resident to see how clean he/she is. Look at the following body areas to see if there is any obvious dirt: eyes, ears, nose, fingernails, hands, and between toes. Was each clean?	Yes No
16.	Were resident's fingernails short enough?	Yes No

Staff Initials: _____

FIGURE 1. Complete Bathing Checklist. An example of a routine duty checklist —this one for bathing a resident—used in both training new staff and giving feedback to veteran caregivers.

MAINTAINING QUALITY: SELF-RECORDING AND
SUPERVISORY FEEDBACK

Once the staff have been trained to the specified criterion of performance (100 percent), it is essential to have explicit, formal procedures for maintaining that quality.

Without such "quality control" procedures performance will drift in directions that are largely unpredictable and sometimes dangerous. Frequently, such drift will be toward "shortcuts" that seem to make the job easier but almost always sacrifice quality. A certain amount of drift is likely to occur without the awareness of either caregiver or supervisor —they simply forget or cease attending to some details of the job. And even if supervisors *do* notice slips in performance, they are likely to overlook them, not wanting to appear picky and incur the displeasure of the employee whose performance must be corrected. Thus, performance may gradually drift until it reaches a crisis point—e.g., a resident is injured, a licensing inspection is failed—at which time the supervisor is forced to take drastic action, an unpleasant situation for both supervisor and employees. Following such "crisis intervention," performance returns to a high level and the process begins again.

To avoid such cyclical fluctuations in performance quality, we use formal procedures for keeping everyone—caregivers and supervisors— attending to *all* of the important details of the job. This involves several types of procedure.

For some activities, caregivers record their own performance. For example, after bathing a resident, caregivers indicate on a bathing chart (Figure 2) that they have conducted a health check (noting health problems such as bruises, fever, etc.) and whether they washed the resident's hair. This checklist serves several functions: First, it visually reminds the caregiver to make health checks and wash hair; second, it gives caregivers feedback (from their own checks or lack of checks) on any residents or duties they have neglected. Third, it provides a continuous public record of what has already been done; thus if an emergency requires a different caregiver to take over an activity from the one who began it, the new caregiver has a readily available record of what remains to be done. Although the supervisor must intermittently check the accuracy of such "self-recording" checklists, they are largely a mechanism for the staff to maintain their *own* attention to details.

Although a limited amount of self-recording and feedback is usually possible, the large majority of the day-to-day performance evaluation and feedback must be done by the supervisor. There are three basic types of supervisory monitoring.

1. Specific Product Measures. One method of performance assessment involves inspecting the quality of performance products and giving

Week beginning _____

Name	Days for Hairwashing	Special Soap or Lotion	Special Clothing Arrangements If Any	Monday			Tuesday			Wednesday			Thursday			Friday		
				Bath	Hair	Hlth	Bath	Hair	Hlth	Bath	Hair	Hlth	Bath	Hair	Hlth	Bath	Hair	Hlth
Ricky L																		
Ronda																		
Laura																		
Judy																		
Ricky O																		
Randy																		
Mary Sue																		
Betty Jo																		

Record "B" for Full Bath
    for Hair Wash
    for Health Check

Routing: 1. Supervisor posts new form Friday;
        2. turn in to External Monitor weekly;
        3. return to Supervisor for filing.

FIGURE 2. Bathing Chart. An example of a "self-recording" checklist—this one for staff to use in conducting the bathing routine.

feedback to those responsible for them. Examples of products checked by the supervisor include bed-making, assembling and organizing materials, and some cleaning activities. One example of how the supervisor checks products of performance is in bathroom cleaning and linen exchange (Figure 3). Each morning and afternoon the person responsible for cleaning the bathroom and exchanging soiled linen for clean linen initials the form once the job is completed. Later, the supervisor checks off items on the checklist and indicates whether each was done properly. Any deficiencies are promptly brought to the attention of the responsible staff member.

2. *Specific Process Measures.* Evaluating some kinds of performance requires the supervisor to watch a performance as it occurs. One example is bathing. A bathing checklist (Figure 1) is used by supervisors to monitor caregiver performance of this routine. This is the same kind of checklist used in the initial training of caregivers; it is derived from the instructions in the bathing section of the procedures manual, and all caregivers are expected to reach and maintain a 100 percent accuracy criterion. Each caregiver is checked once a month on this and all other routines. If any caregiver's performance falls below the criterion level, the supervisor points out the deficiency, explains it or refers the caregiver to the pertinent section of the procedures manual, and conducts another check at the next opportunity (usually the next day) to assure that the deficient performance has been corrected. This same kind of checklist monitoring of "process" is conducted on other routines such as feeding, diapering, and transporting residents.

In addition to these checks on the mechanics of each routine, a supplementary participation checklist (Figure 4, p. 358) is used for all routines that involve caregivers doing something to a resident. Using this checklist, the supervisor can observe whether the caregiver attempts to involve the resident in the activity, giving him an opportunity to participate in and learn from it (incidental teaching) rather than simply having it done to him.

It is important to note that following each check the supervisor discusses the results with the caregiver. This is almost always an occasion for the supervisor to say "Nice job; keep up the good work!" In all cases caregivers initial the checklist to indicate they have received feedback.

Product measures have the advantage of greater intrinsic validity; with a process measure it is possible that the performance might look good and yet—due to undetected deficiencies—fail to produce the desired result. Another advantage of product measures is that they are usually more convenient and less time-consuming, since they can be checked more or less at the convenience of the supervisor; process measures require supervisors to schedule themselves to be available at the times the

Routing: 1. Supervisor checks after AM bathing and PM diapering.
2. Supervisor gives completed checklist to External Monitor weekly.

Code: / = OK; X = No; n.a. = not applicable

	Mon.		Tues.		Wed.		Thurs.		Fri.	
Day:	AM	PM	AM	PM	AM	PM	AM	PM	AM	PM
Staff Responsible:										
Observer:										

Bathroom Cleaning:

1. Tables, counters, and carts free of stickiness, food, or spots along tops, edges, and legs.

2. Slab, sink, and hopper free of stickiness or spots on inside (PM), outside and rim (AM only).

3. Net is dry to the touch.

4. On Wednesdays, after morning cleaning, slab, tub, and commode free of stains and dirt inside and outside.

5. After morning cleaning and PM cleaning, bathroom floor free of dirt, water puddles, piles of hair or lint.

6. Netting over slab free of stains, dirt and BM.

7. Hair brushes clean.

Linen Exchange

1. Mesh diaper bag in garbage can, containing fewer than four dirty items.

2. Linen bag in hamper containing fewer than six dirty items.

3. Under the diaper table, all of the following:
   a. Enough towels to make one pile about 30 inches high.
   b. Enough washcloths to make one pile about 30 inches high.
   c. Enough diapers to make one pile about 30 inches high.
   d. As many plastic pants as possible (maximum of 15).

4. In linen storage area, all of the following:
   a. Enough sheets, pillowcases, and bedspreads to change each bed if necessary.

FIGURE 3. Bathroom Cleaning and Linen Exchange Criteria and Checklist. An example of a product-oriented checklist—this one to record the completion and inspection of bathroom cleanup and linen exchange.

Staff Observed: _____
Observer: _____
Area: _____
Date: _____

Routing: 1. *Supervisor completes this checklist at the same time he or she does checklists (either Training or Monitoring) for: Complete bathing, Sponge Bathing, Feeding, Diapering, Play, Special Activities, or Transporting Residents;*
   2. Staff initials and returns to Supervisor;
   3. Supervisor attaches to corresponding Routine Checklist and gives all completed checklists to External Monitor weekly.

	Circle one answer (or tally if more than one resident is observed)
1. Was the resident positioned so that he/she could see what was happening?	Yes No
2. Did the staff make eye-contact with, and talk to, the resident about what was happening each time something was done to the resident?	Yes No
3. Did the staff give the resident the opportunity to practice the skills he/she has?	Yes No
4. Did the staff prompt (assist) the resident to extend his/her skills? (Does no apply to play manager.)	Yes No
5. Did the staff respond to any initiation of contact or spontaneous movements by the resident?	Yes No
6. If the resident showed a new response, did the staff indicate that he or she watched this by making a circled check on the Master Schedule Board?	Yes No
7. Did the staff help the resident to relax during the activity?	Yes No

Staff Initials: _____

FIGURE 4.   Participation Checklist. The checklist for assessing how well caregivers promote residents' participation in activities of daily living.

performance occurs and to remain throughout the performance. Finally, since caregivers are not aware that their performance is being monitored on any particular occasion, product monitoring does not influence the performance it is measuring, thereby giving a truer picture of "typical" performance. It is difficult to conduct process checks covertly, and therefore caregivers are often self-conscious about their performance while checks are being conducted.

However, there are some situations that require process measurement, either in addition to or instead of a product measure: (1) In some cases, the results of good or poor performance are too difficult to observe (e.g., as in caregivers washing hands before feeding a resident—it is easier and more dependable to watch staff wash their hands than to try inspecting the cleanliness of hands). (2) In some cases a bad product would be so disastrous that it is essential to avoid it by detecting and correcting performance that would lead to it (e.g., if residents are left unattended on a changing table, eventually one will fall off, with disastrous results; the supervisor must correct that performance *before* it has a chance to produce its product). (3) In many cases the product is so long in coming that it is not economical to wait to see it before taking corrective action (e.g., skill training is a very slow process with profoundly retarded, nonambulatory individuals, so it is important to monitor trainers' performance and take corrective action, if necessary, before long periods of time elapse with no product). (4) Finally, many products are jointly determined by the performance of several caregivers, making it impossible to give credit (or blame) to any individual caregiver on the basis of the product alone (e.g., the breakfast feeder may be very skillfully teaching spoon-feeding, but the product—residents' acquisition of that skill—will not reflect the excellence of that caregiver's training if those who feed other meals punish residents for attempting to grasp a spoon).

Initially, the checklists may appear to be exhaustingly long and detailed. We have found, however, that a checklist should specify all of the important aspects of performance; omitting some items risks deterioration of performance in those areas without a significant saving in time or effort for supervisors. (They usually have to watch the performance of the whole routine anyway, so it takes no longer to check all of the details.) Also, the monitoring quickly becomes very easy for supervisors to do as they become very familiar with the routines and checklists. Usually they need not even have the checklist with them while they are monitoring a routine—they simply watch caregivers as unobtrusively as possible, then go and fill out the checklist from memory. It is important to note that the checklist mechanism constitutes a structure and a minimum frequency for evaluating and giving feedback to employees but does not preclude other, more frequent or less formal feedback. In fact, we encourage supervisors to give more frequent informal feedback to their staff on all aspects of their work, even those aspects not covered by formal monitoring procedures.

3. General Monitoring. In addition to the monitoring of specific routine activities mentioned earlier (bathing, feeding, diapering, etc.), the supervisor conducts daily general activity monitoring on a random-interval time-sampling basis. At least once a day, the supervisor makes a near-instantaneous note of (1) what percent of the residents are appropriately engaged (product), (2) whether each of the caregivers are in their assigned locations and conducting their assigned activities (according to the daily activity schedule posted by the supervisor), and (3) which of several categories of behavior each caregiver is engaged in. These categories include social interaction with residents, nonsocial interaction with residents, environmental maintenance, clerical work, "other" activities, and "unaccounted for." In general, the most desirable category is social interaction with residents; the least desirable are "other" and "unaccounted for." By conducting these general checks supervisors keep their attention and that of their staff focused on general activities and goals that are important to the residents' care and development: adherence to the posted activity schedule, social interaction with residents as much of the time as possible, and appropriate engagement of residents with their environment. To give the staff feedback on these dimensions, supervisors post a sheet on the bulletin board displaying the results of these assessments for each caregiver. Although the results of any single check are not very important for overall performance assessment (unless a caregiver is scored "unaccounted for"), over several days and weeks these instantaneous checks eventually begin to give a general picture of how individual employees are spending their time.

Figure 5 shows how data from these checks discriminate good performance from poor: The top graph shows a caregiver who always spends more time in socially interacting with residents than in miscellaneous "other" activities; for the caregiver shown by the lower graph, there is considerable overlap between the amounts of these two classes of activity.

EXTERNAL MONITORING

Although the supervisor's monitoring and feedback to caregivers is the major force influencing ongoing quality of care, it is necessary to support and verify the supervisory monitoring system with an "external" monitoring system for two reasons: (1) Without periodic reminders of what the supervisory role is, supervisors tend to become involved in helping their caregivers do caregiving, and neglect their *supervisory* jobs; (2) because their major on-the-job social contacts are with those they supervise, they tend to come under the social control of their subordinates, which tends to influence them (often subtly) to give positively biased feedback and refrain from giving negative feedback. To overcome these problems, it is important to have an external monitor who is dependable, who is—or represents—a higher authority, and who is socially and administratively insulated from the caregivers.

The external monitor's job involves two things: First, he or she drops in periodically at unpredictable times and does checks on the same areas of staff performance and resident engagement checked by the supervisor. This serves as a visible source of external authority, making clear to all that the supervisor is being held accountable to higher authorities for maintaining standards (rather than arbitrarily setting and enforcing

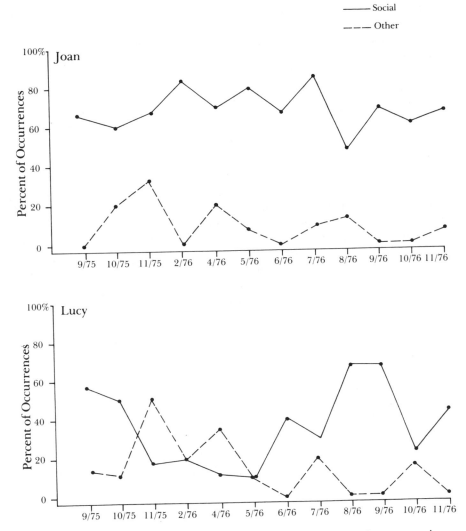

FIGURE 5. Caregivers' Interactions. An example of how data from supervisory monitoring reveal how individual caregivers are spending their time.

standards herself). This allows the supervisor to give corrective feedback, when it is necessary, in terms of *"they* [up there] expect better performance," instead of *"I* [personally] am demanding better performance."

Second, the external monitor meets weekly with the supervisor to review all of the data collected that week (by both supervisor and external monitor). This serves as an occasion for assessment of the "reliability" of the supervisor's data and the thoroughness of her recording of all the various kinds of information.

GENERAL MONITORING CONSIDERATIONS

The following are some general points about the evaluation and feedback system.

1. Frequency of monitoring, both supervisory and external, is a variable that depends to some extent on the staff involved, economic considerations, and so on. However, whatever schedule of monitoring is set, *additional* checks are always scheduled to occur at the first opportunity following discovery of a deficiency; the additional checks should continue daily until the problem is cleared up.

2. The external monitor must be able to conduct all caregiver and supervisory skills as well as have a complete theoretical and practical understanding of the task analysis, behavioral principles, incidental teaching, and so on. The external monitor must also remain somewhat insulated from counter-controlling influences (staff bringing up problems, complaining, etc.). Of course, when possible it is valuable to have a second external monitor available to conduct independent checks.

3. Although we try to specify in advance all important aspects of performance, this is seldom possible. Consequently, checklists and response definitions must be continually refined, particularly in the first few months of operation, and a certain amount of evaluation and feedback must be done informally, especially in the case of complex performance (e.g., behavior shaping).

4. Although the traditional reinforcement model would suggest the importance of tangible backup consequences for staff performance (e.g., Iwata, Bailey, Brown, Foshee, & Alpern, 1976), we have yet to determine their importance. When tangible consequences are available (salary raises, promotions, etc.) we try to utilize them in the system by making them contingent upon performance records. It appears, however, that this kind of system can be very effective with only the social consequences inherent in it.

5. It is probably easier to implement an evaluation and feedback system if one is setting up an operation from scratch than if one is trying to introduce it into an already established institution where staff have become accustomed to sloppy performance. But almost anywhere one implements such a system, one will find a certain amount of skepticism at the prospect of monitoring and feedback. This is probably because most people's experience with feedback has been negative, since in most operations explicit feedback is given only when generated by deficient performance. If feedback is only given when a crisis occurs, it will almost always be negative; if instead it is given frequently, on a schedule that is independent of performance, it will almost always be positive, since it will correct small problems and thereby prevent them from becoming major ones.

6. Formal monitoring and feedback systems will not solve all institutional management problems, but they can be effective in maintaining quality in some basic service areas, thereby freeing administrators and professionals to give more of their attention to some of the more complex, higher-order problems of service delivery.

Conclusion

The protection of institutional residents' rights is clearly an enormous task in terms of the numbers of rights that have been regularly violated, the numerous causal factors from a variety of sources, the numbers of residents and facilities involved, and the slow pace of progress—even with the intense motivation provided by court rulings. To progress farther—or even to maintain the status quo—will require vigorous action on the part of attorneys, regulatory agencies, legislators, and all kinds of advocates. It will also require scientific efforts to develop, refine, analyze, and evaluate systems, such as the one described here, for training staff and managing more effectively the resources that are available for the humane care, education, and treatment of mentally handicapped individuals.

References

BENSBERG, G. J. Administration and staff development in residential facilities. *Mental Retardation*, 1974, *12*, 29–32.

BENSBERG, G. J., & BARNETT, C. D. *Attendant training in southern residential facilities for the mentally retarded.* Atlanta: Southern Regional Education Board, 1966.

BIBLE, G. H., & SNEAD, T. J. Some effects of an accreditation survey on program completion at a state institution. *Mental Retardation*, 1976, *14* (5), 14–15.

BLATT, B., & KAPLAN, F. *Christmas in purgatory: A photographic essay on mental retardation.* Boston: Allyn & Bacon, 1966.

BLINDERT, H. D. Interactions between residents and staff: A qualitative investigation of an institutional setting for retarded children. *Mental Retardation*, 1975, *13*, 38–40.

HARMATZ, M. G. Observational study of ward staff behavior. *Exceptional Children*, 1973, *39*, 554–558.

HART, B., & RISLEY, T. R. Incidental teaching of language in the preschool. *Journal of Applied Behavior Analysis*, 1975, *4*, 411–420.

HERBERT-JACKSON, E., O'BRIEN, M., PORTERFIELD, J., & RISLEY, T. R. *The infant center: A complete guide to organizing and managing infant day care.* Baltimore: University Park Press, 1977.

Iwata, B. A., Bailey, J. S., Brown, K. M., Foshee, T. J., & Alpern, M. A performance-based lottery to improve residential care and training by institutional staff. *Journal of Applied Behavior Analysis,* 1976, *9* (4), 417–431.

Joint Commission on Accreditation of Hospitals. *Standards for services for developmentally disabled individuals.* Chicago: Joint Commission on Accreditation of Hospitals, 1978.

Keith, K. D. Analysis of institutional staff behavior. *Mental Retardation,* 1972, *10,* 44–45.

Keith, K. D., & Lange, B. M. Maintenance of behavior changed in an institution-wide training program. *Mental Retardation,* 1974, *12,* 34–37.

M.A.R.C. v. *Maryland* (Baltimore Cty., Cir. Ct., E. No. 100/182/77676, April 9, 1974).

N.Y.A.R.C. v. *Rockefeller,* 357 F. Supp. 752 (E.D. N.Y. 1973).

O'Brien, M., Porterfield, J., Herbert-Jackson, E., & Risley, T. R. *The toddler center: A practical guide to day care for one- and two-year-olds.* Baltimore: University Park Press, 1979.

Twardosz, S., Haskins, L., Cataldo, M. F., & Risley, T. R. Staff-child ratios and staff-child interactions. *Journal of Applied Behavior Analysis,* in press.

Welsh v. *Likens,* 373 F. Supp. 487 (D. Minn. 1974).

Wyatt v. *Stickney,* 344 F. Supp. 387 (M.D. Ala. 1972); *aff'd* sub nom.

Wyatt v. *Aderholt,* 503 F.2d 1305 (5th Cir. 1974).

CHAPTER 18

Client Rights in Psychiatric Facilities

Joseph E. Hasazi
Richard C. Surles
Gerald T. Hannah

CLIENTS OF PSYCHIATRIC HOSPITALS cannot be deprived of their liberty without due process of law; that is, without a formal legal proceeding during which a full range of procedural rights is afforded. More specifically, they have the right to (1) freedom from cruel and unusual punishment, (2) the least restrictive alternative, (3) treatment, (4) refusal of treatment, (5) confidentiality, and (6) retaining any other legal rights provided by state laws. It has been over a hundred years since Dorothea Dix advocated that the mentally ill be transferred from correctional to psychiatric facilities. For many years this population—which consisted of abandoned children, the uneducated, the poor, and racial minorities as well as the mentally ill—was forgotten. Only recently have the courts, consumer advocates, and mental health professionals begun to take a closer look at the living conditions and treatment given to psychiatric clients. The procedures described in this chapter are designed to ensure that the basic human rights of persons committed to psychiatric institutions are protected while effective treatment options are provided.

Background

The legal rights of clients in psychiatric hospitals—primarily state facilities—have been the subject of increasing concern to legal and mental health professionals during the past decade. Historically, the state and federal courts have been reluctant to involve themselves in the disposition and treatment of the mentally ill, preferring instead to leave disposition and treatment to the discretion of the mental health professions. The substantial body of mental health case law that has developed over the past few years attests to a dramatic change in attitude on the part of the courts. Likewise, almost all state laws pertaining to mental illness have undergone major revisions within the past five or six years. Most of the legal change has been fostered by a growing body of legal professionals who have come to specialize in mental disabilities law. Special interest projects such as the National Mental Health Law Project, based in Washington, D.C., have stimulated changes in both state laws and legal practices on behalf of the mentally ill. Primarily legal advocates now demand that the mental health professional document and prove cause before restricting the rights of a mentally ill person. Without exception, the involvement of the courts and state legislatures has led to an increase in the rights of the client and has diminished the prerogatives of the mental health establishment.

The increased interest in the rights of the client has resulted from multiple factors, including changes in law, medicine, the behavioral sciences, and society itself. A full discussion of these factors is beyond the scope of this chapter, but some discussion is provided in order to place specific issues in a broader perspective.

It is difficult to isolate any single change in attitude on the part of the courts and state legislatures that has prompted the many developments in mental health law. However, it seems both technical and philosophical considerations have been involved. There has been a growing awareness of the relative unreliability of psychiatric diagnoses and the predictions that follow from them. As Judge Bazelon noted in *United States* v. *Browner* (1972), "Psychiatrists have continued to make moral and legal judgments beyond the proper scope of their professional expertise." Beyond this technical consideration, there has been an affirmation of the priority of the person's civil rights over the presumed necessities and demands of treatment. The constitutional rights taken for granted in criminal proceedings have been extended to civil commitment proceedings, due in part to Supreme Court decisions in *In re Gault* (1967) and *Goldberg* v. *Kelly* (1970) which extended due process protections to civil proceedings. The guiding principle of the priority of the individual's civil rights over other considerations was particularly well stated in the case of *Suzuki* v. *Quisenberry* (1976). In this case, the judge ruled that Hawaii's mental health law was unconstitutional, reasoning, "Limiting a person's constitutional rights on the theory that it is in his best interest is questionable philosophy and bad law." On the basis of such considerations, the courts have abandoned their hands-off policy regarding the disposition and treatment of the mentally ill and have increasingly demanded more from the mental health professions in the way of accountability and procedural safeguards. For example, some state courts now periodically review the case of every involuntarily committed client to determine not only if the individual was really mentally ill at admission and continues to be ill, but whether the person is receiving adequate treatment. Furthermore, if treatment is found lacking, the courts have ordered the development of new treatment plans and have in some cases stipulated the nature of the treatment to be rendered.

While the courts have undoubtedly played the major role in bringing about the concern for client rights in psychiatric hospitals and other treatment settings, some credit must also be given to the mental health profession. The interest in community-based treatment of the mentally ill and in de-institutionalization was stimulated by mental health professionals and predates most of the judicial interest in the topic. The development and use of tranquilizing and other psychoactive medications, the development of community mental health centers, the establishment of community-based inpatient psychiatric beds, the success of community group homes, and major advances in diagnostic and psychotherapeutic methods have all contributed to the client rights movement. In fact, the very success of current mental health programs has encouraged and increased the demand for treatment in less restrictive settings. There is no question that the work of physicians, behavioral scientists, such as Szasz (1963, 1970), Goffman (1961), and others, was influential in bringing the plight of hospitalized clients to judicial and public awareness.

Although mental health professionals have helped to increase the interest in client rights, they have not necessarily welcomed some of the involvement of the legal system in the regulation of mental health care. There is a strong feeling on the part of many mental health professionals that the legal system has become too involved in treatment. Lacking the necessary expertise and sensitivity to the realities of mental illness, the legal system is viewed by some as having actually limited the client's access to appropriate care and treatment (e.g., Ennis, 1978; Lebensohn, 1978; Peszke, 1976; Sadoff, 1978; Scott, 1976; Shah, 1975). As Lebensohn (1978) has noted, "Severe mental illness . . . can be as great an impediment to full freedom as iron bars and locked doors. It is one of the great tragedies of our time that countless numbers of mentally ill remain untreated and prisoners of their mental illness all in the name of civil liberty" (p. 29).

Some of the problems of judicial involvement alluded to above are illustrated by the case of *O'Connor* v. *Donaldson* (1975). In this case the Supreme Court ruled that an individual may not be committed involuntarily simply on the basis of mental illness. In addition, the individual must also be shown to present a danger to himself or others. While such a principle advances client rights in obvious ways, it may detract from them as well. As Shah (1975) points out, current definitions of dangerousness as well as methods of predicting such behavior are hopelessly inadequate. Without reliable and valid diagnostic and prognostic methods, the dangerousness criterion could detract from client rights in many ways (Monahan, 1973).

The requirement to use a criterion of dangerousness for admission could also lead to an increase in the prediction of dangerousness by some mental health specialists. Even if the dangerousness criterion could be applied reliably, it still would exclude persons who could benefit from residential treatment but do not meet the legal definition of dangerousness (Sadoff, 1978). The legal interpretations of the *O'Connor* v. *Donaldson* case are but one example of how judicial involvement in mental health areas may create practical problems for the mental health establishment while not necessarily advancing the quality of care provided to the mentally ill.

RESPONSE TO THE PROBLEM

In response to judicial involvement in inpatient mental health care, psychiatric facilities have developed guidelines for safeguarding client rights. Some psychiatric facilities are attempting to develop guidelines that safeguard the rights of the client as well as promote high-quality client care. At times, conflict between the legal and mental health profession may be unavoidable, but both can work together to promote the fullest possible protection of the client's civil rights and mental health.

Mental health case law affecting the rights of the hospitalized psychiatric client can be divided into three broad areas: commitment criteria, procedural rights, and substantive rights. The topic of commitment criteria,[1] while of considerable importance, will not be discussed here, since the primary need for the mental health professional is to develop guidelines that focus on procedural and substantive rights.

The client's *procedural rights* generally are concerned with the legal safeguards surrounding commitment itself. Involuntary commitment procedures are almost entirely statutory. They include emergency and temporary (or observational) commitment procedures as well as indeterminate commitment. However, within recent years most states have all but eliminated indeterminate commitment procedures. Instead, clients are committed for a specified period of time (e.g., ninety days, one year), after which they must be released or recommitted under new proceedings. Criteria in commitment procedures must ensure that due process rights are afforded.

The greatest impact of the courts on the disposition and treatment of the hospitalized mentally ill has been in the *substantive rights* area.

Before discussing the client's procedural and substantive rights and

---

[1] For a discussion of commitment criteria, see Brooks (1974), Kopolow (1974), and Sadoff (1978).

the methods of protecting them, one should note that the protection of these rights is not the sole responsibility of the psychiatric hospital. Client rights are best safeguarded when the efforts of the hospital are complemented by an active public law system, responsible mental health advocacy, and legislative reform. In other words, there must be an impartial and statutory system of review to determine the adequacy of protection for each client.

Due Process

A substantial number of legal cases have dealt with the rights of the client to due process, since commitment, even a civil commitment, does involve the loss of liberty (e.g., *Fhagen* v. *Miller,* 1972; *In re Barnard,* 1971; *In re Gault,* 1967; *Lessard* v. *Schmidt,* 1972; *People* v. *Bailey,* 1966; *Specht* v. *Patterson,* 1967). The legal protections afforded under due process include, among others, the right to a hearing, to counsel, to be present at proceedings, to cross-examine witnesses, to call witnesses, and to receive independent psychiatric evaluation. In response to judicial actions regarding due process, many states and psychiatric hospitals have developed policies and procedures that safeguard these rights, utilizing a very active public law system to insure compliance. Consequently, where an active legal system exists, the protection of client rights under due process is less an issue than the protection of substantive rights.

For psychiatric hospitals, then, the most important procedural safeguard seems to involve the methods used to inform clients of their rights. At a minimum, all clients must be informed in writing of their right to due process at the time of admission. The rights should be stated clearly and succinctly. If necessary, they should be read to the client, and in all cases the client should be encouraged to ask questions and seek clarification; moreover, it makes no sense to inform the client of, for example, his or her right to apply for a "writ of habeas corpus" if the person has no understanding of these words. Safeguarding the client's rights in this area means that hospitals must do more than perfunctorily hand the client a document outlining his or her rights to read and sign. In addition, the hospital must develop procedures that seek to give clients the fullest possible understanding of their rights.

Moreover, informing clients of their rights should not be limited to the time of admission. Clients should continue to be informed of rights on a regular basis throughout the stay at the hospital. Policies should exist that sensitize hospital staff to responding to any signs that the client is unaware of or has misunderstood his or her rights and that staff should provide further information as needed. Hospital staff should be especially responsive to the client's requests to meet with counsel. Facilitating the client's understanding of his or her rights presupposes that all hospital staff are aware of these rights and are encouraged to help the client realize them. As such, in-service training of hospital employees becomes a critical component in the protection process. Ideally, new developments in law that affect the client's rights should be a regular part of staff training and continuing education.

Related to the due process issue are civil rights and general liberties issues. It can be assumed that the client has all of the same rights as any citizen, unless they have been specifically restricted by statute or order of a court (e.g., *Bush* v. *Kallen,* 1973). Clients have the right to vote, to dispose of property, and to communicate by sealed mail, and have the other rights that citizens would normally assume. Since clients may not be aware that they still hold these rights once committed, it is important that this be fully communicated to them. Furthermore, clients should be informed that some civil rights and liberties may not be restricted under any circumstances. Such rights include the right to counsel; to humane care and treatment; to communicate by sealed mail with the state mental health authorities and with an attorney, a clergyman, and the judge who ordered commitment; and to apply for a writ of habeas corpus.

While the focus of this discussion has been on the involuntarily committed client, it must be emphasized that all of the rights outlined above apply as well to clients admitted on a voluntary basis (e.g., *In re Buttonow,* 1968). Unfortunately, there are indications that voluntary clients too are not necessarily fully informed of their rights (Olin & Olin, 1975; Palmer & Wohl, 1972; Szasz, 1972). In the study by Olin and Olin only 8 of 100 voluntarily admitted clients had been fully informed of the terms and conditions of their admission. Procedural safeguards, therefore, should be extended to all clients, including those admitted on a voluntary basis.

Freedom from Harm

The right of hospitalized clients to *freedom from cruel and unusual punishment* has perhaps been most clearly articulated in the landmark Willowbrook decision (*New York State Association for Retarded Children* v. *Carey,* 1975). In that case the court ordered facilities in a state institution for the mentally retarded to be upgraded, based on the constitutional right of the residents to be protected from harm. Courts—including the Supreme Court—have concurred that institutionalized persons have a right to protection from harm.

Safeguarding the rights of the client from harm seems to involve two separate considerations. One obvious consideration involves the quality of care provided. Clients must be provided with adequate living conditions, food, recreation, health care, and stimulation. Safeguarding rights here is complex, since control and protection involves the hospital's environment, policies and procedures, and resources. The hospital may be severely limited in responding to issues of quality, since its operation is controlled by external factors such as legislative appropriations. Safeguards to clients must therefore include the active support of advocacy groups and others who can lobby on their behalf. Nonetheless, hospital policies and procedures regarding the quality of client life must be clearly articulated and should include as much consideration of the social as the physical environment. While research on the quality of care in institutional settings has been limited, recent studies (Balla, 1976; Moos, 1974; Raynes, Pratt, & Rorer, 1977) provide some content for formulating guidelines and procedures. More relevant, perhaps, might be the evaluations of the quality of client care that could be contained in professional reviews of the hospital conducted by such organizations as the Joint Commission on Hospital Accreditation and the state certifying agency for Medicaid/Medicare (usually the state's health department).

A second consideration in protection from harm involves the use of coercive or restrictive management procedures, an issue that overlaps with the client's right to refuse treatment. The most important safeguard to client rights in this area is the development of a clearly articulated policy regulating the use of seclusion, restraint, or physical isolation of clients. Especially important are policies that control the use of medications. Guidelines should specify the conditions under which clients can refuse medication and should include the right to have any decision to administer medications over the objections of the client reviewed by an impartial party. Reviews of coercive or restrictive policy should begin with internal administrative overseeing, which is appealable to higher authority.

Policies regarding protection from harm should indicate, in clear terms, the conditions under which restrictive methods may be used and by whom they may be used. Guidelines should also include a precise description of the manner in which the restrictive method would be applied. Policies and procedures—while drafted by hospital staff—should be reviewed and approved by a human rights committee constituted of individuals who are not employees of the hospital. Frequently, review by legal advocates, such as Legal Aid or an office of the public defender, may improve the due process aspect of the guidelines and reduce the possibility that they will be subject to a legal challenge. All direct applications of the guidelines should be routinely reported to appropriate authorities as a further safeguard against overuse. At a minimum, guidelines should contain the following:

1. formal authorization to administer a restrictive procedure
2. regular monitoring of the implementation and impact of restrictive procedures
3. controls for use of procedures, such as time limitations, or a condition that a less restrictive procedure has been attempted and has failed prior to administering a more restrictive procedure
4. requirements to report all use of most restrictive procedures to higher authority
5. right of appeal of any decision to use restrictive procedures even after application of policy

Merely requiring the authorization of such methods by a qualified mental health professional is inadequate to fully protect the rights of the client against abuse.

The Least Restrictive Alternative

The right of the client to treatment in the least restrictive environment has been established in some legal cases. In the case of *Lake* v. *Cameron* (1966), a woman suffering from chronic brain syndrome was ordered moved from an institutional to a less restrictive setting. The basis of the judgment was that since appropriate care could be provided in other settings there was no justification for the complete deprivation of liberty associated with institutional care. Similarly, in *Dixon* v. *Weinberger* (1975), it was ruled that clients have a statutory right to treatment in the least restrictive environment and ordered that clients who can be treated in community-based facilities be moved to them. The implications of the right to the least restrictive alternative are profound, but have not been generally applied to the mentally ill. The principles, if they become a guiding legal principle, will require greater justification of decisions to commit clients to psychiatric hospitals as well as of any restrictions of freedom within the hospital (such as placing the client on a locked rather than open ward).

The matter of safeguarding the client's right to treatment in the least restrictive alternative raises serious diagnostic questions. The specific problem behaviors or behavioral deficits that prevent the client from receiving community-based care must be identified and given priority in treatment planning. While this issue may seem straightforward, it necessitates an application of clinical procedures beyond traditional methods of diagnosis and assessment; in particular, it calls for a much more direct behavioral assessment process and requires that the assessment outcome be describable in a precise manner for legal testimony during the commitment hearing. The relevant behaviors should be carefully defined, observed, and recorded. As much attention should be focused on the positive skills and abilities required for successful community living as on the social behaviors and emotional status that may be the rationale behind the decision to seek commitment. The principle of the least restrictive alternative should sensitize the clinician to the need for assessing the client's adaptive behavior so that both skills and deficiencies are seriously considered in deciding the most appropriate setting for treatment. Among other judgments, the ability of the client to profit from a less restrictive setting is related to his abilities to care for himself or herself, to secure housing, employment, and transportation, to make purchases, and to handle money— all of which should be considered and made part of the clinical assessment. In Vermont, the Department of Mental Health has developed an instrument, the Vermont Scale for Independent Living Assessment, for assessing an individual's daily activity skills and clinical and maladaptive behaviors across different types of mental health facilities that provide services to the chronically mentally ill. The instrument is used to assist the hospital staff in determining the level of least restrictive environment within the facility and when the client is ready to be discharged to the next level of least restrictive environment.[2]

Finally, the right of the client to the least restrictive alternative suggests that periodic reevaluation of the need for continued hospitalization must be performed. If the initial basis for institutional care has been specified in behavioral terms, the behavioral baseline can form the basis of an ongoing system of measuring progress toward the goal of a less restrictive treatment environment. Typically, hospital policies and procedures call for periodic review of each client's program (e.g., on a monthly or quarterly basis). Guidelines specifying comprehensive periodic reviews alone may not be sufficient. In addition to such reviews, a treatment team should exist to specify other reviews specifically tailored to the needs of the individual client. For example, in the case of a suicidal or assaultive client, it may be desirable to have a daily review of the client's progress in those specific areas. In the section that follows, the importance of this point will be developed further.

Right to Treatment

The right to treatment has been established in several important legal cases (*Rouse* v. *Cameron*, 1966; *Wyatt* v. *Stickney*, 1971; *O'Connor* v. *Donaldson*, 1975). In *Wyatt* it was held that involuntarily committed patients "unquestionably have a constitutional right to receive such indi-

---

2 For a copy of this assessment instrument, contact Dr. Jerry T. Hannah, Commissioner, Department of Mental Health and Retardation, State Office Building, Topeka, Kansas, 66612.

vidual treatment as will give each of them a realistic opportunity to be cured or to improve his or her mental condition." While not yet confirmed or denied by the U.S. Supreme Court, *Wyatt* has had perhaps the greatest impact of any judicial action upon the provision of care in psychiatric hospitals. It reaffirmed the client's procedural and civil rights and specified the general parameters of adequate hospital care.

One of the most important features of the *Wyatt* decision is the concept of the individualized treatment plan. The treatment plan mandated in the *Wyatt* decision includes a statement of the specific problems and needs of the client, intermediate and long-term goals of treatment, a statement identifying staff responsibilities, criteria for movement to less restrictive care, and the condition for ultimate discharge. The individualized treatment plan, as conceptualized in *Wyatt*, can afford the client the highest protection of rights of any single administrative procedure. Construction of the individualized treatment plan necessitates all of the following considerations:

- assessment methods
- specification of goals and objectives
- selection of treatment methods
- evaluation strategies

The issues of assessment methods has been previously discussed in this chapter in the section on least restrictive alternatives. It is important to emphasize again the need to approach assessment from a broad-based perspective. Traditional interview and test methods must be supplemented by measures of adaptive behavior, direct observations in varying settings, and the client's own evaluation of needs and strengths. The purpose of the client assessment must be reconsidered as well: In safeguarding client rights to treatment, the purpose of the assessment must be seen as the identification of needs and strengths rather than simply diagnosis.

In the specification of goals and objectives, two points need to be considered. The first is simply the clarity of the objectives: A well-written objective should include a clear statement of the intended outcome in behavioral terms, as well as of the conditions under which the behavior will be evaluated and the criteria for concluding that the objectives have been met (Mager, 1961). Additionally, it is important that goals and objectives be established in concert with the client to whatever extent possible.

The core of the treatment plan, of course, is the selection and specification of treatment methods. Given the diversity of possible treatment strategies, only general considerations can be stated. Certainly, strategies or methods should be specified in sufficient detail for understanding how they will be applied. The treatment methods should be based upon sound medical or psychological practice and should be the least intrusive or restrictive available. Staff responsibilities should be carefully delineated in the plan and consistent with staff training and professional competence.

Finally, the treatment plan must include provisions for the evaluation of treatment effects. While the types of data collected will vary according to the objectives, sufficient data must be collected to evaluate treatment effectiveness in a convincing and timely manner. In many ways, the evaluation component of the individualized treatment plan is the most important one. It can form the basis for the extremely important decisions of the treatment team regarding changes in approach, discharge, and movement to a less restrictive setting.

The individual treatment plan should be complimented by other quality-assurance devices.[3] For example, the development of peer review mechanisms—internal and external to the hospital—can add an important overseeing dimension. An active and meaningful in-service training program for all hospital staff is also essential. Finally, the involvement of the client's representatives in the development of the treatment plan affords yet another safeguard.

Right to Refuse Treatment

The right to refuse treatment was also established in *Wyatt* v. *Stickney*. In a modification of the *Wyatt* decree, a federal court substantially restricted the freedom of hospital-based psychiatrists to use certain potentially hazardous forms of treatment. For example, psychosurgery was ruled out entirely, while others—such as electroconvulsive therapy (ECT) and aversive conditioning procedures—were permitted only under restricted circumstances. The client's right to refuse treatment is intimately related to the concept of informed consent: In a more recent decision it was held that a client confronted with the alternatives of lifelong commitment and lobotomy could not give truly informed and noncoercive consent (*Kaimowitz* v. *Michigan Department of Mental Health,* 1973). The impact on hospital-based treatment practices of judicial actions in the right-to-refuse and informed consent areas is likely to be substantial. The development of adequate safeguards for the client's right to refuse treatment must be based on a number of distinct issues.

First, many questions and issues must be raised regarding the conditions and types of treatments that the client may refuse. Procedures such as ECT, aversive conditioning methods, and experimental treatments should not be applied without the client's informed consent. As such,

---

[3] See Chapter 17, "A Quality Assurance System for Ensuring Client Rights in Mental Retardation Facilities," for more details.

hospitals must develop explicit guidelines for the regulation of these methods, as well as informed consent procedures. The guidelines should detail the circumstances under which such a procedure may be recommended and, if implemented, how it would be regulated and supervised. In all cases, such recommendations should be reviewed by independent committees constituted for such a purpose. Should the procedure seem warranted, it should then be presented to the client as well as his legal representative for consent. The risks and benefits of the proposed treatment relative to the available alternatives should be carefully delineated. In the case of *Mitchell* v. *Robinson* (1962), a client received insulin shock and ECT therapies for treatment of schizophrenia; this treatment caused the fracture of several vertebrae. Even though the client had given consent, the court held that the client's consent was invalid because the staff had not informed the client of possible serious hazards of the treatment. Needless to say, no attempt should be made to unduly influence the client to accept treatment. The client should be informed that once treatment has begun, he or she may voluntarily withdraw from it at any time without penalty.

The questions of informed consent and the right to refuse treatment become more problematic as treatment methods become more controversial. The *Wyatt* case clearly stated the client's right not to be overmedicated. It should be anticipated that the right-to-refuse and informed consent doctrines will be increasingly applied to drug therapies and other standard modes (Mental Health Reports, 1979). In anticipation of such developments, hospitals would be well advised to develop guidelines for use of all treatment modalities. The guidelines suggested by Martin (1975) and by Stolz and Associates (1978), while meant for behavior modification procedures, serve as good general models.

Confidentiality

The final procedural safeguard to be discussed here is confidentiality. The right of the hospitalized mentally ill to privacy and confidentiality has been affirmed in a substantial number of judicial actions (Brooks, 1974), and has been generally understood and respected for some time. Nevertheless, some discussion of this issue is warranted.

Information regarding clients should be available only to the client, his or her legal representative, and authorized hospital personnel—unless otherwise ordered by the client or the courts. There are some exceptions to this principle—discussed by Shnelsky (1977)—which primarily concern legal actions initiated by the client. The client should be informed of the rules regarding confidentiality and of the exceptions to them. The client should be given access to his or her own records, and be allowed to enter documents if he so desires. In light of the *Tarasoff* v. *Regents of the University of California* (1974) case—in which a psychotherapist was held responsible for failing to disclose the likelihood that his client might commit murder—it may be advisable to inform the client that confidentiality may be violated if there is good reason to believe that he or she may do harm to another.

Summary

The protection of the rights of hospitalized mentally ill persons is an important and challenging task. In the above review of client rights, it may have been difficult to discern any simple overriding principles. Yet all of the procedural safeguards discussed are elaborations of four basic points: (1) Clients should be afforded the same basic respect and dignity as any human being. (2) Hospital staff have a responsibility for specifying clearly to the client and his or her representatives what they are doing and why. (3) Hospital staff have a responsibility to evaluate the effectiveness of what they do. (4) The client's right to appeal decisions regarding his or her treatment to a higher authority must exist.

The following checklist summarizes the specific procedural safeguards that we have discussed:

Due Process
  1. Are clients informed of their procedural rights and civil liberties at the time of admission in a responsible manner? Is information written in language that clients can understand? Are clients reinformed of their rights on a regular basis, and attempts made to facilitate their understanding of them? Do procedures apply as well to voluntarily admitted clients?
  2. Are general hospital policies and procedures consistent with the client's civil rights and liberties? Are attempts made to educate all staff in understanding and respecting client rights? Do hospital policies and procedures spell out clearly the circumstances under which certain rights may be restricted? Is there a human-rights committee that reviews any restriction of client rights?

Freedom from Harm
  3. Do hospital policies and procedures promote the highest quality physical care possible? Do hospital policies and procedures address the quality of the social environment, including client-care practices, staffing patterns, and staff-patient interactions?
  4. Are there clearly articulated policies and procedures regulating the use of seclusion, restraint, physical isolation, and other coer-

cive management practices? Are the circumstances under which these methods may be used specified in clear terms? Have these policies and procedures been reviewed by a human-rights committee? Is the committee routinely informed when the methods are used?

Least Restrictive Environment

5. Can hospital care be defended as the least restrictive alternative? Are the criteria for institutional care spelled out clearly in terms of specific behavioral problems? Can the particular placement within the hospital be defended as the least restrictive alternative at the time of placement?

Right to Treatment

6. Have comprehensive assessments of the client's physical and psychological status been performed? Are the assessments based on recognized tests and procedures? Have traditional psychological assessments been supplemented by methods of behavioral assessment and tests of adaptive behavior? Were the results of each assessment made known to the client or his or her legal representatives?

7. Was the client consulted regarding his own perception of needs, strengths, and goals?

8. Does a list of the client's strengths and needs appear in the record? Are needs stated in terms of what behavior the client should develop or acquire? Are needs representative of the major areas of the client's life, including work, independent skills, use of leisure time, and so on?

9. Have intermediate and long-range goals been specified on the client's needs and strengths? Have behavioral objectives been developed for each goal? Do objectives specify clearly the intended behavior of the client as well as the conditions under which it will occur and criteria for mastery? Do criteria address movement to less restrictive settings and discharge?

10. Has a treatment plan been developed by the treatment team that is responsive to each objective? Are treatment methods spelled out in detail? Are the methods the least restrictive or coercive available? Are methods based on the best currently available scientific opinion? Are staff responsibilities delineated in the plan? Are staff responsibilities consistent with their training and experience?

11. Does a method of evaluation exist for each objective? Does the evaluation method help to demonstrate clearly if progress toward each objective is being made? Are procedures established that insure review of evaluative data on a regular basis by the treatment

team? If progress has not been made, are new objectives of treatment methods substituted?

12. Does the client or his or her legal representative have access to the treatment plan?

13. Has a mechanism been established for periodic review of the treatment plan? Has a mechanism been established for internal or external peer review of treatment plans?

14. Are all staff provided with meaningful in-service training keeping them abreast of new developments in law, program development and evaluation strategies, and treatment methods?

Right to Refuse Treatment

15. Are there hospital policies and procedures regulating the use of potentially hazardous treatments such as medications, ECT, aversive conditioning methods, psychosurgery, and experimental treatments? Are the conditions under which such methods may be used spelled out clearly? Are procedures for regulating and supervising these methods indicated? Are policies reviewed and monitored by an independent human-rights committee? Are procedures for obtaining informed consent clear and responsive to the client's particular state or condition?

Confidentiality

16. Have procedures been established for protecting the privacy and confidentiality of the client? Has the client been informed of his rights to confidentiality as well as of the circumstances under which they may be violated?

Mental illness has been a part of society throughout the history of mankind. It is not a myth as some have contended (Szasz, 1961). The care and treatment of the mentally ill has gone through many phases, ranging from the idea of witchcraft to asylums for criminals to psychiatric facilities. During the past decade, the mentally ill have heard the outcries of many modern-day Dorothea Dixes advocating the rights of clients. It is the hope of the authors that another century does not pass before another Dorothea Dix appears, because there is a lot more to do for safeguarding client rights in psychiatric facilities. The mental health field needs to develop and implement a basic value system in which individuals receiving services will be treated with dignity, in the least restrictive environment, with complete due process of the law.

References

BALLA, D. Relationship of institution size to quality of care: A review of the literature. *American Journal of Mental Deficiency*, 1976, *81*, 117–124.

Barnard, In re. 455 F.2d 1370 (D.C. Cir. 1971).

BROOKS, A. D. *Law, psychiatry and the mental health system.* Boston: Little, Brown, 1974.

Bush v. *Kallen.* 123 N.J. Super. 175, 302, A.2d 142 (App. Div. 1973).

Buttonow, In re. 23 N.U.2d 385, 244 N.E.2d 667, 297 N.Y.S.2d 97 (1968).

Dixon v. *Weinberger.* 405 F. Supp. 974 (D.D.C. 1975).

ENNIS, B. J. Judicial involvement in the public practice of psychiatry. In W. E. Barton & C. J. Sanborn (Eds.), *Law and the mental health professions.* New York: International Universities Press, 1978.

Fhagen v. *Miller,* 29 N.Y.2d 348, 278 N.E.2d 615 (1972).

Gault, In re. 387 U.S. 1 (1967).

GOFFMAN, E. *Asylums.* Anchor Books, 1961.

Goldberg v. *Kelly.* 397 U.S. 254 (1970).

Kaimowitz v. *Michigan Department of Mental Health.* Cir. No. 73-19434-AW (Cir. Ct. July 10, 1973).

KOPOLOW, L. W. Patients' rights and psychiatric practice. In W. E. Barton & C. J. Sanborn (Eds.), *Law and the mental health professions.* New York. International Universities Press, 1978.

Lake v. *Cameron.* 364 F.2d 657 (D.G. Cir. 1966).

LEBENSOHN, Z. M. Defensive psychiatry or how to treat the mentally ill without being a lawyer. In W. E. Barton & C. J. Sanborn (Eds.), *Law and the mental health professions.* New York: International Universities Press, 1978.

Lessard v. *Schmidt.* 349 F. Supp. 1978 (E.D. Wis. 1972).

MAGER, R. F. *Preparing instructional objectives.* San Francisco: Fearon Publishers, 1961.

MARTIN, R. *Legal challenges to behavior modification.* Champaign, Ill.: Research Press, 1975.

Mental Health Reports, vol. 3, no. 19, October 3, 1979, pp. 3–5.

Mitchell v. *Robinson.* 360 S.W. 673 (MO. 1962).

MONAHAN, J. Dangerousness and civil commitment. Testimony before California Select Committee on Mentally Disordered Criminal Offenders, Patton, Calif., December 13, 1973.

MOOS, R. H. *Evaluating treatment environments.* New York: Wiley, 1974.

New York State Association for Retarded Children v. *Carey.* 393 F. Supp. 715 (E.D. N.Y. 1975), 357 F. Supp. 752 (E.D. N.Y. 1973).

OLIN, G. B., & OLIN, H. S. Informed consent in voluntary hospital admissions. *American Journal of Psychiatry,* 1975, *132,* 938–939.

O'Connor v. *Donaldson.* 422 U.S. 563, 45 L.Ed.2d 396 (1975).

PALMER, A. B., & WOHL, J. Voluntary admission forms: Does the patient know what he's signing? *Hospital and Community Psychiatry,* 1972, *22,* 250–252.

People v. *Bailey.* 21 N.Y.2d 588, 237 N.E.2d 205, 289 N.Y.2d 943 (1968).

PESZKE, M. A. Dangerousness not the only measure of need. *Frontiers of Psychiatry,* 1976, *6,* 3.

RAYNES, N. V., PRATT, M. W., & RORER, S. Aides' involvement in decision-making and the quality of care in institutional settings. *American Journal of Mental Deficiency*, 1977, *81*, 570–577.

Rouse v. *Cameron*. 373 F.2d 451 (D.C. Cir. 1966).

SADOFF, R. L. Indications for involuntary hospitalization. Dangerousness or mental illness? In W. E. Barton & C. J. Sanborn (Eds.), *Law and the mental health professions*. New York. International Universities Press, 1978.

SCOTT, E. P. Viewpoint: Another look at the crossroads. *Mental Health Law Project*, 1976, *2*, 9.

SHAH, S. A. Dangerousness and civil commitment of the mentally ill: Some public policy considerations. *American Journal of Psychiatry*, 1975, *132*, 502–505.

SHNELSKY, R. Informed consent and confidentiality: Proposed new approaches in Illinois. *American Journal of Psychiatry*, 1977, *134*, 1416–1418.

Specht v. *Patterson*. 386 U.S. 605 (1967).

STOLZ, S. B., & Associates. *Ethical issues in behavior modification*. San Francisco: Jossey-Bass, 1978.

Suzuki v. *Quisenberry*. 411 F. Supp. 1113 (D. Haw. 1976).

SZASZ, T. S. *The myth of mental illness: Foundations of a theory of personal conduct*. New York: Hoeber-Harper, 1961.

SZASZ, T. S. *Law, liberty and psychiatry*. New York: Macmillan, 1963.

SZASZ, T. S. *The manufacture of madness*. New York: Harper & Row, 1970.

SZASZ, T. S. Voluntary mental hospitalization: An unacknowledged practice of medical fraud. *New England Journal of Medicine*, 1972, 277.

United States v. *Browner*. 417 F.2d 969 (D.C. Cir. 1972).

Vitaly Tarasoff et al. v. *Regents of the University of California*. 529 P.2d 553 (Sup. Ct. Cal. 1974).

Wyatt v. *Stickney*. 324 F. Supp. 781 (M.D. Ala. 1971).

Wyatt v. *Hardin*. Unpublished opinion of July 1, 1975. Reprinted in *Mental Disability Law Reports*, 1976, *1*, 55–57.

CHAPTER 19

The Rights and Treatment of Prisoners

Richard T. Crow

> In the last decade, over three-quarters of a million men and women entered the state and federal prisons and reformatories of the United States. . . . These prisoners, and thousands who preceded them to confinement, were forcibly removed from the social relations in which they were participating and were locked behind walls of concrete and steel where, we are prone to say, they "served their time," "paid their debt to society," and perhaps "learned their lesson." But they did more than pay, and serve, and learn in their prisons. They *lived* in them. [Cressey, 1973, p. 117]

Prisons and jails have been a functional part of Americana since the creation of the Walnut Street Jail in Philadelphia. From its inception the correctional institution has been a futile attempt to provide a "humane" alternative to capital punishment. It has been argued that the very concept of the prison—and indeed the institution itself—is "crimogenic"—a breeder of crime. The debate as to the purpose and function of the correctional institution—punishment versus rehabilitation —has been continual. Philosophers, penologists, politicians, and the public have regularly discussed and influenced the fate of the men and women who have passed through the correctional institutions of this country.

From the colonial period to the present, prisons have categorically been underfunded and understaffed yet over-utilized as a vehicle for influencing the behavior of those who have violated specifically identifiable societal norms. This over-utilization, coupled with the lack of adequate funding and staff, has led to the creation of institutional environments that have been variously described as barbaric, dehumanizing, and in general unfit for human habitation. A U.S. public health officer testifying in a recent federal court case in Alabama found the conditions in Alabama prisons so bad that he stated if he had jurisdictional authority he would close them (*Pugh* v. *Locke*, 1976). Such deplorable conditions are not unique or limited to any one jurisdiction, as substantiated by court decisions reflecting a sad and bizzare uniformity (*Holt* v. *Sarver*, 1971; *Gates* v. *Collier*, 1975; *Rhem* v. *Malcolm*, 1975; *Brenneman* v. *Madigan*, 1972; *James* v. *Wallace*, 1976). As the conditions in American correctional institutions have progressively worsened, the rights of the incarcerated have become the focus of a significant amount of litigation. This chapter will address the rights of the adult prisoner and the role of the prison administrator in ensuring that these rights are protected. It is not intended that all prisoner rights be exhaustively analyzed and discussed; rather, selected rights will be dealt with as illustrative of the broad array of judicial activity in this area. Additionally, attention will be given to what can be done by those charged with the responsibility of managing the correctional institution.

Litigation Dealing with Prisoner Rights

EIGHTH AMENDMENT RIGHTS

The role of the federal court has dramatically changed in recent years relative to the rights of prisoners. For nearly a century, the prisoner was a "slave of the State" (*Ruffin* v. *Commonwealth*, 1871). Thus, the federal courts maintained a "hands-off" doctrine which precluded it from entertaining allegations of unconstitutional treatment (*Robbins*, 1978). However, the swing away from this posture was influenced by the realization that embodied in the Eighth Amendment of the Constitution is the provision that "cruel and unusual punishments could not be inflicted" (U.S. Constitution, Eighth Amendment). The shift away from the hands-off doctrine was significantly influenced by the decision of the Supreme Court in *Trop* v. *Dulles* (1958). In that decision, Chief Justice Warren stated, "The basic concept underlying the Eighth Amendment is nothing less than the dignity of man. While the State has the power to punish, the Amendment stands to assure that this power be exercised within the limits of civilized standards. . . . The Amendment must draw its meaning from the evolving standards of decency that mark the progress of a maturing society."

Robbins (1978) has stated that the question what constitutes cruel and unusual punishment has gone through an evolutionary process. In recent years the courts have used the "shock-the-conscience" test in reviewing conditions of prisons. Thus, the determination of what fosters unconstitutionality has been based on punishment that is so foul, so inhumane, and so violative of basic concepts of decency that people of reasonable sensitivity are shocked or disgusted and often offended beyond fastidious squeamishness or private sentimentalism (*Rochin* v. *California*, 1952; *Holt* v. *Sarver*, 1971; *Wright* v. *McMann*, 1967).

The Eighth Amendment stands as a ready reminder to prison administrators that they must give attention to conditions of confinement. The essence of this responsibility was captured by Gross (1976) when he stated, "Corrections officials have a duty to maintain safe and suitable facilities, and when they are given insufficient facilities and personnel to house and govern too many inmates, the lives of the inmates become less than human and their treatment less than humane." Indeed, this has created what appears to be an untenable situation for the prison administrator, especially in periods of limited resources. However, in several cases the courts have ruled that the lack of adequate resources does not constitute a viable defense (*James* v. *Wallace*, 1976; *Holt* v. *Sarver*, 1971). The legislative and executive branches, particularly at the state level, have given only limited support toward the improvement of the prevailing dehumanizing and inhumane conditions that characterize prison environments throughout the country. Such inattention has accentuated the role of the judicial system to move in when consitutional guarantees have been perpetually violated (Prigmore & Crow, 1976).

In *Monroe* v. *Pape* (1961), the Supreme Court opened the door wider for state prisoners to seek redress in federal courts. Subsequent decisions of federal courts at the district and appellate levels have detailed the rights of prisoners, specifically within the context of the provisions set forth in the First, Eighth, and Fourteenth Amendments.

FOURTEENTH AMENDMENT RIGHTS

Pertinent to the rights of prisoners is the question whether "due process" and "equal protection under the law" pertain to prisoners. The courts have ruled that in specific instances the provisions of the Fourteenth Amendment do apply. In what might be considered a seminal case in regard to due process (*Wolff* v. *McDonnell*, 1974), the Supreme Court set forth the standard relative to the prison population. A prisoner may not be deprived of life, liberty, or property without due process of law (*Haines* v. *Kerner*, 1972; *Wilwording* v. *Swenson*, 1974; *Screws* v. *United States*, 1945). The rights accorded to those outside prison are indeed diminished for those incarcerated within the prison, yet "a prisoner is not wholly stripped of constitutional protections when he is imprisoned for a crime. There is no iron curtain drawn between the Constitution and the prisons of this country" (*Wolff* v. *McDonnell*, 1974). The Court went on to state that there has to be mutual accommodation between the institution and its objectives and the provisions of the Constitution that are applicable (*Wolff* v. *McDonnell*, 1974). The significance of due process is protection against arbitrary and capricious governmental action; therefore, the minimum requirements of procedural due process appropriate for the circumstances must be observed.

The relevance of the Court's decision makes it incumbent that prison administrators develop very specific, detailed, and clearly understood procedures that allow for due process to be honored. It has been conclusively recognized by the courts that the nature of the prison environment does require that prison administrators have the latitude necessary to maintain discipline and control. Yet this must be done in a manner that does not abridge the rights of the prisoner. Illustrative of judicial decisions relative to due process are those in the area of disciplinary action taken by the prison administration. Due process has been mandated to include written notice of the charges; a brief, but realistic, period of time to allow the prisoner to prepare for his or her appearance before the prison officials; delineation of the evidence and reasons for the disciplinary action; a written record of the proceedings; the opportunity for the prisoner to present evidence and call witnesses to testify in his or her behalf—although the Court recognized that inclusion of witnesses to speak on behalf of the prisoner may be disruptive, and allowed for the discretion of the prison administrator to prevail; and some provision for illiterate inmates to have assistance (*Wolff* v. *McDonnell,* 1974). Similar guidelines have been laid out by the courts in regard to parole (*Morrissey* v. *Brewer,* 1972) and classification of prisoners (*Wessen* v. *Moore,* 1973).

The equal protection clause of the Fourteenth Amendment has also been addressed by the courts. In *Washington* v. *Lee* (1968), the court ruled that a prisoner could not be subjected to discriminatory practices on the basis of race. In *McAuliffe* v. *Carlson* (1975), the court found that administrative practices that discriminate on the basis of the offender's sex violate the equal protection clause. This decison precluded action that seems to discriminate against male offenders and is favorable to female offenders.

FIRST AMENDMENT RIGHTS

The protection provided under the First Amendment have been accorded prisoners. Prisoners' right to use the mail has placed the burden of responsibility on prison administrators to show that censorship policies and procedures are justified and do not unduly infringe upon the protections set forth in the First Amendment (*Procunier* v. *Martinez,* 1974). Incoming mail can be inspected for contraband but cannot be summarily withheld from the inmate. If a piece of correspondence is rejected, the inmate must be so notified as well as the communiqué's author. Additionally, inmates have a right to correspond with the court (*Taylor* v.

Sterrett, 1976). Allowance has been made to check for contraband, but only in the presence of the respective inmate. Corollary to this is the right of an inmate to correspond with an attorney: The courts have ruled that prison administrators cannot interfere (*Blanks* v. *Cunningham,* 1966); however, such correspondence has been limited to communications involving legal matters (*Rhinehart* v. *Rhay,* 1970). In the previously cited *Taylor* v. *Sterrett,* the court ruled that inmates have the right to communicate with nonjudicial public officials and the news media. The principle that guided the court was that upon a person's being sentenced to prison his or her right to freedom of speech has not been terminated. It has, however, been recognized by the courts that material of an inflammatory nature can be subjected to control by prison administrators. If such material presents a clear and present danger—as detailed in *Sostre* v. *Ohio* (1971)— it can be withheld from the inmate. This standard was expanded upon in a subsequent case, *Battle* v. *Anderson* (1974), with the court stating that the prison officials had the burden of proving that specific publications presented a "threat to security, discipline, and order within the institution" (Palmer, 1977, p. 49).

Also provided for within the First Amendment is the right to freedom of religion. Case law has not clearly and conclusively been definitive in this area. Basically, guidelines have evolved from the equal protection clause of the Fourteenth Amendment—that is, treating all classes of inmates equally. Palmer (1977) has stated, "Courts have consistently held that where one religious group is permitted to engage in a particular activity, the same right must be accorded all other religious groups within the institution. Thus, it would appear that although prison officials have a right to regulate religious activity in order to promote valid institutional interests, the regulation must in all cases be equally applied to all groups. Likewise, where one group is permitted to manifest its religious beliefs in a certain manner, all other religious groups must be accorded the same privilege."

RIGHT TO LEGAL SERVICES

An inmate has a right to legal services (*Johnson* v. *Avery,* 1969). Whether or not these services are provided by other inmates or attorneys, they cannot be denied. In *Cruz* v. *Beto* (1972), the court ordered the administrator of the state prison system to pay damages to the defendants for interfering with the access of the inmates to legal counsel. While this is a novel decision, it testifies to the fact that the right to legal assistance cannot be administratively precluded. Similarly, inmates have a right to have access to legal materials (*Gilmore* v. *Lynch,* 1971).

PROTECTION AGAINST EXCESSIVE FORCE

The use of excessive force has been brought under some control by the courts. It has been readily recognized that within the prison environment force may need to be employed in specific situations. However, it has been ruled that such use of force must be reasonable and necessary as determined by the facts of the particular case. A companion to the excessive-force issue is that of using corporal punishment to enforce prison discipline. The bellwether case relative to corporal punishment is *Jackson* v. *Bishop* (1968), which effectively eliminated its use within prisons. There are alternatives to corporal punishment that the progressive prison administrator can utilize to maintain discipline and control.

RIGHT TO MEDICAL AND HEALTH CARE

In recent years there has been a marked increase in the court's role in medical treatment cases. The absence of adequate attention to the medical and health needs of inmates has led the courts to conclude that constitutional rights have been violated. The response of the court has been to identify in some detail what would constitute minimum levels of adequate medical and health service to meet the needs of the inmate population (*Newman* v. *Alabama*, 1974; *Gates* v. *Collier*, 1975; *Goldsby* v. *Carnes*, 1973).

Rehabilitation as an Inherent Intent of Imprisonment

Each correctional agency should develop and implement policies, procedures, and practices to fulfill the right of offenders to rehabilitation programs. A rehabilitative purpose is or ought to be implicit in every sentence of an offender unless ordered otherwise by the sentencing court (National Advisory Committee on Standards and Goals, 1973).

The ironic paradox that can be found throughout the country is that in many state statutes rehabilitation of offenders is a stated goal of the correctional system (Georgia Code Annotated, 1964; Indiana Annotated Statutes, 1956; Louisana Revised Statutes Annotated, 1967). In Missouri, the statute states, "In the correctional treatment applied to each inmate, reformation of the inmate, his social and moral improvement, and his rehabilitation toward useful, productive and law-abiding citizenship shall be gu'ding factors and aims" (Missouri Annotated Statutes, 1963). Although such provisions are thus set forth in state law, the other side of the paradox is that limited attention has been given to the achievement of this goal. Influenced by this paradox, the courts have attempted to bring the correctional system into compliance.

It should be noted that the courts have not held that there is an absolute right to rehabilitation. Nevertheless, in several cases the courts have placed the burden on the state to provide programs that allow the inmate to engage in a rehabilitative process (*Holt* v. *Sarver*, 1971; *James* v. *Wallace*, 1976; *Alberti* v. *Sheriff of Harris Co., Texas*, 1975). In *James* v. *Wallace* the court stated that a penal system cannot be operated in a manner that leads to the debilitation of the inmates. Simply put, an inmate should not get worse physically, mentally, or socially for having been incarcerated. In *James* the court detailed what is required of the correctional system to bring it up to basic minimum standards. To achieve this end the court identified eleven specific areas in which improvement is mandated: (1) overcrowding, (2) segregation and isolation, (3) classification, (4) mental health care, (5) correspondence and visitation, (6) protection from violence, (7) living conditions, (8) food services, (9) educational, vocational, work, and recreational opportunities, (10) physical facilities, and (11) staff. In the area of mental health care, for example, the court ordered that those inmates who are psychologically disturbed or mentally retarded must either be transferred to an appropriate facility, or else the respective institution must provide adequate care and treatment, including the hiring of necessary professional personnel to assure adherence to basic minimum standards. The court also stated that meaningful job assignments must be made in accordance with the inmates' interests, abilities, and institutional needs. Additionally, each inmate must have the opportunity to participate in basic educational programs and acquire a marketable skill.

The significance of *James* and its companion case, *Pugh* v. *Locke* (1976), is that it dealt with the totality of prison conditions. That is, it did not limit its finding to a specific question of unconstitutionality relative to one discreet area—e.g., medical care, legal assistance—but ruled that the conditions of the prisons constituted cruel and unusual punishment. It serves as a valuable example "of federal judicial intervention in a state penal system for the purpose of eradicating those unconstitutional conditions" (Robbins, 1978, p. 557). Feldberg (1977) in support of such litigation has recommended that the courts must go beyond delineating the invalidation of specific practices, but must confront the institution of prison in its entirety. If, indeed, rehabilitation of offenders is to have a chance, the environment within which this is to occur must be conducive to rehabilitation efforts having a positive and societally acceptable impact on those subjected to them.

Although rehabilitation may not be an inherent right, the prison administrator must be sensitive to the reality that lack of rehabilitation programs will not be tolerated by the courts. Programs that foster rehabilitation must be available and accessible to the inmate population. To avoid judicial intrusion, prison administrators will need to work toward bringing their institutions up to what is considered the minimum standard. The courts have mandated not the optimum conditions but rather conditions that reflect basic standards of decency and humanity.

Administrative Duties and Responsibilities

Throughout the foregoing discussion an attempt has been made to delineate the impact that the courts have had and undoubtedly will continue to have on the administration of prisons. It is apparent that the courts do not have an interest in "running the prisons"; they recognize that this needs to be left in the hands of the correctional administrator. However, the administration of the prison must be done within the boundaries of constitutional guidelines and must not abrogate the rights of the prisoner. The plethora of litigation and resulting judicial decisions provides the administrator with a framework within which to function. While the responsibility for the administration of the prison rests with the administrator, it should be emphasized that this cannot be accomplished without the support of the executive and legislative branches of government. As has been mentioned previously, such support has not been readily forthcoming. There must be additional resources made available to the correctional system if compliance is going to be achieved.

The context of the prison environment places a very challenging burden on the administrator. It is recognized that the prison administrator has the responsibility of managing those whom society has written off and deemed failures. An additional facet of the burden is that the administrator has little control over who is sentenced to the institution. This being true, it places a heavy responsibility on the prison system and those who administer it to have a meaningful system of classification. It is a foregone conclusion that not all prisoners need the degree of intensive supervision characteristic of the maximum security facilities. In many of the court cases previously cited, arbitrary classification procedures were found invalid. For example, it makes little sense to put a career criminal, repeatedly convicted of crimes against a person in the same facility—and in some instances the same cell—with a young person convicted of possession of marijuana. Most of the major studies dealing with the rights of prisoners and the responsibilities of prison administrators have dealt with this inappropriate approach to the assignment of prisoners.

What then can the administrator do? For illustrative purposes, a closer examination of the classification system as it has an impact on administrative behavior will now be discussed. It should be sufficient to look at selected areas, from which inferences can be drawn and applied to other areas.

CLASSIFICATION

Palmer (1977) has stated that classification is the assessment for rehabilitative and security purposes of an inmate's personality, background, and potential and the assignment of the inmate to a specific status or setting commensurate with these findings. The classification and reclassification of prisoners occurs at various times throughout the offender's involvement with the correctional system. How a prisoner is classified will determine to a great extent what happens to him or her while in the correctional system.

The Commission on Accreditation for Corrections has identified specific standards that relate to the classification of prisoners. If the prison administrator is responsive to these standards, he or she will be taking a giant step toward the improvement of the correctional environment and the recognition of inmate rights. The standards for accreditation in the area of classification include the following:

4372. There is a written plan for inmate classification which specifies the objectives of the classification system, details the methods for achieving the objectives and provides a monitoring and evaluation mechanism to determine whether the objectives are being met. The plan is reviewed at least annually and updated as necessary.

4373. There is a classification manual containing all the classification policies and detailed procedures for implementing these policies. This manual is made available to all staff involved with classification and is reviewed at least annually and updated as necessary.

4374. The written plan for inmate classification provides for maximum involvement of inmates in their classification reviews.

4375. Written policy and procedure provide for special needs of inmates

4376. The written plan for inmate classification specifies that the program and status review of each inmate occurs at least every 12 months.

4377. The written plan for inmate classification specifies criteria and procedure for determining and changing the status of an inmate.

4378. Written policy and procedure require that all inmates appear at their classification hearings and are given notice 48 hours prior to these hearings. [Commission on Accreditation for Corrections, 1977, pp. 72–73]

In discussing Standard 4373, the Accreditation Commission has specified what the classification manual should include:

1. Detailed policies regarding initial inmate classification and reclassification;
2. Instructions regarding the make-up of unit, team or full classification committee, as well as the duties and responsibilities of each;

3. Definition of the various committees' responsibilities for custody, employment and vocational/program assignments;
4. Instructions as to what phases of an inmate program may be changed by the various committee levels;
5. Specific procedures relating to inmate transfers from one program to another and from one institution to another; and
6. Content of the classification interview. [1977, p. 72]

Such a manual should be available to the inmate at the time he or she enters the prison as well as subsequent to initial entry. If the manual itself is not accessible to the inmates, then the policies and procedures governing classification and reclassification should be included in a handbook given to each inmate. The classification process is vitally important to the inmate, and it is incumbent upon the administrator that it be handled fairly and in a just manner, with attention to the due process and equal protection clauses of the Constitution. If attention is given to the above standards then an equitable procedure should be evident.

In arriving at classification decisions those responsible should develop a procedural mechanism that considers the following information:

1. age of the inmate
2. offense for which the inmate was sentenced
3. prior criminal record
4. vocational, educational, and work needs of the inmate
5. physical and mental health care requirements of the inmate
6. presentence investigative reports
7. results of any psychological tests or psychiatric examinations
8. reports from treatment and custodial staff, including progress reports relative to work and treatment programs

The guiding principle should be to acquire and consider all relevant information that would enhance an unbiased, objective, and fair classification and assignment of the inmate.

MEDICAL AND HEALTH CARE

Basic minimum medical attention must be afforded inmates. The correctional administrator must assure that the basic medical needs of the inmates are provided within the institution's medical and dental care programs. This is supported by one of the standards of the Accreditation Commission which states, "The institution provides inmates the medical and dental services needed to maintain basic health" (1977). The services provided within the institution should be comparable to those available to the general public. In the area of medical and health care the courts have mandated minimum standards (*Newman* v. *Alabama*, 1974).

How can the administrator be confident that such minimum standards are being addressed? The American Public Health Association has published *Standards for Health Services in Correctional Institutions* (1976)—a valuable resource to be consulted. To achieve satisfactory compliance the correctional institution is required to do the following:

1. At the time of reception and initial evaluation, the inmate shall be made aware of the health services in the institution. This should be written and also explained to each inmate.
2. The reception evaluation shall be recorded in the individual's medical record which shall be started at this time.
3. Those evaluative procedures clearly necessary to detect health problems requiring immediate action to protect the individual and the institution shall be completed before the inmate is placed in any holding unit or integrated into the institutional population.
4. All other evaluative procedures needed to complete the admitting health profile and to assist in work and activity classification shall be completed in a scheduled manner not to exceed seven calendar days from the date of initial reception and incarceration.
5. A well-defined written plan and orders formulated by the administrative and professional staffs shall exist and be available for the care and disposition of health problems identified upon admission.
6. Any prisoner found to be in acute health stress on admission and in need of emergency care shall be referred to an appropriate treatment facility immediately.
7. Those health problems identified as a result of the assessment during incarceration which need continuing intervention or attention shall be referred to appropriate persons and agencies. [p. 4]

Indeed, the foregoing spells out in specific detail what must be done and how it is to be achieved. These standards provide a guideline to the administrator and would be useful for him or her to be aware of and responsive to in the effort to provide adequate health care. Understandably, the administrator cannot perform these tasks; thus, qualified professionals of sufficient number should comprise the health care staff. All health care providers should be licensed or certified in a respective specialty area. (Inmates should be used in a paraprofessional capacity only under the supervision of a qualified professional.)

The above discussion pertains only to primary health care services. Other areas that must be addressed include secondary care services, mental health care, dental care, environmental concerns, nutrition and food services, pharmacy services, health records, evaluation of services, and staffing (American Public Health Association, 1976).

This discussion of the classification system and medical and health care has been included for illustrative purposes. The concentration on these two areas should not be construed to be anything more than what was intended—providing examples of administrative response. If the same attention is given to the other definable rights of prisoners, then an administrative system will emerge that is humane and promotes an environment within which the rehabilitation of offenders may very well be realized.

One final comment with reference to the needs and rights of the inmates. At the time that the inmate enters the system, he or she should be provided with a handbook. The handbook should address the classification process, provide a description of the physical structure of the institution, provide information regarding the sentence being served, describe policies relating to good conduct credits, give an explanation of parole eligibility, and provide an explanation of the procedures governing disciplinary infractions, including the range of punishments (Krantz et al., 1973).

Summary

Prison administrators have witnessed during the past fifteen years a delineation of the rights of prisoners. There are constitutional safeguards defined by the courts that are applicable to those inside the prison walls as well as to those outside. As Justice Blackmun has stated: "There is no iron curtain drawn between the Constitution and the prisons of this country" (*Wolff* v. *McDonnell,* 1974). Thus, it behooves the administrator to be cognizant of what is expected of him or her and develop appropriate policies, procedures, and practices serving the end of protecting the rights of the prisoner. Administrative systems can be implemented to accomplish this within the prison environment.

This chapter has attempted to identify some of the rights afforded the prisoner and discuss the impact of judicial intervention on the administration of the prison. It is not meant to be exhaustive. The scope of this chapter realistically limited the breadth of discussion. A broader, comprehensive examination of the many intricacies of this important area should be focused on in another forum. Those court decisions discussed should be viewed as indicative of the role the courts will continue to play in assuring that rights are not abridged. Two concerns—classification and medical and health care—were selected to indicate what the administrator can do in developing responsible administrative systems to preclude judicial involvement as well as serve the intended purpose and function of the prison. The administrator is challenged to respond to these responsibilities within the context of a most difficult situation. To rise to the challenge is to ensure the preservation of the rights of those within the prisons.

References

Alberti v. *Sheriff of Harris Co. Tex.,* 406 F. Supp. 649 (S.D. Tex. 1975).

American Public Health Association. *Standards for health services in correctional institutions.* Washington: American Public Health Association, 1976.

Battle v. *Anderson,* 376 F. Supp. 402 (E. D. Okla. 1974).

Blanks v. *Cunningham,* 409 F.2d 462, (5th Cir. 1976).

Brenneman v. *Madigan,* 343 F. Supp. 128 (N.D. Ga. 1972).

Commission on Accreditation for Corrections. *Manual of standards for adult correctional institutions.* Rockville, Md.: Commission on Accreditation for Corrections, 1977.

CRESSEY, D. R. Adult felons in prison. In L. E. Ohlin (Ed.), *Prisoners in America.* Englewood Cliffs, N. J.: Prentice-Hall, 1973.

Cruz v. *Beto,* 405 U.S. 319, 31 L.Ed.2d 263, 92 S. Ct. 1079 (1972).

FELDBERG, M. S. Confronting the conditions of confinement: An expanded role for courts in prison reform. *Harvard Civil Rights–Civil Liberties Law Review,* 1977, *12,* 367–404.

Gates v. *Collier,* 522 F.2d 81 (5th Cir. 1975).

Georgia Code Annotated, 77-139 (1964).

Gilmore v. *Lynch,* 319 F. Supp. 105 (N.D. Cal. 1970), *aff'd sub nom.; Younger* v. *Gilmore,* 404 U.S. 15, 30 L.Ed.2d 142, 92 S. Ct. 250 (1971).

Goldsby v. *Carnes,* 365 F. Supp. 395 (W.D. Mo. 1973).

GROSS, A. N. The increasing scope of federal judicial involvement in state and local correctional facilities. *New England Journal on Prison Law,* 1976, *3,* 227–249.

Haines v. *Kerner,* 404 U.S. 519, 30 L.Ed.2d 652, 92 S. Ct. 594 (1972).

HOFFMAN, H. *Prisoners' rights: Treatment of prisoners and post-conviction remedies, cases and materials.* New York: Matthew Bender, 1976.

Holt v. *Sarver,* 309 F. Supp. (E.D. Ark. 1970); *aff'd* 442 F.2d 304 (8th Cir. 1971),

Indiana Annotated Statutes, 13-123 (1956).

Jackson v. *Bishop,* 268 F. Supp. 804 (E.D. Ark. 1967); *aff'd,* 404 F.2d 571 (8th Cir. 1968).

James v. *Wallace,* 406 F. Supp. 318 (M.D. Ala. 1976).

Johnson v. *Avery,* 393 U.S. 483, 21 L.Ed.2d 718, 89 S. Ct. 747 (1969).

KRANTZ, S., BELL, R. A., BRANT, J., & MAGRUDER, M. *Model rules and regulations on prisoners' rights and responsibilities.* St. Paul: West Publishing Co., 1973.

KRANTZ, S. *Corrections and prisoners' rights.* St. Paul: West Publishing Co., 1976.

Louisiana Revised Statutes Annotated, 15-854 (1967).

McAuliffe v. *Carlson,* 337 F. Supp. 896 (D. Conn. 1974), *mod. on other grds.,* 520 F.2d 1305 (2d Cir. 1975).

Missouri Annotated Statutes, 216.090(1) (1963).

Monroe v. *Pape,* 365 U.S. 167 (1961).

Morrissey v. *Brewer,* 408 U.S. 471, 33 L.Ed.2d 484, 92 S. Ct. 2593 (1972).

National Advisory Commission on Criminal Justice Standards and Goals. *Task force report: Corrections.* Washington: Government Printing Office, 1973.

Newman v. *Alabama,* 349 F. Supp. 278 (M.D. Ala. 1972); *aff'd,* 530 F.2d 1320 (5th Cir. 1974); *cert. denied,* 421 U.S. 948 (1975).

PALMER, J. W. *Constitutional rights of prisoners.* 2d ed. Cincinnati: Anderson Publishing Co., 1977.

PRIGMORE, C. S. and CROW, R. T. Is the court remaking the american prison system? *Federal Probation,* 1976, *50,* 3–10.

Procunier v. *Martinez,* 416 U.S. 396, 71 Ohio Op.2d 139, 40 L.ed.2d 224, 94 S. Ct. 1800 (1974).

Pugh v. *Locke,* 406 F. Supp. 318 (M.D. Ala. 1976); *aff'd and remanded sub nom. Newman* v. *Alabama,* 559 F.2d 283 (5th Cir. 1977); *remanded with instructions sub nom. Alabama* v. *Pugh,* 46 U.S. L.W. 3802 (July 3, 1978).

Rhem v. *Malcolm,* 396 F. Supp. 1195 (S.D. N.Y. 1975); *aff'd,* 527 F.2d 1041 (2d Cir. 1975).

Rhinehart v. *Rhay,* 314 F. Supp. 81 (W.D. Wash. 1970).

ROBBINS, I. P. Federalism, state prison reform, and evolving standards of human decency: On guessing, stressing, and redressing constitutional rights. *Kansas Law Review,* 1978, *26,* 551–569.

Rochin v. *California,* 342 U.S. 165 (1952).

Ruffin v. *Commonwealth,* 62 Va. (21 Gratt.) 790 (1871).

Screws v. *United States,* 325 U.S. 91, 89 L.Ed. 1495, 65 S. Ct. 1031 (1945).

Sostre v. *Ohio,* 330 F. Supp. 941 (S.D. N.Y. 1971).

Taylor v. *Sterrett,* 532 F.2d 462, (5th Cir. 1976).

Trop v. *Dulles,* 356 U.S. 86, 2 L.Ed.2d 630, 78 S. Ct. 590 (1958).

Washington v. *Lee,* 263 F. Supp. 327 (IM.D. Ala. 1966); *aff'd per curiam,* 390 U.S. 333 (1968).

Wessen v. *Moore,* 365 F. Supp. 1262 (E.D. Va. 1973).

Wilwording v. *Swenson,* 502 F.2d 844 (8th Cir. 1974).

Wolff v. *McDonnell,* 418 U.S. 539, 71 Ohio Op.2d 336, 41 L.Ed.2d 935, 94 S. Ct. 2963 (1974).

Wright v. *McMann,* 387 F.2d 519 (2d Cir. 1967); *on remand,* 321 F. Supp. 127 (N.D. N.Y. 1970); *aff'd in part and rev'd in part,* 460 F.2d (2d Cir.), *cert. denied,* 409 U.S. 885 (1972).

PART IV

Safeguarding Research Participants

The preceding chapters have focused on the protection of rights of persons receiving various treatment and educational services. As is evident from these chapters, many rights can be protected in similar ways, irrespective of the service setting and population, and yet many other rights require specific technologies for different settings and handicapping conditions.

This section addresses an issue that is of general concern for all settings and populations—the issue of research involving human subjects. In the chapter to follow, Dr. Kelty provides the reader with (1) an overview of the complexity of the issues surrounding the involvement of humans as subjects in experimentation, (2) a historical perspective regarding the evolution of federal regulations in research, and (3) general guidelines for the encouragement of research and preservation of human rights.

Dr. Kelty's extensive professional work on the National Commission for the Protection of Human Subjects of Biomedical and Behavioral Research has provided her with a unique knowledge regarding the many years of investigation that this now-disbanded commission undertook.

Although many definitions have been devised in an attempt to delineate research, treatment, experimentation, evaluation, education, and therapy, it appears to be increasingly difficult to discriminate one of these from the others. For example, the collection of data is no longer a sole discriminating feature since it is now also considered an integral part of quality education and therapy. Of course, when federal research funds are used in a project, then the institutional review board system is mandatory under current interpretation.

However, a tremendous number of research-like activities are undertaken without the benefit of federal research funds. Thus, the editors of this book suggest that the following guidelines may prove to be very valuable in determining the potential benefits, risks, and protections applicable to almost any applied activity involving human subjects. A researcher, therapist, educator, or human-rights committee could employ these guidelines (in conjunction with those of the following chapter) in identifying areas in which additional safeguards and committee review would be needed in order to protect the persons participating.

Guidelines for Determining Potential Risk and Benefit

1. Potential benefit to society
   a. Will the potential results of this activity benefit our society?
   Benefit greatly   1   2   3   4   5   No Benefit

2. Potential benefit or risk to persons participating
   a. Will benefit accrue to these persons in health, skill development, or general well-being from their participation?
   Benefit greatly   1   2   3   4   5   No Benefit

   b. Have adequate precautions been taken to protect the persons' privacy and preserve confidentiality?
   Adequate   Inadequate
   precautions   1   2   3   4   5   precautions

   c. What is the potential that these persons might be coerced into participation?
   Totally   Potential
   voluntary   1   2   3   4   5   coercion high

   d. Is subject selection being done fairly so that no one racial, ethnic, economic, sexual, or vulnerable group is unduly over-represented?
                                                         Unjust &
   Just & fair   1   2   3   4   5   unfair

e. Is there a clear potential danger to the person's health or general well-being?

No risk   1   2   3   4   5   Great risk

f. Is there is a potential risk? Have adequate precautions been arranged (e.g., special informed consent, special protections)?

Adequate   Inadequate
precautions   1   2   3   4   5   precautions

g. Are adequately skilled and knowledgeable therapists or scientists undertaking this activity? (Have they conducted this type of intervention with a similar population in a similar setting previously? If applicable to this activity, are these persons adequately trained in scientific method and technology?)

                                      Very
Very adequate   1   2   3   4   5   inadequate

3. Impact of intervention variable on persons participating
   a. Have these variables undergone previous experimental analysis (e.g., number of publications, consistency in results, populations and settings previously studied)?

Extensively
tested   1   2   3   4   5   Untested

   b. Does the intervention variable represent an unusual practice for this type of setting? (E.g., How common to this setting? Will this cause a dramatic deviation from normal practice?)

Common to   Unusual
settings   1   2   3   4   5   to settings

   c. Will the intervention be conducted in a public setting (versus in isolation) where others could intervene if the person is in jeopardy?

Public   1   2   3   4   5   Isolation

4. Impact of observation on persons participating
   a. Will the observation system create a serious problem with the person being observed? (E.g., Will the person's anonymity be protected? Is the observation as unobtrusive as possible?)

Person   Person
protected   1   2   3   4   5   vulnerable

5. Potential benefits and risks to other persons directly or indirectly associated with the proposed activity (caregivers, parents, ward aides, siblings, etc.)
   a. Will any potential benefits accrue to these persons from their association with this study?
   Benefit greatly   1   2   3   4   5   No benefit

   b. Is there a clear potential danger to these persons' health or general well-being?
   No risk   1   2   3   4   5   Great risk

   c. Have adequate precautions been taken to protect these persons?
   Adequate   Inadequate
   precautions   1   2   3   4   5   precautions

6. Public review of activity
   a. Has this activity been discussed, designed, and considered publicly with others who are knowledgeable about related research, therapy, education, and professional ethical issues? What are their assessments of the adequacy of the protections for those persons participating?

                                                          Very
   Very adequate   1   2   3   4   5   inadequate

CHAPTER 20

Protection of Persons Who Participate in Applied Research

Miriam Kelty

A CHILD SITS IN A MODULE, designed with a movie screen and a car-like steering wheel and foot pedals. The child activates the computerized machine and the screen lights up, simulating the child driving a modern, streamlined, fast-moving automobile. The child uses these controls to maneuver the car through busy downtown areas as well as country roads. Every time the child is hit by an oncoming car a point is lost from his or her score. However, the score is advanced whenever the child maneuvers the car to hit, maim, injure, or kill a pedestrian.

One can imagine a human-subjects review committee's reaction to reading this in a procedures section of a research proposal. Despite the fact that the experimenter has developed a convincing rationale—perhaps the importance of better understanding the dynamics of "active violence"—the committee would certainly question the appropriateness of earning points for running down other human beings, simulated or not.

Nevertheless, a computerized game of this sort has been introduced into penny arcades. Children, whose parents may be shopping in the mall, bring their quarters to play. For a quarter, children can build their competencies in hitting pedestrians.

Home versions of similar games are available and selling well. On what basis, if any, should an experience freely available at home and in penny arcades be restricted or disapproved in the context of research? What differentiates research from ordinary behavior?

Now consider another situation. In the spring of 1979 a public agency decided to investigate and evaluate community placement of chronically ill psychiatric patients. Lay persons were hired to interview individuals with chronic mental illness who had been released from mental hospitals and placed in homes in the community. Mental health professionals and paraprofessionals did not serve as interviewers because the agency maintained that professional biases and conflicts of interest might influence their findings. The evaluation project was an investigatory activity, part of the audit or overseeing function of the agency involved. If the same project were to be conducted in the context of formal research, would it be permitted? It is almost certain that a human-subjects review committee (i.e., an institutional review board or IRB) might raise some questions regarding (1) the possible psychological stress of the interview on the patients, (2) the possibility that the patients might be disturbed or exhibit psychotic behavior that lay interviewers would be incompetent to deal with appropriately, and (3) the competency of the patients to understand the study for purposes of informed consent. Such a project, if not construed as research, would not be reviewed by an especially constituted committee charged with ensuring that it is conducted in a way such that participants would be protected from harm and invasion of privacy, as well as ensuring that persons to be studied have the option of not participating or of withdrawing at any time.

Research and Human Subjects: Benefits and Risks

Research—a formal investigation designed to contribute to generalizable knowledge—is usually described in a protocol that tests a statement of objectives and procedures (National Commission for the Protection of Human Subjects of Biomedical and Behavioral Research, 1978a). A distinction is sometimes made between basic and applied research. However, for the purposes of this book the focus is on research that involves humans and is designed to examine behaviors that are socially important (Baer, Wolf, & Risley, 1968).

Research and evaluation serve to protect clients to the extent that the objectives include the development and identification of improved service delivery systems, identification of safe and effective practices, development and testing of reliable and objective measures of behavior, and the development of analytic systems useful for interpretation of treatment data. Successful attainment of such objectives contributes to society by protecting people against unsafe or ineffective treatments and programs (Risley, 1969; Stuart, 1970).

Yet, during the past decade the potential benefits of research to individuals and society have taken a back seat to ethical issues raised by biomedical, behavioral, and social research, all of which have been the subject of public concern, debate, governmental regulation, and legislation. Accounts of research abuses and of controversial research projects have been publicized in the media and by congressional hearings. A widely discussed example involved a study initiated in 1932 on the natural course of syphilis. This study was continued until the early 1970s, despite the fact that antibiotics had been developed that could have provided effective treatment for these subjects. In retrospect, consensus is that the benefits of treatment would have outweighed the benefits of adhering to the research protocol. Subjects were deprived of a safe, available, and effective treatment to serve the purposes of research from which they would not benefit, and in fact were being denied treatment. A special panel which examined this project in the 1970s judged that the subjects should have been provided treatment as soon as it became part of accepted medical practice (Ad Hoc Advisory Panel, 1973).

In the social-sciences arena, some projects that have stimulated public controversy involve deception or stress. For example, some research studies manipulated performance by exposing students to failure experiences (Weiner, 1966). The Milgram (1974) study of obedience to authority has been the subject of several articles and at least one television program, and constitutes another example. Other projects have generated concern about invasion of privacy and breaches of confidentiality (Humphreys, 1974).

Another dimension of concern around the use of human subjects in research has been the widespread belief that research subjects are disproportionately drawn from the poor, the racial minorities or those disadvantaged in some way. Barber, Lally, Makarushka and Sullivan (1973) reported that disadvantaged persons were disproportionately involved in high-risk research. More recent and extensive data indicate that a substantial proportion of biomedical and behavioral research projects do involve a sizeable number of poor people. Nonetheless, about the same percentage of poor and minority participants were included in research that produced benefits as were included in nonbeneficial research. The group that was over-represented in high-risk nonbeneficial research was the white males, age nineteen through forty (National Commission, 1978b). Other data collected for the National Commission indicate that racial minorities constitute a small percentage of subjects in some areas of considerable public interest. For example, in one survey of prisoners, minority members participating in research were under-represented by 23 percent (National Commission, 1976). A survey of psychosurgery performed during the last ten years showed that few patients were blacks or other minorities. Most of the psychosurgery done in the U.S. in this period was performed on private patients who had not responded to numerous alternative treatments (National Commission, 1977). Other projects by their very nature involve racial minorities or economically disadvantaged groups, such as the New Jersey–Pennsylvania Income Maintenance Experiment designed to evaluate new social policies by studying their effects on sample communities (Rivlin & Timpane, 1975).

Regulating Research Involving Human Subjects

The issues discussed above, plus the increasingly large role of the federal government in medical, behavioral, and social research, have led to the formulation of guidelines and regulations to govern research involving human subjects. Historically, during the Nuremberg trials for Nazi war crimes it became apparent that medical research had been conducted on persons in concentration camps—unwilling participants. The Nuremberg Code was developed during the trials to provide a standard against which research practices might be evaluated. It has served as a model or a point of departure for later codes.[1] These codes all place major responsibility for ethical behavior, protection of persons involved in research, and compliance on the researcher. However, because of possible biases, conflicts of interest, and uncertainty about untested procedures, some have considered it desirable and even necessary to involve individuals other than the researcher in the judgment whether proposed research is ethical and provides adequate protection of research participants.

Continued public interest in whether research subjects are adequately protected, manifested in congressional hearings (Subcommittee on Health of the Committee on Labor and Public Welfare, 1973), led to the establishment of the National Commission for the Protection of Human Subjects of Biomedical and Behavioral Research in 1974 by P. L. 93-348. The commission was mandated to conduct ten studies, ranging from an identification of the ethical principles that should underlie all research with human subjects, to specific studies of (1) research on the fetus, (2) research involving prisoners and psychosurgery, (3) research involving those institutionalized as mentally infirm, (4) policies and procedures employed by institutional review committees,[2] (5) applicability of ethical

---

[1] Examples of codes for responsible conduct of biomedical experimentation are: the Nuremberg Code (1974); the Helsinki Declaration of 1964 (revised in 1975); and the 1971 Guidelines of the U.S. Department of Health, Education and Welfare, which were codified into Federal Regulations in 1974. Codes for the conduct of social and behavioral research include those of the American Anthropological Association (1973), the American Sociological Association (1972), and the American Psychological Association's Ethical Principle for the Conduct of Research with *Human Participants*, published by the association in 1973 as an addition to its 1953 Code of Scientific and Professional Ethics and Conduct (revised in 1978). The addresses of these organizations are as follows: American Anthropological Association, 1703 New Hampshire Avenue, N.W., Washington, D.C.; American Sociological Association, 1722 N. Street, N.W., Washington, D.C.; American Psychological Association, 1200 17 Street, N.W., Washington, D.C.

[2] The Institutional Review Board (IRB) is a mechanism to regulate research supported by the Public Health Service. It was created in 1966 by the Surgeon General, to subject the researcher's judgment to review by his institutional associates to assure independent determination that rights and welfare of subjects be protected, that appropriate methods be used to secure informed consent, and of probable risks and

principles underlying research to the provisions of health services funded by the Department of Health, Education and Welfare, (6) a study of policies of other federal agencies, and (7) the ethical, social, and legal implications of advances in biomedical and behavioral research, technology, and services (a special study). After the enabling legislation was passed, the commission was given the additional charge to study disclosure of research information.[3]

In several of its reports, the commission emphasized that research should be encouraged to ensure that both research participants and recipients of health services receive the safest and most effective treatments currently possible. In view of the many areas in which full information is not available, more research can contribute in important ways to the improvement of health, education, and human welfare.

The inclusion of behavioral and social research in the commission's mandate—as well as in previously issued guidelines governing research with human subjects—has been met with mixed reaction. Some have claimed that behavioral and social research were included without sufficient thought about similarities and differences between biomedical and behavioral-social research, and without careful consideration whether both should be governed by the same policies (Tropp, 1978). Others have maintained that a single policy would recognize the interaction of bio-behavioral variables and avoid arbitrary distinctions along disciplinary lines. This issue has not been finally resolved. One option currently being presented to federal officials is that research characterized by low risk to its subjects not undergo mandatory review by the institutional review committee. Examples that have been suggested as low-risk research include (1) secondary analyses of data if individual identifiers have been removed, (2) standard educational, aptitude, and achievement tests, (3) educational curricula development and evaluation, (4) survey and interview research, (5) noninvasive psychological procedures, and (6) service delivery research that involves standard and accepted practices. The question whether or not low-risk research should be ex-

---

benefits associated with the research. The Surgeon General's memo referred to medical research, but during the IRB system's initial year he issued a clarification to extend its applicability to behavioral research. In 1971 the Department of Health, Education and Welfare Policy on Protection of Human Subjects was published, again extending the applicability of the basic Public Health Service Guidelines. Regulations issued in May 1974 and revised in 1975 currently govern the IRB system. These regulations and recommendations on the development and policies of IRBs are available from the Office for Protection from Research Risks, National Institutes of Health, Westwood Building, Bethesda, Maryland 20205.

[3] If one wishes to obtain a copy of specific reports issued by the National Commission for the Protection of Human Subjects of Biomedical and Behavioral Research, one should write the Office for Protection from Research Risks, National Institutes of Health, Westwood Building, Room 3A–18, 5333 Westbard Avenue, Bethesda, Maryland 20205.

empted from the review requirement—or whether some other form of expedited review procedures should be initiated—is not yet resolved as of this writing.

Although specific experiments have generated ethical concerns on the part of scientists and the general public alike, debate has often addressed the uses to which research findings are put, rather than the research itself. For example, psychological tests have been claimed to have been used to unfairly discriminate against racial minorities to prevent members of these groups from advancing in their jobs (*Griggs* v. *Duke Power Company*, 1971). Similar claims have been made about the use of psychological test data to place Mexican-American children in classes for the educable retarded (Oakland, 1973; Mercer, 1972). Also, the practices of deprivation, punishment, and psychosurgery have reportedly been used for social control of unconsenting prisoners.

One view of the trend toward regulation of research involving human subjects is that this is part of the human rights movement, which includes expression of interest in civil rights of the disadvantaged, consumers' rights, and patients' rights. Another view is that freedom of researchers to study problems of their own choosing is being limited. Overall, however, most scientists and members of the general public feel that policies for the review of proposed research to protect subjects from harm and assure protection of their civil rights have benefited society. The overwhelming opinion is that currently prevalent review procedures have been accepted (National Commission, 1978a). It is generally agreed that although important research projects have perhaps been slowed, they have not, with few exceptions, been inhibited. The occasional delays experienced because of ethical-review requirements have been a beneficial trade-off on the side of protection of human rights and of persons from physical or psychological harm (National Commission, 1978a). The review requirement that governs research with human subjects may in the long run facilitate the conduct of basic and applied research by generating firmer support for the investment of public funds, if the research itself is considered beneficial to society.

The National Commission, though it was not an investigatory body, collected data from thousands of investigators, review board members, and subjects of research. It also communicated with several thousand interested citizens. During its four-year existence, the commission was impressed by the fact that little abuse was uncovered in research involving human subjects, relative to the potential harm associated with poor care, ineffective treatments, and inadequate services. It became clear, however, that existing policies and practices for reviewing research, to assure that participants are adequately protected from harm and respected as persons, were ambiguous in some instances and poorly understood in others, and differentially interpreted and practiced in institutions around the country.

Research Versus Practice

Particular ambiguity was noted by the commission concerning the definition of research and its differentiation from practice. Practice involves interventions designed to further the well-being of clients, which have a reasonable expectation of success (National Commission, 1978c). The purpose of practice is to prevent, diagnose, or treat conditions in individuals or in those around them. For example, immunization protects the individual but also protects society. Similarly, child abuse programs treat the child abuser and aid the victims. In contrast, research is designed to develop and contribute to generalizable knowledge. In addition, research objectives and procedures are usually explicated in a formal protocol. This last distinction, however, has been further weakened now that most service delivery programs also require a treatment plan similar to a research protocol.

Sometimes the distinction between research and practice is further blurred, largely because the two may occur together. For example, research may be designed to evaluate therapy. Confusion has also arisen from the fact that the word "experimental" is frequently used to describe procedures that are untested, atypical, new, or otherwise depart from "accepted" treatment protocol. However, when a clinician departs from standard or accepted practice, the innovation or departure does not necessarily constitute research—even though for clinical reasons systematic data are being collected (Risley, 1969). The fact that data are collected does not define an activity as research. Nevertheless, when innovations in practice are made, persons should be encouraged to conceptualize them in a research context and request that they be reviewed by the appropriate local group or committee. Researchers, therapists, and educators all might benefit from a systematic consideration of their activities by an appropriate committee for the protection of human rights.

Guidelines for Researchers, Practitioners, and Review Committees

Another area of ambiguity has been the identification of the ethical principles on which a review can be based. The National Commission identified three principles as central: (1) respect for persons, (2) beneficence, and (3) justice (National Commission, 1978c). The application of ethical principles to the conduct of research leads to some guidelines that should be considered when involving human subjects in research projects. Though this chapter focuses on research, the guidelines below may also be helpful to practitioners and review committees.[4]

I. *Respect for persons.* This principle incorporates two ethical convictions: (1) that individuals should be treated as autonomous, and (2) that persons with diminished autonomy are entitled to protection. An autonomous person is one who is capable of both deliberation about personal goals and action in accordance with such deliberation. However, not all people are capable of self-determination. The capacity for self-determination develops during the lifespan, and may be wholly or partially lost because of illness, mental disability, or circumstances that restrict liberty. The loss of self-determination may be permanent or temporary, and should be periodically reassessed. The amount of protection provided may also vary as a function of the risk of harm and the probability of benefit in a given situation. In research, respect for persons generally mandates that individuals participate in the research voluntarily and with adequate information on which to base a decision.

A. *Informed consent.* Respect for persons demands that persons (or an appropriate legal guardian) have the opportunity to decide what shall happen to them. The consent process has three components: information, comprehension, and voluntariness.

1. *Information* (the five-point rating scale addresses the fact that sometimes these issues cannot be answered with a definitive yes or no.)

   Potential subjects should be given adequate information about

   - the research procedures   yes 1 2 3 4 5 no
   - their purposes   yes 1 2 3 4 5 no
   - risks   yes 1 2 3 4 5 no
   - expected benefits   yes 1 2 3 4 5 no
   - alternative procedures (when therapy is involved)   yes 1 2 3 4 5 no
   - an opportunity to question   yes 1 2 3 4 5 no

[4] This statement of the ethical principles that should underlie the conduct of research with human subjects is abstracted from the recommendations of the National Commission. They are more fully explicated in *The Belmont Report: Ethical Principles and Guidelines for the Protection of Human Subjects of Research* (National Commission, 1978c). A summary of this report has been published in the *Federal Register* and is available through the Office for Protection from Research Risks (address given above, p. 405, n.3).

- an opportunity to withdraw from the   yes 1 2 3 4 5 no
research at will
- an opportunity to be informed of   yes 1 2 3 4 5 no
research results

   If complete information about the research will impair its
   validity, is it clear that

- incomplete disclosure is necessary to   yes 1 2 3 4 5 no
accomplish the research goals
- there are no risks that are not disclosed   yes 1 2 3 4 5 no
that are more than minimal
- there is an adequate plan to debrief   yes 1 2 3 4 5 no
subjects upon completion of the research,
and to disseminate results to them

2. *Comprehension*
- is information presented to subjects   yes 1 2 3 4 5 no
in an organized fashion, with
sufficient time for consideration?
- is time allowed between presentation   yes 1 2 3 4 5 no
of information and decision making for
questioning and deliberation?
- if comprehension of the potential subject   yes 1 2 3 4 5 no
is limited because of age, mental
disability, illness, or for any other reason,
has information been presented in a way
to encourage understanding?
- in circumstances as outlined above, has   yes 1 2 3 4 5 no
permission been sought for research
participation of the person of limited
capacity from a third party who is likely
to understand the potential subject's
situation and act in that person's
best interest?
- is the third party authorized to act in   yes 1 2 3 4 5 no
behalf of the subject?
- is the third party offered the   yes 1 2 3 4 5 no
opportunity to observe the research in
progress and to withdraw the subject at
any time if it seems to be in the best
interest of the subject to do so?

3. *Voluntariness*
- is consent solicited under conditions   yes 1 2 3 4 5 no
free of coercion and undue influence?

- have unwarranted rewards been offered   yes 1 2 3 4 5 no
  to obtain compliance with the request to
  participate in research?
- is consent requested by a person in a   yes 1 2 3 4 5 no
  position of authority relative to the
  subject's situation?

II. *Beneficence.* This principle requires that persons not be harmed
and that benefits be maximized and possible harms minimized.
Here problems may arise when research subjects may not benefit
individually but similar persons might derive great benefit in the
future. For example, research designed to identify factors that
facilitate healthy development may not benefit the participating
children directly, but may greatly benefit future generations.

A. *Assessment of risks and benefits.* The assessment of risks and
benefits presents an opportunity and a responsibility to collect
systematic and complete information about the proposed research. Risk-benefit assessments are concerned with the prob-
abilities and magnitudes of possible harms and anticipated
benefits from the research. Risks include possibilities of physical, psychological, legal, social, and economic harm. Benefits
may occur along the same dimensions.

- are risks outweighed by anticipated   yes 1 2 3 4 5 no
  benefits to the subject and to society?
- is the proposed research adequately   yes 1 2 3 4 5 no
  designed to meet its objectives?
- are the nature, probability, and   yes 1 2 3 4 5 no
  magnitude of probable risks clearly
  distinguished and presented so that
  subjects may decide whether or not
  to participate?
- is the researcher's estimate of the   yes 1 2 3 4 5 no
  probability of harm or benefits
  reasonable?
- are the risks necessary to attain the   yes 1 2 3 4 5 no
  research objectives?
- are any inhumane treatments involved?   yes 1 2 3 4 5 no
- if vulnerable populations are involved   yes 1 2 3 4 5 no
  as subjects, is their involvement
  necessary and appropriate?
- are relevant risks and benefits   yes 1 2 3 4 5 no
  disclosed in documents and procedures
  used in the consent process?

III. *Justice.* This principle addresses the question who should receive the benefits of research and bear its burdens. In the selec-

tion of research subjects it is important to determine whether some classes of persons (welfare recipients, racial or ethnic minority groups, institutionalized persons) are being systematically selected because they constitute an available population to study or may be easily manipulated, or are selected for reasons other than those directly related to the problem being studied. Similarly, it is important to consider whether some groups are systematically excluded from the opportunity to participate in research. Justice also demands that those who participate in research be among the beneficiaries of subsequent applications of that research.

A. *Selection of subjects.* The principle of justice demands that there be fair procedures and outcomes in selection of research subjects.

- are individual research subjects selected fairly and justly?   yes 1 2 3 4 5 no
- is social fairness reflected in selection of subjects so that racial, ethnic, economic, sex, and vulnerable groups are not unnecessarily burdened?   yes 1 2 3 4 5 no
- are reasons for involving such groups germane to their particular needs and problems?   yes 1 2 3 4 5 no

Summary

This chapter has focused on the protection of persons who participate in research, whether clients in treatment programs or individuals or groups not associated with particular service programs. The growth of public concern about the protection of rights of research subjects has been documented, and policies developed to assure that research subjects are respected as persons and protected from harm have been reviewed. Guidelines for the protection of research subjects have broad applicability and specific guidelines have been proposed. It has been suggested that clients of researchers, therapists, and educators all deserve substantially similar respect and protections.

References

Ad Hoc Advisory Panel. *Final report of the Tuskegee syphilis study.* HEW, PHS (CDC), 1973.

BAER, D. M., WOLF, M. M., & RISLEY, T. R. Some current dimensions of applied behavior analysis. *Journal of Applied Behavior Analysis,* 1968, *1,* 91–97.

BARBER, B., LALLY, J. I., MAKARUSHKA, J. L., & SULLIVAN, D. *Research on human subjects: Problems of social control in medical experimentation.* New York: Russell Sage, 1973.

Griggs v. *Duke Power Company*, 401 U.S. 424 (1971).

HUMPHREYS, L. *Tearoom trade: Impersonal sex in public places.* Chicago: Aldine, 1974.

MERCER, J. IQ: The lethal label. *Psychology Today*, September 1972.

MILGRAM, S. *Obedience to authority.* New York: Harper & Row, 1974.

National Commission for the Protection of Human Subjects of Biomedical and Behavioral Research. *Appendix to report and recommendations: Research involving prisoners.* HEW Publications No. (OS) 76-009, p. 10–78, 1976.

National Commission. *Appendix: Psychosurgery.* HEW Publication No. 77-0002, 1-169-178, 1977.

National Commission. *Report and recommendations: Institutional review boards.* HEW Publication No. (OS) 78-008, 1978a.

National Commission. *Appendix to report and recommendations: Institutional review boards.* HEW Publication No. (OS) 77-009, p. 1–77, 1978b.

National Commission. *The Belmont report: Ethical principles and guidelines for the protection of human subjects of research.* HEW Publication No. (OS) 78-0013, 1978c.

OAKLAND, T. Assessing minority group children: Challenges for school psychologists. *Journal of School Psychology*, 1973, *11* (4), 294–304.

RISLEY, T. R. Behavior modification: An experimental therapeutic endeavor. In L. A. Hamerlynck, P. O. Davidson, & L. E. Acker (Eds.), *Behavior modification and ideal mental health services.* Alberta, Canada: University of Calgary Press, 1969.

RIVLIN, A. M., & TIMPANE, P. M. (Eds.). *Ethical and legal issues of social experimentation.* Washington, D.C.: Brookings Institution, 1975.

STUART, R. B. *Trick or treatment: How and when psychotherapy fails.* Champaign, Ill.: Research Press, 1970.

Subcommittee on Health (Committee on Labor and Public Welfare). *Quality of health care—Human experimentation.* (Parts 1–4.) Washington, D.C.: U.S. Government Printing Office, 1973.

TROPP, R. A. What problems are raised when the current DHEW regulation on protection of human subjects is applied to social science research? In NCPHSBBR, *The Belmont report: Ethical principles and guidelines for the protection of human subjects of research.* HEW Publication No. (OS) 78-0014, 1978, *Appendix IX*, II:18.

WEINER, B. Role of success and failure in the learning of easy and complex tasks. *Journal of Personality and Social Psychology*, 1966, *3*, 339–343.

Indexes

Index of Authors

Index of Subjects

Accreditation Council for Services for Mentally Retarded and Other Developmentally Disabled Persons (ACMR/DD), 349

Advocacy, 350-51

Alchoholics Anonymous (AA), 128, 158, 170

American Academy of Pediatrics, 217

American Association of Sex Educators, Counselors, and Therapists (AASECT), 125, 129, 131-33

American Civil Liberties Union, 36

American Medical Association (AMA), 113, 159

American Psychiatric Association, 117, 145

American Psychological Association (APA), 113, 125, 128-29, 131-32, 204, 214-15, 269

American Public Health Association, 392

Association for the Advancement of Behavior Therapy, 86

Aversive or restrictive procedures, 6, 76-78, 287

Children
child abuse treatment, 54-57, 144
rights of, 19-21, 24, 247-49
rights in alchohol treatment, 170
rights in counseling, 22, 25
rights in education, 21-22
rights in the social service system, 46-48
rights to handicapped, 61-72

rights to treatment during foster placement, 53
rights within the family, 21, 44-46
treatment of chronically ill children, 286-90

Civil commitment process, 323

Civil Rights Act of 1964, 63-64

Client
admission, 25-29, 111-12, 233-35, 281-86
case records, 12, 112-17
discharge, 290-91
evaluation, 95-96
follow-up, 242-43, 291
representative, 290
review, 31-34
rights in acute-care hospitals, 302-306
rights in alcohol treatment, 161-63
rights in drug addiction treatment, 194-95
rights in group homes, 253-55, 260-63
rights in nursing homes, 325-30
rights in psychiatric facilities, 365
rights in the pursuit of health, 279-81
rights in sex therapy, 125-34
rights of addiction-clients, 188-93
rights of developmentally disabled in vocational settings, 230
rights of handicapped students, 66-75
rights to habilitation, 333

Commission on Accreditation for Corrections, 390

Commission on Accreditation of Rehabilitation Facilities (CARF) in 1973, 222, 229, 247

Index of Court Cases